Technology and Strategy

Technology and Strategy

Conceptual Models and Diagnostics

RICHARD A. GOODMAN
MICHAEL W. LAWLESS

New York   Oxford
OXFORD UNIVERSITY PRESS
1994

Oxford University Press

Oxford   New York   Toronto
Delhi   Bombay   Calcutta   Madras   Karachi
Kuala Lumpur   Singapore   Hong Kong   Tokyo
Nairobi   Dar es Salaam   Cape Town
Melbourne   Auckland   Madrid

and associated companies in
Berlin   Ibadan

Library of Congress Cataloging-in-Publication Data
Goodman, Richard A. (Richard Arthur), 1949–
Technology and strategy : conceptual models and diagnostics /
by Richard A. Goodman and Michael W. Lawless.
p. cm. Includes bibliographical references
and index. ISBN 0-19-507949-3
1. Corporate planning.
2. Technological innovations—Management.
3. Technological innovations—Economic aspects.
I. Lawless, Michael W.
II. Title.
HD30.28.G657 1994   658.4'012—dc20   94-8234

9 8 7 6 5 4 3 2 1

Printed in the United States of America
on acid-free paper

This book is dedicated to
Bunny and Beth
for a multitude of reasons
and with a deep sense of gratitude

Preface

This is a book about the employment of technology in the execution of corporate strategy. It is a conceptual and diagnostic approach. Here we offer conceptual frames and methods of diagnosing the basic nature of an organization—its technological and structural DNA. We describe technical-level methods for analyzing technology, innovation potential, and strategic potential. But, more important, this is a book about a process that explicitly defines strategic action.

The organizational arena that embraces technology and strategy is filled with promising opportunities and fraught with managerial difficulties. Forecasting the eventual performance of a technology often requires a crystal ball. Forecasting the scheduled timing of this performance and the underlying costs to achieve such performance is even more difficult. Those organizations that employ technology as part of their strategic arsenal know that they are running serious risks. This choice clearly increases the uncertainty of organizational performance.

When potential results are not easily estimated, evaluation and selection of strategic action become problematic. The choice process within the organization is exacerbated by intergroup differences. As each group focuses upon its unique perspective, priority and communication disagreements arise. To attenuate the uncertainty associated with the employment of technologically assisted strategic action a *comprehensive conceptual and diagnostic approach* is recommended. This approach helps to reduce the natural technological uncertainty and the artificial organizational uncertainty of specialization.

Such an approach must be diagnostic at a conceptual level as well as at a technical level. It must link environmental analysis to individual project analysis. It must accommodate the forces in the marketplace, the vicissitudes of the financial community, the dynamics of developing technological potential, and the operational needs of the firm. It must bridge the product–process gap as well. Further, it must accomplish its ends in the light of national and international competitive forces.

Management is an ongoing cyclical process: symptom–solution–implementation change–new symptom. It features not just one repeated cycle but many simultaneous repeated cycles—all of differing lengths and intensity. Management is not simply a linear process. Unfortunately, unlike management, a book is a linear process. Thus, the presentation in a book is not the same as real life. One has to start somewhere. One has to take a position. Complexities must be simplified and the simple must eventually be placed into a complex context. This book must conform to such a linear technology, but this book must also convey the essentially nonlinear nature of its subject matter.

For instance, after providing a roadmap to the book, we offer two introductory chapters, both at a conceptual level. They ask the reader to diagnostically explore the underlying thought processes in technology, in strategy, and then in the integration of the two. In philosophical terms they identify the domain of discourse—the so-called ontology of the field. In plain language, they ask the readers to be very clear about the underlying assumptions they are making when dealing with the technology–strategy interface. Then we offer three technical-level diagnostic techniques. These are formal analytic tools but still at a broad level of analysis. They draw the reader from strategy to technology to technology programming. This increasingly specific focus is limited to the technological area. But the firm is more complex than this. So then we offer three chapters that make technological connections with other strategic issues. These explore technological dynamics, core competencies, and quality management issues. This is followed by four chapters on implementation issues featuring technology management techniques, alternative technological substrategies, organizational structuring, and the external acquisition of technology to deal with the complexity of real organizational life. Finally, we conclude with an action-oriented summary.

Los Angeles   R.A.G.
Boulder   M.W.L.
November 1993

Contents

Technology and Strategy

1

A Roadmap to Effective Technology-Strategy Choices

EXPLORING THE CONTEXT OF THE ROADMAP

What is technology? It is a word that has no firm connotative base. Seemingly we all understand the word and yet it is often misused. The word technology commonly conjures up exciting images and fantasies. At the same time, the need to learn about a new technology evokes feelings of apprehension. Technology is simultaneously beneficial and threatening. It will save the world and/or destroy it. It is the engine of increasing employment and competitive ability—it is the source of major economic disruption. Unfortunately, the broad meanings associated with technology serve more as a distraction and confusion than as an aid to decision. For organizational and, in fact, societal action technology must be understood in considerable detail, and the details themselves must be both more precise and more widely understandable. To create an understanding of technology and its role in strategy we first present a roadmap that confirms and solidifies understanding at the general level and then carefully draws the reader toward a more sophisticated understanding.

A roadmap is a simplified picture of the many twists and turns between here and there. The reasons for the actual tracings upon the map are inexplicable unless the background of the territory has also been drawn. In general, this background is a complex matrix of information that permits the viewer a far better understanding of the more simplified route structure. In our roadmap the background we must sketch can be found in the three interwoven issues of organization, technology, and strategy. The textures observed within these background issues serve as the general context to the specific techniques (or route structure) needed for the careful exploration of technology and strategy. Descriptions of the critical textures found in the three areas follow this introduction.

The conceptual and diagnostic approach recommended here is based on the research and experience of an extensive list of scholars and practitioners. Selected work in economics, organization theory, information theory, decision theory, and other substantive intellectual arenas provides the basic theoretical underpinnings. Of equal importance has been the rather robust conceptual and empirical work created in the relevant applied domains of knowledge. Some of these domains represent academic research and some represent the work of thoughtful practitioners.

The roadmap itself is a concise presentation of the interactions among three levels of analysis involved in the diagnostics process. This complex interaction scheme will present the reader with a framework and a touchstone for developing a thorough understanding of the conceptual and diagnostic intent. The appreciation derived from the roadmap is particularly important as the interactions are otherwise difficult to understand due to the linear requirements imposed by the nature of the written medium.

The Organizational Conundrum: Orchestrating among Contending Special Interests

It has become increasingly evident that the modern corporate structure is built upon the benefits of specialization—both technical and functional. Broadly speaking, specialists add unique skills which are increasingly valuable as the corporation grows in size. In general terms, the difference between a rule of thumb and an exact calculation (a heuristic solution and an algorithmic solution) is often small. The seasoned generalist employing a rule of thumb will often come close to the best solution. A specialist employing a formal analytic technique will come somewhat closer. As organizations grow, the importance of the difference between the generalist's and the specialist's solution changes. In a large project, even a small percentage improvement in effectiveness could easily pay back the costs of employing the specialist. Thus, in many circumstances, as size increases, specialization becomes correspondingly valuable.

Unfortunately, the interests of specialists are necessarily focused upon the restricted set of goals that grow out of the techniques and perspectives of their training. Thus, their innate interests are not necessarily congruent with more general goals. The essential corporate conundrum then is to align goals among the various internal functional and technical constituencies. Because of these general characteristics the modern corporation can become cumbersome to direct and not particularly quick to change and adapt.

The cumbersome nature of the corporation is not the only challenge faced by corporate managers in their attempt to reach goal alignment. An additional challenge is that of reaching understanding and comprehension among various units. Each of the functional/technical specialties develops its own language and jargon. Some of it is precise, some is metaphorical, and some is symbolic. "Betas" and "ISDN" mix with "MRP" and "isolating mechanisms." Thus, the trade-offs that must be accomplished to achieve a measure of corporate unanimity must be negotiated through the screen of "foreign" languages. Taken together—the challenges of goal alignment and those of communication—a myriad of dilemmas for planning and for implementation face the corporation.

The normal planning product is a written document which purports to clearly identify the agreement reached among the key organizational participants. It is intended to communicate intent and direction to those organizational members not party to the process. Finally, the plan is intended to serve as a contract for all. Unfortunately, it is unlikely that any plan is sufficiently complete to be followed to the letter. Thus, members of organizations must approximate plans rather then follow them exactly.

Once deviation has occurred, approximation becomes acceptable and the integrity of the agreement begins to fall apart. Depending on their role within the corporation, each constituent has a different set of priorities. Some of these differences are matters of emphasis. They can easily be forecast as they are attributable directly to the group's functional interests. Others are quite a surprise as they are attributable to misunderstandings in the planning and/or implementation processes—misunderstandings that arise from language and jargon difficulties.

Thus, the organizational context of the conceptual and diagnostic roadmap explored here is an arena of contending forces, forces which are split purposefully to attain the benefits of specialization and split unintentionally by the ensuing unique language problems which arise from each technical/functional unit. This contentiousness may lead to the cumbersome and slow character of organizations. Further, it leads to a continual tension among the organizational actors in their attempt to honor an apparently agreed-upon plan of action.

The Technological Landscape: Obscure, Unpredictable, and Dynamic

The second contextual issue that serves to add understanding to the "route structure" of the roadmap is technology. There are three prominent characteristics of technology which seem to explain most of the impact that technology has upon the organization. These are the relative obscurity of technological concepts for many of the organizational members; the often unpredictable results that arise during technological development, and the frequency with which periods of continuity alternate with periods of discontinuity, producing an uneven rate of technological change. In sum, technology adds a significant measure of uncertainty into the organizational calculus.

Non-technologists, who lack the requisite training in science and engineering, find the details of technology and technological progress obscure. This training lapse is further compounded by the unique lexicon of each field. To cope with these communication difficulties technologists may oversimplify the way they speak to nontechnologists. Technologists tend to emphasize the future value of a new development. They speak mainly of the performance they will be able to offer to their users or customers while understating the underlying technological process needed to deliver such potential. Thus, the potential medical value of developments in monoclonal antibodies is not in the hundreds of diagnostic and therapeutic products developed slowly over the next decades. Rather it is the eventual creation of a "magic bullet"—the ultimate of efficacious medicine. Communications which focus on ultimate performance provide little information about the many underlying disciplines that are involved in such a creation. Similarly, the nontechnologist is left with only a sketchy idea of the difficulties inherent in each of the underlying projects.

This problem is further amplified by the unpredictability normally associated with technology projects. Budget overruns and schedule delays are widespread. Even then the final products rarely perform precisely as envisioned. While the performance underrun is sometimes small compared to the cost and schedule overrun, this is not due to technical competence or good technical planning. It is simply an artifact of a process that culls out many technical approaches in advance of proposing them for inclusion in a project proposal. Many false starts are abandoned long before the ultimate performance becomes a meaningful organizational question. Only the most inexperienced organizational member believes that the expected new design can be delivered on schedule.

When the performance characteristics of a technology are charted over time they reveal that improvements occur in fits and starts. In fact, performance improvements are usually the result of several incremental innovations in several different areas of the technology. While occasionally breakthroughs occur, the reduction to practice of a breakthrough is a laborious effort involving both process design and product design. All too often the practical embodiment of a new technology falls significantly below the performance expectations derived from theoretical analyses of the breakthrough. Thus, actual improvements over time will be incremental until a confluence of underlying increments in subtechnologies provides the opportunity to enter a next generation.

The unevenness of the rate of change of development is thus exacerbated by limitations in the communications ability among the technologists and other critical firm participants. In short, the organization's need to meld the internal constituencies into a coherent whole is weakened by the information limitations of performance promises used for planning and/or project implementation.

These issues have begun to find their way into decision theory and from there into planning theory under the simple phrase "unknown unknowns." They wreak havoc with traditional planning approaches that assume we know all we need to know before we begin and that skillful analysis will certainly improve our organizational performance. This technological texture of the roadmap helps explain why the route structure to an effective technology–strategy interface is so complex.

This brief introductory treatment of technology focuses on some of the basic issues that arise when organizations employ technology to obtain either operational or strategic benefits. We can begin to appreciate some of the detail which provides the texture on the roadmap. The technology issues discussed suggest that tensions, communication difficulties, lack of predictability, and frustration are a normal background concern of any technology-based corporation.

The Strategic Essence: Facing Competitors and the Winds of Change

For many firms the normal changes of everyday occurrences are the stimulus to organizational action. This stimulus normally engenders a problem-solving mode of reaction. The events that cause the reaction are quite diverse; they range from changes in supplier prices to declines in customer purchasing patterns. (Occasionally, these stimuli can be positive—supply prices can drop or sales can increase.) Sometimes the stimuli arise from the actions of competitors through the introduction of new products or new prices.

A basic objective of the firm is to provide goods and services to the marketplace. The ability to do so at a profit is related to limitations of time and place. Location often provides a limited geographical sphere of protection. In expanding markets, struggling firms can prosper. In stable markets, effectively managed firms can avoid being victims during an industry shakeout. Declining markets are bad for all save those who produce at the lowest cost.

The story has two messages: one of competition and the other of market change over time. Many of the standard approaches of the business firm can be more loosely characterized as tactics. "Launch new products" sounds a lot like "work harder" not "work smarter." "Cut costs" seems a bit like a reaction to a new competitor rather than a conscious desire to be a low-cost producer. Conversely, strategy is the conscious creation of barriers or of isolating mechanisms—reputation, location, financial constraints, contractual agreements, and so on. Technology provides several approaches to creating such barriers.

The Technology–Strategy Interface

In the successful management of the corporation, a trade-off between the inherent uncertainty of technology and the potential strategic benefits of technology is necessary. The value of good strategy is the shield it provides against competition, ensuring a measure of certainty and allowing an organization to create effective approaches to the needs of the marketplace. Technology is one of the key activities which promise such benefits. The organizational costs of employing technological elements within corporate strategy (technology strategy) are accompanied by the need to cope with an added measure of uncertainty and disruption. This requires a reconsideration of the traditional planning process and a careful integration of the paradigms of the strategists with the paradigms of the technologists.

When strategy is off the mark the stability of the firm's basic processes is weakened. Conversely, when technology is off the mark the resultant organizational uncertainty tends to severely strain the normal planning mechanisms. These tensions require thoughtful attention so that the strategists avoid knee-jerk demands for better planning and technologists avoid knee-jerk demands for less planning. The key premise here is the idea that a well-understood joint position on the nature of technology and the nature of strategy can lead to an effective technology–strategy interface. That's what this book is all about.

UNDERSTANDING THE STRUCTURE OF THE ROADMAP

This roadmap to an effective organizational–technology–strategy interface has been derived from empirical analyses, from an exploration of theoretical constructs from many disciplines, and from a good deal of experience. While the book represents a synthesis and leads to recommendations regarding technique, it is clear that the actual employment of the concepts and techniques described in this work will require interpretation and adaptation. For any specific application within any particular technology, alteration of the technique will be needed in much the same fashion that basic scientific findings (research) must be adapted (development) to a particular application.

A Schematic of the Conceptual-Diagnostic Approach

The underlying approach described in this book can be presented as four loosely inter-connected blocks. First, a *conceptual frame* for diagnosing the potential of technology is presented. Then *techniques for diagnosing* situations and selecting appropriate technology strategies follow. This is followed by a section describing the *technological connections* to other basic strategic issues. Then *techniques for managing* the selected technology strategies are considered. These ideas are summarized in Figure 1-1.

A contextual analysis identifies those elements of a process which need to be understood as a background for management decision and action. A *conceptual frame* extends the benefits of contextual analysis by providing a focal schema—a way of organizing the broader contextual information. The specific conceptual frame required here is one that allows both technology and strategy to effectively interact in service of corporate goals.

Here, the basic nature of technology and its strategic potential must be appreci-ated. Technology is a depreciable asset which can be employed in a variety of fashions to create substantive, albeit erodible, barriers to competition. It is an asset that requires

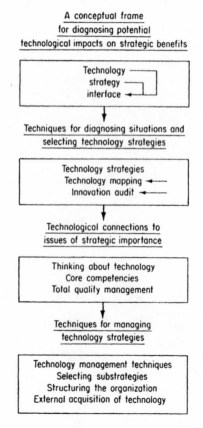

Figure 1-1. Technology-strategy roadmap.

constant reinvestment. At the same time, it is an investment with a high level of uncertainty as to the timing and value of its eventual payoff.

Similarly, the basic nature of strategy and the elements that make strategy work need to be understood. When an organization selects a strategy it is choosing the approach it will employ to isolate its activities from those of its competitors. Strategic choice presumes that the actions selected will more or less provide the firm with an edge in regard to a specified target market. Uncertainty of timing and effect is anathema to the strategist.

The employment of a technological approach in strategic action requires a clear understanding of the paradigmatic conflicts of the technological and the strategic specialist. The interface between strategy and technology must be explored to understand the specific sources of these differences, to devise methods of overcoming intergroup discrepancies, and to meld the two special foci in order to achieve organizational effectiveness.

With this contextual and conceptual understanding the *basic diagnostic process* can begin. Initially, a strategic framework of technology strategies must be constructed. The strategic framework describes common technology strategies in terms of product maturity, market maturity, technological maturity, available actions steps, and defensibility. The resulting gestalts represent viable patterns of strategies for achieving technological leverage.

This framework then is employed as a screening device to sift information derived from a careful mapping of the basic technologies that drive the firm's business. The mapping process identifies the scientific bases of the product line, the impending developments in the scientific base, and the changes in the performance parameters of the product line implied by these developments. Then, by matching the technology framework to the strategy framework, organizations can ascertain areas within the technological base which will present strategic opportunities and initiate appropriate action to take advantage of the revealed opportunities.

Once this initial screening takes place, the sifting then needs to be undertaken at a deeper level—moving from viewing the underlying technology to viewing the firm in an exploration of the firm's innovative skills. An audit of the firm's innovative capability provides the management with a base from which to select opportunities determined by the technology mapping process. The innovation audit uses the strategic conceptualizations to assess which of the opportunities suggested by the mapping exercise are best suited to the firm's abilities. The two analyses taken together with the framing of technology strategies have the capacity to assess the potential impact of the various technologies and technological actions upon strategic positioning—given the firm's innovative capabilities.

The result of the diagnostic process is the selection of actions which are expected to create valuable strategic positioning for the firm. Execution of these actions must be effectively handled or the hoped-for benefits are unlikely to materialize.

The third portion of the roadmap concentrates on the *technological connections* to other strategic issues. Technology is a very important concern of the firm, but it is not the only element of strategy. Other issues of strategic importance often cloud the technological issue and obscure systematic thought about the role of technology. In this third section three collateral strategic issues are raised and the connections between these issues and technology are explored.

Strategic actions can evolve based on a sequence of decisions taken over a number of time periods. On the other hand, strategic action can proceed more rapidly and at the same time be more radical in nature. Thus, a key issue is whether to pursue an evolutionary or a revolutionary model of strategy. This issue can be addressed by looking at certain questions such as the sparsity or munificence of the environment, the rate of technological change, and the complexity of the underlying relevant technologies.

These various ways of thinking about technology provide a broad context for the exploration of a basic strategic question usually labeled core competencies. Core competencies represent the results of a long-term investment process. The firm's core competencies can be in product technology, in financial strength, in marketing position, or in some other area. All of these factors require some form of technology strategy just as they all require some form of a financial and marketing strategy. Technology can assume a leading-edge role in opening markets, in providing customer benefits, and in securing a measure of advantage or it can assume a strong supporting role. This broad decision represents a basic organizational and investment strategy for the firm.

One increasingly important area of competence is the area of quality. Quality per se and "total quality management" have increased their apparent benefits to the firm. The quality improvement programs themselves also have impact upon the corporate use of technology for strategic benefit. Quality represents at one and the same time a force for improvement and an inhibition to change. The use of technology to support the quality effort will reflect the firm's choices about its favored rate of change. The basic strategic issues in this section involve other dimensions of strategy and a firm's proactive or reactive position with regard to the dynamics of change.

The fourth portion of the roadmap explores how the *implementation* of various technology strategies requires unique managing techniques for planning and control systems, substrategy selection, and organizational structure and processes.

Thus, a range of technology management techniques is needed to deal with the general uncertainty that underlies the technology development process. An adaptive planning and control structure blends extant planning models based on certainty with those based on intuition. Such an adaptive rationality model is able to realistically accommodate the uncertainty issues endemic to the employment of technology-based strategies.

The selection of a particular technology strategy requires deep thought and attention to detail in the implementation stage. There are common alternative substrategies regarding technological action steps and action steps in other arenas of the firm. Further analysis is needed in order to select the appropriate technological substrategy.

All these decisions are, of course, carried out within an organization. It is quite clear that organizational structure and processes have a significant effect upon the likelihood of successful implementation of a selected strategy. It is then necessary to have full understanding of the organizational choices so that the organizational embodiment of the strategy does not seriously decrease the theoretical benefits of the strategic choices.

In sum, the *conceptual frames* of technology and of strategy are integrated as a starting place for diagnosis. Technology strategies are characterized as a filter for *diagnosis of technology* (mapping) and for *diagnosis of organizational ability* (innovation audit) in order to select appropriate strategic action. These actions are then *connected* to other strategic issues and concerns. Uncertainty management, substrategy analysis, and structural management are employed to *implement* the actions as specified by the diagnostic process.

Underlying Theories, Conceptualizations, and Empiricism

The theory base presented for the organizational–technology–strategy interface is drawn from two broad arenas of study: economics and organization theory. While it is fair to say that the driving force behind the strategic analysis is economic in nature, this is also somewhat of an oversimplification. Economic theory can be used to explain much activity, but it can also be explained from a behavioral or organizational perspective. Thus, this book presents an amalgam of theory drawn from these basic disciplines.

The economic arguments derive in many ways from two distinct thrusts. One concerns the concept of technology as a driving force within the marketplace and includes work of authors such as Schmookler (1966), Schumpeter (1976), Nelson and Winter (1982), Tushman and Anderson (1986), Porter (1985), and Henderson and Clark (1990). A second thrust comes from the literature of institution economics and argues for organizational activity that is driven to reduce transaction costs and thus tends toward an efficient use of resources. This base is drawn from the origins of the industrial organization literature as represented in some of the relatively recent work of authors such Jensen and Meckling (1976), Klein, Crawford, and Alchian (1978), Dasgupta and Stiglitz (1980), Williamson (1975, 1985), and Eisenhardt (1989).

The organization theoretic base of this book can also be broken down into a set of smaller subgroups. Theories relating to action-taking describe the manager as an actor with a personal set of understandings about the world and how it operates. Action and actor are examined from a range of theoretical perspectives including the early sociological work of Parsons and Shils (1951) and moving through others to the more recent cognitive psychological theories of Argyris and Schon (1978). Similarly, environmental analysis as a technique relies upon a broad range of theoretical bases such as the examination of the texture of the environment by Emery and Trist (1965) and the population perspective posited by McKelvey (1982) and recently applied to technological change by Barnett (1990). Thus, firms' positions and performance are results of an evolutionary process driven by past history and current decisions (Basalla, 1988; Hughes, 1988). Organizational theory combines structure and processes with limited abilities of the individual as represented in the works of scholars like March and Simon (1958), Cyert and March (1963), Thompson (1967), and Galbraith (1973).

As a result of research and scholarly activity there have arisen a series of midrange conceptualizations that fall between theory and empirical findings. They represent a synthesis which integrates several bits of theory with insights derived from several empirical investigations. Much of this book is based on such conceptual material.

For instance, some of the extremely interesting work on the management of technology is found in the Abernathy and Utterback (1978) conceptualization of technological phases which tend to focus the firm on either product-enhancing or productivity-enhancing activities; the White and Graham (1978) project selection analysis involving technological, embodiment, business, and market figures-of-merit; the concern for longer term technology development in Rosenbloom's (1984) work; and the overall technology management question in Twiss (1980) and in publications of Arthur D. Little, Inc. (1981).

At the conceptual level, broad-based strategic guidelines derived from competitor and industry analyses are important elements of Porter's work (1980, 1985). Supplementing these broad guidelines, and still looking outward, are concepts that deal with the identification of relevant environmental domains and understanding their underlying characteristics and potential impacts as found in Dill (1958), Emery (1967), Trist (1968), and Schon (1972). Conversely, concepts that focus on the productive portion of the firm are equally important to the overall understanding of technology and strategy. Some of these ideas can be found in the work of Skinner (1969), Hayes and Abernathy (1980), Maidique and Hayes (1984), and Wheelright and Hayes (1985).

Clearly, much of the work in the field of technology and strategy has an empirical base. Guidelines derived from such a base can make potentially important contributions to actual firm and national planning decisions. These empirical studies can loosely be cast into two broad categories—longitudinal and cross-sectional. Longitudinal research uses as a base data gathered over several time periods in the history of a firm or industry or product. Cross-sectional studies usually compare several projects or firms at a single point in time.

Abernathy's (1978) study of one automobile firm from its founding to current times provides some insights into the tension between productivity and innovation. This work evolved into *Industrial Renaissance,* a forerunner of recipes for industrial renewal (Abernathy, Clark, and Kantrow, 1983). A similar study by Chandler (1962) focused on the chemical industry and led to ideas about the appropriate fit of strategy and structure. Clarke's (1968) study of the liquid propellent rocket engine industry from 1945 to 1966 showed how technology developed over time. The Illinois Institute of Technology Research Institute (IITRI, 1968) study and the Battelle (1973) study on the relationship of science to technology shows the nature of the fits and starts and the complexity of multiple disciplines that underlie many major product breakthroughs. Finally, Sahal (1981) demonstrates the consistency of particular patterns of industrial innovation that have endured over several decades that he studied. This is supported more recently by Basalla (1988) and Hughes (1988).

On the other hand, many empirical studies have an essentially contemporaneous base as they cast about for answers regarding the process of management. Peck and Scherer (1962) examine how the weapons acquisition process occurs and the areas where identified uncertainties have impact. In a study of 150 projects Marquis and Straight (1965) seek to understand the apparent effect of project structure on performance. Freeman and his colleagues (1972, 1974) study the differences between successful innovations and unsuccessful innovations. Hofstede (1980) reports on the effects of national culture in a large multinational technology firm. Dess and Beard (1984) categorize some 52 industries on the basis of their task environment. Schoonhoven (1983) reports on the relationship between strategy and performance in electronics firms. These examples and many more are woven into the conceptual and diagnostic approaches found in this book.

Resultant Synergies and Values Added

Within this book, synergies arise from the combination of the theoretical, conceptual, and empirical material as well as from the integration of the economic and the organizational literature withthe technological and the scientific literature.

The value added by this work is the specification of a soundly based, detailed approach to analyzing technology, to understanding the implications of that technology in the light of a range of strategic options, and to making appropriate technological choices to add value through more effective strategic positioning.

THE BOOK: COMPLEXITY SIMPLIFIED—SIMPLICITY ELABORATED

The remainder of the book conforms to the roadmap in structure. It contains three sections plus a summary chapter and follows the outline below.

Part I, a description of the contextual analysis schema, is entitled "Broad Guidance for Technological and Strategic Praxis: Conceptual Frameworks and Contextual Analysis." These conceptual frames are built in two chapters, "Strategy as Defensible Competitive Advantage" and "The Technology–Strategy Interface."

The second part "Techniques for Diagnosing Situations and Selecting Technology Strategies," provides the detailed technique material for the diagnosis and selection of appropriate strategy. This part contains "Success Conditions for Technology Strategies," "Mapping Technological Potential for Defensible Positioning," and "Evaluating Your Advantage: The Innovation Audit."

Part III broadens the concepts by looking at "Technological Connections to Other Strategic Issues." This section begins at a broad level with a chapter entitled "Thinking about Technology." It then becomes more specific by exploring the concept of core competencies, finally becoming even more specific by looking at the innovative implications of total quality management.

The final section concerns implementation issues. "Techniques for Managing Technology Strategies" contains "Technology Management Techniques," "Selecting Appropriate Technology Substrategies," "Structuring the Organization for Advantage" and "The External Acquisition of Technology." "The Elements of Strategic Action" is then offered as a summary overview of the book.

REFERENCES

Abernathy, W. 1978. *The Productivity Dilemma: Roadblocks to Innovation in the Automobile Industry.* Baltimore, MD: Johns Hopkins University Press.

Abernathy, W. J., K. Clark, and A. Kantrow. 1983. *Industrial Renaissance.* New York: Basic Books.

Abernathy, W. J., and J. M. Utterback. 1978. "Patterns of Industrial Innovation," *Technological Review* 80:40–47.

Argyris, C., and D. Schon. 1978. *Organizational Learning: A Theory of Action Perspective.* Reading, MA: Addison-Wesley.

Arthur D. Little, Inc. 1981. "The Strategic Management of Technology." Boston: Arthur D. Little, Inc.

Barnett, W. 1990. "The Organizational Ecology of a Technological System," *Administrative Science Quarterly* 35:31–60.

Basalla, G. 1988. *The Evolution of Technology.* Cambridge: Cambridge University Press.

Battelle 1973. "Interactions of Science and Technology in the Innovative Process: Some Case Studies." Columbus: Battelle, March 19.

Chandler, A. 1962. *Strategy and Structure: Chapters in the History of the Industrial Enterprise.* Cambridge, MA: MIT Press.

Clarke, R. W., 1968. "Innovation in Liquid Propellant Rocket Technology," *Final Report Task 7910-05.* Holloman Air Force Base, NM: Office of Aerospace Research, March.

Cyert, R., and J. March. 1963. *A Behavioral Theory of the Firm.* Englewood Cliffs, NJ: Prentice-Hall.

Dasgupta, P., and J. Stiglitz. 1980. "Industrial Structure and the Nature of Innovative Activity," *Economic Journal* 90(358):266–93.

Dess, G., and D. Beard. 1984. "Dimensions of Organizational Task Environments," *Administrative Science Quarterly* 29:52–73.

Dill, W. 1958. "Environment as an Influence on Managerial Autonomy," *Administrative Science Quarterly* 2:409–43.

Eisenhardt, K., 1989. "Agency Theory: An Assessment and Review," *Academy of Management Review* 14(1):57–74.

Emery, F. E., 1967. "The Next Thirty Years: Concepts, Methods and Anticipations," *Human Relations* 20(3):21–32.

Emery, F. E. and E. Trist. 1965. "The Causal Texture of the Environment," *Human Relations* 18(1):21–32.

Freeman, C. 1974. *The Economics of Industrial Innovation.* Baltimore, MD: Penguin.

Freeman, C., et al. 1972. *Success and Failure in Industrial Innovation.* Centre for the Study of Industrial Innovation, University of Sussex.

Galbraith, J. 1973. *Designing Complex Organizations.* Reading, MA: Addison-Wesley.

Hayes, R., and W. J. Abernathy. 1980. "Managing Our Way to Economic Decline," *Harvard Business Review,* July–August, pp. 67–77.

Henderson, R., and K. Clark. 1990. "Architectural Innovation: the Reconfiguration of Existing Product Technologies and the Failure of Established Firms," *Administrative Science Quarterly,* 35:9–30.

Hofstede, G. 1980. *Culture's Consequences: International Differences in Work-Related Values.* Beverly Hills, CA: Sage.

Hughes, T. 1988. *Networks of Power.* Baltimore, MD: Johns Hopkins University Press.

IIT Research Institute. 1968. *TRACES (Technology in Retrospective and Critical Events in Science).* Chicago: IITRI, December 15.

Jensen, M., and W. Meckling. 1976. "The Theory of the Firm: Managerial Behavior, Agency Costs, and Ownership Structure," *Journal of Financial Economics* 11:5–50.

Klein, B., R. Crawford, and A. Alchian. 1978. "Vertical Integration, Appropriate Rents, and the Competitive Contracting Process," *Journal of Law and Economics* 21:297–326.

Maidique, M., and R. Hayes. 1984. "The Art of High Technology Management," *Sloan Management Review,* Winter, pp. 17–31.

March, J., and H. Simon. 1958. *Organizations.* New York: Wiley.

Marquis, D. G., and D. M. Straight, Jr. 1965. "Organizational Factors in Project Performance." Working paper, School of Management, MIT, Cambridge, MA, August.

McKelvey, B. 1982. *Organizational Systematics: Taxonomy, Evolution, Classification.* Berkeley: University of California Press.

Nelson, R., and S. Winter. 1982. *An Evolutionary Theory of Economic Change.* Cambridge, MA: Belknap Press.

Parsons, T., and E. A. Shils. 1951. *Toward a General Theory of Action.* Cambridge, MA: Harvard University Press.

Peck, M. J. and F. M. Scherer. 1962. "The Weapons Acquisition Process: An Economic Analysis." Division of Research, Harvard University.

Porter, M. 1980. *Competitive Strategy.* New York: Free Press.

Porter, M. 1985. *Competitive Advantage: Creating and Sustaining Superior Advantage.* New York: Free Press.

Rosenbloom, R. S., 1984. "Managing Technology for the Longer Term: Notes from a Managerial Perspective." Boston: Harvard Business School. (mimeo)

Sahal, D. 1981. *Patterns of Technological Innovation.* Reading, MA: Addison-Wesley.

Schmookler, J. 1966. *Invention and Economic Growth.* Cambridge, MA: Harvard University Press.

Schon, D. 1972. *Beyond the Stable State.* London: Maurice Temple Smith.

Schoonhoven, C. 1983. "Strategy and Performance in High Technology Corporations." Paper presented at the annual meeting of the Western Academy of Management, Santa Barbara, CA.

Schumpeter, J. 1976. *Capitalism, Socialism and Democracy,* 5th ed. London: Allen and Unwin.

Skinner, W. 1969. "Manufacturing—Missing Link in the Corporate Strategy," *Harvard Business Review,* May–June, pp. 136–45.

Thompson, J. D. 1967. *Organizations in Action: Social Science Bases of Administrative Theory.* New York:McGraw-Hill.

Trist, E. 1968. "Urban North America." Toronto: Town Planning Institute of Canada. (mimeo)

Tushman, M., and P. Anderson. 1986. "Technological Discontinuities and Organizational Environments," *Administrative Science Quarterly* 31:439–65.

Twiss, B. 1980. *Managing Technological Innovation.* London: Longman.

Wheelright, S., and R. H. Hayes. 1985. "Competing through Manufacturing," *Harvard Business Review,* January–February, pp. 99–109.

White, G., and M.B.W. Graham. 1978. "How to Spot a Technological Winner," *Harvard Business Review.* March–April, pp. 146–52.

Williamson, O. 1975. *Markets and Hierarchies: Analysis and Antitrust Implications.* New York: Free Press.

Williamson, O. 1985. *The Economic Institutions of Capitalism.* New York: Free Press.

I

BROAD GUIDANCE FOR TECHNOLOGICAL AND STRATEGIC PRAXIS: CONCEPTUAL FRAMEWORKS AND CONTEXTUAL ANALYSIS

"The world is complicated—and our responses to it are similarly complicated, but the human tendency is to proceed as if this complicated reality were not so. . . . [We do this through] the necessary and desirable simplification of relationships. . . . Yet life remains without the model's elegance. It is exceedingly complex, characterized by ever changing pressures, and . . . frequently surprising" (Goodman and Huff, 1978).

Conceptual frameworks are a method of structuring our experiences and providing coherent ways of thinking about relationships. They are potentially beneficial for problem solving in domains which are overly complex. In such domains, formal analytic approaches (structural or algorithmic) do not capture enough variance to provide reliable guidance. Decisions are then heavily reliant on the application of judgment—judgment which has been constructed from personal experience. Often this experience base has been neither systematically developed nor systematically examined. This lack of "system" or "logic" or "assumption base" creates an opportunity for disagreement without a base for resolution. The application of conceptual frameworks creates mechanisms for assisting with the resolution of contending personal experience bases. Such frameworks provide the organization with both context and structure for organizing and employing an otherwise randomly developed set of beliefs.

One method to create appropriate conceptual frames is to engage in a study of the specific intellectual domains that bear directly upon the given problem. Part I therefore contains both contextual analysis and conceptual framing of the two domains most relevant to the issues at hand: technology and strategy. The conflicts, compatibilities, and potential synergies of the domains are blended through analysis of the underlying paradigms.

2

Strategy as Defensible Competitive Advantage

When the formulation of strategy is considered, many of us have an image of issues carefully hammered out by a set of thoughtful executives. This image often includes the resolution of conflicting forces, philosophical elements, and a reflective atmosphere. Unfortunately such a philosophical or armchair image of strategy formulation omits some of the central realities of organizational life. Executives and the organizations that they run are constantly buffeted by an ever-changing world; as a result, their ability to pause for substantial reflection is severely hampered. A contextual analysis of the dynamics of organizations indicates that everyday pressures often distort strategic intent (Mintzberg, 1973).

This chapter begins by examining several approaches used to describe the everyday pressures that serve to distort strategic action. It is then argued that these problems can be ameliorated through a broad understanding of the strategic choice and the organization's commitment to this choice. Commitment is rather straightforward—and detailed discussion is reserved for Part IV. Understanding refers to both the general idea of strategy and specifics of a particular strategy. In this chapter the focus is on the underlying concept of strategy itself. (Chapter 4 will look closely at the specifics of individual strategies.) A clear definition of strategy is the foundation of understanding. Thus, the chapter surveys alternative definitions of strategy and finally settles upon the idea of defensible competitive advantage. Then this foundation is extended through the careful examination of the conceptual bases that underlie the choice of definition. In the next chapter the focus is on analyses of practices and concepts that are valuable tools for developing an effective technology–strategy interface.

ORGANIZATIONAL PRAGMATICS AND STRATEGY

To help explore organizational pragmatics and strategy it is instructive to consider the conditions under which the strategy-making executive labors. Perhaps this is best accomplished by delving into a rather rich description drawn from the works of Tolstoy. In *War and Peace* (1863–69/1941), Tolstoy provides a fascinating and detailed description of the defense of Moscow from General Kutusov's perspective. He examines Kutusov's chosen strategy in light of the dynamics of the real situation. In this passage he concludes that Kutusov's limited abilities to determine what was really occurring and to process such information under the day-to-day, minute-to-minute pressures of command meant that no "strategy" was likely to exhibit sufficient leverage to actually affect the outcome of the battle. That is, strategy could neither be easily formulated nor, if formulated, be actually implemented.

> For people accustomed to think that plans of campaign and battles are made by generals—as any one of us sitting over a map in his study may imagine how he would have arranged things in this or that battle—the questions present themselves: Why did Kutusov during the retreat not do this or that? Why did he not take a position before reaching Fili? Why did he not retire at once by the Kaluga road, abandoning Moscow? and so on. People accustomed to think in that way forget, or do not know, the inevitable conditions which always limit the activities of any commander-in-chief. The activity we imagine to ourselves when we sit at ease in our study examining some campaign on the map, with a certain number of troops on this and that side in a certain known locality, and begin our plans from some given moment. A commander-in-chief is never dealing with the beginning of any event—the position from which we always contemplate it. The commander-in-chief is always in the midst of a series of shifting events and so he never can at any moment consider the whole import of an event that is occurring. Moment by moment the event is imperceptibly shaping itself, and at every moment of this continuous, uninterrupted shaping of events the commander-in-chief is in the midst of a most complex play of intrigues, worries, contingencies, authorities, projects, counsels, threats and deceptions, and is continually obliged to reply to innumerable questions addressed to him, which constantly conflict with one another.
>
> Learned military authorities quite seriously tell us that Kutusov should have moved his army to the Kaluga road long before reaching Fili, and that somebody actually submitted such a proposal to him. But a commander-in-chief, especially at a difficult moment, has always before him not one proposal but dozens simultaneously. And all these proposals, based upon strategies and tactics, contradict one another. A commander-in-chief's business, it would seem, is simply to choose one of these projects. But even that he cannot do. Events and time do not wait. For instance, on the 28th it is suggested to him to cross to the Kaluga road, but just then an adjutant gallops up from Miloradovich asking whether he is to engage the French or retire. An order must be given to him at once, that instant. And the order to retreat carries us past the turn to the Kaluga road. And after the adjutant comes the commissary-general asking where the stores are to be taken and the chief of hospitals asks where the wounded are to go, and a courier from Petersberg brings a letter from the sovereign which does not admit of the possibility of abandoning Moscow, and the commander-in-chief's rival, the man who is undermining him (and there are always not one but several such), presents a new project diametrically opposed to that of turning to the Kaluga road, and the commander-in-chief himself needs sleep and refreshment to maintain his energy, and a respectable general who has been overlooked in the distribution of rewards comes to complain, and the inhabitants of the district pray to be defended, and an officer sent to inspect the locality comes in and gives a report quite contrary to what was said by the officer previously sent, and a spy, a prisoner, and a general who has been on reconnaissance, all describe the position of the enemy quite differently. People accustomed to misunderstand or to forget these inevitable conditions of a commander-in-

chief's actions describe to us, for instance, the position of the army at Fili and assume that the commander-in-chief could, on the 1st of September, quite freely decide whether to abandon Moscow or defend it: whereas with the Russian army less than four miles from Moscow, no such question existed.

This passage highlights the circumstances that make it difficult to execute any particular strategy—endemic "information unevenness" in terms of both accuracy and timing; actions that change what was previously known; the ability to conceive of multiple and contradictory projects from the same strategic base; and real-time decision overloads placed upon the commander-in-chief. While most chief executives do not live quite such a harrowing existence, there are many periods when such pressures are evident.

Diversity

To respond to complex and changing markets, firms must have a variety of resources, routines, and robust intellectual processes. Even when the immediacy of battle is over and longer time perspectives can be contemplated, there exist natural conditions that make coherent strategic action difficult. In a world that can be only imperfectly "known," achieving total coherence in planning can be accomplished only by denying the existence of underlying complexity. In the face of underlying complexity, monolithic strategies are replaced with a "set" of diverse strategies. This is not all bad. There are even some authors who argue that diversity is not only necessary but even beneficial.

McKelvey (1982) argues the need for diversity from two quite different theoretical bases. Both biological theory and cybernetic science tell us that survival is dependent on maintaining a requisite variety of possible alternatives (Ashby, 1964). The organization must have many alternative ways of achieving its goals in case a route becomes blocked. Without the requisite variety the potential for survival is limited. Thus, the conscious use or unconscious existence of diversity increases the organization's survival potential.

The studies on value conflict within organizations demonstrate the unfortunate difficulty of sustaining diversity. In examining conflict between employees and their organization, McKelvey (1969) found that organizations tend to reward employees who follow the organizational norms rather than rewarding divergent thinkers. At each promotional level there is a selection bias toward homogeneity. Thus, the closer they get to the top the more likely the management is to be in mutual agreement. If senior managers see the world in much the same way, they are unlikely to adopt diverse strategies. McKelvey argues that lack of variety in outlook is likely to reduce the organization's ability to cope with and adapt to changing external situations and to weaken the organization.

This view is further supported by Warren Bennis in *The Unconscious Conspiracy* (1976), a book based to a large extent on the author's experience as president of the University of Cincinnati. The inadvertent result of management's discomfort with conflict creates a "doppelganger" effect—the development of an executive team whose members all think like one another. Bennis's experience suggests that such uniformity of perspective filters out early warnings of changing situations and prohibits the development of necessary contingencies.

Given these natural restraints, how can the value of diversity be transformed into guidelines with potential for directing managerial thought and underlying managerial action? To answer this question the basic arenas of diversity within the organizational setting must be articulated. Below we briefly scan several types of diversity as exhibited within the organization.

Organizations engage in many diverse activities. At times they vary from the mission statements that they have formulated to articulate their commitments and goals. A firm's intent and its observable or emergent behavior are often distinct (Mintzberg, 1973; Argyris and Schon, 1978). Organizations employ mixed strategies in pursuing their business opportunities and product mix. And, of course, they continually adapt and change tactics in response to variances in their results. Within each firm it is normal to demonstrate diverse approaches, even within firms that seem to have clear dominant themes.

Organizational Diversity. The idea of organizational diversity can be illustrated through the experience of one European automobile manufacturer. This company's attempt to bring a totally new model to market was thwarted by its inability to coordinate its engine, assembly, and marketing divisions. As a result the introduction of this model was very difficult and contributed to poor market performance for the first year or two. Only then did the firm engage in a serious and long-term study to determine the source of these problems and to find ways to overcome them in the future.

The problem was identified as a misunderstood mismatch of technologically driven organizational cultures and their resultant innovation mechanisms. The assembly division was easily able to comply with the technical demands of launching the new car as it normally handled a very high rate of change made necessary by yearly model changeovers. The engine division did not normally experience such a rapid rate of change and was not prepared to meet the new demands. Since the engine manufacturing system was a process with very limited flexibility and new engines were only infrequently introduced, the division's development system was also relatively inflexible and the development system's inflexibility was in turn not compatible with the flexibility and adaptability of the assembly division. The marketing division was used to planning its approaches without detailed coordination as its task focused upon the car's image, not its details.

The two technical divisions worked under considerably different senses of time priorities, which posed additional problems. The longer time horizons of the engine division did not fit smoothly with the quick reaction needs of the assembly division and created serious coordination problems. The differences between the two divisions were further intensified by the capital-intense characteristics of one division versus the relative labor intensity of the other.

Whereas this type of firm needs to coordinate its major units in order to function, other firms can choose to separate them if they prefer. It is not uncommon to have separate divisions for the limited production of somewhat customized, high-value products and longer production runs for generic products—even when they are based upon the same product technology (Prahalad and Hamel, 1990). The diversity of the product, process, and market of such divisions would allow each to coexist while pursuing distinctly different strategies. But this would continue to create problems when all three divisions had to complete their work to meet a common target date.

Product Diversity. Single-product firms almost all inevitably consider line extension and/or capacity utilization steps. Line extension represents limited diversity using size, color, and modest functional differences to satisfy a wider range of customers. The selection of products to improve utilization of capacity often creates a significant diversity in the pattern of resource application. Capacity utilization usually creates a wider gap between the original products and those selected to more effectively use either productive capacity or distributive capacity.

A soft drink manufacturer, for example, added potato chips to its line to better utilize its existing distribution system. Both products were sold through the same outlets although the lines had opposite seasonal sales peaks: soft drinks were summer products; potato chips were winter products. Unfortunately, although the distribution channel was better utilized, manufacturing under capacity (in winter) was unaffected. The added costs of purchasing, warehousing, spoilage, and so on, did not provide the additional profit margins needed to create the necessary return on the new capital investment (delivery vans, racks and point of purchase material, etc.). Additionally, the potato chip peak was not as high as that of soft drinks and the maintenance of potato chip delivery during the summer interfered with the higher profit margin soft drink line. The resulting strain on the organization was quite high and the potato chip line was soon abandoned. This kind of diversity in the pattern of resource application can put pressure upon the organization's management system. Ideally, product mix selections do have a satisfactory return on investment even with the additional managerial complications, and in many instances this is the case.

Life Cycle Diversity. Product life cycles are a well-known phenomenon. Appropriate organizational activities during each phase of a product life cycle are quite different, and so managerial activity and focus must change as the product moves from the growth phase to the mature phase and finally into decline. When a firm has several products in different phases of the product life cycle this problem is exacerbated. Large potential is observed in the growth phase and often inordinate amounts of managerial time and resources are consumed. During the mature phase management is often "by exception," even though large amounts of resources are consumed. The results in this phase are most often positive and corporate funds are accumulated. In decline, management is faced with an exit strategy question. In this phase price and often profit margins are on the decline, requiring careful management attention and timely decision making about culling the product from the line. Thus, life cycle effects add a dimension to the diversity of the product mix effects.

Customer Diversity. Not all customers are alike. They often purchase the same product for a variety of reasons. Some purchases are determined by price, others by location, some by functional features, others by habit, and so on. Methods of purchasing are equally diverse: cash or credit, by mail or in person, under formal contract or by informal handshake. While this natural diversity is understandable, it does not necessarily have to be the driving force in determining the firm's response. The firm can act to limit the diversity to some extent by better targeting the customers it wishes to attract and/or to determine the terms and conditions to be offered.

Strategic Business Unit Diversity. Another form of diversity is the mix of strategic business units within a division. Here the divisional strategy relates to resource allocation among the units and/or to infrastructure investments to serve all the units. Each of the units has a character of its own, based to some extent on the characteristics of (or types of) diversity listed previously.

Commitment

One method of overcoming the combined effects of action-taking complexity and normal diversity is to demonstrate strong commitment to basic values and/or underlying systematic approaches to the organizational situation (Ghemawat, 1991). Here are two quite different examples of such commitment.

The structural reshaping of General Motors under the leadership of Alfred P. Sloan, Jr., provides an example of a, then counterintuitive, response to a problem which was endemic to all large organizations. In his autobiography, *My Years with General Motors* (1963), Sloan reported on his continual struggle as General Motors tried to find an operational formula to balance the need for coordination with the need for motivation. By focusing upon the relationships between strategy and structure, Sloan was able to begin solving the problem. He saw the value of decentralization and the use of the profit center concept as a method for creating executive motivation. At the same time he employed a clear product line concept as a method of reducing the costs of coordination. He committed what was then considered a business heresy by allowing his divisions to go head-to-head against one another in the marketplace. He encouraged this situation to hone the competitive edge he felt had been missing in his large, functionally organized firm. This business heresy has since become conventional wisdom after meeting both the test of the market and that of the academy (Chandler, 1962; Thompson, 1967; and Rumelt, 1979; among others).

By contrast, John L. Lewis, president of the United Mine Workers (UMW), selected a strategy unique within the American labor movement. Responding to the pressures of his constituency and pressures from the industry, Lewis and his union adopted a bargaining position that encouraged technological innovation and productivity improvement. By making this choice the UMW opted for fewer miners, safer mines, and higher wages per miner—a trade-off requiring real courage as a large number of UMW members were not only displeased but also displaced by the choice. Clearly a significant, long-term difference in the overall economic picture of mining was created by virtue of this radical alteration of the very structure of the industry.

Though Sloan and Lewis solved their problems differently, there are some interesting similarities in their style of taking action. Successful implementation of the strategies can be attributed to their personal commitment to the options they selected. It is clear that an executive's personal determination often makes the difference in overcoming implementation problems with an otherwise well-selected strategy. This commitment develops dedicated structures and processes that effectively institutional-ize (Selznick, 1957) the strategy. (Determination, though, is not enough to compensate for selecting an inappropriate strategy.) The power of commitment is supported by Goodman and Huff (1978), who recommend strategic action based upon formal analy-sis, multiple assessment perspectives, and executive commitment. They conclude that the amount of personal energy expended by an executive in pursuing a selected course of action is quite likely to be more important in determining the success of that action than is an assessment of the "correct timing."

The concept of commitment was echoed by Winston Churchill in his last will and testament. Churchill is reputed to have given a large donation to his alma mater in sup-port of the *not* well-rounded student. The homogenization of modern liberal education was anathema to Churchill, who contended that the people who make a difference are narrowly focused but vigorous special-interest proponents.

Action, Diversity, and Commitment

The complex issues of information unevenness, change, decision overloads, commit-ment, and diversity serve to highlight the action-oriented contextual background of strategy. These issues often confuse what the firm is really about. Crisp communica-tion of purpose can provide a touchstone for management. The next two major sections amplify on this theme. They discuss alternative definitions of strategy and the underly-ing conceptual paradigms associated with a chosen definition of "defensible competi-tive advantage."

DEFINITIONAL BASES OF THE STRATEGIC CONCEPT

This section focuses upon how the definitions employed to describe strategy clearly alter the types of decisions taken by the firm to formulate and to implement strategy. It is important to harness this power through the development of an appropriate definition of strategy-making, a definition that can employ the inherent power-of-metaphor to communicate and direct activity.

The wide variety of strategic definitions illustrates an evolving understanding as various writers engage in thoughtful presentations of their strategic explorations.

The Merriam-Webster dictionary defines strategy as

> a careful plan or method especially for achieving an end, tactics is the art or skill of using available means to reach an end.

This definition suggests the possibility of developing new means to an end, means dif-ferent from those "available means"—thus the distinction between strategy and tactics. The power of the definition is contained within the idea that the future is not a simple extrapolation of the present and that, assuming the ends are known, management has the power to change the operational means of the organization. Thus, the definition is adaptive as the possibility for change is suggested. It is also conservative and stabiliz-ing as the ends are accepted as given.

Steven Brandt (1981) uses this definition in a text that focuses upon emerging corporations:

> Strategy is a summary statement of how objectives will be pursued.

This is a considerably more conservative definition. That is, the "summary statement" provides the executive with an economical instrument for the overall guidance of the organization. Within this definition neither change nor innovation is suggested. Further, it does not convey a search for objectives; ends and means are presupposed.

George Steiner (1969) suggests that

> strategic managerial planning is a philosophy, a process, a structure of plans which deal with the futurity of current decisions.

Steiner focuses upon planning. He conveys an important idea with the phrase "futurity of current decisions." This idea focuses the attention of the executive upon the impact of current decisions. A particular current decision may allow the organization to cope well in some future situations but will preempt (or at least weaken) effective coping in others. A decision to construct an inflexible but highly efficient manufacturing facility, for example, will be excellent if the future represents price competition and continuing high levels of demand but will be poor if the future requires wider variety and/or a reduced demand. The weakness of this idea lies in the executive's failure to focus on the examination of the future per se or upon the selection of ends in light of various possible future outcomes. Nor does it suggest to the executive a dynamic in the means of operation over time.

Correcting for the overlooked dynamic is the definition used by John Grant and William King (1982):

> A strategy is a timed sequence of internally consistent and conditional resource allocation decisions that are designed to fulfill an organization's objectives.

The conditional resource allocation decision suggests to the executive that change will be needed. Thus, this definition can be innovative in its function, but it is also conservative or status quo oriented in that the objectives are treated as givens.

Richard Vancil and Peter Lorange (1977) use another definition:

> Strategy is a conceptualization of long-term objectives, broad constraints and near term plans set by the executive and currently in operation.

The definition here is one of power and analysis. The executive sets in motion a short-term plan derived analytically from the executive's selection of long-term objectives and the existing broad constraints. This definition does not accept the ends as given but requires that the executive select the ends. The definition is limited because the selection of ends is left to the executive rather than derived from an analytic framework.

A definition taken from Rowe, Mason, and Dickel (1982) addresses the goal-setting process:

> Strategic management is the decision process that conjoins the organization's capability with the opportunities and threats it faces in its environment.

Here the goal-setting process is derived from an analysis of organizational capabilities and environmental threat and opportunities. The definition lacks power since the executive is enjoined to analyze and select rather then to be proactive and create, yet this definition implies the art of the possible.

Another definition that includes goal formulation is used by Porter (1980):

> A competitive strategy is a broad formula for how a business is going to compete, what its goals should be, and what policies are needed to carry out those goals.

This definition deals with the determination of goals, the methods of attack, and an analytical framework necessary for creating policy. The executive has to determine the goals.

The final definition cannot be attributed to any specific person. It has been the lingua franca of the academic for a number of years.

> Strategy is the creation of a defensible competitive advantage.

This definition suggests that organizations are and/or should be seeking positions in which they can exhibit a measure of monopolistic power. This limited position of finding and/or creating market imperfections implies an environmental analysis and study of current strengths and weaknesses, a creation of barriers to imitation, and a host of other activities. In this definition, executives must be both reactive and proactive within the environment in which they function and must alter the nature of the organization in reaction to both opportunities and threats.

The definition which encompasses the fullest range of those activities that are necessary components of a successful organization is the one that should be chosen. The final definition does this quite well. It implies that strategy requires a careful study of the reasons for existence and success along with considerations of the actions required to meet and accomplish one's stated mission.

DEFENSIBLE COMPETITIVE ADVANTAGE

The value of defensible competitive advantage is best explored through what is basically a commonsense approach. It illustrates the ideas of complexity and diversity and provides a base for subsequent actions. Then the theoretical underpinnings of defensible competitive advantage are explored to provide a framework for suggesting appropriate managerial choices.

A Commonsense Approach

In practice, the variety of means available for creating a defensible competitive advantage is immense. In the simplest sense, however, knowing whether you have been successful or not is measured by survival. Survival implies an adequate return on investment in comparison with other opportunities. It permits the continued employment of the firm's assets in their current pattern. The corner cleaning establishment can create a defensible competitive advantage as well as Royal Dutch Shell. What do these two companies at opposite ends of the corporate spectrum have in common? They exist and look as if they will continue to exist. Additionally, both appear to have a high enough level of business acumen to account for their continued existence. This rather far-fetched comparison of the large and the small, the sophisticated and the naive, is intended to point out the concept's premise; that is, a defensible competitive advantage is not a single masterstroke like the apocryphal story about Joe Kennedy having cornered the rum market just before the end of Prohibition. Rather, the concept incorporates a multitude of variables such as product, process, location, and organizational and resource qualities. It also has dynamic dimensions, such as timing, rate of change, and the advantages of being first.

To elaborate on the ideas of Richard Normann (1969), an organization is a unique bundle of assets, contracts, and relationships. Its products exhibit more or less variety, are better or less well designed, are expensive, moderately priced, or inexpensive, and deliver a certain level of efficacy to the user. Its production processes can be more or less efficient, unique, or adaptive. It can have organizational qualities regarding innovation, market knowledge, technology sensing, project management skills, and so on. Its location can be a key determinant of labor costs, raw materials, and/or customers. Its resource strength can come from the availability of personnel, technical facilities, financial strength, supplier power, and the like. Each of these dimensions is valued differently by each customer, but the successful firm does attract, through this bundle of assets, customers who choose to buy from it rather than from others.

The corner cleaning establishment that offers an undifferentiated product at a standard price depends on variables such as location, parking, and courteous service to attract customers. Some use the corner cleaner because the owner is a character. Some use the cleaner because it sells coupon books. Others use the cleaner across the street in the shopping center and do two or three errands without moving the car. Royal Dutch Shell also offers an undifferentiated product at a standard price. It attracts customers solely because of location. This simple one-dimensional argument is, of course, specious. Some patronize Shell because its price is no more than two cents higher than other major brands and its stations accept credit cards. Others do so because the Shell station is open 24 hours, and some swear that Shell gas gives higher mileage than any other brand. Shell's customer base clearly responds to diverse dimensions of the firm's product and business approach.

A constellation of diverse reasons permits firms to operate successfully; that is, to earn an acceptable return on investment. But many of these reasons are conscious choices on the part of the business executive, albeit often taken at diverse times in the history of the firm and developed at functional levels of the firm not necessarily dependent upon a strategic vantage point. Some factors such as changing traffic patterns in the neighborhood are unpredictable but have a collateral effect.

A Theoretical Approach

Competitive advantage results from a failure of the perfect market, which, depending on the situation and the firm's actions, could have relatively long or short duration. Failure of the perfect market arises from several conditions: information delays and blockages, the costs of information, imperfect imitability, artificial differentiation, preemptive situations, regulatory barriers, and poor "market potential–to–investment needs" ratios.

Market Imperfections and Temporary Competitive Advantage. Adam Smith (1776) believed that all producers would eventually adopt the least-cost approach. All firms eventually would look the same, theoretically eliminating the possibility that any one would enjoy a long-run advantage. In general, competitive advantage arises from an imperfection in the market system—an imperfection that might be found on either the production or the consumption side of the market. Being the first producer of new goods or services (the first mover) stems either from purposeful strategy or from random interests on the part of an individual entrepreneur or innovative firm. Either way the market imperfection can be said to exist as little or no information is available about this market. Other producers cannot enter the market until they notice the first mover's activities and recognize that the market exists. Then they incur delays involved initiating a new business unit. Thus, the first mover's competitive advantage can be viewed as the sum of the two time lags: the time it takes to recognize a new product has been introduced and the time it takes to respond. The nature of the first mover's "temporary competitive advantage" then stems from delays in market information and business delays in setup and entry. The first mover often can stake out a reputation for innovation, quality, and cost which extends the temporary advantage beyond the initial monopoly time period created by the information and setup delays (Lawless and Fisher, 1990).

On the consumer side, market imperfection arises from delays and blockages of information about the product's or service's existence, its availability, and its performance and use qualities. These information delays relate to the knowledge a consumer has about the product per se and/or to one or another firm's variations upon the intrinsic product. With some delay in communication, the end result is the sharing of information about the product and the temporary competitive advantage disappears—unless the cost involved to obtain the information is too high.

Market Imperfection and Stable Competitive Advantage. Neither temporary production- nor consumption-based market imperfections are significant departures from the perfect market. For instance, on the production side, production costs of the individual firms exhibit no learning and no experience effects, and the sharing of information is the final result, albeit with some communications delay. Similarly, temporary market imperfection due to consumption effects assumes that essential characteristics of the product eventually can be communicated with certainty. Neither of these conditions is consistent with everyday knowledge of the nature of markets.

The temporary imperfection argument can be extended to a "stable competitive advantage" by studying the sources of permanent market imperfection. Philosophically speaking, all advantage will eventually pass as the need satisfied by a product or service waxes, then wanes, and finally disappears. Thus, the words "stable" and "quasi-permanent" have been selected to more realistically state the case—to describe a situation that is far from temporary but short of immortal (Schumpeter, 1976). Theoretical conditions for quasi-permanent market imperfection can be discussed under several categories—information economics, imitability considerations, preemptive conditions, regulatory barriers, and market size versus investment costs.

The Economics of Information and the Market. The cost of obtaining information is frequently found to be a nontrivial expenditure. In this circumstance market imperfections often result. The costly information means that consumers cannot easily know the variety of products or services available, their performance qualities, their use qualities, or even their costs. Individual firms can take advantage of the consumers' difficulty and thus reap the benefits of an apparent competitive advantage. Costly information on the production and market position can prevent rivals from duplicating a successful strategy.

For example, consumers' costs of acquiring information in the personal computer market is extremely high, and firm reputation seems more important than the specific characteristics of the product. After purchase, the new computer owner is often bombarded with opinions of friends suggesting features for which they should have looked—and/or waited.

The cost of obtaining information on how to manufacture a product also represents a market imperfection which results in firm competitive advantage on the price and/or quality dimensions. Manufacturers thus compete by creating or replicating "best practice" strategies. While this focus does occur in many organizations, it is risky because not all consumers want the same functional results from their purchases. Even under conditions of a perfect market, consumer differences in preferences and utility functions for various features would allow several firms to exist because the customer differences would lead to market segmentation. In segmented markets the cost of obtaining information on competitors' manufacturing processes reduces the organization's motivation to focus on such a strategic approach when a less expensive product differentiation strategy might be sufficient to create competitive advantage. Additionally, the very process of following the "success factors of others" changes the conditions under which they led to success. In the extreme, if all rivals follow an identical strategy, they could create perfect competition.

Firm Imitability. In some industries product differentiation is limited. The recent uncoupling of service stations from their sources of petroleum product supplies was an admission that the products were not really differentiable—gasoline is just gasoline. Many chemical products are also undifferentiable. In these situations, the high cost of obtaining and employing competitor manufacturing process information can create a market imperfection allowing competitive advantage to develop between and among the firms in such process-oriented industries. Much more secrecy about manufacturing plans and processes and investment levels is evident in the process industries than in many other industries.

Sometimes an otherwise comparable product can be differentiated by successfully conferring upon it attributes which are psychological in nature. This is the effect of advertising and is often referred to as an investment in brand name capital. The advertising effect as commonly understood is one that accumulates with continual reinforcement. That is, the effect of an advertisement is strengthened when repeated within a short period of time. Unfortunately, the repeat does not double the effect of the first advertisement and soon a maximum impact is reached. After advertising is terminated the impact wanes. Thus, advertising must be maintained for a product to continue to benefit from a such a reputationally based market imperfection.

Another aspect of information economics involves imperfect imitability—the difficulty of duplicating some successful strategies. Fundamentally, each firm is a unique bundle of assets. This bundle is multifaceted with regard to the firm but also with regard to the firm's products or services. The actual dimensions of a firm's bundle of assets are both hard to determine and hard to measure. Often the elements which make a venture successful are so complex they can be known only imperfectly—even by the firm's own management (Lippman and Rumelt, 1982). In such a circumstance, perfect imitation is not possible and another condition for perfect market competition is unsatisfied. There exist opportunities for the creation of a defensible competitive advantage. This suggests that executives' starting points when pondering competitive moves should be their unique bundle of assets and their competitors' ability to imitate.

Preemption. If a firm can preempt, or deny access to rivals, a critical resource (input to the firm's production function) or a market, then a market imperfection can occur and the benefits of a defensible competitive advantage are possible. The resource might be personnel, supplies, raw material, technology, or the like. When extended over a sufficient time horizon, preemption may be quite valuable.

Regulatory Barriers. A variation on this notion of preemptive position can be seen in the market failures which result from regulatory barriers. Some, the so-called natural monopolies, clearly present a defensible competitive advantage. Under the current rush to deregulation, these advantages are more sparse. Patents, copyrights, trademarks, and so on, are other examples of quasi-permanent legal or regulatory barriers to the perfect market. Another side of the regulatory barrier can be seen in cases where less efficient firms use antitrust legislation to keep prices high enough for them to stay in business.

Investment Costs versus Market Size. In some circumstances, the size of the market cannot justify rivals' investments necessary to enter. Thus, the first mover can create sufficient capacity to meet demand in the entire market segment and preemptively block competition. This works only when the production function exhibits increasing returns to scale, that is, when major cost savings occur as the volume of production increases. With increasing returns to scale, the second mover must match the capacity size of the first mover in order to potentially be price competitive. Otherwise the first mover will always be able to reduce price to a level that is not profitable for the new entrant but is still profitable for itself. This situation, with all honors going to the first mover based on efficiency, holds only if the product is undifferentiated. Technological (product characteristics) or psychological (advertising effects) differentiation will certainly provide opportunities to segment the market and will be valuable if the cost of information to the consumer is low enough for these effects to be realized.

The basic result of market imperfection for those firms that can create or locate such a condition is the opportunity to earn higher than average profits—so-called supernormal returns. When facing an advantageous situation, a firm theoretically can maximize supernormal returns by a pricing strategy that is unique to each customer. The price would represent the value added to the customer of acquiring the firm's product. Of course, value-added pricing is complicated and potentially costly itself and is seldom practiced in favor of the simpler cost-plus pricing system.

Thus, market imperfection provides the opportunity for supernormal return under circumstances which arise from several conditions: information delays and blockages, the costs of information, imperfect imitability, artificial differentiation, preemptive situations, regulatory barriers, and appropriate market size–to–investment costs ratios.

THE CREATION OF ADVANTAGE: REALITY TESTING THE CONCEPT

Advantage is achieved within a dynamic context of evolving organizational and environmental forces. These forces create information unevenness, change, decision overloads, and diversity, which can be attenuated through commitment and through the clear communication of strategic intent. The definition of strategy as defensible competitive advantage illustrates the potential for reactive and proactive interactions with the environment as well as the need to alter organizations' response to both opportunities and threats.

This definition suggests that organizations seek positions in which they can obtain a measure of monopolistic power. This limited position of finding and/or creating market imperfections implies an environmental analysis and study of current capabilities and creation of barriers to imitation.

REFERENCES

Argyris, C., and D. Schon. 1978. *Organizational Learning: A Theory of Action Perspective.* Reading, MA: Addison-Wesley.

Ashby, R. 1964. *An Introduction to Cybernetics.* London: Methuen.

Bennis, W. 1976. *The Unconscious Conspiracy: Why Leaders Can't Lead.* New York: AMA-COM.

Brandt, S. C. 1981. *Strategic Planning in Emerging Companies.* Reading, MA: Addison-Wesley.

Chandler, A. 1962. *Strategy and Structure: Chapters in the History of the Industrial Enterprise.* Cambridge, MA: MIT Press.

Ghemawat, P. 1991. *Commitment.* New York: Free Press.

Goodman, R., and A. Huff. 1978. "Enriching Policy Premises for an Ambiguous World." In John Sutherland, ed., *Management Handbook for Public Administrators.* New York: Van Nostrand Reinhold.

Grant, J., and W. King. 1982. *The Logic of Strategic Planning.* Boston: Little, Brown.

Lawless, M., and K. Fisher. 1990. "Sources of Durable Competitive Advantage in New Products," *Journal of Product Innovation Management* 7(1):35–44.

Lippman, S., and R. Rumelt. 1982. "Uncertain Imitability: An Analysis of Interfirm Differences in Efficiency under Competition," *Bell Journal of Economics* 13:418–38.

McKelvey, B. 1969. "Expectational Noncomplimentarity and Style of Interaction between Professional and Organization," *Administrative Science Quarterly* 14(1):21–32.

McKelvey, B. 1982. *Organizational Systematics: Taxonomy, Evolution, Classification.* Berkeley: University of California Press.

Merriam-Webster Dictionary, ed.

Mintzberg, H. 1973. *The Nature of Managerial Work.* Englewood Cliffs, NJ: Prentice-Hall.

Normann, R. 1969. "Some Conclusions from Thirteen Case Studies of New Product Development." Stockholm: Swedish Institute of Administrative Research, UPM-RN-100.

Porter, M. 1980. *Competitive Strategy.* New York: Free Press.

Prahalad, C., and G. Hamel. 1990. "The Core Competence of the Corporation," *Harvard Business Review,* May–June, pp. 79–91.

Rowe, A., R. Mason, and K. Dickel. 1982. *Strategic Management and Business Policy.* Reading, MA: Addison-Wesley.

Rumelt, R. 1979. "Evaluation of Strategy: Theory and Models." In D. Schendel and C. Hofer, eds., *Strategic Management.* Boston: Little, Brown.

Schumpeter, J. 1976. *Capitalism, Socialism and Democracy,* 5th ed. London: Allen and Unwin.

Selznick, P. 1957. *Leadership in Administration: A Sociological Interpretation.* Evanston, IL: Row Peterson.

Sloan, A. P., Jr. 1963. *My Years with General Motors.* New York: Doubleday.

Smith, A. 1776. *An Inquiry into the Nature and Causes of the Wealth of Nations.* London: W. Strahan and T. Cadell.

Steiner, G. 1969. *Top Management Planning.* New York: Macmillan.

Thompson, J. D., 1967. *Organizations in Action: Social Science Bases of Administrative Theory.* New York: McGraw-Hill.

Tolstoy, L. 1941. *War and Peace,* translated by Louise and Aylmer Maude. London: Oxford University Press. Originally published in 1863–69.

Vancil, R., and P. Lorange. 1977. *Strategic Planning Systems.* Englewood Cliffs, NJ.: Prentice-Hall.

3

The Technology–Strategy Interface

Technology and strategy represent two very complex areas of thought. The interface between the two becomes a concern when technology significantly affects performance. The ensuing integrative difficulties are based on contrasts—of worldviews, techniques, and time horizons. This chapter offers two broad foci for responding to the challenge of integration under complexity. We discuss first the basic nature of the contrasts that underlie the challenge; then we focus upon guidelines to ameliorate the ensuing conflicts and to integrate the results.

ISSUES OF TECHNOLOGY–STRATEGY INTEGRATION

For a strategic program to be successful a number of factors—some controllable, some not—must be present. When the strategic program involves technology, this factor set expands due to uncertainty and integrative complexity. The very nature of the technological process adds significant uncertainty regarding both performance and timing. This natural uncertainty causes further problems when integrated with strategic "planning." As a result, significant tensions between the technological and the strategic communities are frequently exhibited. More critically, it is common for these tensions to remain unexamined, resulting in inappropriate corrective action. To overcome this deficiency it is helpful to examine three key perspectives.

The main perspective focuses on the role of technology in strategy. This concept is enhanced by two complementary perspectives: the strategist's view of technology and the technologist's view of strategy. A simple story—an organizational parable—of the steel industry is a good introduction to these concepts and illustrates the performance issues that arise from the complexity involved in integrating technology and strategy.

The Parable of Steel

This story may very well be apocryphal, but it is alleged to have occurred in the mid-1960s. It describes the research and development (R&D) divisions of three different steel companies, each pursuing its own unique portfolio of projects. Each R&D division independently and simultaneously succeeded in creating a virtually identical specialty steel. Since the developments were independent—no firm had knowledge of the others' activities—each firm's further choices could also be seen as independent.

Since they had the same starting point, it might be reasonable to expect that each of the firms would reach the same ending point (although this expectation belies the unique capability discussion of the previous chapter). Even though all three corporations had the same *technological* opportunity, different *strategic* decisions led to divergent results. By normal measures, one firm did quite well. It entered the marketplace with the product and achieved a dominant share with strong profit margins. A second firm made the same entry decision but achieved only a small market share and earned limited returns on its investment. Interestingly, the third corporation chose not to enter the marketplace at all.

Why were such different choices made and how were such different results obtained? The first corporation developed a well-articulated corporate strategy based on market, product, and technological concerns. The R&D program focused upon the development of products which the firm could market well and which the firm could manufacture effectively.

The second corporation seems to have allowed its R&D program to deviate significantly from its areas of marketing and manufacturing expertise. It also seemed unaware of the impact of this drift. As a result, it misspent *both* its R&D resources and its marketing resources.

The third corporation also permitted the drift but recognized its impact and minimized the error by choosing to stay out of the market. Even though the firm eventually recognized that this specialty steel was not a viable part of its product strategy, it still was responsible for inefficient use of R&D resources.

A careful and extensive examination of the real-world facts would enrich the story but would also reduce the simplicity of the point being made. Strategy formulation and implementation depend on close articulation among various functional specialties in order to cope with a set of complex issues and to realize organization-wide potential. Not only must functional specialties be coordinated, but the technology must be clearly integrated into the strategy formulation and the implementation processes.

The Role of Technology in Strategy

Within the literature on the management of research, development, and innovation is a remarkable degree of agreement about the need for technology areas to be integrated with strategy-making and planning. For reasons illustrated by the steel parable, lack of integration often leads to wasteful employment of resources, while integration eventually translates into better performance.

The rationale for integration is quite broad and includes the promise of more successful product introduction, greater production economies, protection of products from appropriation by competitors, and more. The literature usually cites one or more of the following general statements as justification:

> Integration of technology and strategy has direct strategic and competitive effects.

Investment in integration (both coordination and information costs) is a significant claim on the firm's resources.

Integration is required to achieve goal congruence.

Technology Decisions Are Often Strategic in Nature. When reviewing the menu of technological choices, executives are often struck by the serious implications of their decisions. Many of these decisions span long time frames and deploy large portions of a firm's available resources. These decisions are frequently difficult to change once commitments are made and if the choices do not contribute to the firm's success or become a constraint on its flexibility they will, perforce, alter the corporate strategy. In the very first phase of committing resources to technological programs, these concerns must be recognized and consciously considered. If resources do not earn appropriate returns, management is forced to accept costly redeployment decisions and/or lower returns on technology investment. Resources committed to technology must be considered strategic in nature (Wheelwright, 1984).

Technology Directly Affects Competitive Position. Production decisions have significant technological bases. Choices regarding maintaining currency in process innovation or lowering the costs of manufacturing and transportation have direct impact on the firm's competitive position (Skinner, 1978). These decisions can provide direct benefits, provide the firm with the ability to alter the bases of competition, or may provide margins to engage in more costly marketing strategies. Defining the firm's technology as it affects the ability to maintain distinctive competitive advantage is therefore central to market success (Frohman and Bitondo, 1981; Williams, 1983).

Technology Competes for Resources within the Firm. Each firm must decide how to deploy its resources in light of opportunities available. Selection of one investment area normally precludes an investment in another. Thus, technological investment projects must be arrayed alongside other opportunities or demands within the firm. There should be an allocation method that provides a far-ranging view of the company's ability to support the mix of proposed activities. Lack of integration in making these decisions will inevitably result in uneven progress and increased competitive risk (Ramsey, 1981; Buggie, 1982; Hertz and Thomas, 1983).

Structures and Processes for Promoting Innovation Are Costly. The administrative costs of organizational structures and processes intended specifically to promote innovation are generally high (Quinn, 1979; Cooper, 1981; Lawless, Feinberg, Glassman, and Bengston, 1981). There are usually opportunity costs and external effects to consider as well. These costs may either limit or enhance the firm's ability to execute its other critical tasks.

Information Systems for Managing Technology Are Costly. In the technology functions, there is often high task uncertainty and a corresponding intense need for information to be gathered, processed, and transferred during task performance (Galbraith, 1973, 1977). Managing the uncertainty and developing adequate information systems to support the technology functions are strategic issues not only because of choices of substance and content but also because of the significant cost implications.

Integration among Diverse Organizational Units Is Often Required. Effective coordination among several departments is a necessary condition for successful commercialization of new products (Mansfield, 1981). Product innovation requires interaction
among R&D, marketing, product engineering, and production (Ford and Ryan, 1981;
Buggie, 1982). There is, however, a natural tendency for organizational units, including those involved with the technology functions, to suboptimize. They pursue
parochial goals with little appreciation of the impact those goals may have on other
units, and perhaps on the organization as a whole (Cyert and March, 1963). The tendency for specialists to narrowly focus on the specifics requires a countervailing formal integrative effort (Lawrence and Lorsch, 1967).

*Divergence in Worldviews between Managers and Researchers Requires Special
Attention.* The values, worldview, and corporate goal orientation of scientists are
liable to differ from those of managers and from what the firm needs to ensure its competitive success. (Parker, 1977; Petroni, 1983). While the importance of this issue
varies with the technology function to some degree (Ritti, 1982), it poses problems of
communication and goal congruity in all organizations.

Strategy–Technology Integration Is a Dominant Need. Weil and Cangemi (1983)
clearly identify integration as the dominant theme in their comprehensive review of the
strategy-technology literature. In many organizations, strategists and technologists
exist as two separate communities. Ideally, these communities maintain close communication on matters of planning and decision making. Rarely are the two groups well
integrated. Differences—in temperament, in training, in location within the corporate
hierarchy, in roles regarding budgeting—all detract from integration. These factors
reduce the likelihood of an effective strategic–technological integration without purposeful, if not formal measures imposed by management.

Even in firms in which technology is recognized as a competitive weapon, serious
friction may still exist. Managers in key nontechnological positions often do not understand the nature of technology and are uncomfortable with the uncertainty that arises
from the unanticipated problems created by the technological functions. Technology
creates problems for decision makers because of the uncertainty it generates, an uncertainty which almost guarantees that planners will have to revise and re-revise their
plans as unpredictable obstacles continue to occur.

Careful analysis of the integration difficulties is more likely to yield good solutions than is symptom-oriented problem solving. The first step in such analysis is the
creation of a common understanding of the basis of the differences between the two
communities.

The Strategist's View of Technology

In general terms, the strategist's view of technology revolves around the three linked
issues of constraints, worldviews, and complications. In many circumstances specific
technological choices prove constraining as they preempt flexibility. These constraints
are often exacerbated by the impact of inherent uncertainties that accompanies techno-

logical choice. Finally, the constraints and the accompanying uncertainty further complicate the strategy-making process.

The Technology Base as a Constraint. Technological constraints inherent in choices of capital investment, product design, and production process are potentially frustrating to strategic purpose. In the steel and automotive industries, technological progress is seemingly slowed by capital intensity. Some chemical works exhibit similar resistance to change. Large markets and substantial capital investments permit the development of finely tuned, highly efficient manufacturing processes. Fine-tuning of manufacturing creates resistance to "revolutionary" change. Similarly, finely tuned manufacturing processes can become a limitation to the rapid introduction of product changes or variations (Abernathy, 1978). The obvious converse to this is that if revolutionary change is to occur, it is likely to arrive from vested incumbents (Tushman and Anderson, 1986).

A similar argument can be made about the constraints imposed by some product designs. A highly complex design often prompts a firm to vary and extend a current product rather than redesign it (Goodman and Abernathy, 1978). Rather than quickly moving on to a next-generation product many firms "tweak the parameters" of an existing design to find a low-cost way of extending the life cycle. Unfortunately, adopting this strategy can mean falling behind. For example, an electronics firm that specialized in radar navigation was unable to compete in that market when the technology shifted to inertial guidance systems. By continually improving the accuracy and reducing the weight, volume, and power of the current design the firm was initially able to upgrade existing equipment and maintain a marginal lead over the inertial technology. Eventually, however, the firm was overshadowed by newer technology and withdrew from the navigation marketplace. Thus, current product technology served as a serious barrier to the firm's ability to move to the next wave of technology.

Interaction between product design and manufacturing process design can also create resistance to change. Choosing a design approach that allows flexibility in product function often restricts manufacturing efficiencies and can reduce potential low-cost strategies. Adopting a low-cost strategy is a common way to extend the product life cycle after market saturation has been achieved. In the later phase of the product life cycle, attempts to extend the cycle range from upgrading product performance qualities to reducing price. This end-of-life-cycle, low-cost strategy can be limited if the firm has to start from a diverse base—a base that is a natural consequence of serving multiple specialized market segments.

Thus, technological choices of the past can be viewed by strategists as either enabling or constraining. Such constraints to adaptation create tension and frustration in strategy formulation and implementation.

Worldview Conflicts. Strategists are commonly distressed by technologists' unreliable estimates of performance, cost, or schedule. Strategists' normal response is to compensate for the unreliable estimate problem by requesting that technologists produce increasingly detailed planning documents. While the strategist's response is common, it is based upon an important misunderstanding of the essence of technological work.

Technological development is a process of "discovery"—of appropriate interrelationships among a large number of variables. It is a discovery process that firms enter even when it is not clear, a priori, that any successful combination of variables actually exists. Success is uncertain, and even the proper approach to the problem is unclear. Such a process needs to be pursued with many contingencies (Quinn, 1985).

In short, strategists often do not understand the work, the worldview, or the iterative nature of the technological development process; thus, they naively believe that by paying closer attention to planning and control they can remedy the situation. When this does not prove true, frustrated strategists often reduce communication with the apparently recalcitrant technologists, although effective management of the firm mandates quite the opposite approach.

One CEO expressed his exasperation by explaining that his development people were late even when he doubled their own time estimates. He did not seem to realize that since the technologists felt they had been given double the time necessary (substantial schedule slack) they would not begin the new task until more pressing assignments had been completed. Thus, in spite of the additional time, their normally encountered unanticipated obstacles were uncovered too late in the schedule to be able to complete the given task on time.

Similar situations exist in firms where technology takes a back seat to functions like finance and marketing. The research director of a major food products division put it very well: "In the face of exceptionally good sales, the CEO only remembers this year's efforts. Since these efforts are at the marketing end of the development cycle, marketing is commended for a job well done. Conversely, the CEO seldom looks at exceptional sales and commends research for a product that was well conceived five years ago." This research director then explained how he coped in such a marketing-driven environment: "When I sit down with the CEO, I select an exceptional product in our current product line and remind him of the early research results that we got five years ago. Then I compare that product to the new one and suggest that the new one has as much potential even though it is still at the early, amorphous stage. I remind him of the skill my staff has demonstrated in pursuing other amorphous ideas and producing effective products which have done well in the marketplace." Even with such sensitivity and finely honed ability to communicate with a technologically naive CEO the value of research to corporate strategy was undervalued and the research director was not a part of the strategic planning apparatus of the firm.

Product and process development are often viewed as having little relevance to the strategic decision-making process. Their jargon and unique problems often create distance between them and the rest of the firm in which they operate. In a 1982 meeting of manufacturing vice presidents from a group of Fortune 500 companies, the advent of CAD/CAM (computer-aided design/computer-aided manufacturing) was being discussed. The group consensus was that CAD/CAM would have no strategic impact. This opinion makes sense only if it is presumed that these senior technologists have a simplistic understanding of strategy. Their strategic naïveté is the mirror image of the strategists' technological naïveté. The two blind spots taken together cause much of the communication gap that exists between the strategic and the technological communities.

Complications to the Strategy–Making Process. Planning a strategy involves laying out directions for future decisions based upon projections about the economy, antici-

Table 3-1. Impact of Technological Change on the Planning Process

Effects of Change	Firm's Response	Resultant Costs and Problems
Short planning horizons	Incremental decision making	Losing sight of overall strategy
Short decision time frame	"Firefighting" decisions	Costly: quick fixes can lead to future problems
Multiple possible futures	Contingency planning	Costly: complex to implement and monitor
Unexpected opportunities and threats	Flexible strategies More integration Flexible organizational structure and staff	Costly: reliant on finding and retaining good people

pated moves by competitors, and a wide range of other internal and environmental variables. Among these, none is more likely to produce surprises than technology. Uncertainty resulting from technological change reduces the time frame available for decision making while simultaneously complicating plans and the planning process. As the level of uncertainty increases, so does the amount of information that must be processed during implementation. Uncertainty increases the complexity and difficulty of all the strategists' tasks from planning through execution. Table 3-1 summarizes these effects.

Firms must adapt quickly to new, unforeseen situations. The ability to move rapidly requires effective communication and integration mechanisms. The lack of this skill is evidenced, however, by the many high-technology firms which bring products to market prior to compiling complete documentation. One well-known computer firm brought a new-generation system to market without complete testing. The system then needed modifications several times during its first year of sale. This continual change created havoc with third-party software and hardware producers, and the resulting incompatibilities were the source of numerous customer complaints.

Overly stringent organizational rules and procedures, which are efficient in a stable environment, make it harder to react quickly in the face of rapid technological or competitive change. Conversely, technological change has the potential to sink a rigidly bureaucratic organization. Such change calls for flexible methods and structures and extremely competent managers.

The Technologist's View of Strategy

Stories about the nature of scientists and engineers abound. They are viewed as people who march to the beat of a different drummer, as daydreamers or "gold-platers." Serious examination of their personal traits reveals tendencies which are not too far off the mark. Technologists have high standards because they employ as reference groups other technologists and because they focus on relatively long-term time horizons. One division executive explained it in these terms: "All of my technologists were extremely good students and came to us with very high grade point averages. I have to remind them constantly that the quality standard for their work here is 'C.' When they strive for 'A' level work they are not being cost effective and they are wasting the customer's funds. Only when they begin to take this seriously are they likely to do well in our firm."

It is only after technologists make the transition from the use of "science" as a reference to the use of the firm as a primary reference that the issue of technology versus strategy can be joined. The newer engineers and scientists and the more recently trained engineers and scientists use the scientific standards of the classroom as a way of judging the quality of their own work. As they gain experience, they find that the firm has multiple objectives, not merely the singular touchstone of science. Finally, schedule, performance, coordination, financial, and resource constraints become an explicit part of the standards used for judgment. Adoption of these standards normally occurs after technologists move up to the third level of technical management.

There is a strong bias against activities that take discipline-oriented technologists away from their technical work and into planning and administration. Technologists often view these tasks as a waste of time. A survey of both electronic and mechanical designers in a moderate-sized firm revealed this prevailing attitude. Consider this typical survey response: "Each technical task we undertake is unique and thus its results cannot be known—not as to time, nor cost nor performance. But the managers keep asking whether it is similar to X or to Y. 'Can't you budget and plan by analogy and then deliver to this plan?,' they ask. This attitude is nonsense so we ignore attempts to force careful detailed planning into such a unique and uncertain arena. We feel that 'management' gets in the way of excellence in engineering." Attitudes such as these create tension and distance between the strategists and the technologists.

A second problem faced by the two groups is reflected by the frequent conflicts between their two methods. Technologists have rigorous methods which allow them to prove unambiguously that a design approach works. The problem they face is not then the ability to assess the quality of the design approach but rather the creativity required to invent an appropriate design approach. Technologists believe the strategists' methods to be "squishy," unreliable, and often not worth the effort. With such differences in basic attitude, it is easy to see why a technologist might shy away from the strategy-making process.

Technologists are also deeply rooted in their historic roles—the frequency with which they are called on to participate in strategy-making processes, the type of involvement, and the way their contributions have been treated in the past. Technologists classify their participation in the strategy process as either integrated or isolated. It is integrated when management regards technology as a means to obtain a competitive advantage and actively involves representatives from the technology functions in planning and decision making. When technology is neglected or regarded as a constraint on strategy and not as important as marketing and finance, it is classified as isolated. In general, a tendency toward the isolation extreme is the norm, and this results in strategic plans that are less effective than in an integrated approach.

THE STRATEGIC PROCESS: COMPLEXITY AND DYNAMISM

The potential of technology both as an enabling condition for and as a constraint upon strategy is clear. The added difficulty of merging a "discovery" process with a "foresight" process under uncertainty and change is similarly clear. This section sets forth some guidelines to assist in this challenge.

A paradigm represents a worldview and a set of methodologies which have been derived from that worldview. In simple terms there are two competing underlying paradigms for strategy making: analytic and intuitive. Arguments abound as to whether the strategy-making process should be approached with rigor and method or creativity and flair. The two paradigms can be best explored within a broader view of the strategy-making process. The five-phase strategy-making overview presented leads to a recommended "adaptive rationality model" which balances the two paradigms through an iterative application process. More important, adaptive rationality provides an organized mechanism for balancing discovery processes with foresight processes.

In this section, basic tasks of strategy making are specified and discussed. This concept of the tasks involved in the strategy-making process is based upon models of cybernetic or control systems. In its most general sense an open system—that is, the firm—must maintain equilibrium to survive in a changing environment. To accomplish this dynamic equilibrium, the firm uses feedback and adjustment. These basic postulates have been used rather widely by writers who apply cybernetics in their work on corporate strategy and planning (e.g., Ackoff, 1970).

To achieve its stated objective, a firm must maintain acceptable performance levels while simultaneously dealing with changing conditions. The control system model applied to business strategy leads to the five tasks shown in Table 3-2 and Figure 3-1. The strategy-making process should set standards, monitor performance, and identify variances. Where there are variances, the process should find and identify the causes in ways that allow for the creation of a responsive strategy. Identification of feasible strategies and assessment of appropriate strategies for implementation must follow. The process then cycles back to the monitoring phase as the strategists gather information about the effect of the selected actions on desired performance and further iterations occur until performance matches expectation.

Evaluation of Performance. In one way or another all organizations examine their performance from the top level to see if they are on the "right track" or to determine

Table 3-2. The Basic Tasks in Strategy Making

1. Performance evaluation, standard setting, and monitoring	The routine observation of performance (e.g., periodic sales, profit, return on investment [ROI] reports) and comparison with planned goals and standards.
2. Issue identification, issue statement formulation	The examination of an issue in response to a variance from expected performance or when a new opportunity arises. The issue must be analyzed and then stated in a fashion that permits the decision maker to create a responsive strategy.
3. Strategy identification	The development of alternative courses of action to take in response to the issue.
4. Strategy evaluation/selection	The emergence of the strategy to implement through analysis and/or negotiation.
5. Implementation	The introduction of the chosen strategy and the adaptation of the strategy as necessary for maximum effectiveness.

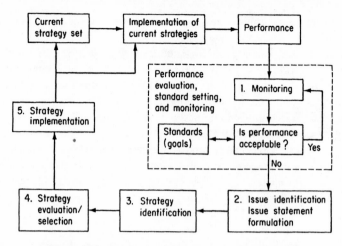

Figure 3-1. A cybernetic model of strategy making.

whether changes are needed. Performance evaluation is a natural place to begin when examining strategy formulation.

As shown in Figure 3-1 and Table 3-2 the strategy formulation process is comprised of three activities. First is the setting of standards for expected performance. These are typically expressed as goals or objectives. Strategic standards are determined during the planning process. They reflect management's intended level of performance as constrained by the firm's resources and its environment. Monitoring, simply stated, is a data collection process intended to gauge actual performance, comparing intended results with the outcomes of implemented strategy. Variance between the two provides the impetus for changing the current strategy. This process is complicated by uncertainty.

In goal setting, uncertainty makes it hard to predict eventual outcomes or to set reasonable performance levels. Monitoring is complicated by uncertainty as well, since knowing what data to collect, how to account for unexpected effects, and sometimes even how to measure are not intuitively clear. Additionally, evaluation is often based on data with built-in variations that are difficult to interpret. In short, it is often difficult to know exactly how the firm is doing.

In general, however, the more stable a firm's environment, the more certain its information will be and the less need there will be to modify previously successful strategy. The strategist in a high-technology environment, on the other hand, is in a more difficult position since the information is less reliable and harder to evaluate. At the same time, there is a greater likelihood that current strategy may require some adjustment.

Issue Identification, Issue Statement Formulation. Gathered under this heading are activities that lead to the diagnosis of the performance variances previously identified. The essence of the work at this stage is to frame the issue in operational terms rather than abstract terms so that a strategy for resolution can be reasonably determined. If the new strategy is sound, there is a good chance that the performance variance will be reduced or eliminated.

Framing the issue into appropriate operational terms is likely to be difficult, especially when strategists are compelled to make choices under time pressures and with scarce information. This situation, more typical than not for managers in high-technology environments, is characterized by the following conditions: (1) insufficient information to trace symptoms back to causes, (2) few precedents to guide the analysis and avoid false starts, and (3) multiple possible forms that an issue statement might take. Under these conditions, strategists tend to define issues in terms of the clearest and most urgent symptoms, postponing investigation of root causes for another time or ignoring them completely.

The error in focusing upon symptoms rather than root causes is illustrated in this example. A well-known multinational manufacturing firm which occupies a dominant position in a stable market used a technology strategy and constructed a large fixed-capacity factory. During the first year of operation, sales were 26 percent lower than anticipated. The initial framing of the issue was incorrect and the firm responded to the downturn as if it was a marketing problem. It continued to use a symptom-oriented perspective for two additional years before finally beginning to seriously investigate the root cause of the sales shortfall. At that point, the firm realized that the power in the marketplace had shifted from seller to buyer as a result of customer consolidation into larger buying units. It discovered that a new process developed overseas had suddenly made raw materials available at prices which allowed smaller competitors in the home market to become price competitive, and that consumer tastes had shifted so that the stable market was actually shrinking. Having discovered root causes rather than merely identifying symptoms, the firm was finally able to correctly frame the strategic issue (Emery and Trist, 1965).

Whether pressed for time or not, strategists must be especially adaptive when diagnosing issues under conditions of uncertainty. It is more comfortable to have clearly stated issues than ambiguous ones, yet strategists must remain receptive to alternative explanations, and to new information as it becomes available.

Strategy Identification. Having identified the issues, the rational policymaker's next step is to identify ways of resolving them. Depending upon how familiar the issues appear, this step can be either routine or highly creative. According to Simon's (1957) concept of strategic problem solving, a repertoire of solutions develops around issues that recur and that have been successfully dealt with in the past. Conceptually, the decision maker matches the current problem to one solved earlier, then applies some version of the old solution.

Unprecedented issues are especially challenging. If they are misdiagnosed as routine, then selection of an answer from an existing repertoire of solutions can be counterproductive. Even if the unprecedented nature of the issues is correctly identified, it is still difficult to predict with absolute confidence the result that any one strategy will produce. In such situations strategists must compensate by developing contingent strategies for possible alternative outcomes. Additionally, since some of these outcomes are themselves virtually unpredictable, given available information, strategies must be flexible enough to permit modification after implementation.

Strategy Evaluation/Selection. In formulating strategies it is important to ask whether the strategy is likely to resolve the issue at hand and yet fit within the constraints imposed by the situation. There are always limits on the kind of strategy that can be adopted based on available budget, personnel, and the like. Competing projects often claim the same resources. This constraint problem has been brought into the formal analytic process by established evaluation methods such as expected payback periods and present value analysis.

Normally, however, rational strategy-making models such as these do not say enough about the involvement of stakeholders. The process of strategic assessment is one of identifying preferences, searching for universally acceptable strategies, and negotiating a stable strategy. Strategy identification and implementation are, in this view, inseparable. Indeed, the design of strategy is more importantly a process of negotiation than of the analysis of rationally constrained opportunities. The strategy maker who recognizes the role of stakeholders in strategy creation and who implements measures responding to stakeholder concerns is more likely to obtain strategies that can be effectively implemented.

Implementation. Strategy making is not complete without implementation. Experienced managers know that a formulated strategy is no more than a set of guidelines for the future waiting to be put into action. Implementation is key to the achievement of desired performance.

To a great extent, implementation is an art. It requires, even in routine situations, large measures of intuition and judgment. Additionally, the academic literature on implementation is fragmented, attesting to the complexity and diversity of the subject. For example, Galbraith and Nathanson (1978) define implementation as the achievement of congruence among strategy, structure, process, rewards, and people. Steiner, Miner, and Gray (1982) call implementation the design and management of a system created to achieve the best possible integration of people, structure, processes, and resources in reaching organizational purposes. Both emphasize consistency among these elements and between them and the strategy to be pursued. It is clear that the successful firm's functional systems—production, finance, personnel, marketing, and so on—must evolve into a structure consistent with the strategy it has selected.

Henry Mintzberg (1978) writes about the influence of past decisions on current strategy making. He says that strategy cannot be defined in the present, as it is only by tracing the sequence of earlier decisions that a pattern emerges. The pattern itself extends to the firm's structure and resource deployment. The term "infrastructure" is borrowed from economics to further describe the phenomenon. In its original context, it is the foundation—the roads, waterways, airlinks, communication media, and so on—that allows commerce to exist. In a firm, a "strategic infrastructure" is the particular configuration of functional systems that develops in support of the firm's strategy. Distribution, for example, may be national or regional, achieved through exclusive dealers or discount stores. Manufacturing may be labor- or capital-intensive. Each function both reflects and influences the firm's strategy.

The relation between strategy and infrastructure is reciprocal. Strategy is constrained by the existing infrastructure as much as the infrastructure is constrained by existing strategy. It is a relatively simple matter to maintain strategies that are in place. The same infrastructure, however, precludes selection of certain strategies when they diverge from the status quo.

Examples of this potential constraint are found in two *Business Week* articles on minicomputer manufacturers, both written in 1984. These manufacturers historically used proprietary products and extensive customer service as means of maintaining market share. In 1983, the market for minicomputers matured and demand for more powerful microcomputers grew. This was followed by demand for super minicomputers. Firms that had succeeded in the minicomputer market needed to make adjustments in their strategies. They had to invest in new-product development, assuring that new products were compatible with the older, proprietary systems while simultaneously maintaining service levels for their older customers.

As new strategies diverge further and further from old ones, more effort and planning must go into implementation. Rather than assuming such strategies will be put into effect, managers should borrow from Lewin's change model (1947) and give special attention to "unfreezing" existing strategies and infrastructure before changing them and refreezing the new strategies and infrastructure.

Companies that frequently adjust their strategy as a normal course of doing business can simplify implementation with adaptive structures and processes such as task forces, or the project and matrix organizational structures that have been used in the aerospace and defense communities for over thirty years. In recent years greater attention has been given to innovation as a means for successful competition. For example, in a 1982 address, Alan J. Zahan, CEO of the Boston Consulting Group, suggested that lowering hurdle rates for new projects and reducing penalties for mistakes by managers were conditions necessary for increasing adaptability and innovation.

Comparing Two Strategy-Making Models

As shown in Table 3-2, the main tasks required in formulating strategy are constant regardless of the application. In particular firms and certain kinds of decisions however, the ways in which these strategy-making tasks are performed can vary considerably. Strategists, explicitly or not, tailor the way they make decisions to their own decision styles, training, available time and money, and other existing constraints. They perform their strategy-making tasks in ways that conform to their assessments of the situation.

Two virtually opposite examples illustrate the range of valid strategy-making methods. One is called "synoptic," or rational. It is the comprehensive, systematic method of problem solving taught in business and engineering schools. The other is the "incremental" method, otherwise known as crisis management or "firefighting."

Using the steps laid out in Figure 3-1, Table 3-3 summarizes the differences in the two as the strategy-making process unfolds. In each stage there are critical differences. In monitoring, the rational approach has a structured, systematic view of potential problem areas. The incremental approach has no such well-defined system but uses a combination of rational measures and intuition. It does not call for analysis of symptoms or determination of root causes; instead it tends to define the symptom as the problem. March and Simon (1958) call this "problemistic" search.

In the next two strategy-making tasks, the essential contrasts between the two approaches is clear. The rational strategy maker is an optimizer. After the competing strategies are compared to one another, the *best* one is chosen and implemented.

The incrementalist, on the other hand, arrives at one strategy at a time and selects

Table 3-3. Comparative Strategy Models

Problem-Solving Task	Strategy-Making Approach	
	Synoptic/Rational	Incremental
1. Monitoring	Comprehensive scan of internal and external environment for critical issues	Wide range of factors scanned opportunistically, sometimes rational, often by "gut feel"
2. Issue identification	Comprehensive analysis to identify causal issue	Action–response–feedback converge on causal issue
3. Strategy identification	Rigorous search for full set of feasible strategies	Short search for strategies; relies upon repertoire of previously successful responses; zeros in on correct strategy via action and adjustment
4. Strategy evaluation/ selection	Comparison of competing strategies with each other using consistent criteria	Trial-and-error process; one strategy at a time implemented and evaluated
5. Implementation	Problems with change and structure are forecasted and responses are planned	Problems are resolved as they are encountered through adjustment
Pros	Higher certainty that real issue is addressed; "best" strategy is used; control more structured	Faster, cheaper, efficient in routine decisions
Cons	Expensive, time consuming, inflexible	Can lead to conflict among decisions, inconsistencies over time

the first one that specifically addresses the issue at hand. The criterion for selection is the estimate that the strategy will meet the minimum requirements of the problem. There is virtually no attempt to find the best response. Implementation employs anticipation and planning if the synoptic/rational model is followed, and the action/feedback/adjustment process under the incremental model.

Both these approaches and the many combinations in between have been offered as descriptive and/or normative models of strategy making. Each is a valid and appropriate mode under different conditions. Referring to Table 3-3, it is clear that the rational approach increases the certainty that a causal issue will be framed and that the best strategy will be used to resolve it. The incremental model guarantees neither, but it is more economical and allows decisions to be made quickly.

The Adaptive Rationality Model

Normative models for strategy making in technology-rich environments cover a full spectrum of options that range from the rational to the incremental approaches. At the synoptic/rational end are techniques such as quantified scheduling algorithms for new-venture planning (Dean, 1984), while at the incremental end are loosely defined ways to conceptualize the demands of environmental change. Although there are many strategy formulation techniques in the literature, little information is provided to guide decision makers as they struggle to determine the appropriate strategy for any particular context. Some explanation of how the range of methods can be used to complement each other to make for a sounder, more adaptable overall approach to strategic decision making is still needed as well.

One analysis of strategy making under ambiguity (Goodman and Huff, 1978) points to the analyst's need to be both a creative and a rigorous problem solver. At times, an abstract global view is needed; at other times, a rigorously defined microview is required. The analyst is frequently called on to shift from perspective to perspective while striving and to keep the two in balance, avoiding the rigorous but trivial issue statement *and* the inclusive but ambiguous issue statement.

The adaptive rationality (AR) model presented here helps both to provide better insight into the issues of context and to indicate ways in which various techniques can be employed in complementary fashion. It describes the strategy-making process appropriate to high-uncertainty environments. Rather than asking the decision maker to choose either a synoptic/rational or an incremental approach to strategy making, it calls for the analyst to alternate between highly structured methods and more loosely structured ones, using each to complement the other for the best overall resolution. The model employs feedback both from strategy formulation (a theory-based control loop) and from implementation (a data-based control loop) to converge on an acceptable set of strategic decisions. This model is shown in Figure 3-2.

The model is composed of seven elements: appreciation, differentiation, micro formulation, integration, strategy checking, implementation, and performance checking. In its initial stage, the model combines rigorous and intuitive viewpoints upon the issues of concern. Technique and experience are explored to look at both issues and context. Then the task of strategy formulation is divided into various functional elements. That is, the overall issues are decomposed into simpler, more manageable elements. These elements are then examined with functionally based rigorous techniques and the results are micro-level strategic formulations. The micro formulations are then merged and tested against the larger appreciation in a strategy check. This process

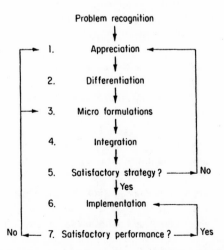

Figure 3-2. Adaptive rationality model flow diagram.

allows the rigorous and the intuitive to come into play. As long as significant progress is being made to reduce the discrepancies that arise from the micro analysis, this process is repeated over and over again. The iterative nature of this process provides an important vehicle for the discovery process of the technologists and the foresight process of the strategists to engage in a dialogue and mutual problem solving. This iterative process continues until progress in resolving of discrepancies slows and then stops. The implementation phase and the performance check require the same iterative work effort.

In summary, the AR model is a procedural model for strategy formulation in highly uncertain, complex environments like those of high-technology industries. It provides the strategists a framework with which to evaluate and fit together the various analytic models. It gives the technologists a look at the context and meaning for the organization of their efforts. As knowledge is gained prior to implementation and during actual performance this model allows strategists to adapt and change.

SUMMARY

In the broadest terms, technology helps to define the firm's range of possible futures. It presents planners with some environmental constraints and determines the kinds of competitive weapons, new products, and markets that they will face.

Many of the questions emerging from the firm's technological functions and technological environment have organization-wide implications. These widespread, significant implications have led many experts to argue that technology plays a key role in strategic planning. It is clear, however, that the opposite is also true, that strategic planning plays a key role in technology.

Technology's most dramatic effects have been seen in microcomputer industry, but it is a strong influence in determining the competitive position in a wide range of industries. Competitive moves based on technological threats have been studied by a number of theorists, among them Cooper and Schendel (1976). They suggest that industry-level growth and decline are also based on technological change and that strategic decisions about entry, exit, and continued investment must be based on industry projections. Firms must decide whether to invest in technology in order to remain current with product and process improvements or to compete on other dimensions. They may have to decide to develop a technology that leads them away from their core business, or to exploit a noncore technology through alternative means such as licensing. This was argued forcefully by William Abernathy, whose book on the automobile industry (1978) demonstrated the tension among product-, process-, and market-driven innovation.

According to Christensen et al. (1982), the internal evolution of the firm is tied to technology as well. Organizational structure and the various aspects of culture found within corporations are fundamental parts of a company's mission statement. Structure can be defined by many variables—centralization, formality, divisional or functional form, and the like. The particular structure a management adopts will, of course, have an impact upon its current effectiveness. Similarly, the ease with which the corporation can exploit its technology is affected by these same structural choices.

An organization's culture—its internal atmosphere—is also closely related to technology. The impact of the various elements of corporate culture on technological innovation ranges from resistant to supportive. They can either promote or deter effective innovation and the overall positioning of the firm with regard to technology.

Decisions made at the top levels of a firm both direct and constrain the effectiveness of its technology as a competitive weapon. Similarly, decisions on the use of technology have far-reaching effects for the firm that argue for treatment by strategic-level decision makers.

Frohman (1980) has used the term "strategic balance" to describe the phenomenon of maintaining effective relationships among technology and the firm's other internal functions. Top management must keep in touch with the technological aspects of its environment to create a balance of technological and strategic planning.

This chapter was intended to present a critical point of view on strategic management, analysis, and planning in a technologically enriched environment. The chapters that follow move from the broad, historical role of technology in corporations to specific techniques for managing technology in individual firms. Along the way a variety of issues and viewpoints are examined, but the focus throughout is on strategic decision making.

REFERENCES

Abernathy, W. J. 1978. *The Productivity Dilemma: Roadblocks to Innovation in the Automobile Industry.* (Baltimore, MD: Johns Hopkins University Press.

Ackoff, R. 1970. *A Concept of Corporate Planning.* New York: Wiley.

Buggie, F. 1982. "Strategies for New Product Development," *Long Range Planning* 15(2):22–31.

Business Week. 1984. January 16, pp. 78–82.

Business Week. 1984. January 30, pp. 50–58.

Christensen, C. R., K. R. Andrews, J. L. Bowers, R. G. Hammermesh, and M. L. Porter. 1982. *Business Policy,* 5th ed. Homewood, IL: Irwin.

Cooper, A. 1986. "Strategic Management: New Ventures and Small Business," *Long Range Planning* 14(3):39–45.

Cooper, A., and D. Schendel. 1976. "Strategic Responses to Technological Threats," *Business Horizons,* February, pp. 61–69.

Cyert, R., and J. March. 1963. *A Behavioral Theory of the Firm.* Englewood Cliffs, NJ: Prentice-Hall.

Dean, B. 1984. "The Management of Innovative Start-up Firms," *Technical Memorandum No. 548.* Cleveland: Case Western Reserve University.

Emery, F. E., and E. Trist. 1965. "The Causal Texture of the Environment," *Human Relations* 18(1):21–32.

Ford D., and C. Ryan. 1981. "Taking Technology to Market," *Harvard Business Review,* March–April, pp. 117–26.

Frohman, A. 1980. "Managing the Company's Technological Assets," *Research Management,* 23:20–24.

Frohman, A., and D. Bitondo. 1981. "Coordinating Business Strategy and Technical Planning," *Long Range Planning* 14(6):58–67.

Galbraith, J. 1973. *Designing Complex Organizations.* Reading, MA: Addison-Wesley.

Galbraith, J. 1977. *Organizational Design.* Reading, MA: Addison-Wesley.

Galbraith, J., and D. Nathanson. 1978. *Strategy Implementation: The Role of Structure and Process.* St. Paul, MN: West.

Goodman, R. A., and W. J. Abernathy. 1978. "The Contribution of 'NEW BOY' Phenomena to Increasing Innovation and Development in New Technology," *R & D Management* 9(1):31–41.

Goodman, R. A., and A. S. Huff. 1978. "Enriching Policy Premises for an Ambiguous World." In John Sutherland, ed., *Management Handbook for Public Administrators.* New York: Van Nostrand Reinhold.

Hertz, D., and H. Thomas. 1983. "Decision and Risk Analysis in a New Product and Facilities Planning Problem," *Sloan Management Review,* Winter, pp. 17–31.

Lawless, M. W., A. Feinberg, A. Glassman, and R. Bengston. 1981. "The Role of the Change Agent in Management Science Implementation," *Omega* 10(2):107–14.

Lawrence, P., and J. Lorsch. 1967. "Differentiation and Integration in Complex Organizations," *Administrative Science Quarterly* 12(1):1–47.

Lewin, K. 1947. "Frontiers in Group Dynamics: Concept, Method, and Reality in Social Science, Social Equilibria and Social Change," *Human Relations* 1(1):5–41.

Mansfield, E. 1981. "How Economists See R & D," *Harvard Business Review,* November–December, pp. 98–106.

March, J., and H. Simon. 1958. *Organizations.* New York: Wiley.

Mintzberg, H. 1978. "Patterns in Strategy Formulation," *Management Science,* 24(1): 934–48.

Parker, R. 1977. "Human Aspects of the R & D Organization," *Research Management* 20:34–38.

Petroni, G. 1983. "Strategic Planning and Research and Development—Can We Integrate Them?" *Long Range Planning* 16(1):15–25.

Quinn, J. 1979. "Technological Innovation, Entrepreneurship, and Strategy," *Sloan Management Review,* Spring, pp. 19–30.

Quinn, J. 1985. "Managing Chaos," *Harvard Business Review,* May–June, pp. 73–84.

Ramsey, J. 1981. "Selecting R & D Projects for Development," *Long Range Planning* 14(1):83–92.

Ritti, R. 1982. "Work Goals of Scientists and Engineers." In M. Tushman and W. Moore, eds., *Readings in the Management of Innovation.* Boston: Pitman.

Simon, H. 1957. *Administrative Behavior.* New York: Macmillan.

Skinner, W. 1978. *Manufacturing in the Corporate Strategy.* New York: Wiley.

Steiner, G., J. Miner, and E. Gray. 1982. *Management, Policy and Strategy.* New York: Macmillan.

Tushman, M., and P. Anderson. 1986. "Technological Discontinuities and Dominant Design: A Cyclical Model of Technological Change," *Administrative Science Quarterly,* September 31(3):439–465.

Weil, E., and R. Cangemi. 1983. "Linking Long Range Research to Corporate Planning," *Research Management* 26:32–39.

Wheelwright, S. C., 1984. "Manufacturing Strategy: Defining the Missing Link," *Strategic Management Journal* 5(1):77–91.

Williams, J. 1983. "Technological Evolution and Competitive Response," *Strategic Management Journal* 4(1):55–65.

II

TECHNIQUES FOR DIAGNOSING SITUATIONS AND SELECTING TECHNOLOGY STRATEGIES

Increasing effectiveness of the technology-based firm begins with mastery of the *conceptual frame* that was presented in Part I of this book. This expertise must extend to relevant organizational members in each of the firm's functional areas. It is then important to master the *techniques for diagnosing* situations to be able to select appropriate plans and activities to meld the technological with the strategic.

Part II outlines several techniques that can be employed for diagnosis and selection. These several techniques represent three different but interrelated levels of analysis. Chapter 4, "Success Conditions for Technology Strategies," focuses upon the strategies per se. A framework is presented to define common strategies in terms of product maturity, market maturity, technological maturity, available actions steps, and the resulting bases of defensibility.

The second level of analysis maps the product and process technologies that are relevant to the firm's product line. This technique is presented in Chapter 5, "Mapping a Technology's Antecedents," Chapter 6, "Mapping Technological Potential for Defensible Positioning," and Chapter 7, "Some Examples of Strategic Technology Maps."

The third level focuses upon the firm's innovative capabilities and is covered in Chapter 8, "Evaluating Your Advantage: The Innovation Audit," Chapter 9, "Detailing the Innovation Audit Technique," and Chapter 10, "Some Examples of the Innovation Audit."

The strategic framework is used at the technology and the firm level as a filtering device for the choice of strategies. The basic diagnostic process begins with a framework describing various technologically assisted strategies. This framework has been created from both theoretical and practical bases and is used to sift information derived from a careful mapping of the basic technologies that drive the firm's business. The mapping process identifies the scientific bases of the firm's product line, the anticipated developments in the scientific base, and the way the performance parameters of the product line may change as the relevant science base develops. This map is then compared to the strategic framework to ascertain areas in the technological base that present opportunities.

This sifting process is repeated once again with a focus on the firm rather than the underlying technology. This time the firm's innovative skills are explored. An audit of the firm's innovative capability provides managers with a base from which to select opportunities that have been determined by the technology mapping process. The innovation audit uses the strategic conceptualizations to assess the opportunities suggested by the mapping exercise and identify those that are best suited to the firm's abilities. The two analyses taken together specify the potential impact of various technologies and technological actions on strategic positioning.

The end result of the diagnostic process is the selection of activities which are expected to create valuable strategic positions for the firm. The third part of the book deals with issues of effectively managing and implementing the selected strategic activities in order to achieve the desired results.

4

Success Conditions for Technology Strategies

In the real world there are numerous anecdotes demonstrating the brilliance of one or another executive's deft positioning of his or her firm. Upon more detailed analysis of these success stories, the same behavior is often described as basically fortuitous or, in the vernacular, "dumb luck." Academics like to believe that effective strategic action requires a combination of analytic thinking and managerial judgment. Both views may very well be true, but there do not seem to be enough "brilliant" and/or "lucky" executives to go around. Thus, we must offer the "merely excellent" executive some assistance. In particular, this executive needs a framework which both drives strategic analysis and a provides a context for the exercise of judgment.

This chapter offers a description of nine technology strategies and the normal conditions under which they appear to be successful. The theoretical bases of these strategies are drawn mainly from the industrial organization literature; the practical bases of these strategies are drawn mainly from observed organizational practice. It is these strategies which form the basis of the recommendations that are part and parcel of the following chapters on technology mapping and on innovation auditing.

The analytical comments presented here lead to practical methods for selecting a technology-based strategy for organizational action. More specifically, the analysis examines several existing technology strategies, indicating optimal conditions for the use of each strategy—conditions that might be found "in nature" (Smith, 1776) or created purposefully in the organizational equivalent of Lamarckian mutation (Kuhn, 1963; Lamarck, 1963; McKelvey, 1982). The strategic guidelines are derived from theory and from practice, from an enriched definition of "defensible competitive advantage," and from an understanding of the nature of technological development over the longer term (Sahal, 1981; Rosenbloom, 1984).

CONCEPTUAL UNDERPINNINGS OF STRATEGY SELECTION

Strategy selection most commonly arises either from an analysis of "fit" or an analysis of "action potential." Utilizing the first approach, the manager judges whether the firm's activities are consistent with (fit) a particular strategy. The latter approach asks the manager to consider the strategic potential of various possible actions. Fit analysis tends to be rather static in character because it implies the need to achieve coherence in all elements of the firm. Such a static approach to strategy limits the firm's ability to adapt to changing technological and marketplace conditions. As Abernathy suggested in *The Productivity Dilemma* (1978), coherence seriously inhibits innovation and change. The action potential analysis recognizes that the firm must often use different strategies dependent upon the nature of the specific product/market life cycle and the basic state and change dynamic of various relevant technologies. As such the action potential approach to strategy selection has a more dynamic and changing character.

Miller (1988) summarizes the common strategy classification systems by employing some generic technological concerns to achieve a more basic level of appreciation. He blends three ideas about technology: Woodward's (1965) production methods schema (batch, mass, and continuous), moderated by rate of innovation (Abernathy and Utterback, 1978) and product sophistication (Liebler, 1976). These three ideas then lead him to propose six types of production systems and permit him to correlate these systems with the strategy classification systems of Ansoff and Stewart (1967), Freeman (1974), and Miles and Snow (1978). It should be noted that recent work in this area emphasizes the "gestalten" character of strategies as represented by clusters of attributes or relationships that are internally cohesive (Miller and Friesen, 1984) or as "design archetypes," which are described as interpretive schemes embodied in structures and systems (Hinings and Greenwood, 1988).

As shown in Table 4-1, these classifications are oriented toward a description of observed firm behavior. Thus, they seem to pose the question of fit: Is the firm's behavior internally consistent? Are the organizational strategies sensible in light of existing production systems? It appears, though, that it is important to go beyond "fit" to add an action oriented-perspective.

From a theoretical perspective there are two cost-oriented issues that create the envelope of advantage. Reducing the full cost incurred by your customer when purchasing your products and increasing the cost to your competitors of serving your customers creates barriers—that is, defensible positions. The nature of each of these costs

Table 4-1. Four Technology-Based Strategy Classification Systems

	Ansoff and Stewart (1967)	Freeman (1974)	Miles and Snow (1978)
Established batch	Follow the leader	Defensive Imitative	Analyzer
Innovative batch	First to market	Offensive	Prospector
Flexible line	Applications engineering	Opportunist	Analyzer
Fixed line	"Me too"	Imitative Traditional	Defender
Unaltered process	"Me too"	Dependent Traditional	Reactor Defender
Modified process	Applications engineering	Dominant	Analyzer

Adapted from Miller, 1988, p. 248, by permission.

is, of course, quite different. There are a number of technologically based actions that can affect these costs and thus provide the basis for a technology strategy.

Cooper and Schendel (1976) suggest seven strategic responses to technological threats. Two have low cost implications: "do nothing" or "monitor external technological development vigorously." Two serve to increase competitor costs: "defend with public relations and legal action" or "improve current technology." Three reduce customer costs: "increase flexibility," "leave submarkets," and "cut prices or promote." Linked to each of the seven responses are specific technological actions. Their approach is a good beginning to understanding an "action" but perhaps a bit more systematic treatment might be more helpful.

At a broad level, it is possible to logically identify seven technologically based actions that can be linked with the several sources of barriers described earlier. This action list simplifies the concept of "action and barriers" mainly for reasons of ease in description. The seven actions are presented in Table 4-2 along with the basis upon which the actions help create barriers to competition. These seven actions can be observed in the discussion of the alternative technology strategies that are the core concepts of this chapter.

An investment in productivity drives costs down and permits price reductions, which in turn lowers the cost to the customer and requires the competitors to respond by making a similar investment, thus increasing their costs. Alternatively, the increased margin can be employed by the firm to differentiate its product through a variety of advertising and/or service actions, also raising the cost to the competitor.

An investment in capacity normally has a cost reduction effect and a potential preemptive effect. The cost reduction benefits are the same as those just noted. A preemptive effect occurs when the new capacity brings down the unit cost while simultaneously creating a capacity or overcapacity condition in the industry. Under these circumstances, the relative cost to competitors is driven up.

Investment in flexibility reduces costs to the customer when high change rate or niche strategies are called for and, of course, drives up costs to competitors who would need to make the same investment in order to compete.

The three product R&D strategies all create informational barriers to the competitors by developing proprietary knowledge, creating higher costs for the competitors, who have to respond in kind. Experience curve benefits can also be associated with these developments as the firm becomes increasingly sophisticated and better understands the technologies involved in product development.

The final category deals with benefits of formal contractual, or informal techno-

Table 4-2. Technology Actions and Competitive Barriers

Action	Type of Barrier Created
Invest in productivity	Cost/price or cost/reputation
Invest in capacity	Cost/market size
Invest in flexibility	Cost/market size
R&D for new general products	Information barriers
R&D for new niche products	Information barriers
R&D for hierarchical design	Information barriers
Negotiate hierarchical governance	Contractual/regulatory barriers

logical, vertical integration (Goodman, 1989). By definition, these actions create contractual or regulatory barriers to competitors as they formally preempt certain markets or market segments.

NINE TECHNOLOGY STRATEGIES

We now examine a number of existing technology strategies, looking for the conditions of success. To facilitate comparisons each is discussed within a similar general format. First, examples of the strategy are presented; then, the nature of the situation is identified in terms of both market and product characteristics. Corporate actions relevant to the extant situations are indicated, as are the dimensions of implied defensibility attendant with such actions. Finally, anticipated results are indicated and some cautions are addressed.

Each strategy is presented as if it were being attempted by only a single firm. We know from the strategic group literature that this is seldom the case, but the results argued here are based on the assumption that the size of the market is sufficient, given the costs of a particular strategy, for any of the well-managed firms within the strategic group to obtain the indicated result. These analyses suffer from oversimplification, which is a necessary condition for lucid exposition as a firm is often able to have a complex mix of strategies under way simultaneously.

In this section, the technology strategies are examined along a number of different dimensions. These include three market dimensions: uncertainty, size, and purchaser sophistication; two product dimensions: uncertainty and complexity; and seven actions: three in manufacturing development, three in product development, and one in governance. The permutations available for twelve dimensions would be over four thousand, and to totally enumerate them would be foolish at this juncture. One problem is that the dimensions themselves are generally continuous functions rather than bimodal categories. The more commonly found combinations are reported here. It would be possible to trace back through the multidimensional analyses suggested here to explain anomalies in a specific situation by noting that they represent a different combination of dimensions than the more commonly occurring situations described below. A portion of the multipart Table 4-3 is inserted within each strategy discussion to summarize the discussion in a common format.

Technological Commodity Search

The Spanish electronics firm PIHER was faced with a combination of problems when it considered expansion. Although the beneficiary of governmental regulations requiring that imported products include a significant measure of local content (a regulatory quasi-monopoly), it had been effectively limited to the Spanish market by this situation. As entrepreneurial pressures built inside PIHER, it sought an innovative approach to overcome this limitation. It chose to take advantage of one of the contemporary distinctive advantages of Spain, low labor cost, by developing products whose low cost would create a defensible competitive edge. Thus, it chose to invest in manufacturing excellence by increasing its quality to meet international standards and then focusing its research and development on manufacturing processes. The products it selected for this strategy were stable and well-understood standard electronic components such as carbon film resistors and standard microcircuits, high-volume products in a relatively stable global market.

A number of firms focus their attention upon the trailing edge of the product life cycle. In their respective industries, they search for products that have developed commoditylike characteristics; that is, the products are standardized, well understood, and technologically undifferentiable. Typically these products face stable or secularly declining markets. Such a market situation discourages new entrants and provides competing firms with relatively good information about competitors through normal market scanning.

Successful firms in this arena focus their technological strategy upon their manufacturing processes. They continually invest in cost-reducing manufacturing process improvements while engaging in little or no product development. To maintain low selling prices they focus on creating low manufacturing costs. It is unlikely that firms not dedicated to maintaining low cost will be able to imitate the many subtle characteristics that mark these firms. A manufacturing process built around products with high margins, for example, will usually have too much slack to effectively operate some of its lines on a purely low-cost approach.

The low-price strategy has more than a competitive effect. It also extends the product life cycle by allowing marginal consumers to remain in the market rather than incur the switching costs needed to adapt to new products. The major defensible competitive advantage arises from constantly investing to continue to drive costs down. Continual cost reduction and the ensuing low-price strategy preempt new firms from entering the market as their investment costs will be too high when compared to the returns available from a shrinking market. Additionally, the constant cost reduction provides increasing margins for "reputational" differentiation of branding and/or customer service.

As competitors find opportunities to better employ their capital they will withdraw from the market. If competitors do continue, then the competitive balance can be maintained and normal returns can be expected. If a competitor withdraws, then a higher margin can be obtained. That is, supernormal returns are possible. Here the technological strategy is the enabling condition for the investment in brand name capital and other service qualities for the purposes of differentiation. The major caution in

Table 4-3. Technology–Strategy Matrix

A. Technological Commodity Search

Market/Product Situation	Actions/Defensibility	Results	Example
Stable or declining/ well known or standard	Invest in productivity/low-cost firm exhibits uncertain imitability/market size–to–investment cost ratio favorable/potential for reputational differentiation	Normal to supernormal returns	PIHER

this situation is the problem of selecting products that are declining. Thus, new trailing-edge products have to be sought continually in order to maintain the effectiveness of the overall strategy.

Preemption

In a 1966 article that appeared in *Chemical Week,* industry specialists speculated about the cost of the new Monsanto chemical plant at Chocolate Bayou, Texas. By driving around the outside of the construction site, they attempted to estimate capacity that would be coming on line when the facility opened. As construction continued, the estimates were refined and the industry began to reshape its plans in light of the soon to be realized change in industry capacity.

Under certain conditions, these speculations provide opportunities for preemptive moves for certain segments of the industry. In 1980, Joel Goldhar, then with the National Research Council, indicated that there was evidence in the chemical industry of what he termed "a preemptive megaplant strategy." Firms would estimate the market demand for a product and then build a plant that could produce twice the market demand. This action usually resulted in a "micro-monopoly" situation as potential competitors stayed on the sidelines (Dasgupta and Stiglitz, 1980).

The distinction between this strategy and the commodity strategy discussed previously is its reliance upon the steepness of the returns to scale versus unit price curve. Here low cost is not sufficient to be an effective barrier. When the plant size versus unit cost curve is quite steep, a preemptive entrant into a market constructs a manufacturing facility as large as or larger than the entire market. This means that competitors must be willing to make equal investments in order to become cost competitive. Selecting a smaller investment will mean that the competitors' manufacturing cost will be significantly higher. The preemptive entrant will thus maintain a cost advantage. This advantage can then be used to control the market through a low-price strategy. With an equally large investment, the competitor can at best expect to split the market and then only after start-up delays. The market may not be large enough for two competitors to make normal returns on their total investment. Thus, the first mover, having avoided information leakages about its new product and its plant construction project, obtains a substantial barrier to entry.

It is only after release of the product that competitors become aware of the first mover's activities. Even when, as is often the case, the product itself in easily copied, second and third entrants are faced with significant funding and construction delays,

Table 4-3. Technology–Strategy Matrix

B. Preemption

Market/Product Situation	Actions/Defensibility	Results	Example
Industrial/easily copied	Invest in megacapacity plant/ competitor investment too high given market size	Supernormal returns	Monsanto

which provide the initial defensibility. If the steepness of the returns-to-scale curve is appropriately coupled with a narrow customer base, effective competitive response is blocked until either the customer base widens or competitors create superior product technology. Both market developments and competitor actions must be carefully scanned to identify changes in the situation which have potential for destroying this strategic advantage.

Productive Efficiency

Henry Ford's assembly line is commonly touted as the first major example of the doctrine of productive efficiency. Ford's attention to the manufacturing process as a defensible competitive edge was revolutionary and quite effective—for several years. His apocryphal statement, "You can have it in any color you want as long as it is black!" was the forerunner of what Abernathy termed *The Productivity Dilemma* (1978). The original advantage enjoyed by Ford was whittled away by competitors who offered variety in size, shape, color, and function. As Ford and his industrial followers discovered, a mass market can best be served by those firms that are low-cost producers *if*. . . . The *if*, of course, assumes that competitors will compete on the price dimension alone. *if* this is true, then, with continuing investment in the manufacturing process, the experience curve of the first firm will keep it ahead and provide the expected edge. This *if* does not always occur, even in the most traditional mass production industries.

The automotive industry can be described with very-long-wave innovation cycles. First, a major product redesign occurs and, if effective, the market swings toward the product innovation. Then, as competitors copy this innovation, the industry leader focuses upon the manufacturing process to drive down costs. Eventually the market power of both the original product innovation and the later cost reductions begins to wane, and the firm faces the tail end of the product life cycle. Attention then shifts to the marketing dimensions leading to an increase in the variety of the product offerings. While an increase in variety usually reduces the manufacturing effectiveness, it also succeeds in staving off the impending decline in market position. Then another cycle starts. This simplified summary of Abernathy's work also fits reasonably well the activities of major marketing firms such as Carnation, Procter & Gamble, and General Foods.

The technological strategy which focuses upon productive efficiency represents the generalized low-cost approach. It can be effective in highly competitive situations when there is a large mass market. Earlier manufacturing-oriented strategies differ here in regard to the markets in which they seem best suited. The preemptive strategy focuses upon niche markets and the commodity strategy focuses upon markets at the tail end of the product life cycle. This general productive efficiency approach usually occurs only in mature industries or with mature, well-understood products. Many firms are extremely well versed in low-cost production processes—whether by virtue of low-cost materials or effective process design, planning skills, or work force supervision. Low per-unit cost is generally a requirement of other strategic needs. In mass market/commoditylike industries, competitive differentiation tends to be created by the marketing aspects of the firm's strategy. Heavy advertising and promotional expendi-

Table 4-3. Technology–Strategy Matrix

C. *Productive Efficiency*			
Market/Product Situation	Actions/Defensibility	Results	Examples
Mature mass market/stable and well-understood product	Invest in manufacturing process/competitor faces information delays regarding manufacturing technique–experience curve effect	Normal returns	General Foods Alberto-Culver

tures require an extremely low manufacturing cost to provide appropriate profit margins. The recent "Intel inside" advertising campaign demonstrates the shifting emphasis of even high-technology firms as their market matures.

Cosmetics and hair care products and breakfast cereals are two widely different examples of mature mass market items. It has been said by executives of firms such as General Foods and Alberto-Culver that the low-product-cost, high-margin structure of their respective industries makes as little as 1 percent market share profitable. In the mature mass market the manufacturing volumes are quite high and further learning curve effects are minimal. Although manufacturing skill is a necessary condition for competition, there is little defensible edge as information is widely shared and imitation is relatively easy. This industrial structure is as close to pure competition as one might find and thus only normal returns are to be expected. Here the technological strategy of investing in manufacturing processes is an enabling condition for the employment of the high-cost marketing strategies which are necessary for some form of competitive edge.

Producer Preference

New product offerings, whether entrepreneurial or intrapreneurial, are often categorized as producer preference strategies. When the new product has a functional value significantly in excess of substitute products and the firm's ability to supply the market is limited, the firm is in control of the market. Here the firm can choose which customers to prefer and which variations on the product to introduce first, thus the producer preference nomenclature.

This is sometime referred to as first mover advantage and may be either a short- or a long-term situation. New microprocessors and/or new computers are not often available at the level of initial demand due to early manufacturing yield problems and/or a conscious decision to create manufacturing capacity for the forecast steady state, rather than the initial spike in the demand.

Other examples of producer preference come from situations of patent protection or situations in which demand exceeds manufacturing capability. Still others emanate from manufacturing processes that cannot be easily replicated. Polaroid was originally protected by its patents and as a result had complete control of the instant photography

Table 4-3. Technology–Strategy Matrix

D. Producer Preference

Market/Product Situation	Actions/Defensibility	Results	Examples
Early stage/ complex product	Invest in product research/ early steep learning curve provides information delay and early uncertain imitability	Supernormal returns until new entrants	Polaroid Michelin Volkswagen

business for the lifetime of the patents. When Polaroid stopped making film for its early cameras it instantly created an antique camera market. The consumer in that period was constrained by what Polaroid chose to offer or not offer. When demand outpaced supply, other new products were rationed either by price or by quotas. Michelin radial tires sold at a premium until competitive tires narrowed the perceived gap between Michelin and the competitors. As late as the 1960s, Volkswagens had to be ordered months in advance.

The producer preference strategy is commonly adopted in the early stages of a new technologically complex product. The producer focuses upon product design and thus presumably provides a significant increase in customer functional satisfaction. Thus, demand is created but the firm approaches its investments in manufacturing process conservatively. The market will take what is available and bid up the price in accordance with general supply and demand characteristics. Barriers to penetrating the actual technological design or the actual manufacturing process provide a defensible condition and make profits greater than normal.

The barriers may exist, however, only for the length of time needed by the competition to "reverse engineer" the product and design and construct a competitive manufacturing facility. In the fashion industry this can happen relatively quickly, whereas in industries with strong patent protection the process is longer. When the experience curve is steep and the relative complexity of the technology high, the firm can earn greater than normal returns until new entrants flood the market (Lawless and Fisher, 1990). The critical caution here is that the industry will eventually become competitive. Early high-handed and/or exploitive behavior must be moderated by the need to sustain the product later in the competitive marketplace. Thus, for example, Polaroid extended itself a great deal to build initial customer satisfaction and loyalty. Eventually, when the market matures, other strategies become necessary.

Production Flexibility

Computer-aided design and computer-aided manufacturing (CAD/CAM) are techniques necessitated by needs for product flexibility. As a result CAD/CAM is employed in such diverse settings as the fashion industry and the aircraft industry. The aircraft industry invests heavily in major capital assets, which must be used in a

Table 4-3. Technology–Strategy Matrix

E. Production Flexibility—Seasonal/E'—Custom Design

Market/Product Situation	Actions/Defensibility	Results	Examples
Seasonal or low volume/custom design	Develop flexible manufacturing approaches planning and CAD/CAM/ takes advantage of normal product information delays to the competition	Normal returns	Lockheed Levi-Strauss

"batch" process to maintain a reasonable return on investment. In addition, its production rate is low, in tens to hundreds per year.

In the fashion industry the product line is completely redesigned each season. Participants are constrained, however, by its inability to obtain more than a single order of raw fabric from the mills per season. Even when a particular style is extremely popular, it is impossible to obtain additional fabric in order to meet an otherwise welcome demand. To attenuate the impact of this ordering risk, many firms in the industry build clothing only to meet customer orders rather than building inventory. Each customer's order represents a unique mix of sizes and colors. Using CAD/CAM approaches allows a great deal of flexibility and facilitates both rapid turnaround and a major reduction of fabric wastage, from 25 to 12 percent.

A flexible approach to manufacturing creates an opportunity to move quickly from design to production. It is this speed that enables the firm to get its product to market before the competition has had much time to react. If the market is small or seasonal, this ability is preemptive in nature. As such this strategy enables an effective custom design strategy. The profitability of the strategy itself is limited by the ease with which it is copied or by the existence of many similarly equipped competitors. If the very nature of the markets demands flexibility, as in the foregoing examples, then all competitors will invest in flexibility. Thus, only normal profitability can be expected from this technological assist to custom design strategies. Of course, the custom design strategy could be executed quite well and above-average returns could then be reasonably expected. On balance, however, the flexible approach is an enabling condition rather than a driver of high potential returns.

Flexible manufacturing involves the extensive use of CAD/CAM, which significantly reduces cost by reducing waste in several different operations—tool proving, material usage, work-in-process, machine loading and planning, and the like. In addition, there are limited learning curve effects, since a computer-operated machine is as efficient the first time as the tenth time or the hundredth time. The fashion industry uses this capability to customize its production for marketing purposes and to combat offshore cost-cutting competition. Aircraft manufacturers use this approach because of the extremely low volume of end products and the high capital assets required by the nature of the product. The flexible approach produces the productivity benefits otherwise available only to large-scale, high-volume manufacturers.

Table 4-3. Technology–Strategy Matrix

F. Customer Preference

Market/Product Situation	Actions/Defensibility	Results	Example
Mature-moderate to high volume/ standard	Develop ability to manufacture with limited flexibility	Better than normal returns	Apple

Customer Preference

Apple Computer has long passed the point when employing a producer preference strategy is sufficient, although, with introduction of each new product, there is a period when output must be allocated until pent-up demand has been satisfied. The market for the basic Apple products has matured somewhat and more routine production processes must be adapted to a customer-driven flexibility. This flexibility must be encouraged in order to widen the otherwise stagnant market through customizing, but it must be limited to provide opportunities for low-cost production in a highly competitive market.

The essence of the strategy is to tailor the product to the special needs of groups of customers. The efficacy of this targeted process relies upon the ability to set competitive prices. This ability in turn relies on an effective manufacturing process that permits flexibility at a small increase in cost. This "customizing" strategy does provide some sense of a protected niche and allows better than normal returns.

Product Pioneer/Product Leader/Product Follower

With the development of Metrecal, the ethical drug manufacturer Mead Johnson simultaneously created a new product, a new market, and a new industry. Metrecal is a weight reduction product (a six-ounce flavored liquid) which is intended to substitute for a meal and provide limited calories while still assuring nutritional balance. As the product pioneer Mead Johnson did quite well until Pet Foods entered the industry. Pet Foods selected a product leader strategy for the development of its competitive entry, Sego. Product leadership is a complex strategy which requires sophisticated interaction among the many product and marketing decisions. Sego was able to achieve a dominant position in the market through changes in distribution approaches, product taste, serving size, and advertising/promotional investment. Other product leaders, as well as a number of product followers, entered the industry. The complexity of the product allows different product leaders to focus on different product or market dimensions and thereby to create some measure of a defensible position in a nichelike portion of the market. Product followers provide a less than comprehensive copy of the mainline product and differentiate themselves either by attacking a micro niche or by providing a lower priced version.

Table 4-3. Technology–Strategy Matrix

G. Product Pioneer/G'. Product Leader/G". Product Follower

Market/Product Situation	Actions/Defensibility	Results	Examples
Latent/new and technologically complex	Invest in product development/experience curve advantages competitor delays due to product complexity and market uncertainty	Early supernormal returns	Mead Johnson Apple
Growing/ technologically complex	Heavy investment in product and market development/ better solution to large portion of market needs	Normal returns	Pet Foods IBM
Mature/ multipurpose products	Invest in special-purpose design/niche benefit of market size not worth competitor's investment	Limited supernormal returns	Others

This model also fits the personal computer industry. Apple was the product pioneer, IBM is a product leader, and the many other lookalikes are the product followers in the personal computer industry. In this case the product pioneer was not a well-established firm venturing afield but a start-up company. Entrepreneurial firms are often the source of pioneering products. Conversely, only well-established larger firms such as IBM can select the role of product leader while smaller firms and later entrants often select the product follower strategy, as illustrated by the proliferation of personal computer clones. Another way of characterizing the product leader is the firm or firms that de facto establish the dominant designs.

The pioneer strategy benefits from the experience curve and can achieve a significant payoff until established firms become aware of the fuller market opportunities. The pioneer must of course shoulder a risky initial investment until market acceptability reaches significant proportions. When product leaders enter the market, their leverage comes primarily from the fact that it costs the customer less to continue using their product than it does to switch products.

While pioneers have an initial opportunity to select a producer preference strategy they begin to lose position in face of the product leader's customer preference strategy. The product leader can be expected to earn only normal returns as it enters into an increasingly competitive situation. This strategy can pay off for more than one firm in the same industry as complex products do not have a simple one-dimensional effectiveness measure. The cost of this strategy is an inability to react quickly to technological and/or product changes. IBM's and DEC's late entry into the personal computer field can be accounted for by lack of technological experience and uncertainty that potential volume would support their more expensive marketing and service support systems without pricing themselves completely out of the market. They were also hampered by an unwillingness to risk their overall reputation by entering the market too quickly. The experience curve concept suggests that the product leader must invest heavily when entering new markets. The other special-purpose product followers can earn a higher than normal return by customizing for a specific niche. The niche size, however, will limit the total profitability available to the product follower.

Vertical Integration

The story of IBM's new personal computer is well known. Initially, this device was designed with a number of subcontractor-supplied critical components. For some of these components there were alternate sources of supply, and for some there was only a sole-source supplier. The IBM PC is a complex design which was uniquely tailored to accept only the specific components supplied. Thus, the components purchased from sole-source suppliers such as Rolm were interrelated with the PC's design. Because of the complexity of the design interface, the replacement of Rolm as a supplier would necessitate an expensive and extensive redesign effort. The possibility of problems arising between IBM and Rolm or within Rolm itself posed a significant risk, and IBM chose backward vertical integration. This alternative is often selected when there is a single supplier of a technologically complex product that is an integral and necessary part of the larger system.

Another reason for backward vertical integration is better utilization of available technological resources. McDonnell Aircraft Corporation (MAC) normally subcontracted production of a large portion of the electronics required for its various flight vehicles. The development of the basic subsystem specifications, the negotiation of the subcontracts, the supervision of the subcontractors' developments, the design and implementation of acceptance tests, systems tests, flight test procedures, and so on, required MAC to maintain a large, technically competent staff. Given this in house capability, it seems natural that the firm would shift some of the subcontract development in house, leading to more effective use of the technical staff and enhanced profitability as a larger portion of the overall product was designed, developed, and produced by MAC.

In considering backward vertical integration, MAC had to be careful not to overstep certain limitations. The business benefit to the firm was constrained in the first instance by issues of technological complexity and capacity—and in the final analysis by regulatory issues. The complexity of many of the subsystems manufactured under subcontract prevented MAC from easily developing the in-house depth to create them. There were, though, many less complex electronic subsystem developments that were

Table 4-3. Technology–Strategy Matrix

H. Vertical Integration: Forward/Backward

Market/Product Situation	Actions/Defensibility	Results	Examples
Large or growing/ technologically complex	Enter into cooperative agreement/contractual regulatory	Normal returns	IBM MAC

clearly within the firm's manufacturing capability. An additional constraint arises from government regulations that do not support a new business area within one firm when existing firms can provide the product or services required in a cost-effective manner. MAC is limited to manufacturing less complex products, which can be produced with current technical expertise and do not necessitate major investment in replicating the experience curve of potential outside suppliers. On balance, MAC chose a technological vertical integration strategy by moving a step backward in the supply chain.

Many entrepreneurial high-technology firms base their claims for support primarily on long-term contracts for a large portion of their production with an original equipment manufacturer (OEM). Some OEMs insist upon contract language that allows manufacture of the purchased component, subject to license fees, should they choose to exercise the clause. While these contracts provide a measure of financial stability, they also provide a significant risk. The firm's future is dependent upon the success of the OEM, and the investor is deprived of the risk diversification that goes along with a broad customer base. Such firms are often best served by developing some proprietary end product using their own device or by amalgamating with their main OEM. Thus, a forward vertical integration might be indicated when the power is in the hands of a single customer.

The underlying structure of this situation is a combination of uncertain imitability, normally derived from the effects of the technological experience curve, and the market. In a technologically complex product there may be a number of complex subsystems. The combination of subsystem parameters and the system design philosophy results in the unique properties of the final system product. If the various subsystems can be procured from many sources, then a buyer's market exists. If they can be procured from only one source and they cannot be easily replicated, then the market power lies with the subsystem supplier (Porter, 1985). This is evident in the IBM situation or in the new entrepreneurial high-technology firms. An attempt to balance the market power is the driving force behind the various attempts at reaching a cooperative agreement. These agreements ranging from contract to outright merger provide contractually based defensible positions for both parties. These agreements, though, are only an enabling condition for the continued existence and cost structure of the larger system product. Thus, the agreement does not provide a competitive edge, and normal returns are to be expected.

Complementary Technology

Gene Amdahl was interested in starting a new computer firm to compete with IBM. He understood quite clearly that he needed a technological design, a service and support system, and a good library of software. The service and support system was not hard to design and could be rolled out with the main product. The large library of software was a different story, however. IBM has created its software base over many years. For Amdahl to wait that long would make his business plans infeasible. His chose instead to design his computer to be IBM-compatible. That is, regardless of the technological wonders he designed into his new computer, it would operate all the existing IBM software. This complementary technology reduced not only his barrier to entry into the

Table 4-3. Technology–Strategy Matrix

I. Complementary Technology

Market/Product Situation	Actions/Defensibility	Results	Example
Large market for complex product (computer/car)	Design product to be compatible	Normal returns	Amdahl

mainframe computer business but his potential customer's switching costs as well (Teece, 1987).

This particular approach reduces barriers to entry for a firm. In general, the market size for a complementary technology strategy is smaller than that of the mainline producer. Here the firm must compete directly with the mainline producer, with other firms using similar strategies, and possibly with customers who do not purchase any complementary technology at all. Often, the mainline producer controls the rate of change and complementary firms must continually change their product design to remain compatible. Thus, high product redesign costs and small markets require a large mainline market to make this strategy economically feasible. The lower barriers are necessary for the firm to make a reasonable return and only normal returns are expected for the firm that selects a solely complementary technology strategy.

USING TECHNOLOGY STRATEGIES AS AN ANALYTIC SCREEN

This chapter was developed to enrich the thought process by which executives approach strategy. Key elements of technology were discussed to indicate how they might characterize one or another strategy gestalt. It should be clear from this summary that specific situations often call for a combination of the strategies described here. Technology is complex and so is strategy. Technology-strategy solutions require an ability to thoughtfully interrelate two very complex ideas in order to create a defensible competitive advantage. In particular, the multiple dimensions characterizing these technology strategies can be applied to the results obtained from technological mapping (Chapters 5, 6, and 7) and from innovation auditing (Chapters 8, 9, and 10) to assess the strategic potential of the various actions discussed here and to thus provide guidance for managerial action.

REFERENCES

Abernathy, W. J. 1978. *The Productivity Dilemma: Roadblocks to Innovation in the Automobile Industry.* Baltimore, MD: Johns Hopkins University Press.

Abernathy, W. J., and J. M. Utterback. 1978. "Patterns of Industrial Innovation," *Technology Review,* June–July, pp. 41–47.

Ansoff, I. H., and J. M. Stewart. 1967. "Strategies for Technology Based Business," *Harvard Business Review,* November–December, pp. 71–83.

Cooper, A. C., and D. Schendel. 1976. "Strategic Responses to Technological Threats" *Business Horizons* 19:61–69.

Dasgupta, P., and J. Stiglitz. 1980. "Industrial Structure and the Nature of Innovative Activity," *Economic Journal* 90(358):266–93.

Freeman, C. 1974. *The Economics of Industrial Innovation*. Harmondsworth, England: Penguin.

Goodman, R. A. 1989. "Dual Perspectives on the Strategic Employment of Technological Vertical Integration: As National Policy and as Corporate Policy," Los Angeles: Graduate School of Management, University of California, Los Angeles.

Hinings, C., and R. Greenwood. 1988. *The Dynamics of Strategic Change*. New York: Basil Blackwell.

Kuhn, T. S. 1963. *The Structure of Scientific Revolutions*. Chicago:University of Chicago Press.

Lamarck, J. B. 1963. *Zoological Philosophy*, translated by H. Elion. New York: Hafner.

Lawless, M., and K. Fisher. 1990. "Sources of Durable Competitive Advantage in New Products," *Journal of Product Innovation Management* 7(1):35–44.

Liebler, W. J. 1976. "Impact of Public Policy on Drug Innovation and Pricing." In *Public Policy Research in the Drug Industry*. Washington, DC: American Enterprise Institute.

McKelvey, B. 1982. *Organizational Systematics: Taxonomy, Evolution, Classification*. Berkeley: University of California Press.

Miles, R. E., and C. C. Snow. 1978. *Organizational Strategy, Structure, and Process*. New York: McGraw-Hill.

Miller, A. 1988. "A Taxonomy of Technological Settings, with Related Strategies and Performance Levels," *Strategic Management Journal* 9:239–54.

Miller, D., and P. Friesen. 1984. *Organizations: A Quantum View*. Englewood Cliffs, NJ: Prentice-Hall.

Porter, M. 1985. *Competitive Advantage: Creating and Sustaining Superior Advantage*. New York: Free Press.

Rosenbloom, R. S. 1984. "Managing Technology for the Longer Term: Notes from a Managerial Perspective." Boston: Harvard Business School. (mimeo)

Sahal, D. 1981. *Patterns of Technological Innovation*. Reading, MA: Addison-Wesley.

Smith, A. 1776. *An Inquiry into the Nature and Causes of the Wealth of Nations*. London: W. Strahan and T. Cadell.

Teece, D. 1987. *The Competitive Challenge*. New York: Ballinger.

Woodward, J. 1965. *Industrial Organization: Theory and Practice*. London: Oxford University Press.

5

Mapping a Technology's Antecedents

Thus far this book has addressed two issues: what is competitive advantage and how does an organization obtain it? In Chapter 4, product issues and market issues were introduced as the critical dimensions underlying the appropriate technology-strategy archetypes or gestalts. Now the technological elements must be pursued in some detail. A practical aid to in-depth analysis of the detailed technological situation, a strategic decision-making technique called *technology mapping,* is helpful. A technology map is a time-based descriptive of technological change that helps management to exercise judgment regarding potential development.

It combines historical analysis with the basic tenets of strategic analysis—the strategic screen of Chapter 4. This combination provides a new lens from which to view the development of a technology and/or an industry. By understanding the likely shifts in the bases of competition due to technology and the time frames in which these shifts might occur, implications for strategic action can be ascertained.

The basic objective of technological mapping is the creation of competitive advantage—through the analysis of strategic options—in light of expected technological development. The basic building block required to achieve this objective is the technological forecast. Since forecasters are not omniscient, forecasts can represent only guesses about the future, based on a forecaster's idea or model about which indicators from the past best foreshadow future developments. A model helps to simplify the forecaster's problem by directing attention toward some elements and deemphasizing others. Technological mapping—one of the centerpieces of this book—represents just such a model. To appreciate the many perspectives which were blended into this forecasting approach, we examine many earlier approaches for their contributions and drawbacks.

A common type of technological forecast depicts the basic trends of important variables and projects their development with linear or curvilinear models. This approach has the benefit of using conveniently available data and smoothing the unevenness of day-to-day developments. Conversely, such a broad analytic approach obscures the myriad of detailed developments that underlie progress. More detail often is needed. For instance, at the firm level, decisions must be taken about where defensible technological advantage can be obtained. Thus, effectively forecasting the future of technology for strategic purposes requires a quite different approach.

Understanding how technologies progress and develop is required for strategic decision making. The basic sciences that underlie the firm's product portfolio continue to develop and to alter the range of possible technological solutions. The product portfolio itself will often evolve as new application areas and thus new markets (and new competitors) are located. Issues in the larger society often create pressures which stimulate a search for new solutions. These and other detailed issues are important concerns as the firm engages in its strategy formulation.

This chapter, through the presentation of many different "maps," or perspectives of technology, provides a broad background. The many maps presented here reflect the very diverse needs of analysts. Nevertheless, this diversity provides a very rich context which is essential to understand technology mapping.

The technology maps presented in this chapter begin with the purely historical views that were initially constructed for academic purposes and/or as a step toward the development of national technology policy. These are followed by the various treatments of technology qua technology, which finally relate underlying science to technology. These later maps were also created to explore national policy issues.

Other maps have specific firm application as they explore long-run benefits and downstream payoffs of individual, project-driven technological advances. These maps show how ideas flow from project to project and illustrate the complex interrelationship between yesterday's projects and today's possibilities. The final maps show the results of competitive pressures and the notions of passive interfirm technological development. All these maps form a background upon which dimensions of strategy can be built.

When studying the maps presented in this chapter the most important concern is how one might employ them as a basis of forecasting. Extrapolation from a trend line is not particularly useful to the firm as the trend line concept masks many underlying sources of competitive advantage. Attending to the basic technologies which drive one or another parameter and observing the growing diversity of applications for the product provide a better basis for prognostication. Consciously investing in specific technologies which create higher speeds, or better reliability, or smaller size entails strategic actions and creates potential experience curve benefits. Similarly, investing in product design for a unique high-end niche could very well do the same. The question for the forecaster remains what will be the key elements of advantage in the future—technology, niche experience, or something else. But this is the subject of Chapter 6; here the background for technology mapping is laid out by starting with simple issues and then adding complexity to increase the sophistication and appreciation of the actual recommendations presented in the following chapter.

SOME HISTORIES OF TECHNOLOGICAL DEVELOPMENT

Are there patterns of technological innovation? If they exist, can they be anticipated or accelerated? Questions such as these were the focus of some significant work by Sahal

Table 5-1. Technical Characteristics of Passenger Ships, 1840–1961

Date	Vessel	Length (feet)	Beam (feet)	Tonnage	Horsepower
1840	Acadia	206	34	1,136	425
1850	Atlantic	276	45	2,860	850
1861	Scotia	379	47	3,871	1,000
1881	City of Rome	560	52	8,415	17,500
1889	Teutonic	565	57	9,984	17,000
1900	Deutschland	661	67	16,502	35,000
1911	Olympic	853	93	46,439	55,000
1921	Bismarck	916	100	56,621	80,000
1931	Empress of Britain	733	98	42,348	60,000
1950	Queen Elizabeth	1,031	119	83,673	200,000

Adapted from Sahal, 1981, p. 351, by permission.

(1981), Basalla (1988), Hughes (1983), and others, all of whom developed several technological histories. One of Sahal's histories, shown in Table 5-1, involves passenger ships from 1840 to 1961. The table lists the world's largest ships and the dates when the next largest ship was constructed. This rudimentary "map" develops rather smoothly as size, tonnage, and horsepower continue to increase in general proportion from one to the next. It suggests that in the long term size parameters can be expected to continue to grow if there is a market need for such growth. Many studies continue to focus on change in measurable features as a surrogate for underlying trends. Thus, price, speed, and the like, are featured in analysts' reports on the development of specific industries and the expected role of the various competitors.

On the other hand, the measures do not indicate the nature of various underlying technical breakthroughs in the changed characteristics. Using gross measures may also mask performance and other attributes which are significant to customer populations. Since strategic action is aimed in part at maximizing the likelihood that the firm's products will be purchased, underrepresenting buyer value is problematic.

Table 5-2 is a different sort of a technology map; it focuses on performance parameters rather than the gross size parameters. This map of energy efficiencies also provides only current status information. A drawback to this approach is that the cross-sectional method does not allow any analysis of *development potential*. Thus, one cannot ascertain the possibility of more efficient uses of the various energy forms. The "status" report mode of technological map also does not allow analysis of the potential benefit or value to the customer and/or user populations except in the most rudimentary sense.

The third of the series of maps selected from Sahal is a true development history. It describes the underlying technical changes which provide either increased customer satisfaction or a wider range of functional performance. These ideas are critical to the full development of the strategic technological mapping process.

Table 5-3 traces the development of the farm tractor from a stationary steam engine, to a mobile vehicle with towing capability, to a vehicle with power takeoffs for driving other implements. The reader can begin to appreciate that the technological shifts in the basis of competition were neither bigger nor more efficient in the narrow

Table 5-2. Efficiencies of Energy Use

Source of Energy	Efficiency of Use (%)
Electricity	100.0
Fuel wood	20.4
Lumber mill waste	40.0
Bagasse	39.9
Other vegetal fuels	20.0
Coal and briquettes	39.4
Lignite	48.6
Lignite briquettes	44.6
Peat	29.6
Coke	52.4
Liquefied petroleum gas	57.1
Aviation gasoline and jet fuel	20.0
Motor spirit	45.8
Distillate fuel oil	47.3
Residual fuel oil	41.7
Refinery gas	80.0
Natural gas	71.6
Oven gas	74.2

Adapted from Sahal, 1981, p. 355, by permission.

sense but were more effective. That is, technological advancements which increased the range of applications seemed critical in the customers' purchase decision process. Functional differentiation helped to alter the bases of competition within the industry and is the direct result of technological development.

After many maps and technological development histories, Sahal developed several broad concepts. First, innovations seemed to occur in cycles whose lengths correspond to the lengths of normal economic cycles. This has some value to macro-level analysis for national policy actions. Second, he theorized that the development of a

Table 5-3. Major Innovations in Tractor Technology, 1800–1971

Innovation	Date
1. Stationery steam engine for farm use	1808
2. Portable steam engine for farm use	1849
3. Self-propelled steam engine for farm use	1870
4. Gasoline track-type tractor	1908
5. Farm tractor equipped with power takeoff	1918
6. Cultivating or tricycle-type general tractor	1924
7. Farm tractor equipped with mechanical power lift	1929
8. Diesel-powered tract-type tractor	1931
9. Low-pressure rubber tires for tractors	1934
10. Three-point hitch for tractor	1938
11. Continuous running or independent power takeoff	1947
12. Hydraulic remote control of drawn implements	1947
13. Power steering for tractor	1953
14. Auxiliary front-wheel drive and four-wheel drive	1967
15. Electric remote control of drawn implements	1970

Adapted from Sahal, 1981, p. 331, by permission.

technology seems to occur as a result of improvements in a myriad of underlying technical areas. He further argues that the development process can be seen as a series of disjoint and incremental performance enhancers. The resulting mastery of diffuse technologies leads to further product improvements when the interrelationships between the technologies are better understood. This last premise underlies the experience curve.

TECHNOLOGY AND TECHNOLOGY MAPS

Table 5-4 is a technology map for life cycle costing. The broad categories suggest the wide range of performance parameters with which users might be concerned. The details of R&D costs versus investment costs versus operating costs highlight the technological complexity suggested earlier. It is clear that there are interrelationships among the three categories. More R&D expense may reduce annual operating expense and the like. Some design choices increase the level and number of personnel to operate the system while other choices would have the opposite effect. This sort of map highlights design and strategic issues but has limited use in technology-strategy formulation. It ignores typical performance measures such as speed, range, and payload. Although cost implications of any new development cannot be estimated without detailed technology analysis, the cost focus is still rather narrow. For strategic purposes this map is also limited by being a "point in time" construct rather than a longitudinal construct. Development of a long-term technological thrust, technological life cycle effects, and other dynamic questions is left unattended by this particular approach.

Another technology map that provides insight into the complexity of the technological dimension is shown in Tables 5-5 and 5-6, which represent a product–technologies matrix for the electronic components sector. The data were gathered through a series of extensive interviews with representatives of the firms in the industry, research

Table 5-4. Cost Categories for Aircraft

Research and Development	Initial Investment	Annual Operation
Design and development	Facilities	Facilities R&M
Airframe/special AGE	PME	PME replacement
Engines/special AGE	Airframe	Airframe
Avionics/special AGE	Engines	Engines
Systems test	Avionics	Avionics
Flight test vehicle production	Unit support aircraft,	PME maintenance/POL
Flight test operations	AGE, stocks spares	Unit support aircraft maintenance and
Flight test support	Personnel training	POL
	Initial travel and	AGE replacement and maintenance
	transportation	Personnel pay and allowances
		Personnel replacement training
		Annual travel, transportation, services

Key: AGE = aerospace ground equipment; R&M = replacement and maintenance; PME = prime mission equipment; POL = petroleum fuel, oil, and lubricants.

Adapted from Mooz, 1965, p. 19, by permission.

Table 5-5. Technologies Necessary for the Production of Electronic Components

1. Applied chemistry
   1.1 Analysis
      1.1.1 Physical analysis of chemical elements
      1.1.2 Specific analysis of material (structural, localized)
   1.2 Surface treatment
      1.2.1 Chemical rinsing and degreasing
      1.2.2 Chemical interventions (isotropic and anisotropic)
      1.2.3 Plasma treatment
      1.2.4 Surface chemistry
2. Physicochemistry
   2.1 Solid-state technology areas
      2.1.1 Growth of volume—crystals
      2.1.2 Doping
         2.1.2.1 Diffusion
         2.1.2.2 Ionic implantation
         2.1.2.3 Alloy
      2.1.3 Epitaxy
      2.1.4 Metal deposits
      2.1.5 Dielectric and refractory deposits
   2.2 Ceramics technology areas
      2.2.1 Ceramics formation
      2.2.2 Sintering
   2.3 Glass technology areas
      2.3.1 Formation
      2.3.2 Vitrification process
   2.4 Encapsulating and coatings
      2.4.1 Plastic encapsulation
      2.4.2 Glass encapsulation
      2.4.3 Metal encapsulation
      2.4.4 Ceramic encapsulation
      2.4.5 Lacquer and varnish coatings
      2.4.6 Resin coatings
3. Vacuum technology areas
   3.1 Metallization in high vacuum
   3.2 Pyrolisis
   3.3 Impregnation process
4. Design and reproduction
   4.1 Modeling and computerized hand design of components
   4.2 Reproduction
      4.2.1 Microphotography
      4.2.2 Photolithography (optical, X-ray, electron)
      4.2.3 Serigraphy
      4.2.4 Image transference
      4.2.5 Thermoprinting
      4.2.6 Photoprinting
      4.2.7 Developing
   4.3 Technologies with resolution better than 1 micrometer
5. Instrumentation
   5.1 Instrumentation of measurements in manufacturing processes
      5.1.1 Length and surface measurements
      5.1.2 Atom density measurements
      5.1.3 Measurements of electrical characteristics
      5.1.4 Evaluation of seams
   5.2 Automatization of the manufacturing process
      5.2.1 Cinematic systems
      5.2.2 Pneumatic systems

Adapted from Goodman and Pavon, 1984, pp. 357–60, by permission.

Table 5-6. Semiconductor Product–Technology Matrix

	Product			
Technology	Small-Signal Diodes	Field Effect Transistors	Digital Integrated Circuits	Piezoelectric Circuits
Applied chemistry				
Analysis	Nec	Ess	Imp	Nec
Surface treatment	Imp	Ess	Ess	Ess
Physical chemistry				
Solid state	Ess	Ess	Ess	Ess
Ceramics				Ess
Glass	Nec			
Encapsulation/coating	Ess	Ess	Ess	Ess
Vacuum				
Metallization	Ess	Ess	Ess	Ess
Pyrolisis				
Impregnation				
Design/reproduction				
Model	Nec	Ess	Ess	
Reproduction	Ess	Ess	Ess	Imp
High-resolution			Ess	
Instrumentation				
Instrument manufacturing	Ess	Ess	Ess	Ess
Automatation	Ess	Ess	Ess	Imp
Control				
Antiparasite technologies				
Fluids				
Purification	Imp	Ess	Ess	Ess
Conditioning	Imp	Ess	Ess	Imp
Water treatment	Imp	Ess	Ess	Imp
Treatment residual gases	Nec	Nec	Nec	Nec
Treatment residual liquids	Nec	Nec	Nec	Nec
Treatment residual liquids for impregnation				
Welding				
Macro				
Micro	Ess	Ess	Ess	
Engineering				
Chemical				Ess
Mechanical	Nec	Nec	Imp	Ess
Electromagnetic manufacturing techniques				
Alternative materials			Ess	
Quality control and reliability	Imp	Imp	Imp	Imp

Key: Nec = necessary; Imp = important; Ess = essential to product world-class components.

Adapted from Goodman and Pavon, 1984, p. 366, by permission.

establishments, and the industry's trade association. The intent of the study was to create a data base to stimulate industrial activity and to provide a basis for recommended national policy positions for development.

Included in Table 5-5 are those technologies that must be mastered before a firm can participate. Many can be mastered at the technician level, but each firm needs state-of-the-art competence in a dozen or so areas.

Table 5-6 indicates technological areas and their criticality to the development of one or another electronic component. The firm must estimate the difficulty and the cost of achieving the appropriate mastery. Then it must estimate potential parameter performance improvements from the general development of the technology and/or from competitive pressures. This type of map provides a good starting point for a two-stage inquiry. Questions about the firm's ability to enter a particular product market can easily be framed. Questions about competitiveness require other maps with dynamic dimensions. Nevertheless, technology strategies can be undertaken only if an enormous amount of technical detail is first mastered.

The Illinois Institute of Technology Research Institute (IITRI, 1968), under a contract from the National Science Foundation, developed a dynamic mapping technique for science and technology. This technique was employed in the study of several diverse developments such as the electron microscope, the oral contraceptive, and the biological matrix. This mapping approach was then applied to additional technological areas by Battelle (1973). Figure 5-1 is a map from the Battelle study.

Figure 5-1 represents a map of the development of the videotape recorder. This map shows the confluence of work in six basic technologies: control theory, magnetic and recording materials, magnetic theory, magnetic recording, electronics, and frequency modulation. Control theory began at Battelle in the 1920s with studies on feedback and then servomechanisms. After three decades of research work on theory and two decades of work in parallel on the reliability of manufacturing processes a decisive event occurred at the IIT Research Institute when in 1950 Camras developed the concept of rotating heads. It was this concept that became the heart of the new system.

Magnetic recording materials began in 1882 when an accidentally formulated iron–silicon alloy was found to exhibit extreme hardness. By 1913 it was transformed into permalloy, an iron–nickel alloy with remarkable properties. In the same decade the magnetic properties of iron oxides were studied closely. Investigations into the chemical structure of oxides and plastics led in 1927 to a two-layer paper tape. In the 1940s two-layer plastic tape was developed, followed in the 1950s by the development of tape with improved oxide coatings yielding a reliable wideband tape. The theoretical underpinnings began in the 1850s with the development of ferromagnetic theory. In 1888, Smith envisaged the use of magnetically coated material to record information. That idea led to the design and development of a wire recorder patented in Copenhagen in 1897. By the 1920s there were numerous publications of data on the ferromagnetic medium.

By 1930, wire and steel recorders were in general use. In 1935, AEG's Magnetophon produced a plastic tape machine, which was developed into a device sufficiently reliable for instrumentation recording by the 1950s. The electronics development stream carried through with the vacuum tube of Edison in 1883, the diode by Fleming in 1904, the triode by DeForest in 1906, enhancement of DeForest's basic design by 1915, and, decisively, by the inauguration of regular television broadcasts by the BBC in 1936. This event of course created the basic need. FM theory was sparked by Hertz in 1887, patented in 1902 for transmission of signals, became practical by 1920, and led to the transmission of television images by 1949.

Parallel developments were pursued by Ampex and RCA. Ampex selected the FM

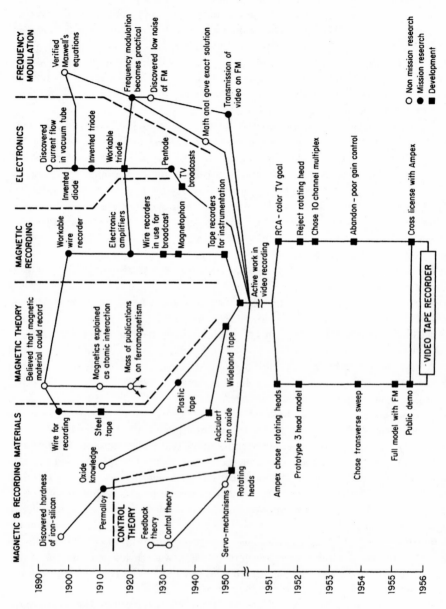

Figure 5-1. The scientific and technological history of the video tape recorder. Adapted from Batelle, 1973.

approach and the transverse recording techniques while RCA focused on the linear techniques, multiplexing, and color. Ampex achieved the first practical result, which led to CBS's monochrome videotape recorder in 1956. This machine was originally used to cope with shifts from live U.S. east coast broadcasts to delayed broadcasts on the west coast. The main function of the first videotape recorder was to "shift the time" of viewing. The first users of this videotape recorder were broadcast engineers—technically trained, professional customers.

Following the Ampex success, RCA changed its design philosophy. Cross-licensing between the two firms resulted in a videotape recorder with color capability by 1958. Further developments in the broadcast medium included time zone planning, storage, program planning, instant replay, and color.

Figure 5-1 traces the long-term development of a particular innovation, the videotape recorder. This innovation initially required basic research, then applied research or mission-oriented research, and finally development efforts. Significant events occurred in the United Kingdom, Germany, Denmark, Switzerland, the United States, Italy, and elsewhere. Universities such as Illinois Institute of Technology, Columbia, City College of New York, and MIT were involved. Private industry assistance came from Helca Steel, Battelle, RCA, AT&T, I.G. Farben, AEG, and finally Ampex. While this map indicates the ebb and flow of scientific progress, it falls short of identifying developments that shift technological competitive advantage. Science and technology in a myriad of areas continue to increase the potency of specific products, but consumer value is created through both parameter growth and functional diffusion. Thus, the videotape recorder as a network engineer's time-shift device and as a home playback machine requires dramatically different embodiments of the basic technology. Thirty years after the introduction of the videotape recorder, Ampex has not been able to achieve significant market share in the home market.

Figure 5-2, derived from the same study, illustrates the development of the oral contraceptive. This innovation draws upon developments in three scientific fields (physiology of reproduction, hormone research, and steroid chemistry) and increasing awareness of the need for contraception. Focused research was stimulated by a social issue in combination with technical development. This awareness–technology interface was seen as early 1931 when Taylor first suggested using hormones for temporary male sterilization. In 1937, Kurzrok suggested the use of hormones in contraception. In 1945, Albright suggested estrogen for this purpose. The decisive event in this stream of awareness occurred in 1951 when McCormick and Sanger requested a population control proposal from Pincus, who was then with the Worcester Foundation.

Male hormone was discovered in 1849, female hormone in 1896. From this beginning, the relationship of hormones to reproduction and to menstrual functioning could be pursued. In the early 1920s, attention was focused directly on the relationship of hormones and ovulation. The active role of progesterone was identified in 1929, and in 1931 ovarian hormones were used to prevent conception in animals. For the next decade, animal studies were conducted on the effects of estrogen and progesterone on ovulation and the menstrual cycle. By 1948, it was clear that estrogen and progesterone were ovulation inhibitors. In 1951, Pincus was able to propose the oral contraceptive as a device to control population growth in response to the McCormick-Sanger request.

Meanwhile, other hormone research work was being independently undertaken.

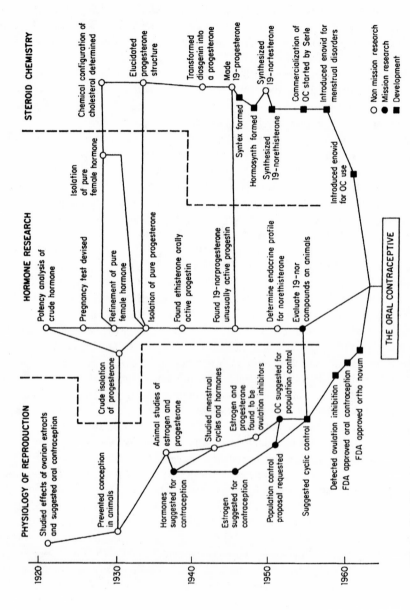

Figure 5-2. The scientific and technological history of the oral contraceptive. Adapted from Batelle, 1973.

Work in the 1920s in Ithaca, St. Louis, and various laboratories in Germany led, in 1938, to the discovery of ethisterone as an orally active progestin. In 1944, 19-nor-progesterone was discovered to be an unusually active progestin. The late 1940s and early 1950s saw the determination of the endocrine profile for norethisterone and norethynodrel. Finally, after Chang and Pincus evaluated the 19-nor compounds on animals, and evaluated the 19-nor compounds on women in 1954, Pincus suggested cyclic controls.

Steroid chemistry was created as a field in 1903. By 1934 Butenandt and colleagues had elucidated the progesterone structure. The chemical conversion of cholesterol to male hormone occurred two years later, followed in 1941 by the transformation of diosgenin into a progesterone. In 1944, 19-norprogesterone was made from strophanthidin. The same year Syntex was formed in Mexico to produce sex steroids. Birch synthesized 19-nortestosterone in 1949, followed by Syntex's synthesis of 19-norethisterone in 1951. The period from 1954 to 1960 resulted in a collaboration of Pincus with Searle to introduce Enovid in 1960, followed closely by Syntex's offering and Johnson and Johnson's introduction of Ortho-Novum in 1962. These products were initially used for menstrual disorders until they received full approval for use as an oral contraceptive.

The flow and development of this innovation involved research at Göttingen, Cornell, Washington (St. Louis), Pennsylvania State, Columbia, and Harvard universities. Research was carried out in Germany, Mexico, and the United States. Searle, Syntex, Johnson and Johnson, and Parke-Davis participated. The Worcester Foundation with various hospital associates and the National Institutes of Health were critical to this development, as were the efforts of Planned Parenthood.

The initial follow-up work required was the study of "side effects" in the short and long term, evaluation of other methods of birth control, research into the metabolic effects of hormones, and the test and approval of other commercial products.

This map has shown the confluence of science and technological events with strong public awareness of the need. The discovery of biological mechanisms, the understanding of the role hormones play in these mechanisms, the creation of a field of steroid chemistry, the ability to synthesize hormones, and finally the conceptualization of a delivery system in concert with a public need and desire all were required and all occurred over a thirty-five year period ending in 1960.

The unevenness of development as well as the need to monitor many disciplines and opportunities is fairly clear. Still, the essence of the strategic process remains to be identified, and some attention must be given to performance parameter improvement and functional diffusion.

These maps are particularly useful in tracing the development of an innovation, but they focus little attention on the development of a product family. Both performance parameter improvement and functional diffusion occur as various projects and various firms leapfrog one another.

MAPPING THE DOWNSTREAM PAYOFFS OF TECHNOLOGY

Abernathy conducted a study of a relatively common project strategy, the parallel pursuit of several technical approaches as a hedge against failure. In his 1969 publication, Abernathy reported that such parallel approaches were often pursued at the subsystem level when the ultimate performance characteristics of the specific subsystem were problematic. Sometimes an almost completely new approach was attempted to improve the system's performance. Under these circumstances, the new approach was often found to have shortcomings that would require much time to resolve. In such a cases, the new approach was abandoned and an older approach was substituted.

Abernathy was concerned with developing a reasonable definition of success. The study site (U.S. Naval Ordnance Test Station, Pasadena) produced rather complicated systems (torpedoes). The major subsystems included the warhead, target acquisition and guidance technology, control systems, stored energy systems, energy conversion systems (engines), and propulsion systems (mechanical systems for water coupling). How could one relate a system developed in 1958 to one developed in 1967? The measure that he finally selected combined a contractual view, a marketing view, and a contribution to technology view. Evaluation of the product's ability to meet the technical specifications was supplemented by a measure of product acceptance, an evaluation of whether the customer accepted the product. Did the fleet really like the product or was the fleet slow to adopt it and quick to demand a newer version to overcome its shortcomings? In this case, wide fleet acceptance was a measure of the marketplace reception of the product. Finally, he evaluated the degree to which the later subsystem improvements were stimulated by the earlier learning derived from abandoned approaches. Figure 5-3 is a map showing the influences of earlier approaches upon later results.

Later work by Clarke (1968) concentrated on 237 liquid propellant rocket engine

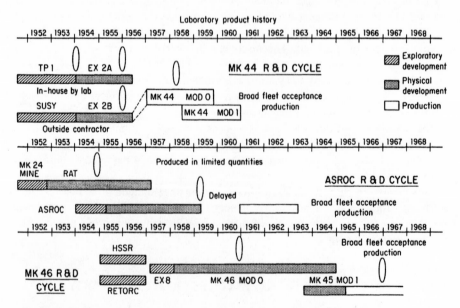

Figure 5-3. Naval ordnance test station product history. Adapted from Abernathy, 1969.

(LPRE) projects conducted during a 25-year period from 1942 to 1967. The projects were clustered into some ten application areas such as deep space or assisted takeoff. A key aspect of the study was the creation of diffusion maps showing projects which were sources of technology and projects which received technology.

Figure 5-4 is a diffusion map depicting the 1940–1954 period of the Aerojet General Corporation's work in the assisted takeoff (ATO) application area. It shows both interfirm and intrafirm movement of technology. Intrafirm movement looks very similar to any long-term development program. Interfirm movement is also traditional, but it is seldom emphasized in studies on development. The technologies that make a difference are subsystems-level transfers. For instance, the first interfirm transfer from the AL-500 project was the heat sink thrust chamber. Similarly, the Jet Propulsion Laboratory's AL-2000 contributed an aerojet rotating thrust chamber pump drive to Aerojet's AL-6000 project. This map and the one in Figure 5-3 indicate how subsystem development flows from project to project and the value of development occurring outside the firm.

While both maps reflect several companies' participation in an individual innovation, they pay little direct attention to competitive effects. This oversight can be partially redressed by looking at Abernathy's (1978) study of the automobile industry. Table 5-7 summarizes the innovations occurring in Ford engines from 1903 to 1970. The focus of the engine innovations shifts back and forth between manufacturing process and product design.

A second look at this automotive cycle is provided in Figure 5-5. In this figure,

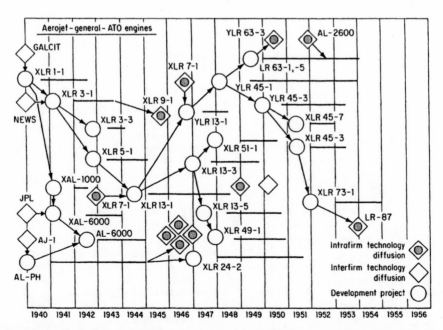

Figure 5-4. An example of a diffusion map showing competitive affects of technological developments. Adapted from Clarke, 1968.

labor productivity spikes upward a year or two before a major model changeover. Abernathy explains the figure by suggesting a three-phase competitive cycle that begins with a product innovation (new model). Complexity of the new product and lack of manufacturing experience make initial manufacturing costs rather high. In this first phase the firm's competitive positioning is based upon the innovative quality of the new product's design.

In the second phase, manufacturing improvement programs drive the costs down. This technology-assisted cost strategy uses a pricing strategy as the leading edge of competitive positioning. As long as major cost savings can be attained this low-cost–low-price strategy can continue. Unfortunately, after several years, the new product reaches a point where further productivity improvement is very costly. Enabling conditions for the pricing strategy begin to fade.

Phase three is a struggle to extend the life of the new product. The firm begins to create design variations. These market-oriented variations widen the appeal of the product by capturing sales from various niches in the marketplace. Introduction of these variations, however, begins to reduce manufacturing advantage by driving costs up. Eventually the forces underlying product life cycle extension weaken and the firm begins the cycle over again with introduction of a new-generation product.

This mapping and the underlying analysis show how the Ford Motor Company reacted to competitive pressure. It also traces historical trends in applying technology to corporate strategy. Thus, the nature of competition is an important element in the choice of technology and its use to create a defensible edge. Aside from competitive pressures, firms face opportunities which arise as elements of the industrial system progress.

Table 5-7. Major Design, Process, and Organizational Changes or Innovations in Ford Engines

Year	Application	Change or Innovation
1903	8-hp 2-cylinder (opposing engine)	Adjustable spark advance
1907	149-CID IL-4 engine	Cylinder head removable
1908	New 177-CID Model T engine	First mass-produced, lightweight, reliable engine
1924	Engine manufacturing inspection	Constant temperature
1927	New 200-CID V-8 engine	Aluminum pistons, mushroom valve stems
1932	Engine manufacturing	First in-line transfer device
1932	New 448-CID V-12 engine	
1941	New 226-CID IL-6 engine	First IL-6 since 1907
1952	New 215-CID overhead valve	Start of "horsepower race"
1952	Cleveland engine plant	First fully automated by transfer lines engine plant Start of decentralization of engine manufacture
1959	Thin-wall, gray cast iron engine introduced	Improved casting technology permits weight reduction
1960	Merger of Lincoln–Mercury and Ford engine lines	Consolidation of divisions into corporate-wide line
1970	New 4-cylinder metric engine	Metric engine introduced for Pinto at Ford Germany

Adapted from Abernathy, 1978, p. 95, by permission.

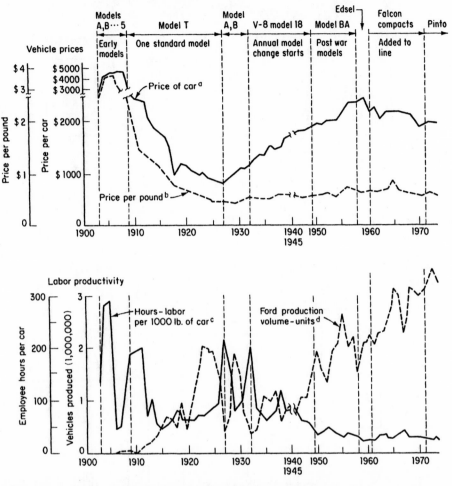

Figure 5-5. Operating trends, Ford Motor Company: North American operations. *Sources:* Corporate Reports; Ford Archives; *Automotive Industries* Statistical Issue, various years; and U.S. Bureau of Labor Statistics. a Retail price for median-priced car in 1958 dollars. b Price per pound of car for curve (a). c Ford employee hours (nonsalaried) per 1000 lb of vehicles produced. d Unit production volume for North American operations—Ford. Adapted from Abernathy, 1978.

TECHNOLOGY MAPPING OF MULTIFIRM EFFECTS

A variety of forecasting techniques can be employed to forecast the future of technology. Scattered through the published literature are numerous prognostications about the possibilities of sending people to the moon, driving under the English channel, or the like. Such forecasts are built upon some sense of the technical possibilities and an equivalent sense of socioeconomic priorities. They are normally approached by observing the rate of change of a few broad parameters, for example, in computing, the increasing number of active elements that can be placed upon a single chip. Broad trend extrapolation has limited value at the firm level.

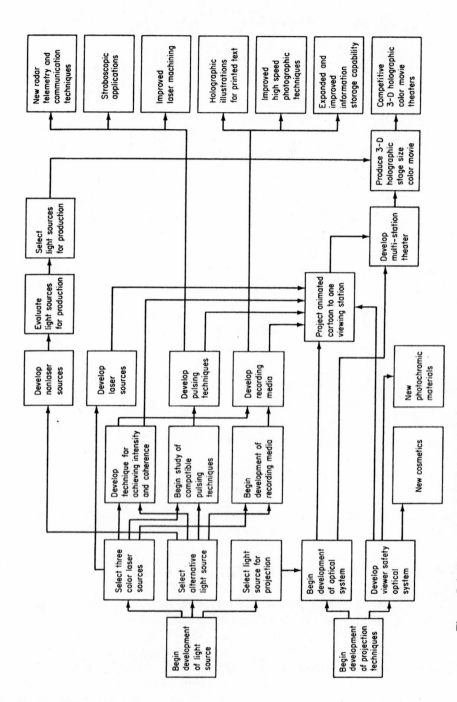

Figure 5-6. Forecasted technological map for 3-D holographic color movies. Adapted from North and Pike, 1979.

More functional to the firm is a forecast technique that can build upon detailed levels of analysis. Many of the mapping techniques presented in this chapter are based upon the premise that technology progresses unevenly through improvements in several underlying technologies. An ambitious project begun by North and Pike at TRW (1969) posed the problem of technological forecasting as a detailed question rather than a broad trend analysis. Using the Delphi technique (Dalkey and Helmer, 1963), they set out to study the technological developments in seven technologies and eight systems/subsystems areas drawing experts from twenty-seven areas within the firm's four basic divisions. Although the four divisions were automotive, electronics, equipment, and systems, there were relevant experts in each division for all but three study areas—oceans, personal and medical, and urban and international. This is indicative of the wide range of underlying technologies needed for new-product development.

Of particular interest was the way that TRW used these results in their strategic research and development planning. Results were initially presented in the traditional format. "Electric automobiles will be marketed commercially by the year X plus or minus Y years." Faced with such information, management continued essentially to employ its normal planning process. In a second approach, the reporting forecast's format was extensively redesigned. A more detailed mapping technique was used, as shown in Figure 5-6, and management took a new approach to the R&D resource allocation process.

The map idea had some very interesting characteristics. The map reveals events that were part of the firm's research and development program and were required precursors of desired technological developments. Thus, critical steps along the way to an innovation are identified. One particularly intriguing idea is the identification of technology which is a precursor needed for an innovation but which needs to be developed outside the firm. This latter information provides a focus for the firm's technology monitoring and for deciding to defer certain research programs. TRW could choose to delay its internal investment until the precursor events seemed well under way.

Many technological developments needed to create a specific technological innovation would be the stimulus of sequential opportunities in several other areas. In the version of such a map as shown in Figure 5-6 the development of pulsing techniques and the development of recording media are of particular interest. For "two of the technical developments essential for the development of 3-D holographic color movies are likely to be accompanied by improvements in radar, telemetry, photographic techniques, communications and so forth" (North and Pike, 1969, p. 75). This more detailed mapping was seen as a major information breakthrough with more understanding of the technical dynamics underlying their managerial responsibilities.

SUMMARY

Parameter estimation techniques (range, speed, etc.) as a historical analysis or as a current status comparison or as a development forecast must be accompanied by buyer value issues. The concept of performance parameter must include interaction with other attributes in the purchase decision. Similarly, history must be seen as a precursor to forecast. Strategic analysis must be forward-looking. Additionally, there must be no underestimation of complexity as reflected in the myriad of underlying technological details or of interorganizational flows of technologies. In the next chapter these are interwoven with strategic analysis to arrive at strategic action program selections.

REFERENCES

Abernathy, W. J. 1969. *Decision Strategies in R & D Projects.* LosAngeles: Graduate School of Business, University of California, Los Angeles, August.

Abernathy, W. J. 1978. *The Productivity Dilemma: Roadblocks to Innovation in the Automobile Industry.* Baltimore, MD: Johns Hopkins University Press.

Basalla, G. 1988. *The Evolution of Technology.* Cambridge: Cambridge University Press.

Battelle. 1973. "Interactions of Science and Technology in Innovative Processes: Some Case Studies." Columbus: Battelle, March 19.

Clarke, R. W. 1968. "Innovation in Liquid Propellant Rocket Technology," *Final Report Task 7910-05.* Holloman Air Force Base, NM: Office of Aerospace Research, March.

Dalkey, N. C., and O. Helmer. 1963. "An Experimental Application of the Delphi Methods to the Use of Experts," *Management Science* 9:458–67.

Goodman, R. A., and J. Pavon. 1984. *Planning for National Technology Policy.* New York: Praeger.

Hughes, T. 1983. *Networks of Power.* Baltimore, MD: Johns Hopkins University Press.

IIT Research Institute. 1968. *TRACES (Technology in Retrospective and Critical Events in Science.)* Chicago: IITRI, December 15.

Mooz, W. E. 1965. *The B-X: A Hypothetical Bomber Cost Study.* Santa Monica, CA: Rand Corporation, July, RM-4635-PR.

North, H. Q., and D. Pike. 1969. "Technological Probes of the Future," *Harvard Business Review*, May–June, pp. 68–83.

Sahal, D. 1981. *Patterns of Technological Innovation.* Reading, MA: Addison-Wesley.

6

Mapping Technological Potential
for Defensible Positioning

The various maps presented Chapter 5 provide a foundation upon which to consider strategic issues. Unfortunately, truly strategic appreciation of technology requires supplementary information such as competitor's technological status and thrust, environmental factors that will encourage or inhibit certain technological developments, manner and rate at which product and/or service parameters are changing, and the rate of change of functional diversity and diffusion. Such additional considerations are the domain of this chapter. Most important, this chapter explains the application of the nine technology strategies introduced in Chapter 4 as a screening device—to make explicit the strategic implications of the mapping process.

In Chapter 7, the strategic screening technique is demonstrated by two case examples, one drawn from the electronics arena and one from biotechnology. They also indicate some of the adaptations necessary when applying such a general tool in specific situations.

TECHNOLOGICAL MAPPING FOR STRATEGIC EFFECTIVENESS

A technology map is a historical document to forecast future technological achievements. It helps build the foundation for the exercise of managerial judgment and decision making. With appropriate information and analysis, management can more effectively engage in the selection of well-founded strategic activities. It must be quite clear that the art of employing this technique ultimately relies upon judgment. Managers must accept the responsibility of blending past trends with current status and with the informed reading of signals about the future. Information and analysis—in this case technology mapping—can provide a surer foundation for the exercise of judgment.

The Exercise of Judgment and Relevant Time Horizon

A major barrier to a firm's ability to effectively anticipate changes in the marketplace is the lack of a shared vision or consensus about the firm's strengths and directions among key executives. Equally important is consensus about the effects of potentially shifting conditions in the firm's environment. Such shared visions promote swift and smooth adjustments. Conversely, in periods of shifting strategy divergence creates difficulty in fully articulating the necessary interactions among these units. Lack of consensus dampens responsiveness to change. Consensus formation is handicapped by different assessments of the level of uncertainty in the forecast, by lack of agreement on basic assumptions, and by differences among executives vis-à-vis their planning time horizon.

Judgment and Forecasting

What sort of faith is possible in a forecast? Eminent futurists have, in one way or another, identified diverse current events and their synchroneity—their interrelationships. This has led Emery (1967), after studying many forecasting techniques, to conclude that forecasting successes generally depend on a common understanding of the values represented the arena of interest. Successful forecasters have all recognized that the seeds of the future were sown in the past. Their job therefore was to recognize hardy early growths and then to estimate rates of growth and interaction effects among the competing strains.

Technology mapping focuses explicitly on past technological development to achieve perspective and then employs this perspective as a basis for looking forward—for obtaining "prevision."

Alternative views of this proposition are found in Forrester's simulation models. In his landmark book, *Industrial Dynamics* (1961), Forrester describes a modeling technique that employs only continuous variables. He contends that discrete events can be modeled as having ever-increasing probability of occurrence. Thus, discontinuities, normally seen as surprises which create a natural distrust of forecasts, can be anticipated through an appropriate understanding of the past and the present. In his approach, uncertainty is reduced by admitting to uncertainties and explicitly building such events into the forecasting simulation. Potential interactions are immediately evaluated, and it is only the occurrences that are estimated. Explicit treatment of uncertainty provides a medium for engaging various executives and thus helps construct consensus visions.

RELATIVELY STRONG CONSENSUS

Forecasting, technological or otherwise, represents an arena of uncertainty for the firm. To take action effectively, technologists, strategists, and the entire top management team must engage in the forecasting exercise, so that residual uncertainties are clearly recognized. In this technology mapping exercise strategic factors can be added only through interaction between the firm's strategists and technologists. This joint effort can be very helpful in clarifying the various issues that face the two groups and in dealing with the inevitable differences in their perspectives. Participants must eventually agree on patterns of development and possible competitive positions indicated by the development.

Variable Time Horizons

Das (1986) notes that time horizons create problems in strategic judgment. Confidence in the estimate of future events may vary even among top management members within a single firm. Attending to the different time horizons of individuals is important in moving toward consensus. Agreement is more likely in the creation of a strategic technology map when careful attention is paid to the selection of an appropriate time horizon. Basically, the time horizon must be sufficiently long for the participants to identify patterns in the data. Without them events appear unique and thus not predictable. Participants have little basis upon which to form a consensus. The time horizon issue has a double-edged quality which can positively or negatively affect the perspective and the value placed upon the eventual outcome of the mapping process. In practice, the team setting out to create a strategic technology map must make time horizon decisions in three distinct arenas: historical, managerial, and financial.

The *historical* dimension requires looking backward far enough to gain a realistic perspective on the rate and change of technological development and the rate and change of industry structure. The TRACES study (IITRI, 1968) of major innovations found an average of thirty years from an advance in basic science to a commercial innovation. Similarly, Sahal (1981) reports patterns of innovation occurring in long waves (Kondratieff cycles) of approximately fifty years, medium-term waves (Kuznets cycles) of fifteen to twenty-five years, and short-term waves (Juglar cycles) of seven to eleven years which correspond to the cycles found in the analysis of basic economic time series. Thus, from business, economic, scientific, and technological perspectives, it is necessary to study several decades to identify the patterns and to sort out the random events that temporarily distort underlying processes.

For *managerial* purposes, the value of the map is derived from the rather long view of the way the business will develop given the forecast of technological developments. With a normal perspective, managers can anticipate changes in the bases of competition and reposition the firm. To gain an existential sense that the nature of the industry is shifting, the time horizon of thought must project conditions a decade forward, more or less. For instance, as the personal computer revolution grew, it became clear that IBM would eventually enter the industry. Far in advance of IBM's entry into the market, other firms faced decisions about how to position themselves for this event. It is possible to successfully engage strategic concerns only if the time horizon extends beyond the probable life of the current product line. It is only in this area "beyond the present" that the question of the critical variables that affect a sale can be thoughtfully asked.

The *financial* time horizon relates to shareholders' interests. While investors vary considerably in the rate of portfolio turnover, their interest in a firm is usually much shorter than management's. The average stockholding position is about a year and a half, while venture capitalists speak in terms of cashing out in five years. Thus a five-year horizon is a good basis for this perspective. Underlying this financial perspective is a basic question: Why should an outsider keep resources tied up in your firm rather than invest them with a competitor? This very discomforting question forces the firm to directly face the strategic and business dimensions of its plans and activities and to be clear about the five-year time horizon when looking at investor support.

THE TECHNOLOGY MAPPING TECHNIQUE

The technology mapping technique consists of seven steps shown in Figure 6-1. In the first step, the basic technologies underlying a firm's product line are retrospectively mapped for application events, mission-oriented events, and basic science events. In the second step, the firm's products are represented by a block diagram of the system within which they are employed. In the third step, key parameters of customer value for each block are identified. In the fourth step, technologies of relevance are identified vis-à-vis the parameters. (Steps 2, 3 and 4 can be termed key parameter analysis.) In the fifth step, the organization of the industry is assessed and the competitive forces in the industry are identified. Functional diversity of the firm's products is then assessed. Finally, strategic issues are addressed and appropriate technology strategies are defined.

A Map of Science and Technology Building Blocks

The development of the videotape recorder discussed in Chapter 5 relied upon magnetic theory, magnetic recording, electronics, frequency modulation, magnetic and recording materials, and control theory (for details refer to Figure 5-1). The development of the oral contraceptive's science and technology building blocks could be categorized into the physiology of reproduction, hormone research, and steroid chemistry. These are examples of the starting points for the creation of a strategic technology map.

To create the first portion of such a map, it is necessary to trace a product's several scientific bases. These bases are then followed backward from technology to science in

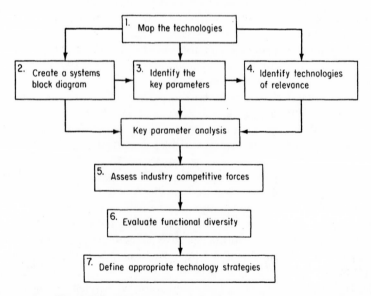

Figure 6-1. The seven steps of technological mapping.

order to build the broad historical map of the product area's underlying supports. Data for such an exercise are normally available in collegiate texts and trade association publications and through interviews. In general, this portion of the map will point the way to the basic innovation and will provide the basis from which improvements might be expected.

A Three-Step Key Parameter Analysis

A *key parameter* is a dimension affecting the outcome of the purchase decision. Thus, value to the customer is the focus of the analysis. This parameter approach is also one way of describing the past, current, and future bases of competition in the industry.

A History of Performance Parameter Improvement. In the early days of the aircraft industry, three parameters—speed, range, and payload—provided a common way to evaluate performance. Over time, other measures such as fuel efficiencies, reliability, and lifetime cost-effectiveness, were added. In the computer industry, the earliest parameters were cycle time, RAM, and storage memory size. To these were added physical size, power usage, compatibility, and the like. In liquid propellant rocket engines, the original buyer value parameters were payload, range, and reliability. Eventually thrust, thermal efficiency, and mechanical efficiency were added. In industrial practice, several performance parameters can be identified as a reasonable measure of value to the customer and determinants of competitive edge. Over time, performance on these parameters of buyer value will normally improve. Additionally, the set of buyer value parameters will vary as new concerns surface in the marketplace and thus the basis for competitive edge shifts.

A history of the improvement along product performance parameters, plus the introduction and measurement of additional buyer value parameters, helps explain the shifting fortunes of various members of the industry. If an industry were considered as a series of products whose performance improves over time and whose performance is measured with increasing complexity over time, then its structure could be explained by the shaping of these two forces. Change, after all, provides opportunities for the founding of new enterprises or the conditions for the foundering of old enterprises and thus provides the impetus for the restructuring of the industry.

The map must explicitly show parameter improvement as a function of time. This should be in the form of a time line with branching to include other parameters and commentary on the circumstances that created the developments—both improvement in old parameters and the demand for new buyer value parameters.

Key Parameter Analysis, Step 1: Block Diagraming. In step 1, the product line is analyzed in terms of the various subsystem elements of the design. In systems analysis this is known as block diagraming. A printing press will have a transport mechanism, a printing mechanism, a die cutting mechanism, and a control system. A radar altimeter will have an antenna, a transmitter, a receiver, a computer, a display, and a power supply. An electronic funds transfer system will have input devices, transmission systems, computer data processing systems, and output devices. There may be several different elements in each of the major blocks.

It should be clear that the three block diagrams represented in Figures 6-2 to 6-4 could be executed with considerably more detail. The diagrams provide a concrete visualization of the block diagraming process. While sparse and simple in their level of detail, they provide a starting place to explain next steps in key parameter analysis. As usual, the level of detail employed in practice will require managerial judgment.

Key Parameter Analysis, Step 2: Identify Key Parameters. The next step in this process is to list the key parameters of each of the blocks. These key parameters should directly reflect the concerns of the buyers and affect customer's purchase decisions. Using the electronic funds transfer block diagram as an example, the analyst would list the key parameters of the input blocks, the transmission blocks, the computer block, and the output blocks.

One such list might be as follows:

INPUTS

> *Style:* print data, keystrokes, voice, magnetic strips, microprocessors, visuals (face or fingerprint)
>
> *Use Characteristics:* simplicity, user friendliness, speed, reliability, ruggedness
>
> *Costs:* investment, operating

TRANSMISSION

> *Use Characteristics:* speed, security, reliability
>
> *Costs:* investment, operating

COMPUTER

> *Use Characteristics:* speed, size-memory, reliability
>
> *Costs:* investment, operating

OUTPUTS

> *Style:* print, voice, video, magnetics, microprocessor input, cash, paper products, analyses
>
> *Use Characteristics:* simplicity, user friendliness, speed, reliability, ruggedness
>
> *Costs:* investment, operating

This list is meant to be suggestive and not necessarily exhaustive. It is at a level of detail consistent with the electronic funds system block diagram (Figure 6-4).

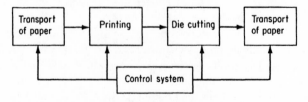

Figure 6-2. Printing press block diagram.

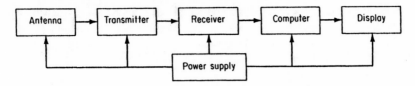

Figure 6-3. Radar altimeter block diagram.

Key Parameter Analysis, Step 3: Identify Technologies of Relevance. Here the analyst tries to identify the technologies that potentially affect the parameters identified in step 3. Again turning to the example of electronic funds transfer, the analyst can array the technologies that have potential for improving the parameter performance of each the blocks.

INPUTS

    Sensors: keyboards, scanners—print, voice, fingerprint, etc.

    Converters: analog-to-digital conversion, etc.

    User Technology: psychology of cognition, consumer behavior, human factors

TRANSMISSION

    Hard-wired, networked—LAN\WAN, phone line, microwave satellite linked, fiber optics, spread spectrum, software, redundancy, encryption

COMPUTER

    Architecture: standard, RISC, parallel processing, thinking machine versus Cray, centralized versus distributed

    Speed: millimicrometer lithography, optical memory

    Software: data bases

OUTPUTS

    Transient: video, LED, electroluminescence, signals for smart cards and magnetic strips

    Permanent: impact printing (fixed font, dot matrix), laser printing, on/off line, etc.

    Physical Items: cash and merchandise handling mechanisms

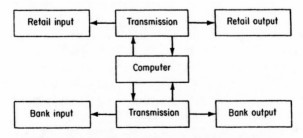

Figure 6-4. Electronic funds transfer block diagram.

These lists represent first-level analysis and require the analyst to consider the ways in which these technologies affect the parameters identified in the second step, the speed with which they will be available to the marketplace, and the way these changes may affect the bases of competition.

Assessment of Industry Competitive Forces

The mapping technique should assess technological dimensions of competitive advantage by focusing on two broad characteristics of the competitors: membership (both entrance and exit) and technological thrusts. The history of both early and later entrants helps to clarify the conditions that favored these actions. The history of exits helps identify business or technological elements which prevented success. In pursuing this analysis it is helpful to divide the competition into two groups: firms directly competing against each other and firms offering substitute products. The technological benefits and limitations of each should be examined and their potential proprietary claims and/or other forms of defensible position should be assessed.

A History of the Industry Participants. Who were the early participants? Who left early? Who stayed? Who came later? Who is likely to enter the industry? What are their reasons for staying and for leaving? Why are new entrants likely? This series of questions helps the analyst to better understand the competitive structure of the industry. If the reasons are understood, then undercapitalized and poorly managed firms can be weeded out. The remaining firms made "apparently right" strategic choices.

The map must explicitly show a history of industrial participants. Given such a history, the patterns of competitive moves can be understood and the potential for future competitive moves can be anticipated.

Identifying Sources of Innovative Stimulation. Early studies from which this mapping technique evolved often detected strong external pressures for new rounds of innovative stimulation. Improvements in prostheses seem to be stimulated by dramatic increases in demand, the unfortunate result of active military engagements. Broad social pressure for population control seems to have stimulated Pincus to bring together the three technological streams that resulted in the creation of the oral contraceptive. The development of the transistor has had revolutionary impact upon many industries and products.

There are numerous government programs directed explicitly at advancing science and technology. These vary from the superconducting supercollider to mapping the human genome, nascent programs in superconductivity and high-definition TV. Many of the major high-technology products available today were stimulated indirectly by other needs. Until the late 1970s World War II still served as a major stimulator of technological progress. Similarly, the Korean War was an impetus, as were major governmental initiatives such as the NASA space program. In some industries increasing numbers of environmental issues force the pace; in others the pace is set by broad economic expansion. Clearly, basic scientific breakthroughs lead to increased activity and eventual technological payoff, albeit often over a longer time period than initially anticipated. Thus, industry and technological history needs to be scanned carefully to reveal sources of unusual activity.

These events of science and serendipity, of war and economics, of persistence and perspicacity—all illuminate patterns of the developments in the industry. Whether as commentary or as an explicit additional time line, it helps to identify the apparent sources of innovative stimulation on the map.

A History of Functional (Use) Diffusion

The videotape recorder was originally designed as a time delay device for network broadcast use. The original design approach was predicated upon the assumption that the machine would be operated by a broadcast engineer. When use widened into the consumer marketplace, this assumption had to be abandoned. Diffusion of functional use also resulted in a shift of the parameters that expressed buyer value. To create a history only of parameter value would have overlooked this normal diffusion process. In similar fashion, computers originally created for scientific application evolved into computers for operating wristwatches. Generally the evolution of functional diffusion provides opportunities for widening the product's market base while at the same time providing opportunities for creating defensible niches.

The strategic technology map must include a time line showing the widening and diffusion of the use of the generic products being studied. This will of course be a branching list with commentary to identify technological opportunities as they are created and demand as it develops. Data for such a study should be easily found in trade journals.

Define Appropriate Technology Strategies

The final step in the creation of a technology map is to help define the strategies appropriate to a given technological thrust. Assuming first the perspective of the manager and then of the investor, we use a modified decision tree approach to select appropriate strategies for each. Here the investor perspective represents the medium term or three- to five-year time horizon. Conversely, the managerial perspective represents a longer term or five- to eight-year time horizon.

While the decision tree may appear a mechanistic solution to the strategy screening problem, it is important to note that judgment is a critical ingredient of the process. The attempt to synthesize such a broad range of information is clearly a creative act. As such, the synthesis represents a judgment or a best guess about those features of the future that were detected in the present.

A Decision Tree for Selecting Appropriate Strategies. The dimensions of the nine technology strategies in Chapter 4 focused on three major categories: the nature of the market, characteristics of the product, and potential action programs. Uncertainty about the market, size of the market, and level of purchaser sophistication are key dimensions of the market. Uncertainty about characteristics and the overall complexity of the product

Table 6-1. Technology Actions and Competitive Barriers

Actions	Barriers
Invest in productivity	Cost/price or cost/reputation
Invest in capacity	Cost/market size
Invest in flexibility	Cost/market size
R&D for new general products	Information barriers
R&D for new niche products	Information barriers
R&D for hierarchical design	Information barriers
Negotiate hierarchical governance	Contractual/regulatory barriers

are the two dimensions employed in the product category. Seven potential action programs specified in the action category are depicted in Table 6-1 (a duplication of Table 4-2). For ease of reference the nine technology strategies originally arrayed in Table 4-3 are collected in Table 6-2. For the modified decision tree analysis these strategies will be referred to more simply by their alphabetic identification.

The technology map provides a solid historical background for forecasting. Judgment is required in order to forecast the rapid changes or slow evolution of technologies relevant to key parameters. Differences in rate of development will sometimes suggest different strategies depending upon investors' (medium term) or managers' (longer term) time horizon. The modified decision tree begins with the nature of the basic product and/or product ranges in the mapping process. One "generic" question should be asked: Is the product in its early or introductory phase, in its growth phase, or its mature phase? The answer to this question determines which of the previously described strategies fit, and which are excluded. Table 6-3 lists the specific strategies included.

The second series of questions concerns the nature of the marketplace for the product/product range under study. There are three market-oriented questions. Is the nature of the market well understood? Is the size of the market large? Is the purchaser sophisticated? The strategic selections from each of these questions are shown in Table 6-4.

As indicated in the earlier chapter on the nine technology strategies it is possible to simplify the analysis or selection process by asking a few guiding questions. These analytic questions can be combined to create a sparsely populated but otherwise reasonable strategic screen (see Table 6-5). These strategies form a screen which can be applied to the map analysis and can lead to appropriate managerial and investor actions, depending upon their respective time frames.

It is extraordinarily important at this junction to remind the reader of the "scientific" evidence supporting this analytic approach. This decision tree represents a "logical" manipulation of the categories selected to "describe" the nine technology strategies. Thus, this is a descriptive device being used as a prescriptive or normative device. Any solution derived from this "decision tree" must be filtered through several layers of judgment.

There are two main benefits to this logical solution process. The first is to provide the analyst with a starting point for strategy determination. (In many applications of this approach the findings showed consistent face validity with the circumstances and the industry.) The second is provide the analyst with a starting place that requires attention to underlying phenomena rather than stopping at a gross level of generalization.

There are substantial cautions about this logical solution process. These cautions fall into two categories. First, our scientific knowledge of strategy formulation and

Table 6-2. Technology–Strategy Matrix

Market/Product Situation	Actions/Defensibility	Results	Examples
A. Technological Commodity Search			
Stable or declining/ well known or standard	Invest in productivity/low-cost firm exhibits uncertain imitability/ market size–to–investment cost ratio favorable/potential for reputational differentiation	Normal to supernormal returns	PIHER
B. Preemption			
Industrial/easily copied	Invest in megacapacity plant/competitor investment too high given market size	Supernormal returns	Monsanto
C. Productive Efficiency			
Mature mass market/stable and well-understood product	Invest in manufacturing process/competitor faces information delays regarding manufacturing technique–experience curve effect	Normal returns	General Foods Alberto-Culver
D. Producer Preference			
Early stage/ complex product	Invest in product research/ early steep learning curve provides information delay and early uncertain imitability	Supernormal returns until new entrants	Polaroid Michelin Volkswagen
E. Production Flexibility—Seasonal/E'—Custom Design			
Seasonal or low volume/custom design	Develop flexible manufacturing approaches planning and CAD/CAM/takes advantage of normal product information delays to the competition	Normal returns	Lockheed Levi-Strauss
F. Customer Preference			
Mature-moderate to high volume/ standard	Develop ability to manufacture with limited flexibility	Better than normal returns	Apple

Table 6-2. Technology–Strategy Matrix *(continued)*

Market/Product Situation	Actions/Defensibility	Results	Examples
G. Product Pioneer/G'. Product Leader/G". Product Follower			
Latent/new and technologically complex	Invest in product development/experience curve advantages competitor delays due to product complexity and market uncertainty	Early supernormal returns	Mead Johnson Apple
Growing/ technologically complex	Heavy investment in product and market development/better solution to large portion of market needs	Normal returns	Pet Foods IBM
Mature/ multipurpose products	Invest in special-purpose design/niche benefit of market size not worth competitor's investment	Limited supernormal returns	Others
H. Vertical Integration: Forward/Backward			
Large or growing/ technologically complex	Enter into cooperative agreement/contractual regulatory	Normal returns	IBM MAC
I. Complementary Technology			
Large market for complex product (computer/car)	Design product to be compatible	Normal returns	Amdahl

Table 6-3. Product Technology Decision Tree Strategy List

In which phase is the product technology?
  Early: select strategy D or G
  Growth: select strategy B, E, or E'
  Mature: select strategy A, C, E, F, G', G", H, or I

Table 6-4. Market Dimension Decision Tree Strategy List

Is the nature of the market well understood?
  Yes: select strategy A, B, C, F, G", H, or I
  No: select strategies D, E, E', G, G', or H
Is the size of the market large?
  Yes: select strategy A, B, C, G', G", H, or I
  No: select strategy D, E, F, or G
Is the purchaser sophisticated?
  Yes: select strategy D, E, G, or I
  No: select strategy A, B, C, E, F, G', G", or H

Table 6-5. Product Technology and Market Dimension Decision Tree Strategy List

	Product Life Cycle		
	Early	Growth	Mature
	D, G	B, E, E'	A, C, E, F, G', G'', H, I
Is the market well understood?			
Yes		B	A, C, F, G'', H, I
No	D, G	E, E'	E, E', G'
Is the market large?			
Yes		B	A, C, G', G'', H, I
No	D, G	E, E'	E, E', F
Is the purchaser sophisticated?			
Yes	D, G	E'	E', I
No		B, E	A, C, E, F, G', G'', H

implementation to date has very limited prescriptive validity. That is, the broad changes in the industrial landscape have far outstripped our ability to adjust our research programs and thus we have a scientific base which has more historical significance than future-oriented strengths. Second and more important, actual strategies exist at very complex and detailed levels, as shown in Chapter 15, where we demonstrate how strategies differ from one another on at least fifteen dimensions.

Thus, the strategic decision tree analysis recommended above must be treated as an aid to dig below the level of grand strategy and a starting point for the thoughtful consideration of the more complex issues that lie below the surface of strategy formulation and implementation. Again, judgment is still a most important ingredient in the strategic process.

SUMMARY

Technology mapping begins with a historical investigation of the various underlying technological developments and their contributions to the product/product range parameters. This is enhanced (or strengthened) through an exploration of the industry's competitive forces and the ever-expanding diversity of functional applications for the basic product/product range. Then managerial judgment is applied to the sense of evolving technologies and competitive situations to select broad technology strategies which are appropriate to the situation and the managerial forecast of developments.

To make the rather abstract nature of this chapter more concrete two examples of the way this tool is applied are presented in the following chapter.

REFERENCES

Das, T. K. 1986. *The Subjective Side of Strategy Making: Future Orientation and Perceptions of Executives.* New York: Praeger.

Emery, F. E. 1967. "The Next Thirty Years: Concepts, Methods and Anticipations," *Human Relations* 20(3) 71–92.

Forrester, J. 1961. *Industrial Dynamics*. Cambridge, MA: MIT Press.

Goodman, R. A., and A. S. Huff. 1978. "Enriching Policy Premises for an Ambiguous World." In John Sutherland, ed., *Management Handbook for Public Administrators*. New York: Van Nostrand Reinhold.

IIT Research Institute. 1968. *TRACES (Technology in Retrospective and Critical Events in Science)*. Chicago: IITRI, December 15.

Sahal, D. 1981. *Patterns of Technological Innovation*. Reading, MA: Addison-Wesley.

7

Some Examples of Strategic Technology Maps

In this chapter two examples of technology mapping are presented. The first traces the development of machine vision, a manufacturing process control system. The system optically creates a digital image of a manufactured part and compares the image with a previously computerized standard. The second example describes the development of monoclonal antibodies (MOABs) as a tool for cancer diagnosis and treatment. These two technologies illustrate the mapping process as applied in two distinctly different arenas.

For each of these examples, the seven steps of technology mapping are carefully treated. As a convenience to the reader, the block diagram of the basic technology mapping technique from Chapter 6, is reproduced here (Figure 7-1).

MACHINE VISION

The following analysis draws heavily on the work of Phillips and Pulos (1986). Machine vision involves an optics system and a computer to automatically acquire an image, store it in the form of digital signals, and compare it with a standard. The outcome of the process is a decision about the acceptability of the image, an adjustment to the manufacturing process creating the imaged item, or change in the machine movement pattern required for the production of the item.

Map the Technologies

The basic scientific history of machine vision as shown in Figure 7-2 can be reported in three categories: computers, microcomputers, and television cameras.

From the 1930s until the mid-1980s, the basic computing power of mainframe computers increased in speed as measured in operations per second and in size of ran-

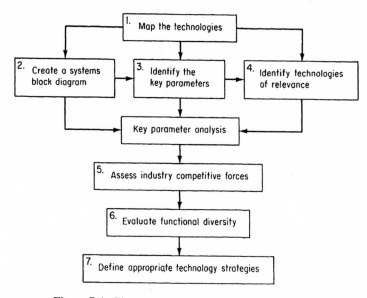

Figure 7-1. The seven steps of technological mapping.

dom access memory (RAM). In the mid-1940s operations per second were in the range of 300–400. By the mid-1960s they had increased to 100,000, and by the mid-1980s they were in the billions. RAM increased from 98 K (thousand) bytes in the mid-1960s to 2,000,000 KB in the mid-1980s. Microcomputers by the mid-1980s could handle 5,000,000 operations per second with a RAM of 512–640 KB. Television cameras evolved from the early cathode ray tube of the 1900s to the color capabilities in the

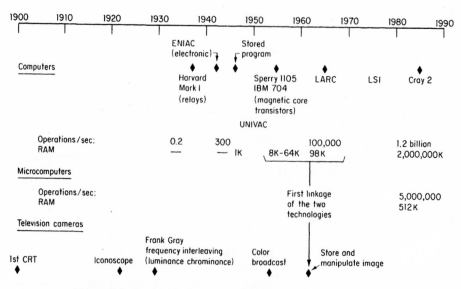

Figure 7-2. Engineering developments leading to machine vision.

1950s. In the early 1960s computers and televisions were first linked together to store and manipulate images. Eventually this led to the ability to use computers to enhance and process images for a variety of applications.

Create a Systems Block Diagram

The basic building blocks of a machine vision system are systems for sensing, image processing, flaw analysis, and process control. The sensing system has an illumination subsystem, which might be an incandescent light or a laser, and a sensor subsystem such as a television vidicon camera or a charged couple device. The image processing system contains a microprocessor, which digitizes the image into discrete gray levels, isolates the object of interest, and compares the object to a known standard. The flaw analysis system has a part classification subsystem and a reports and disposition subsystem. This is shown in Figure 7-3.

Identify Key Parameters

In designing machine vision systems, eight issues represent the design trade-offs. Improvement of one parameter degrades another parameter unless there is underlying technological progress. With faster computer processing the final parameter measures would improve, but it would remain necessary to trade off, for example, speed for accuracy or speed for complexity.

The first parameter issue is image size. The standard size is the current television standard of 512 by 512 pixels (picture elements). Smaller sizes result in reduced processing and memory requirements permitting faster and cheaper systems to be developed. The smaller size though reduces the accuracy of the system.

The second design issue involves the trade-off between field of view and resolution. Having defined the image size, the system can look at a wide field of view with

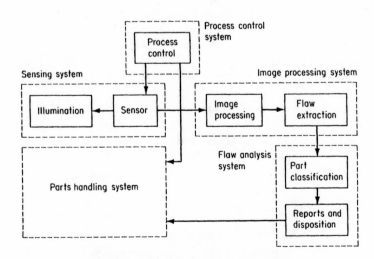

Figure 7-3. Machine vision block diagram.

limited detail or a narrower field of view with more detail. The level of detail required helps specify the design. In some cases, a scanning system will permit several sectors to be viewed in detail and then added together in the computer to provide a larger high-resolution picture. This requires more memory and more processing time and slows the process.

The third design parameter is the number of gray levels. When looking simply for the edge of an object, a binary approach of only black and white is sufficient, and it requires only 1 bit per pixel. For surface feature evaluation, greater detail is necessary and 64 (6 bits per pixel) or 256 (8 bits per pixel) may be required.

The fourth issue is processing speed. The microprocessor determines the number of operations per second possible. Image size and the gray levels required then determine the processing speed of the system. The lowest acceptable limit is the speed of the production line using the system. The highest possible limit is the real-time speed of the sensor (60 Hz for a vidicon camera).

The next issue parameter is decision accuracy. Given a specific choice regarding detail of the image, there remains some level of error which permits "good" products to be rejected and "bad" product to be accepted. Greater detail results in fewer incorrect decisions. But increasing the level of detail necessarily slows decision processing. Additionally, gray levels are not continuous scales. The sensor must make a choice about how to record any intermediate readings, but these choices are imprecise by definition. This then necessitates trade-offs between rejecting some good products to ensure all bad products are rejected or vice versa.

Another parameter—and a particularly troubling one—is the question of standardized versus customized design. Designers must grapple with the trade-off between achieving a standardized design for a broad range of applications or customized design for unique applications. In this situation, hardware standardization does not obviate the need for software customizing. As a result of the manufacturing efficiencies, standardized systems are available for a significantly lower cost than customized systems.

Another general parameter involves questions of durability and reliability. This is particularly important when the equipment moves out of the manufacturing "clean rooms" and onto the factory floor, where interference is common at all levels—electromagnetic, dust and dirt, vibration, changing light levels, and so on.

Finally, the eighth key parameter is flexibility. How widely can the machine adapt to accommodate multiple products? How quickly can the machine shift from batch to batch? How quickly can the machine be reprogrammed to accommodate product changes?

These eight key parameters (image size, resolution, gray levels, process speed, decision accuracy, standardization, durability, and flexibility) must be added to the other standard parameters of investment cost and operating cost to augment information regarding the basic decision trade-offs.

Identify Technologies of Relevance

The increase in computer operational speeds and the concurrent decrease in computer costs continue to have significant impacts on machine vision. The increased ease with which color is utilized should improve accuracy. Increased image size potential from the high-definition TV (HDTV) developments will contribute to added precision and resolution. Integrated optics and fiber optics for illumination and transmission to the sensors also increase performance possibilities. Charged couple devices and charged injection devices as alternative sensor subsystems may permit lower power consumption and exhibit shorter lags and permit random access of pixels. Computer-aided design/computer-aided manufacturing (CAD/CAM) compatibility will increase the functional value of machine vision in the future as the CAD/CAM systems develop not only tooling but quality control templates for the machine vision system. Additional coordination between the machine vision and the control system will lead beyond accept–reject decisions to actual process control adjustments, thus further increasing the value of the machine vision system.

Evaluate Competitive Forces

As a starting point, comparisons among North America, the Pacific Rim nations, and the European Community show some dramatic productivity differences. In many manufacturing areas, the Japanese are basically more productive than their North American and European counterparts. Competitive pressure for productivity and quality are pushing all parts of the manufacturing process, machine vision included.

Second, consider national-level programs that focus on several technologies: semiconductors, CAD/CAM, HDTV, supercomputers, superconductivity, and so on. Each of these programs could contribute to parameter growth within the machine vision sector. Some will have more direct applications and their effects will be felt more quickly. There is also continuing substantial private investment in developing computers and software. Introduction of more extensive vision systems for more sophisticated robotics systems reflects further functional diversity.

Output of the machine vision industry has been increasing at a rate of almost 100 per-

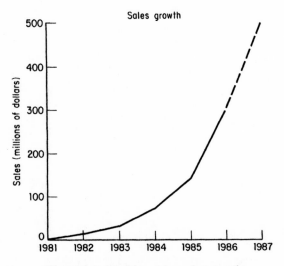

Figure 7-4. Machine vision sales growth.

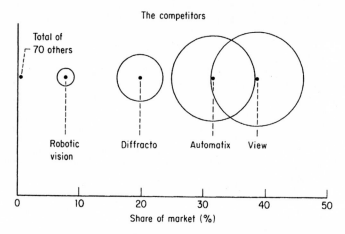

Figure 7-5. Machine vision competitive map.

cent per year. It far outstrips any likely return on investment and thus requires continued infusion of large capital sums to continue on such a track. (See sales data in Figure 7-4.)

Additionally, the market has numerous participants, but few with any significant part of the market. Meanwhile, large companies are on the prowl to assimilate potential new technologies. Aside from the machine vision firms that have been integrated within General Motors and other large firms, the freestanding competitive situation can be depicted as in Figure 7-5.

Evaluate Functional Diversity

Figure 7-6 depicts the functional diversity of machine vision developments. The chart describes the changes or growth in methodology, in application, and in cost. Figure 7-7 describes a forecast of the widening functional diversity in the industry in similar terms.

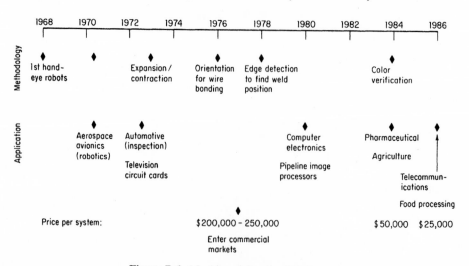

Figure 7-6. Machine vision developments.

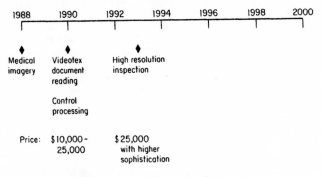

Figure 7-7. Machine vision projections.

Define Appropriate Technology Strategies

The medium term and the longer term are considered separately. As Figure 7-5 indicates, currently there are four major competitors and approximately seventy minor competitors; View and Automatix are the largest followed by Diffracto and Robotic Vision. In addition, there are a number of now captive operations owned by very large firms.

To proceed to a general understanding of the marketplace and technology strategies, it is necessary to look at product and market dimensions as articulated in the previous chapters. This step of technology mapping requires judgments on several levels. One involves the nature of the future technological development. The map leads one to believe that the relevant technologies affecting key parameter performance are in a great state of flux. While equipment will still be ordered and delivered, opportunities for standardization will be limited. Technology will still offer surprises, thus complexity of the interactions among subsystems will continually be a problem. It will be further complicated by widening functional diversity as new potentially promising applications arise.

These judgments are summarized in Table 7-1. The product life cycle will be moving from early to growth over the three- to seven-year time period. The market characteristics are relatively poorly understood and the purchaser will focus more on performance (whether the offered system actually fits the specific needs) than on price. The strategy selection shown in this table is drawn from Table 7-2 (a reproduction of the strategy selection matrix of the preceding chapter). Table 7-2 suggests a producer preference or a product pioneer strategy in the medium term and a production flexibility (custom design) strategy in the longer term.

Table 7-1. Machine Vision Strategy Selection

	Medium Term (3–5 years)	Longer Term (5–7 years)
Product life cycle	Early	Growth
Market characteristics		
Well understood	N	N
Large	N	N
Sophisticated buyer	Y	Y
Strategy	D (producer preference) or G (product pioneer)	E′ (production flexibility—custom design)

Table 7-2. Strategy Selection Matrix

	Product Life Cycle		
	Early D, G	Growth B, E, E′	Mature A, C, E, E′, F, G′, G″, H, I
Is the market well understood?			
Yes		B	A, C, F, G″, H, I
No	D, G	E, E′	E, E′, G′
Is the market large?			
Yes		B	A, C, G′, G″, H, I
No	D, G	E, E′	E, E′, F
Is the purchaser sophisticated?			
Yes	D, G	E′	E′, I
No		B, E	A, C, E, F, G′, G″, H

As we said in the preceding chapter, this decision tree approach is simply a logical reconstruction of the nine technology strategies. This approach, then, is a starting point for a more thorough consideration of the strategic implications of the mapping process. Such a discussion follows.

The producer preference and the product pioneer are, at first blush, very similar. The producer preference strategy is for a product that has some market value, but where serious scaling up of the manufacturing process is premature. Rather than accommodating the customized needs of specific customers, the firm must remain focused on the product. Product development efforts continually broaden the application range of the basic product. This product investment takes advantage of competitive barriers in the form of experience curve benefits. The more the firm knows about relevant technologies, the more the firm can stay ahead of others through both grand and subtle moves.

Conversely, the product pioneer strategy, which is derived directly from technological familiarity, can be seen as a solution looking for a problem. The application specifics are less well defined, the nature of the market is less well known, and manufacturing issues take a back seat.

The production flexibility strategy for custom-designed products admits to a reasonably clear market which cannot support long production runs of standardized products. Thus, the investment focus begins to shift to the production function. Benefits are derived from standardization of parts and component assemblies. Implementation of CAD/CAM and other detailed planning and information systems approaches reduces setup and changeover costs.

Evaluation of these strategies can also be explored in terms of the size of the industry participant and the managerial versus investor time horizon being employed here. Firms purchased as technology investments by the industrial giants will be under pressure to meet new owners' return on investment (ROI) targets. They tend to follow strategies that are not suggested directly by an industry analysis. They will look for an internal market, and thus reduce market uncertainty. They may find a market large enough to act as a niche-oriented product follower. Thus, relevant technology advantage will tend to decrease and standardization to increase.

Success of this niche strategy will lead often to a tight, vertically integrated operation. Preemptive purchase of technology, which is a form of vertical integration, is often premature and a handicap to the later intellectual development of the acquired firm. Failure to achieve the ROI target may mean that the acquired firm will be shut down and/or spun off.

An investor in one of the larger freestanding firms should consider whether the firm has captured enough of a niche to participate in a growth industry. This would indicate that the investor should look for a firm with production flexibility strategy. If the larger firms eschew the production flexibility strategy, then the analysis here suggests that they might exhibit a producer preference strategy. Finally, all of the smaller firms are expected to follow a product pioneer strategy. They represent a purer form of risk for the investors than the larger firms.

In summary, the diagnostic properties of the technology mapping procedure were explicitly demonstrated using the machine vision industry as an example. Throughout the seven steps of the analysis, managerial judgment continues to be necessary as each step requires input as to what is important (what parameter, what competitor) and how elements deemed important are evaluated.

MONOCLONAL ANTIBODIES FOR CANCER

This second example is an adaptation of the technology mapping process in a biologically based technology area, monoclonal antibodies (MOABs). It is drawn from Clemens et al, (1984). This recent but rapidly advancing technology has broad medical applications. This particular technology map centers on applications for the diagnosis and treatment of cancer.

Map the Technologies

The basic scientific history of MOABs, as shown in Figure 7-8, has several separate research tracks. Some of the research tracks relate to developments in the understanding of the disease itself—its cause, its diagnosis, its treatment, and its cure. Other tracks feature the development of what can be broadly defined as "tools." Some of these tools opened up new lines of scientific research and other tools permitted the scale-up of laboratory procedures to obtain larger quantities at reasonable costs—that is, tools for research and tools for manufacture. Specifically, the map can be divided into five technological areas: cancer etiology, cancer treatment, immunology, tissue culture, and manufacturing scale-up techniques.

The study of the causes, that is, the etiology of disease, usually begins with early folk wisdom and then develops as a scientific subject only when tools and concepts become available—and when the efficacy of folk wisdom is found to be insufficient. Hippocrates in 400 B.C. identified two classes of tumor: benign and malignant. In 1665 high-powered microscopes were used to establish that cells were the basic structural unit of all living things. In 1838 it was discovered that cancer tumors were also cellular in construct and "cell theory" became the basic paradigm of the cancer researcher. The development in 1905 of the ability to transplant tumors to animals allowed experimental research to begin. The etiology of cancer reflected major progress in the 1940s

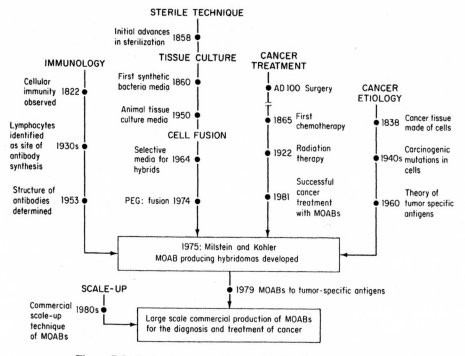

Figure 7-8. Technology map of monoclonal antibodies for cancer.

when cancer was identified as a cellular-level genetic mutation. Certain cells were seen to change (mutate) and then reproduce themselves and spread rapidly. It was this finding that directed research toward the genetic paradigms and the discovery that transformations of DNA were the key to such mutations.

Immunological approaches were added in the 1950s as the ability to transfer cancer immunity through the lymphoid cells was identified. This line of causal understanding was further enriched in the 1960s by the theory of tumor-specific antigens. The body develops antibodies to fight disease. This activity is a normal response to a foreign antigen entering the bloodstream or an antigen created through a cellular mutation. Unfortunately, the body must generate many different antibodies in search of one that acts on any specific antigen. The body's "shotgun" approach is normally effective—if not efficient. The idea that specific tumors contain specific antigens means that the medical scientist could hope to increase the efficiency of the body's reaction by searching for a way of identifying or attacking unique antigens.

Early cancer treatment evolved from Hippocrates' (400 B.C.) use of caustic pastes to burn away tumors (chemotherapy). By A.D. 100 Cilcus had developed surgical techniques (mastectomy). The invention of the X-ray and the discovery of the radioactive nature of radium in the 1890s led to the development of radiation therapy, which was established by 1922. Modern chemotherapy was developed some thirty years after the human impact of mustard gas was observed. Farber in 1947 employed a nitrogen mustard derivative and achieved leukemic remissions.

Immunology began with the first observation of cellular immunity in 1822. In a more formal sense this field began in the 1880s and 1890s with studies focusing on infectious diseases, cellular immunity (phagocytosis), and the development of the first vaccines by Louis Pasteur. During this period two types of immunity were identified: cellular and humoral. Cellular responses directly destroyed foreign cells or substances. Humoral responses were mediated by antibodies (immunoglobulins).

In 1953 Coons identified plasma cells as the site of antibody production. In 1958 the structure of antibodies was determined. They were found to have constant regions common to all antibodies and variable regions specific to a particular antigens. When these discoveries were added to knowledge of the factors stimulating antibody production and knowledge of the relationship between antibody and antigen, the foundations of the later monoclonal antibody development were in place.

The production of antibodies requires a culture medium with appropriate nutrients for growth. The work on tissue culture techniques began with improvements in sterilization techniques occurring around 1858. Pasteur began the work on synthetic bacteria media in 1860. As the field progressed effort was centered on enrichment media and selective media, which would support the growth of only certain organisms. By 1950, animal tissue culture media were developed, which then made it possible for scientists to support the growth of cells, not just bacteria and fungi.

Normal antibody-producing plasma cells can be isolated but do not survive. Cancer cells on the other hand can be grown continuously and indefinitely. If the two types of cells can be fused into a hybrid, then the resulting cell line will survive and grow and will produce antibodies. Such fusion is a normal bodily process but occurs all too infrequently to be a major tool in the body's resistance to disease. Media that supported only hybrid cells, allowing scientists to select or isolate such naturally occurring hybrids, were added to the scientist's arsenal by 1964. Finally, by 1974 the discovery that polyethylene glycol (PEG) caused cells to fuse allowed scientists to more effectively work in this arena. Now they could actually create hybrids (hybridomas) rather than patiently searching their petri dishes for naturally occurring hybrids.

These four streams of events were brought together in 1975 when Milstein and Kohler develop MOAB-producing hybridomas. Their process begins with the immunization of mice with human antigens. Antibody-producing plasma cells are generated by the host and are located primarily in the spleen. When the spleen cells are removed they are found to contain many types of cells. Next, a PEG fusion process is initiated to create hybridomas. A selective medium is then employed to encourage the growth of the hybridomas while not supporting the growth of other types of cells. At this point the cell lines can be screened to determine which contain the antibody of interest, and finally these hybridomas can be grown in large quantities. By 1979, MOABs for tumor-specific antigens were developed. In 1981 successful cancer treatment with MOABs was inaugurated.

Manufacturing scale-up followed quite different paths depending on which company was driving the research. The four most promising are Damon Biotech's microencapsulation technique, Bio-Response's recycled bovine lymph in its mass culture technique, Celltech's large batch fermentors, and Amicon's hollow fiber cell culture system. All of these scale-up developments occurred since the early 1980s.

Create a Systems Block Diagram

This second step in the technology mapping model does not appear to have any leverage for the analyst studying MOABs for cancer. While one might consider elements of molecular structure as a block diagram, doing so requires a sizable stretch of the imagination and has little value in helping the analyst gain focus.

Identify the Key Parameters

The mutation of normal cells to create cancer cell often leads to some cell surface antigens. The bonding of an antibody to an antigen has been described by some as similar to fitting a jigsaw puzzle piece into a puzzle. A particular antibody may bond to one cell surface antigen but not another, and where some antibodies will exhibit a better fit with a specific antigen others will not fit well or at all. This character or parameter is one of the keys to efficacy.

Other parameters here include potency of the antibody to generate the immune reaction, purity, safety with respect to various side effects, manufacturability, and cost. Added concerns include tumor specificity, the ability to act as a delivery system (i.e., to bind to radioimmunoglobulins or immunotoxins), and the ability to bind to cancer cells when used in a scavenging mode.

Identify Technologies of Relevance

In this field the technologies of relevance are basically scientific and rather specific. Uniqueness of the research interests is derived from the need to be absolutely tumor-specific to avoid cross-reaction with normal cells. Thus, the technologies of relevance include basic biotechnology research techniques needed for the identification and cloning of antigen-specific antibodies. A second technological interest area relates to the ability to bind with various radioimmunoglobulins and other immunotoxins and then deliver them to the specific cancer sites. (This permits more powerful drug therapy as the concentration on the specific tumor cells greatly reduces the cross-reactions with normal cells and/or systemic side effects.) Additionally, the firm might develop skills in medical treatment and research and the concomitant abilities to work with the Food and Drug Administration (FDA) in order to bring a diagnostic or a therapeutic product to market. Manufacturing scale-up techniques are a third area of technological relevance.

Assess Industry Competitive Forces

Four outside sources of innovative stimulation can be identified: increasing life spans, war, increasing market potential, and FDA policy. With the twentieth century, increases in life expectancy have brought to light a number of diseases associated with old age, such as cardiovascular disease and cancer. World War I led to an increased emphasis on wound sepsis, the bacteriology of gas gangrene, and advances in culture media techniques. Also, the damaging effects of mustard gas upon bone marrow and lymph systems suggested that a nitrogen mustard derivative might retard or cure some cancers. This line of research led to the first human leukemia remission in 1947. World War II created a need for preserved packaged foods, which led to food dehydration and then to the commercial development of dehydrated culture media.

These two causes of stimulation operated directly upon medical and scientific bases of innovation. The remaining two causes operate indirectly to stimulate innovation. The five most frequently occurring cancers (prostate, lung, breast, colon, and leukemia/lymphoma) account for 1.3 million new cases each year in the United States, Europe, and Japan. The estimated market potential for dealing with these five cancers is in the range of a billion dollars annually. Recognition of this potential has clearly stimulated increased focus on this area of innovation. On the other hand, the FDA regulations for testing an in vivo versus an in vitro product are quite different. Any product which is administered within the human body (in vivo) requires very extensive testing before being approved for sale. In contrast, products used outside the human body (in vitro) require considerably less testing before approval for sale. Firms seeking earlier payback for their investment are focusing upon diagnostics, normally done in vitro. Pursuing treatment applications of MOABs, which must be done in vivo, requires a decidedly longer time perspective and thus less work on treatment is under way.

There are six major players in the cancer-related monoclonal antibody industry. The field, established only in the 1970s, has exceedingly long product development and approval processes. As this was well understood, financing has been adequate and there have been relatively few exits. The major pharmaceutical firms in this business are Abbott Laboratories and Becton-Dickinson. Start-up firms include Centacor (1979), Cetus (1971), Genetic Systems/Oncogen (1983), and Hybritech (1978). Abbott seems to be focusing on the higher speed diagnostic capability of MOABs over conventional culture media while Becton-Dickinson seems to have focused upon infectious diseases. Centacor has focused in the diagnostic area on cancer, immunoregulation, and hepatitis. Cetus has focused upon infectious diseases and solid tumor diagnosis and therapeutics. Genetic System/Oncogen has chosen infectious diseases, blood and tissue typing, and cancer. Hybritech has been working on immunodiagnostics followed by work on immunotherapy.

Evaluate Functional Diversity

The functional diffusion of monoclonal antibodies led to early pregnancy tests and early ovulation indicators, to fast means of determining venereal disease, and to new methods of blood typing. It seems that the MOAB will be important in diagnostics, monitoring, and treatment in a wide range of medical arenas from subfertility to diabetes management to cancer. In the narrower realm of cancer, progress is being made rapidly with regard to diagnosis and more slowly with regard to treatment. Diagnostic work currently focuses upon leukemia and cancer of the gastrointestinal track, pancreas, ovaries, breast, lung, and prostate. MOAB treatment applications appear to be focused upon leukemia/lymphoma.

Another view of the functional diffusion process can be seen in three different paths of commercial exploitation:

1. The use of MOABs with immunotherapy and immunotoxins to bind to specific cancer antigens.
2. The localization of therapy with MOABs delivering other extant treatments such as radioimmunoglobulins or immunodrugs to the cancer cells in lethal levels of toxicity without creating systemic lethality.
3. The removal of pathogens from the bloodstream.

Define the Appropriate Technology Strategies

Broad management recommendations must accommodate several factors. These factors relate to the nature of the business itself and to the nature of the technology. As the typical drug approval cycle is on the order of seven years, the management recommendations have to be seen as long-run concerns. Intellectual property regulations, particularly the use of either patent or "trade secret" principles, can be used to legally protect monoclonal antibodies. While this advantage is real, it has not yet provided much comfort to the firms in this arena as little litigation has occurred to substantiate the kinds of claims that will hold up. Thus, this protection is felt to be rather narrow. On the other hand, the discovery of a more efficacious MOAB would obviate even this limited advantage. This latter possibility suggests that high R&D expenses must be a continual management strategy to broaden product line, improve efficacy, and maintain a presence in the marketplace.

Manufacturing costs are not normally critical as the competition in this arena is not as price-sensitive as that in consumer products. Techniques of scale up are important in providing the firm with the ability to serve the market at all, particularly if the product is beneficial in any of the disease areas that have a heavy incidence in the population. Thus, concern with scale-up techniques should not be overlooked. In the beginning, wide distribution of a MOAB that has clear value and little or no competition could be accomplished with few problems. As MOAB products multiply, an expected result of the widespread work in these areas by small and large firms and university research laboratories, access to effective distribution systems will become a critical business parameter. New firms will need massive funding if they are to enter the therapeutic portion of the market. Many have selected the diagnostic area to avoid the longer approval cycle of therapeutics and to potentially create an income stream that can be employed to fund a longer run R&D program and to encourage interest by the investment community.

To restate this analysis more formally, the specific nature of the product and market conditions must be assessed. These conditions are presented in Table 7-3 along with the conclusions drawn from the strategy selection matrix presented earlier in Table 7-2. The conclusions drawn from this process require a deeper discussion, such as the one that follows.

In the medium term, with few product offerings available, the product life cycle is clearly in its early phase. The nature of the market is relatively poorly understood by

Table 7-3. Monoclonal Antibodies for Cancer Strategy Selection

	Medium Term (2–5 years)	Longer Term (7–9 years)
Product life cycle	Early	Growth
Market characteristics		
Well understood	N	N/Y
Large	N	N/Y
Sophisticated buyer	Y	Y/N
Strategy	D (producer preference) or G (product pioneer)	B (preemptive) or E (production flexibility— custom design)

the start-up companies as they are offering new technological solutions that either may replace older solutions or may be solutions to problems that are currently unsolved. By choosing diagnostics rather than therapeutics firms are more likely to face a replacement market with a sophisticated purchaser and a relatively small number of outlets (in the thousands rather than the millions). The strategy indicated here is the producer preference or product pioneer strategy. The distinctions between the two were described in the study of the development of machine vision.

In the longer term, the field will be entering its early growth phase with some products well established and other new ones continually being created. Either a preemptive strategy or production flexibility will be expected. Preemption will be a "first-to-market" strategy for therapeutics, which depend to some extent on luck based upon heavy expenditure and high-level expertise. Production flexibility refers to a manufacturing strategy which requires flexibility; since actual manufacturing levels of a single MOAB will seldom support the scale necessary to obtain FDA approval, the facilities will have to be initially planned to accommodate a range of MOABs. The production flexibility strategy for custom-designed products admits to a reasonably clear market which cannot support long production runs of standardized products. Thus, the investment focus here begins to shift to the production function, and benefits are derived from some standardization of process steps and other detailed planning and information systems approaches which reduce setup and changeover costs and/or tightly control variable operations.

The advantage of adopting one of these strategies can also be explored in terms of the size of the industry participant and the managerial versus investor time horizon being employed here. Firms which have been purchased as technology investments by an industrial giant will be under pressure to meet the new owner's ROI targets and will tend to follow strategies that are not suggested directly by an industry analysis. There will be a tendency to look for a larger market and thus take advantage of existing distribution and FDA procedure familiarity.

The investment expectations in this field are rather straightforward. Investors will place their funds in firms that already have a product with a large market potential and need funding to support the approval process. Obviously, betting on early stages in the cycle involves higher risks where investing after the approval phase in a public stock offering is significantly less risky.

STRATEGIC TECHNOLOGY MAPS AND MANAGERIAL ACTION

It is clear that any one of several strategies can be effective in a given industry. Thus, the general objective of the technology mapping exercise is to identify patterns and then to suggest viable alternative strategies. Later chapters will suggest how to apply these potential choices to a specific firm. Development of the technology maps of machine vision and monoclonal antibodies for the diagnosis and treatment of cancer leads to quite different technology and strategy expectations, although both are in early phases of the industry life cycle.

In summary, the technology mapping technique provides the manager patterns for understanding the developing technology. However, the mapping technique still requires the thoughtful engagement of managerial judgment throughout the process. It will reveal much about the changing conditions of competition and when coupled with an individual firm innovation audit, described in a later chapter, will provide the executive with sound planning tools for executive action.

REFERENCES

Clemens, D., M. K. Ganobcik, E. Gerhardt, and L. McCracken. 1984. "Monoclonal Antibodies for Cancer." Los Angeles: Graduate School of Management, University of California, Los Angeles.

Phillips, P., and A. M. Pulos. 1986. "Machine Vision." Los Angeles: Graduate School of Management, University of California, Los Angeles.

8

Evaluating Your Advantage:
The Innovation Audit

Technology mapping provides an essential tool for strategic action taking. While the results derived from mapping set forth the technological opportunities, other considerations must also be evaluated. Only after the firm matches its own resources and competencies to the identified opportunities will the analysis become useful for strategy formulation.

One approach to this matching question is the "innovation audit." The audit is a two-stage method that analyzes the firm's competencies and then explores the match with the previously identified opportunities. More specifically, the innovation audit is a systematic approach to determining the firm's innovation potential.

Within the next three chapters the underlying concepts of the innovation audit and the detailed techniques involved in conducting the audit are outlined. In this chapter the overall framework is described and the concept of "technology programming" is developed. In Chapter 9, the specific audit methods are presented and discussed. Finally, to demonstrate the application of the audit technique, two diverse examples—one in medicine, the other in electronics—are described in Chapter 10.

EXCELLENCE IN THE ORGANIZATION

Corporate strategy represents the deployment of the corporation's resources—financial, technical, physical, and human. The essential substance of strategy is choice and direction. Good strategy results in good earnings and long-term viability. Adequate strategy creates either good earnings or long-term viability. Poor strategy creates neither. The domain of strategic thinking is the intersection of operational effectiveness and market viability. The objective of the corporation is to make choices and deploy resources to create opportunity and erect barriers to competition within its market area.

Technology has a significant potential for creating a strong earnings stream and for erecting barriers to competition. But technology should not be considered a panacea and should not be pursued for its own sake. Technology must be understood in terms of the many different roles it can play in support of corporate strategy. Excellence in technology strategy does not imply the finest products imaginable. *Rather, it implies the corporation's ability to **balance** technological potential against the needs of operational effectiveness, the market viability of the results, and the nature of the barriers to competition.*

The world's third largest producer of carbon film resistors focuses its entire research budget on the manufacturing process. It extends the life cycle of electronic components that are in their declining phase by driving the manufacturing cost down and competing solely on the basis of lowest price. A major producer of "carriage trade"—high-quality—ovens and waste disposal units does not have a qualified engineer on its staff. It competes on product features and product reliability created by highly qualified and very experienced designers. Do these companies show excellence in their technology functions? Of course they do! The quality and focus of their technological efforts is a perfect match to their corporate strategy, and their corporate strategy is a match to the outside market environment. Excellence in these terms represents the balancing of efforts and resources to serve both the operational system and the marketplace.

WORLD-CLASS COMPETITORS

The idea of excellence as achieving coherence between organizational and marketplace issues provides strong intellectual linkage for the integration of strategy and organizational effectiveness. As a beginning point, examine the concept of becoming a "world-class" competitor. To be a world-class competitor, it is argued, requires excellence across all of the firm's functional areas. Unevenness among functional areas will lead to vulnerabilities that can be exploited by competitors. For the firm to achieve a world-class rating, the various technology functions in market research, product development, manufacturing, and distribution must be pursued in a consistent and coherent manner along with the basic functional areas of marketing, finance, human resources, and the like.

Much of this argument is drawn from the Wheelwright and Hayes (1985) study of Japanese and German competitive skills. Their study was aimed at understanding the sources of sustainable advantage achieved by firms in both these nations. Wheelwright and Hayes initially reported and interpreted the results from a single functional perspective, manufacturing, viewing the firms' respective manufacturing approaches as key to their competitive advantage. Since then they have broadened their ideas to address the needs for excellence in all functional areas and to examine these needs at different stages of competitive positioning. They present their ideas as a four-stage model of firm development that eventually leads to the achievement of a world-class competitive position.

During stage one, a firm is flexible and reactive. It requires a fleet-footed product design skill coupled with a manufacturing process which is at best internally neutral, that is, one that doesn't interfere with the precedence accorded to the driving forces of engineering design.

In stage two, industry practice is the touchstone and product design must reflect such a standard. At the same time, manufacturing costs must be reduced from the earlier higher costs needed to support flexibility and reactivity. This is accomplished through interaction with engineering design to select more common components and assemblies to lower costs by increasing the scale of some of the operations.

These first two stages are basically reactive or short term. Stages three and four reflect longer time perspectives and the merger of product design and manufacturing design into an overall competitive or strategic plan aimed at creating and sustaining advantage. In these stages serious long-term investment is made in scale economies and broad agreements must be forged among the engineering designers, the manufacturing designers, and the corporate strategists.

Consistent with stages one and two and the technology strategies described in Chapter 5, it can be seen that achieving world-class status, while a fundamentally sound objective for many firms, is not a necessarily desirable status for all firms. Depending upon the specific nature of the firm's business and the nature of a firm's competitors, many other defensible positions can be attained. PIHER, a basic electronic component manufacturer, focuses upon manufacturing excellence, not product R&D, for its competitive advantage. Thermador/Waste King employs limited technical resources for its product design as there are relatively few technical difficulties in the oven and disposal lines. For this firm marketing skills and distribution are the functional areas of excellence which allow it to dominate its portion of the market.

If the Wheelwright-Hayes perspective is twisted a bit, these firms could very easily be considered candidates for a world-class rating. In these firms the quality of engineering and/or manufacturing and the other technology functions are a perfect match to the corporate strategy. That is, they are entirely consistent with an appropriate allocation of the firm's resources in order to pursue the firm's chosen strategy. In turn, the selected strategies themselves seem to be matched well to the external market environment which the firm faces.

The innovation audit technique developed in these chapters is built upon the "perfect match" twist of the Wheelwright-Hayes argument. The technique is used to evaluate the innovative potential of a firm and then to recommend action steps that are consistent with the firm, the industry, the marketplace, and the rate of development of product and process technology. The recommendations that emerge from such an innovation audit are a blend of direction derived from the Chapter 5 presentation of technology strategies and the application of managerial judgment.

THE CONCEPT OF TECHNOLOGY PROGRAMS

Insight into the firm's "excellence," or balance and coherence, can be ascertained by studying the answers these two basic questions:

1. How should technology assist corporate *strategy?*
2. How should technology be developed to assist in the creation of corporate *operational effectiveness?*

The intersection of these two questions is firm-specific. That is, these question will generate unique answers for each firm studied.

A "technology program" perspective provides an effective framework for examining this intersection. The framework is initially explained as a "generic" process upon which all the firm's deployment of technology is based. Then several levels of detail are presented to explain the specific nature of technological programs.

Figure 8-1 depicts the firm's technology programs in a unique fashion. It depicts the major output of technology programming to be the development of individual and organizational intellectual capital. It shows new products and new processes as by-products of the technology programs. This conceptualization of the operations of the firm, emphasizing the intellectual development aspect, is an important variation to the traditional product and process focus.

In this figure science and technology developed outside the firm represents one source of input to the process. Data about customer needs represents a second stream of inputs. The process is further tempered by the broad impact of the external environment. The firm is considered to engage in technology programs which involve research and development efforts on both products and processes.

This generic conceptualization evolved from an earlier study by Abernathy and Goodman (1972). They were interested in the strategies adopted by project managers when faced with serious uncertainty about the performance of subsystems. That study was aimed at understanding the implications of pursuing few or many parallel technological projects under such conditions.

Typically, when a new-generation product is required the design staff identifies each of the necessary subsystems and assigns performance specifications to each. The subsystem designer then considers the needed performance level to determine whether it can be attained by existing approaches. If this evolutionary approach does not seem viable, subsystem developers must then decide if there are other new approaches that might yield the required performance. The system designer must then determine whether all of the selected subsystem concepts can be reduced to practice within the time frame available. (Reduced to practice includes both meeting operational specifications as a subsystem and working appropriately within the larger system.) Finally, the subsystem approaches must work in the real use environment, not just the laboratory, and must be reliably manufactured for a reasonable price within a reasonable time frame.

Common sense borne out by this study suggests that it is unlikely that any particular approach incorporated into a new-generation product can be reduced to practice in the time available to the product development program unless it has been pursued at

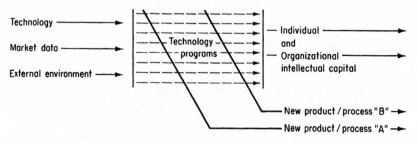

Figure 8-1. The generic flow of technology programs.

some length prior to its selection for inclusion. One good example from the study is the selection of propulsion subsystems. When a new propulsion approach was selected with only analytic work to back up its feasibility then trouble was almost assured. The designers often found it necessary to fall back, late in the product development, to a more traditional propulsion approach. This need to fall back to old technology was seldom encountered when the propulsion system concept had not only been analyzed but in addition some prototype work had ensued and the approach had been tested in a reasonable approximation of the use environment. Thus, to some extent ongoing development work on various subsystem approaches is critical to the smooth creation of a new-generation product.

These findings are most effectively presented when the normal product/process development approaches were turned on their side and the development of intellectual capital was emphasized as shown in Figure 8-1. The interaction between level of previous subsystem development work and smooth new product/process creation means that the technology programs as depicted in Figure 8-1 are at the intersection of strategic thrust and operational effectiveness.

THE NATURE OF TECHNOLOGY PROGRAMS

What precisely are technology programs? The nature of technology programs has to be appreciated on their many levels in order to explicate the link between them and firm performance. In this section a rich, multifaceted description of the nature of technology programs is presented and the links from these ideas to the firm's operational effectiveness are drawn out.

Levels of Existence

Several authors offer categorizations of the various levels of technology programs. Among them is a common distinction between basic and applied research. Few firms engage in much basic research. The vast preponderance of basic research is undertaken by universities or research establishments. The essence of basic research might well be termed phenomena exploitation and the search for basic understanding of the workings of the universe. Operationally, the pursuit of basic research is constrained by available resources, perceived scientific benefit, and the belief that one idea or another is providing the spark by which real progress might be accomplished (Barber and Fox, 1962). Applied research has traditionally been accomplished in firms driven by a real or imputed customer need, constrained by resource availability and inventiveness.

As a variant of this traditional set of categories the IIT Research Institute in a study of the critical events in science leading up to major innovations adopted a tripartite distinction among basic research, mission-oriented research, and applied research (IITRI, 1968). Here basic research was identical to the traditional definition, but mission-oriented research was undertaken with a broad, product-oriented goal such as magnetic recording or medical research aimed at a specific disease. Applied research was focused on the development of a specific product such as the Ampex videotape

Table 8-1. Levels of Technological Programs

Science	Basic research
Application to subsystems	Applied research
Application to whole systems	New product/process development

recorder. In light of these definitions it appears that mission-oriented research is often carried out in universities or research establishments, although more firms are represented at this level than at the basic research level.

Alfred Brown, president of Celanese Research, offered another thoughtful counter to the traditional research dichotomy. He suggested a categorization of defensive research, offensive research, and continuing research (1972). For him, the business objectives or intent of the research is the most important way that executives should categorize their research programs. Defensive research referred to product extensions, which usually took the form of modest performance increases (new improved, now useful for, etc.) or cost decreases brought about by manufacturing improvements. Offensive research described the process of bringing a significant new product or new-generation product to market or dramatic improvements in manufacturing costs. Continuing research was similar to basic research as it focused on technological programs for the more distant future.

Chauncey Starr (personal communication, 1970) offered a somewhat more pragmatic categorization that was based upon the construct of system and subsystem. His three levels of technology programs are basic research, which is intended to elucidate basic scientific phenomena; applied research, which is intended to improve the performance of a component or a subsystem; and development, which is intended to improve the performance of a whole system.

For application in this chapter the Starr three-level categorization has been slightly modified. As shown in Table 8-1, the categories are science—basic research; application to subsystems—applied research; and application to whole systems—new product/process development.

Intensity of Technology Programs

Whereas level of technology program is simply an explanatory concept that helps clarify the specific program intent, intensity of technology program is an operational concept. The appropriate intensity of a specific technology program can be related to its potential for strategic advantage and to the operational effectiveness questions of deployment within a specific development project. Level of intensity—that is, the depth to which a technology should be pursued in anticipation of eventually employing that technology in a new product and/or process development—is explicitly a management decision, a decision which is normally affirmed or reaffirmed on a yearly basis. Later sections of this chapter will focus first on operational effectiveness and then on strategic thrust as reasons to select a specific level of program intensity. For now, however, the chapter focuses upon the need for understanding that the intensity of pursuing technology programs is a conscious choice on the part of management.

Table 8-2. Technology Program Intensity

Low cost	Monitoring activities
Moderate cost	Active experimentation
High cost	Major development

To expand slightly on the question of intensity, a simplified scale might be suggested. The scale has three levels, each of which has dramatically different cost implications as well as considerably different work statements. The least cost and lowest level of technology program relates to monitoring activities, which may range from simple periodic literature search activities, to data base accumulation and computer-aided continuous update activities, to attendance at appropriate scientific conferences to speak directly with relevant sources. A moderate cost activity might include active experimentation with new phenomena, new components, new systems approaches. Here prototypes are constructed and attributes varied in accordance with an experimental protocol. The data gathered provide the firm with considerable hands-on experience about the potential of the chosen technology in an actual use situation. The third and most costly level is full investment in a major development effort. Here full analysis and testing is followed by full product design and manufacturing design along with the creation of full process and product specifications. (See summary in Table 8-2.)

OPERATIONAL EFFECTIVENESS

In earlier chapters the power of metaphor was explored. In this chapter the metaphor of operational effectiveness will be explored by contrasting the different measures that have been suggested by diverse management researchers. Within the broad definition of operational effectiveness as the ability to "reduce to practice" a set of subsystem concepts within an overall systems design, a simple but more subtle measurement (metaphor) will be explicated.

Measurement as Metaphor

Measurement of the technology function serves management as a tool for directing the efforts of the firm's work force. Thus, selecting appropriate measures is quite important. Unfortunately, for management the evaluation of the various technology functions has always been problematic. During the 1960s and 1970s the available measurement approaches became increasingly sophisticated. The adoption rate of these more sophisticated measures, though, has been slow.

The most commonly employed measure has been that of cost or schedule performance—all too often in terms of overruns. Peck and Scherer's (1962) work on the weapons acquisition process has employed reported many of their findings in just such terms—cost and schedule overruns. Within a firm the management focus commonly is on budget and schedule, and variance analysis is one of the major tools used to evaluate the effectiveness of the technology functions. This focus is logically equivalent to that of Peck and Scherer. These measures are based on an underlying concept of meeting expectations rather than one of performance or of productivity. While upper management and the various technology managers *do* focus on good technical practice, they are more often called to task by management for not meeting expectations.

In response to the need to make interproject comparisons, technical performance began to be employed as part of the measurement approach. This occurred when Marquis and Straight (1965) expanded the cost and schedule performance question to include technical performance. They created a scale that involved ranking of both technical and administrative contracting officers in an overlapping fashion. This scale provided them with a method for comparing diverse projects occurring in several different firms. Such comparisons are imperative if progress is to be made in understanding which management practices are better than others.

Concurrently, Knight (1963) was at work extending the technological measurement concept from a "comparative judgment" to an "unambiguous measure." He proposed an explicit technical structural–functional measure of technological progress. This concept was employed in a study aimed at understanding the progress in computational effectiveness delivered by different firms' mainframe computers. Clarke (1968) extended the Knight construct in a study of liquid propellant rocket engine development from 1945 to 1966. Clarke used thrust, a figure of merit for mechanical efficiency, a figure of merit for thermal efficiency, and a scale of mechanical innovativeness, all normalized against a three-year moving average. Sahal (1981) further extended these concepts by developing a "technological progress function" and constructing what he terms a technometric. The underlying metaphor of Sahal's concern is a measurement of phenomena that contribute to pushing the state of the art.

What management needs is an easily conceived measure that captures both of the metaphorical dimensions of pushing the state of the art and meeting expectations. Lawrence and Lorsch (1967) add a corporate or a strategic dimension to these measures when they ask what percentage of current sales is accounted for by product that did not exist five years ago. This suggests a somewhat more direct measure of the role technology might play in corporate performance.

In reflecting upon the range of technology strategies offered in Chapter 4 it is clear that pushing the state of the art in not always required. But as product and process development is necessary for many of the strategic thrusts suggested by the theory, a longer run view of developing intellectual capital must be tempered by a look to the short run. There still exists an important need to focus on the shorter run design and development of specific projects which also deliver strategic value to the firm.

The ability to simultaneously build for the future while satisfying present needs is represented in the measurement metaphor recommended here. Operational effectiveness is represented by the combination of *meeting specifications*, *broad customer acceptance*, and *downstream payoff* for next-generation products and processes (Abernathy and Goodman, 1972). The first phrase refers to meeting expectations. Here the specifications concept is meant to explicitly cover the technical, schedule, and cost dimensions. Broad customer acceptance refers to success in planning and/or market research because it indicates that the specifications were correctly chosen in the first place. Downstream payoff for next-generation products and processes relates current developments to the longer run technology programs that serve to keep the firm moving forward.

A GENERAL THEOREM OF OPERATIONAL EFFECTIVENESS

To be operationally effective critical questions must be answered and appropriate responses must be undertaken. Simply stated, the managers must *identify areas of relevant uncertainty* in the firm, the business, new products, or new processes and then must devise activities to *reduce these areas of relevant uncertainty as early as is practical.* Related to the idea of achieving objectives is the notion of relevant uncertainty: What are those factors that would prevent a firm or a development effort from achieving its goals?

This issue has two parts to it. One is the identification of uncertainty, the other is the earliest possible reduction of the uncertainty. The second part of the question is rather obvious but is often overlooked in most firms. Typically, as projects develop, more and more personnel become involved, so that coordination of the development becomes more and more of a challenge. As a result, the cost of change escalates. Thus, it is considerably less expensive to explore areas of uncertainty early in order to reduce the cost of corrections to the project approach. This is true not only for the generation of new products or new processes but also for handling the organizational stresses of changes in strategy.

Three Types of Uncertainty

A brief typology of uncertainty is useful to understand more about the identification of uncertainty. In the past it has been useful to focus upon uncertainty as it is differentiated among technology, use, and process. Uncertainty is a factor of the specific personnel assigned to accomplish a task as well as of the task itself.

With regard to the *technological* approach there are three diagnostic issues for identifying technological uncertainty: the knowledge level of the technology, the analytic potential for grappling with the technology, and the depth of experience with the technology. If the technical approach to a new development is an old concept adapted to different performance parameters, then the approach will have low technological uncertainty. If the selected approach is originally created to solve the problem at hand, then the technological uncertainty is high. The first use of a pulsed laser beam to replace a pulsed microwave system for navigation purposes is a clear example of an approach that should work in theory but represents high technological uncertainty.

What is the analytic potential of specific technology in a problem-solving or design situation? Analytic methods can define some technologies quite well. Other technologies are only approximated by analysis. Then a trial-and-error, test-and-evaluation process must be employed. The third diagnostic question focuses on experience level. A crude experience level scale might begin with analysis only, grow through testing components to testing a full prototype, and end with full field test of production equipment. A low experience level (only analysis) signifies high uncertainty, while a high experience level (field test) signifies low uncertainty.

Of course, even an approach with inherently low technological uncertainty does not guarantee low actual uncertainty. For such a guarantee, the specific personnel assigned to the design staff must have a high experience level with the technological approach. Complex ideas for sophisticated applications cannot be communicated by simply reading the scientific literature. Technological concepts are, more often than not, subjects that can be learned only by extensive experience. The so-called NIH (not invented here) factor arises from failure at attempts to use an approach about which the personnel have only a reading knowledge. Thus, in addition to the technological, diagnostic questions, management must ask about the specific experience of the project team.

This minor diversion suggests that technology programs should work toward reducing technological uncertainty in anticipation of need as well as to provide development opportunities for technical personnel who will be called upon to bring some of these technologies forward. (Specific project strategy to accomplish these ends can be found in Balderson, Birnbaum, Goodman, and Stahl, 1984; additional information on professional technological development is available in Goodman, 1981.)

Similar to technological uncertainty is the uncertainty that is related to the actual *use* or employment of the new product. When a new product, process, or service is envisioned, an idealized image of the new idea's use is created. This simplification of the actual use situation provides a powerful communication device that can ease the explanation of the essential features of the new concept. But in developing this concept, much attention is required to adapt it to the multifaceted details of actual use. The less a project team knows about the rich details of use, and possible misuse, the more "use" uncertainty exists.

As an example, one development program of some flight line test equipment for the Air Force was considered extremely successful by the customer. The success was related not to the basic technological design but to several added features which were not required by the customer's design specification. For instance, the specification required a device that could be towed to the airplane at speeds not to exceed 5 MPH (this is the posted speed limit on the aprons and runways). Experienced design personnel recognized that the "real" drivers of the tow vehicles usually violated the speed limit and made sure that the design was stable at considerably higher speeds than required. Similarly, the test equipment specification did not consider the idea of training in a flight line environment. By adding a simple headphone system to the test set the flight line noise level was overcome and training procedures were facilitated. A third issue was designed around industry behavior and knowledge of the fact that cable connectors were commonly out of stock. Maintenance personnel frequently "borrowed" connectors from one piece of equipment in order to repair another. To prevent this the connector and the cable were encapsulated together. As a result the test equipment had one of the highest readiness scores of the entire test equipment inventory.

Process uncertainty is the uncertainty introduced into the development by less than ideal management processes. In general, communication and control systems are not developed in light of the foregoing uncertainty analysis and many of the more critical issues are exacerbated by the difficulties of coordination and timely information sharing. Although the selection and design of technological programs is not an effective antidote for management process failure, such design and selection can be directed at overcoming technological and use uncertainty questions.

TECHNOLOGICAL ASSISTS TO STRATEGY

When further exploring the intersection of strategy and operational effectiveness, it is necessary to keep a few concepts in mind. Technology programs should anticipate the needs of the firm and provide the head start that is necessary to achieve the operational effectiveness requirements. Technology programs should be driven by competitor analysis, particularly as shaped by the use of technology mapping techniques. Thus, technology programs must consider the changes in product performance parameters which are expected from each of its competitors. How can the firm meet or exceed these performance challenges? Again the basic question, how can the technology programs create a defensible competitive advantage?

One schema for beginning to answer such questions is to build a technology program priority matrix. Table 8-3 depicts just such a matrix as a two-dimensional program versus investment level chart. The decision to invest at the various levels in each technology is determined by analyzing the state of each potential technology in comparison to the technological component of current products and processes, the technological promise of underlying science and technology, and the technological nature and promise of competitive products and substitute technologies. Taken together these three questions lead to the decision to monitor, to experiment, or to develop.

Current or future product technological potential can be assessed using a conceptualization developed by White and Graham (1978). Their structure for this evaluation is shown in Figure 8-2. Although they applied the structure only to new-product development, it does have good value in determining current as well as future technological potential.

Working down the left-hand side of Figure 8-2, the evaluator is initially asked to examine the basic physical or chemical constraints that limit the product performance. As an example, aircraft speed was limited by the physics of the air pressure buildup on the leading edges of the airframe prior to the discovery of the "Coke bottle" fuselage shape. The evaluator then is asked to state the next physical or chemical limitation on product performance. After the Coke bottle fuselage design was introduced the speed of the aircraft was then limited by the temperature performance of the materials used on the leading edge of the wings. This problem was itself initially limited by the ability to machine titanium; that is, a manufacturing process was an obstacle to overcoming the next limiting factor. The inventive merit of a new product or the inventive potential of a current product is thus limited by the performance improvement possible when resolving one constraint and reaching the limit imposed by the next constraint.

These questions about various technologies and their performance implications present the organization with the ability to assign priorities to various technology programs as the answers identify the order in which various problems need to be solved to increase performance.

Table 8-3. Technology Program Priority Matrix

Activity:	Monitor	Applied research	Product development
Investment level:	Low	Moderate	High
Technology 1	X		
Technology 2	X		
Technology 3		X	
Technology 4		X	
Technology 5			X

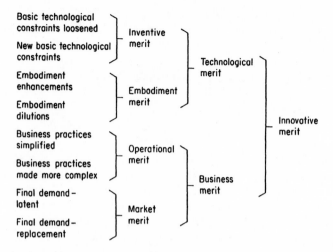

Figure 8-2. Technology evaluation matrix. Adapted from White and Graham, 1978.

Embodiment enhancement and embodiment dilution ask the evaluator to examine ways in which the actual design or embodiment of the basic physical phenomena dilutes the actual performance from the theoretical ideal or enhances the application value of the theoretical performance limits. Such an evaluation can be a basis for directing technological programs so that current design performances can be responsibly maximized.

The remaining sectors of the White and Graham schema suggest that the product fits with the firm either by complicating or simplifying the nature of the business and with the market environment either by representing a replacement market (with a clear set of competitors) or a latent market (with no competitors at the outset). This schema provides another window on the technology–strategy interface.

A second general technique useful for assisting the design and selection of technology programs for improving the strategy–operational effectiveness intersection was developed by the consulting firm of Arthur D. Little, Inc. (1981). ADL recommends a broad analysis of the firm's product and process technologies in order to classify these technologies under one of four categories. *Base* technologies constitute the technological foundation of the business but are technologies which are also widely available to competitors. *Key* technologies are those that have the greatest impact upon competitive performance. *Pacing* technologies are those in early development which have the demonstrated potential to change the basis of competition. *Emerging* technologies are those which hold long-term promise to alter the basis of competition.

In a simple connection of these categories to the idea of technology programs the following schema is shown in Table 8-4. The firm's technology program for base technologies needs little investment. Here the focus is normally upon small increments in performance capability and continual recruitment to replace technical personnel when they move on. Key technologies require a considerably different investment level. The shift upscale in microprocessors from 8 bit to 16 bit to 32 bit requires that computer and software firms engage in systematic development of new hardware and software embodiments in the new capabilities. Systematic investment in next-generation tech-

Table 8-4. Technology Category and Technology Program Investment Level

Technology Category	Investment Level
Base technology	Needs little
Key technology	Systematically built
Pacing technology	Selective investment
Emerging technology	Monitored

nology includes main products, complementary products, distribution strategies, and coordination with major customers. Investing in pacing technologies needs to be done on a selective basis. The firm needs to have some hands-on experience with the core elements of such technologies in order to reduce technological uncertainties in anticipation of more effective deployment in a systematic development effort when the pacing technologies achieve key technology status. Emerging technologies need only be monitored through a variety of literature review and scientific meeting attendance activities.

But the ADL schema has one more element of note, the addition of a technology strategy matrix. The technological competitive analysis matrix of Figure 8-3 helps to assign priorities to the firm's technology programs by expanding the managerial vantage point to include industry position. In answering the question of whether the introduction of a particular technology will shift the product, process, or service to a better competitive position, two dimensions—industry maturity and firm competitive position—seem to be especially important. Figure 8-3 depicts four stages of industry maturity: embryonic, growth, mature, and aging; it also depicts five levels of competitive position: dominant, strong, favorable, tenable, and weak. The appropriate strategic thrust for a firm depends on the combination of industrial maturity and competitive position. Broadly speaking the firm can invest in natural development, selective development, or turnaround, or it can abandon the area completely.

The matrix is way of describing a window of opportunity for technological assistance. Implied action is aimed at moving the firm upward toward competitive dominance. The matrix compares the strength of the firm's positions against the increasing

Competitive position	Industry maturity			
	Embryonic	Growth	Mature	Aging
Dominant				
Strong				/////
Favorable			/////	//// 0000
Tenable		/////	/// 00000	000 XXXXX
Weak	000000000	0000 XXXX	XXXXXXXXX	XXXXXXXXX

XXXX – Abandon //// – Selective development
0000 – Turnaround ☐ – Natural development

Figure 8-3. Technological competitive analysis. Adapted from Arthur D. Little, Inc., 1981.

or decreasing opportunities within the industry. With this in mind the construct suggests generic actions to improve the situation.

According to this construct, a firm in a weak competitive position should abandon the industry if the industry has slowed its growth, matured, or is aging. In fact, turnaround seems possible for such a firm only if the industry is embryonic or is in the early growth phase—a situation of evolving opportunities. A firm with a tenable hold on the market can, through natural development, improve its position in embryonic or early growth phases of the industry but faces the need for selective development in the later growth and early maturity phase. Presumably this might be accomplished with a niche strategy. A turnaround situation is indicated if the position is tenable only in the mature phase, whereas early abandonment is suggested if the tenable position is carried into the aging phase. In these later two phases opportunities are decreasing and a tenable competitor is unlikely to be able to make a dramatic difference against stronger, more dominant competitors.

This construct provides one approach to the setting of technology program priorities by permitting the industry and competitive situation to be connected to the idea of a technology program and allowing the management to push the type of program that will help move the firm up the chart into a more dominant position. Thus, the construct helps to connect the technology program concept with the strategic concept as drawn in the earlier chapters.

SUMMARY

In the introduction to this chapter it was argued that excellence could be considered as an effective match between the firm's competencies and the environment. This matching concept was then restated as the integration of strategic thrust and operational effectiveness. A discussion of several perspectives which provide a background for the innovation audit technique was then presented and technological programming was suggested as a framework for organizing the results of the several analyses presented. These sets of concepts then represent the background for the innovation audit. The next chapter presents a series of instruments that blend the various ideas into an operational tool which provides a strong basis for the exercise of managerial judgment in the selection of appropriate technology strategy.

REFERENCES

Abernathy, W. J., and R. A. Goodman. 1972. "Strategies for Development Projects: An Empirical Study," *R & D Management* 2(3):125–29.

Arthur D. Little, Inc. 1981. "The Strategic Management of Technology" Boston: Arthur D. Little, Inc.

Balderson, J., P. Birnbaum, R. A. Goodman, and M. Stahl. 1984. *Modern Management Techniques in Engineering and R&D.* New York: Van Nostrand Reinhold.

Barber, B., and R. Fox. 1962. "The Case of the Floppy-Eared Rabbits: A Case of Serendipity Gained and Serendipity Lost." In B. Barber and W. Hirsch, eds., *The Sociology of Science.* New York: Free Press of Glencoe.

Brown, A. E. 1972. "New Definitions for Industrial R & D," *Research Management* 15:55–57.

Chandler, A. 1962. *Strategy and Structure: Chapters in the History of the Industrial Enterprise.* Cambridge, MA: MIT Press.

Clarke, R. W. 1968. "Innovation in Liquid Propellant Rocket Technology," *Final Report*

Task 7910-05. Holloman Air Force Base, NM, Office of Aerospace Research, March.

Goodman, R.. 1981. *Temporary Systems: Professional Development, Manpower Utilization, Task Effectiveness and Innovation.* New York: Praeger.

IIT Research Institute. 1968. *TRACES (Technology in Retrospective and Critical Events in Science).* Chicago: IITRI, December 15.

Knight, K.. 1963. "A Study of Technological Innovation—The Evolution of Digital Computers." Ph.D. diss., Graduate School of Industrial Administration, Carnegie Institute of Technology.

Lawrence, P., and J. Lorsch. 1967. "Differentiation and Integration in Complex Organizations," *Administrative Science Quarterly* 12(1):1–47.

Marquis, D. G., and D. M. Straight, Jr. 1965. "Organizational Factors in Project Performance." Working paper, School of Management, MIT, Cambridge, MA, August.

Peck, M. J., and F. M. Scherer 1962. *The Weapons Acquisition Process: An Economic Analysis.* Division of Research, Harvard University.

Rumelt, R. 1976. *Strategy, Structure and Economic Performance.* Cambridge, MA: Harvard Business School Press.

Sahal, D. 1981. *Patterns of Technological Innovation.* Reading, MA: Addison-Wesley.

Wheelwright, S., and R. H. Hayes. 1985. "Competing through Manufacturing," *Harvard Business Review*, January–February, pp. 9–119.

White, G., and M.B.W. Graham. 1978. "How to Spot a Technological Winner," *Harvard Business Review,* March–April, pp. 146–52.

9

Detailing the Innovation Audit Technique

This chapter provides the details of a technique for auditing the innovative capacity of a firm. The innovation audit strengthens managerial judgment in the creation and maintenance of a technologically based defensible competitive advantage. The audit benefits fall into three categories. First, the audit process provides a convenient technique for the *structured collection* of information about innovative potential. Second, this information can be *analytically linked* to the nine technology strategies featured in Chapter 4. And finally, this analytic linkage provides *substantial input to managerial judgment* in the selection of short- and long-term strategic actions. In Chapter 10, two extended examples of the innovation audit are presented to demonstrate the application of the techniques described in this chapter.

The specific objective of the audit is to provide recommended action to the firm's management in order to achieve both short- and long-term benefits. The managerial judgment required should be framed by both strategic and valuation considerations. On the one hand, the manager should be concerned with defensibility. On the other hand, the manager should be concerned about the implied change to the valuation of the firm over the short, medium, and long term. Thus, the actions drawn from the analysis need to be viewed from the internal or managerial perspective and the external or investor perspective. This use of these two perspectives considerably strengthens the guidance provided to the firm's management by the audit process.

The initial part of the audit is an introductory section which is basically an executive summary. The body of the audit employs three different audit frameworks. This is followed by an interpretive section which begins with comments and analysis of each of the three instruments. It then concludes by linking the audit data to relevant strategy sets and then employing the internal and external perspective on which conclusions and recommendations are based.

THREE ANALYTIC FRAMEWORKS

Characterizing the basic nature of the innovation audit is the combination of three analytic frameworks. One framework is drawn from the wide range of literature on project success and provides an internal look at the firm's innovative processes. The second framework is a competitive one and contrasts the firm's innovative abilities with those of its competitors. The third framework, an internal–external comparison, highlights the firm's position in regard to the industry technology base.

Thus, the main body of the audit contains three interview protocols, a technological innovation process audit (TIPA), an innovative comparison audit (ICA), and a technological position audit (TPA). Each of these audits represent a structured way of summarizing the extremely wide range of research extant on the management of R&D, the role of technology, and the like.

The Technological Innovation Process Audit

Table 9-1 is the questionnaire employed to solicit responses from the organization being studied. The introductory section to the process audit is followed by questions on

Table 9-1. Technological Innovation Process Audit

The basic objective of the audit is to reduce the downside risks of investing in technological innovation. While the instrument can be applied to a single new project, it has additional power when a sampling of the firm's innovative project activities is undertaken. This latter perspective provides management with a method of assessing the organization's innovative abilities and processes. The audit is meant to be a technological supplement to financial and managerial judgment. It has value for existing organizations, for new ventures, and for new projects.

Technology

The technology section of this audit requires judgment about the length and depth of prior experience with basic technological approaches. Technology is assessed through analysis at the subsystem level; the highest scoring subsystem is the highest risk area and is considered the limiting factor for further analyses.

1. The length of experience that the firm has with the basic technological approach it has selected is:

	<1 year	1–2 years	2–3 years	>3 years
Subsystem A _____	4	3	2	1
Subsystem B _____	4	3	2	1
Subsystem C _____	4	3	2	1
Subsystem D _____	4	3	2	1
Subsystem E _____	4	3	2	1
etc.				

Question 1 score equals highest subsystem score   _____

2. The depth of technical experience that the firm has with the basic technological approach it has selected is:

	Analysis	Prototype	Use test	Production
Subsystem A _____	4	3	2	1
Subsystem B _____	4	3	2	1
Subsystem C _____	4	3	2	1
Subsystem D _____	4	3	2	1
Subsystem E _____	4	3	2	1
etc.				

Question 2 score equals highest subsystem score   = _____

Table 9-1. Technological Innovation Process Audit *(Continued)*

3. The source of innovative stimulation for the project is:

technical literature.	4
the organization itself.	3
competitors.	2
customers.	1

4. The promised performance character of the project is:

an order of magnitude increase.	4
a shift of primary performance focus.	3
a substantial increase.	2
a modest increase.	1

Project technological risk is sum of questions 1–4   = _____

Market

5. The project faces:

an undifferentiable replacement market.	4
a modestly differentiable replacement market.	3
a significantly differentiable replacement market.	2
a latent market.	1

6. The market perception is derived from the:

producer.	4
producer with limited user input.	3
user with limited producer input.	2
user.	1

7. The level of market uncertainty is due to the project:

being never sold in the market before.	4
being sold by others in the market before.	3
being sold through others in the market before.	2
being sold and serviced by the firm before.	1

8. The project is intended:

to leapfrog the competition.	4
to improve performance.	3
to keep up with competitive performance.	2
to catch up with competition.	1

Project market risk is sum of questions 5–8   = _____

Organization

9. The project's match to the organization's objective is:

not at all.	4
good, but represents a major new idea.	3
good, but represents a minor new idea.	2
good and in direct support of current mainline work.	1

10. The project is an important idea of:

a single project champion.	4
a small team of technical personnel.	3
a small team of technical and marketing personnel.	2
a systematically defined objective development.	1

11. Cross-functional communication is achieved by:

formal memo.	4
informal liaison.	3
regular face-to-face meetings (or physical colocation).	2
all of the above.	1

12. The project requires:

dramatic changes in normal business practices.	4
significant changes in normal business practices.	3
little change in normal business practices.	2
no change in normal business practices.	1

Project organization risk is sum of questions 9–12   = _____

Table 9-1. Technological Innovation Process Audit *(Continued)*

Environment

13. The environment is:
    subject to major changes in competitors and outputs.   4
    subject to uneven but rapid evolution of outputs.   3
    subject to smooth but rapid evolution of outputs.   2
    subject to gradual, well-understood evolution.   1
14. The regulatory climate is:
    extremely complex and strict.   4
    complex but well understood.   3
    well understood and reasonable.   2
    loosely constraining and indirect.   1
15. The underlying technological bases are:
    changing rapidly and unevenly.   4
    changing rapidly and smoothly.   3
    changing smoothly.   2
    changing gradually.   1
16. The firm depends on a supplier:
    for complexly compatible input.   4
    for unique parts or services.   3
    for high-value parts or services with second sourcing.   2
    for commonly available parts and services.   1

Firm environment risk is sum of questions 13–16   = _____

Industry Structure

17. Substitution for the firm's products and services by other technologies or from other industrial sectors:
    is making rapid inroads in the industry.   4
    occurs frequently.   3
    occurs only occasionally.   2
    is not expected to occur in the medium term.   1
18. The industry is reshaping to require:
    new competence outside its mainline technology core.   4
    widening its mainline technological core.   3
    deepening its mainline technological core.   2
    no change in its mainline technological core.   1
19. The basic industry structure has:
    many participants and diverse integration strategies.   4
    many participants and common integration strategies.   3
    a moderate number of participants.   2
    few participants.   1
20. The firm's products and services are:
    complexly integrated into a systemic innovation.   4
    simply integrated into a systemic innovation.   3
    part of synergistic innovation.   2
    autonomous.   1

Firm industry structure risk is sum of questions 17–20   = _____

Firm Analysis

If a firm-level analysis is to be attempted, the analysis should be replicated for large and small product innovations and for large and small process innovations. This affects only the technology, market, and organization sections of the evaluation. The outline below suggests weights that should be given to each of the findings. These would then be used to plot the risk profile below.

Table 9-1. Technological Innovation Process Audit *(Continued)*

Firm technological risk is weighted average of large and small project samples from product and process innovation areas.

	Score	Times	Weight	
Large project product innovation	_____	X	4	= _____
Large project process innovation	_____	X	3	= _____
Small project product innovation	_____	X	2	= _____
Small project process innovation	_____	X	1	= _____
Subtotal				_____
Firm technological risk score is subtotal divided by 10				= _____

Firm market risk is weighted average of large and small project samples from product and process innovation areas.

	Score	Times	Weight	
Large project product innovation	_____	X	4	= _____
Large project process innovation	_____	X	3	= _____
Small project product innovation	_____	X	2	= _____
Small project process innovation	_____	X	1	= _____
Subtotal				_____
Firm market risk score is subtotal divided by 10				= _____

Firm organization risk is weighted average of large and small project samples from product and process innovation areas.

	Score	Times	Weight	
Large project product innovation	_____	X	4	= _____
Large project process innovation	_____	X	3	= _____
Small project product innovation	_____	X	2	= _____
Small project process innovation	_____	X	1	= _____
Subtotal				_____
Firm organization risk score is subtotal divided by 10				= _____

Risk Profile

The firm's risk profile can be plotted below:

	1	2	3	4	5	6	7	8	9	10	11	12	13	14	15	16
Technology																
Market																
Organization																
Environment																
Industry structure																
TOTAL																

= _____

technology, market, organization, environment, and industry structure, and the audit concludes with a summary section that shows how to analyze the firm's answers and construct a rudimentary risk analysis.

The basic questions employed in this analytic instrument represent a synthesis of the literature on the management of technological innovation. Questions 1, 2, and 7 are drawn from Abernathy and Goodman's "Strategies for Development Projects" (1972); questions 5 and 12 from White and Graham's "How to Spot a Technological Winner" (1978); question 9 from Twiss's *Managing Technological Innovation* (1980), question 10 from Freeman's "Project Sappho" (1972), question 11 from Lorsch and Lawrence's "Organizing for Product Innovation" (1965); question 17 from Porter's *Competitive Advantage* (1985); questions 18 and 19 from Lawless's "The Structure of Strategy: A

Taxonomic Study of Competitive Strategy and Technology Substrategy" (1987); question 20 from Goodman's *Temporary Systems* (1981). The remainder of the questions represent extant conventional wisdom.

The Innovative Comparison Audit

Table 9-2 represents an assessment of the innovative abilities of the firm as compared to the competitors in the industry. This audit, was drawn from the work of A. Rubenstein, represents the extensive research program carried out under his direction at Northwestern University's Technological Institute (personal communication, 1982).

The Technological Position Audit

In Table 9-3 a way of assessing the firm's position in relation to the broad developments of the technologies relevant to the firm's business is depicted. This analysis is drawn from the extensive technological consulting practice of the Arthur D. Little (1981) corporation—particularly the work undertaken in its European practice area.

Table 9-2. Innovative Comparison Audit

This questionnaire should be evaluated by senior executives in marketing, manufacturing, R&D, and general management in order to achieve a balanced perspective on the firm. Serious discrepancies in answers should be explored to better understand the factors that underlie the differences in perspective.

Compared to your leading competitors (or to all your competitors), how does your firm rate on each of these questions?

	Much below average	Below average	Average	Above average	Much above average
Track Record					
New-product introductions	____	____	____	____	____
Costs of production	____	____	____	____	____
Success of new products	____	____	____	____	____
First mover record	____	____	____	____	____
Contribution of new products to sales and profits	____	____	____	____	____
Capability of Staff					
Size of R&D staff	____	____	____	____	____
Discipline diversity	____	____	____	____	____
Experience level of staff	____	____	____	____	____
Reputation of staff	____	____	____	____	____
Strength of R&D Organization					
Flexibility	____	____	____	____	____
Anticipation skills	____	____	____	____	____
Ability to execute long-term projects	____	____	____	____	____
Reliability of communication	____	____	____	____	____

Table 9-2 Innovative Comparison Audit *(Continued)*

	Much below average	Below average	Average	Above average	Much above average
Idea Generation					
Robustness of ideas	——	——	——	——	——
Breadth of base in firm from which ideas arise	——	——	——	——	——
Mechanisms for evaluating new ideas	——	——	——	——	——
Time to Commercialize					
Time from start to market introduction	——	——	——		——
Time from introduction to full-scale marketing	——	——	——	——	——
Time to derive learning curve benefits on costs	——	——	——	——	——
Costs/Benefits of R&D					
R&D costs relative to life cycle revenues	——	——	——	——	——
Relations among functional areas					
Smoothness of transfer from R&D to marketing and manufacturing	——	——	——	——	——

Adapted from Rubenstein, 1982, by permission.

Table 9-3. Technological Position Audit

This audit begins with a classification of the technologies needed by the firm. It should begin with a broad analysis of the firm's product and process technologies in order to classify these technologies under one of four categories. Base technologies, *which are the technological foundation of the business, are technologies that are also most widely available to competitors.* Key technologies *are those that have the greatest impact upon competitive performance.* Pacing technologies *are those in early development which have the demonstrated potential to change the basis of competition.* Emerging technologies *hold long-term promise to alter the basis of competition.*

List of Product Technologies
Base   Investment level

Key   Investment level

_____   _____

_____   _____

Pacing   Investment level

_____   _____

_____   _____

Emerging   Investment level

_____   _____

_____   _____

List of Process Technologies
Base   Investment level

_____   _____

_____   _____

Key   Investment level

_____   _____

_____   _____

Pacing   Investment level

_____   _____

_____   _____

Emerging   Investment level

_____   _____

_____   _____

_____   _____

Note: Investment levels include little (L), systematically built (SB), selective investment (SI), and monitoring (M).

INTERPRETATION

The interpretation step of the innovation audit leaves considerable room for managerial judgment. The interpretation is achieved in three steps. Initially it is important to provide a commentary on the three audit instruments to help the reader understand the firm in greater depth than the numerical results can portray. The second step is the employment of the strategy selection matrix as a screen for the data developed in the audit. This step will analytically link the data to potential strategy selections. The third step is the application of internal (managerial) and external (investor) perspectives to the analysis and the application of the required managerial judgment in the selection of an appropriate course of action.

Audit Instrument Comments

Comments about the audit instruments are intended to be explanatory in nature. Comments about the TIPA instrument fall into two categories, one focusing on context and one on specifics. The relationship between the projects analyzed by the instrument and the firm also needs to be explicated and questions about other firm contextual factors such as resource strength and market power need to be explored. These contextual issues are one source of judgmental contribution that management should factor in. The second area of comments should explain the various risk scores found in the analysis.

    The ICA is intended to measure the firm's current skills in comparison with those of its major competitors. Here the comments simply reiterate the strengths and weaknesses that have been identified. Additionally, it is very useful to add comments that may explain why scores of the various functional areas do not agree. Such disagreement, when found, often reflects differences in time horizons among the functional areas. But the interviews from which the scores are derived may suggest other explanations. The TPA focuses upon the appropriate nature (or lack therefore) of the firm's investment in technology and how that investment promises to reposition the firm among the competition.

Linkages to Technology Strategies

Here the strategy selection matrix can be employed in much the same fashion it was used in the technology mapping exercise. The matrix is reproduced here as Table 9-4. The operative questions are specified and the resulting selection then follows from the structure of the matrix. Again, it is important to exercise managerial judgment as a supplement to the formal linkage steps that are suggested here.

Internal (Managerial) and External (Investor) Perspectives

The judgment called for here requires simultaneous focus upon the managerial perspective and the investor perspective. The investor is searching, more or less, to

Table 9-4. Strategy Selection Matrix

Product Life Cycle	Early D, G	Growth B, E, E'	Mature A, C, E, E', F, G', G'', H, I
Is the market well understood?			
Yes		B	A, C, F, G'', H, I
No	D, G	E, E'	E, E', G'
Is the market large?			
Yes		B	A, C, G', G'', H, I
No	D, G	E, E'	E, E', F
Is the purchaser sophisticated?			
Yes	D, G	E'	E', I
No		B, E	A, C, E, F, G', G'', H

increase the market valuation of the firm over the short to medium term. The manager, on the other hand, must look to these issues but can consider the longer term as well. When the early investors cash out, the manager is faced with day-to-day stock market vicissitudes and the need to put in place longer term projects to ensure the long-term future of the firm. These two broadly drawn perspectives can then be employed as additional factors in considering the recommendations that may be appropriate to the situation revealed by the audits.

A BLENDING OF THE THREE TECHNIQUES

The concept of blending the three measures together is an attractive thought but must be pursued with considerable caution. As indicated earlier, the first instrument, the technological innovation process audit (TIPA), looks at the internal innovative potential of the firm. One question frequently comes up at this point: Just what does each risk score mean? The risk assessment scores have meaning at three levels: the individual question, the category, and overall.

First, the individual questions highlight specific areas of concern. Thus, any question which draws a 4 for an answer indicates considerable risk and suggests strongly to management that they should alter the nature of the project and/or invest in some contingency approaches to deal with this specific issue. A 3 suggests that some caution be exercised and that this specific issue be carefully monitored. A 2 suggests either a conservative choice on the part of the management or an issue which will not be a basis for competition. A 1 then is usually an indicator of a low-risk, low-innovation firm. (Many firms which are low-risk, low-innovation are highly profitable, though.)

At the category level a similar analysis can be made. Scores above 12 show very high risk in the area of the category and should serve to focus management attention on the category itself in order to reduce such risk. Scores in the 9–12 range are normal scores for high-technology firms and rather high scores for firms competing in mature market segments. The 5–8 scores are normal for mature market competitors and conservative for high-technology firms. The lowest range tends to represent either a competency that is widely shared and thus not a basis for competition or a conservative approach.

The overall risk score is usually more informative for its components then for its summary. For instance, the two examples in the next chapter score 47 and 48.8 respectively. But the firm with the lowest score overall has the highest category score, a 12 in regard to the industrial structure risk, while the apparently more risky firm evaluates its industrial structure risk as a 7. It faces instead a rather high environmental risk. The data gathered thus far from a wide range of firms in many different industries show a clustering in the overall risk evaluation but widely divergent underlying profiles. The mean is approximately 45 with a standard deviation of 4. Thus, a firm with a score over 49 is showing a serious risk and a firm under 41 is probably not competing on its technological innovation skills.

How can this analysis blend with the innovative comparison audit? The TIPA provides the analyst with a baseline understanding of the firm. Although using simple mechanical devices to blend the two together is highly questionable because of the immense loss of information and the reduction of opportunity for the exercise of managerial judgment, it is possible to consider the ICA as a potential weighting factor for the TIPA risk assessment. If your firm is above average is some areas vis-à-vis competition, your risk is somewhat lessened.

The three clusters of track record, capability of staff, and R&D cost–benefit ratio could be used to weight the technology scale. Above-average scores would reduce the risk while below-average scores would increase the risk. Similarly, the idea generation cluster could be used to weight the marketing category. The strength of R&D organization, the relation among function areas, and the time to commercialize could be used to weight the organizational category.

The technological position audit does not directly blend with the other two. This audit, in many ways, looks to current resource allocation and the future implications of these decisions. Inappropriate allocations can be seen as raising the future technological risk and the future organizational risk. Thus, the analyst should use the TPA analysis to make suggestions or offer judgments about the future and the shifting risk factors foreseen.

SUMMARY

This chapter outlined three instruments which serve as aids to decision making: the technological innovation process audit, the innovative comparison audit, and the technological position audit. The data gathered by these instruments should be further elaborated by commentary, analytically linked to appropriate technology strategies, and then viewed from an internal (managerial) and an external (investor) perspective. Taken together—instruments, commentary, analysis, and perspectives—these conceptual devices provide the manager with a solid base upon which to select strategic actions for the deployment of technology to create defensible competitive action.

The next chapter presents two examples of how the tools can be employed. One of the examples is drawn from the medical products industry; the other is drawn from the industrial electronics industry.

REFERENCES

Abernathy, W. J., and R. A. Goodman. 1972. "Strategies for Development Projects: An Empirical Study," *R&D Management* 2(3):125–29.

Arthur D. Little, Inc. 1981. "The Strategic Management of Technology." Boston: Arthur D. Little, Inc.

Freeman, C., and et al. 1972. *Success and Failure in Industrial Innovation*. Centre for the Study of Industrial Innovation, University of Sussex.

Goodman, R. 1981. *Temporary Systems: Professional Development, Manpower Utilization, Task Effectiveness and Innovation*. New York: Praeger.

Lawless, M. W. 1987. "The Structure of Strategy: A Taxonomic Study of Competitive Strategy and Technology Substrategy." University of Colorado working paper.

Lorsch, J., and P. Lawrence. 1965. "Organizing for Product Innovation," *Harvard Business Review*, January–February, pp. 109–22.

Porter, M. 1985. *Competitive Advantage: Creating and Sustaining Superior Advantage*. New York: Free Press.

Twiss, B. 1980. *Managing Technological Innovation*. London: Longman.

White, G., and M.B.W. Graham. 1978. "How to Spot a Technological Winner," *Harvard Business Review*, March–April, pp. 146–52.

10

Some Examples of the Innovation Audit

To more clearly demonstrate the value and use of the innovation audit techniques examples have been selected from the medical products and the industrial electronics industries. These examples have been disguised in order to maintain corporate confidentiality. The medical products firm produces devices that involve the cardiovascular system. The electronics firm is involved in advance microchip production. While the presentations are necessarily brief, they do demonstrate in some detail how the instruments are interpreted and then how these details are framed in order to make recommendation based upon the dual criteria of short- and long-term valuation increase (the so-called investor and management perspectives).

AN INNOVATION AUDIT OF VASCULAR SYSTEMS INC.

Vascular Systems Inc. (VSI) produces a range of disposable blood oxygenators with ever-increasing technical performance capabilities. Additionally, the firm produces physiological pressure transducers. VSI's latest innovations include the introduction of a biocompatible vascular access system and the adoption of gamma ray sterilization to replace the ethylene oxide gas sterilization technique as an important manufacturing process innovation.

The technological innovation process audit requires an analysis of a large and a small new-product innovation as well as a large and a small new-process innovation. The large new-product innovation available for analysis is VSI's new vascular access system (VS). The large new-process innovation is the employment of the gamma ray sterilization procedure (GS). Data on smaller innovations in each of the arenas were not available. The three audits are presented in Tables 10-1, 10-2, and 10-3. This is followed by Table 10-4, which shows the industrial placement of the firm in regard to its other competitors. The analysis of these four figures follows directly.

Table 10-1. Vascular Systems Inc. Technological Innovation Process Audit

Technology

1. The length of experience that the firm has with the basic technological approach it has selected is:

	<1 year	1–2 years	2–3 years	>3 years
Vascular access system	4	3	2	1
Gamma ray sterilization	4	3	2	1

2. The depth of technical experience that the firm has with the basic technological approach it has selected is:

	Analysis	Prototype	Use Test	Production
Vascular access system	4	3	2	1
Gamma ray sterilization	4	3	2	1

3. The source of innovative stimulation for the project is:

technical literature.		4
the organization itself.	[VS, GS]	3
competitors.		2
customers.		1

4. The promised performance character of the project is:

an order of magnitude increase.	[VS]	4
a shift of primary performance focus.		3
a substantial increase.	[GS]	2
a modest increase.		1

Project technological risk is sum of questions 1–4 = VS 9, GS 10

Market

5. The project faces:

an undifferentiable replacement market.		4
a modestly differentiable replacement market.	[GS]	3
a significantly differentiable replacement market.	[VS]	2
a latent market.		1

6. The market perception is derived from the:

producer.	[GS]	4
producer with limited user input.	[VS]	3
user with limited producer input.		2
user.		1

7. The level of market uncertainty is due to the project:

being never sold in the market before.	[VS, GS]	4
being sold by others in the market before.		3
being sold through others in the market before.		2
being sold and serviced by the firm before.		1

8. The project is intended:

to leapfrog the competition.		4
to improve performance.	[GS]	3
to keep up with competitive performance.	[VS]	2
to catch up with competition.		1

Project market risk is sum of questions 5–8 = VS 11, GS 14

Organization

9. The project's match to the organization's objectives is:

not at all.		4
good, but represents a major new area.	[VS]	3
good, but represents a minor new area.		2
good and in direct support of current mainline work.	[GS]	1

10. The project is an important idea of:

a single project champion.		4
a small team of technical personnel.	[VS]	3
a small team of technical and marketing personnel.		2
a systematically defined objective development.	[GS]	1

11. Cross-functional communication is achieved by:

formal memo.		4
informal liaison.		3
regular face-to-face meetings (or physical colocation).		2
all of the above.	[VS, GS]	1

12. The project requires:

dramatic changes in normal business practices.	4
significant changes in normal business practices.	3
little change in normal business practices.	2
no change in normal business practices.	1

Project organization risk is sum of questions 9–12 =   VS 10, GS 6

Environment

13. The environment is:

subject to major changes in competitors and outputs.	4
subject to uneven but rapid evolution of outputs.	3
subject to smooth but rapid evolution of outputs.	2
subject to gradual, well-understood evolution.	1

14. The regulatory climate is:

extremely complex and strict.	4
complex but well understood.	3
well understood and reasonable.	2
loosely constraining and indirect.	1

15. The underlying technological bases are:

changing rapidly and unevenly.	4
changing rapidly and smoothly.	3
changing smoothly.	2
changing gradually.	1

16. The firm depends on a supplier:

for complexly compatible input.	4
for unique parts or services.	3
for high-value parts or services with second sourcing.	2
for commonly available parts and services.	1

Firm environment risk is sum of questions 13–16   =   11

Industry Structure

17. Substitution for the firm's products and services by other technologies or from other industrial sectors:

is making rapid inroads in the industry.	4
occurs frequently.	3
occurs only occasionally.	2
is not expected to occur in the medium term.	1

18. The industry is reshaping to require:

new competence outside its mainline technology core.	4
widening its mainline technological core.	3
deepening its mainline technological core.	2
no change in its mainline technological core.	1

19. The basic industry structure has:

many participants and diverse integration strategies.	4
many participants and common integration strategies.	3
a moderate number of participants.	2
few participants.	1

20. The firm's products and services are:

complexly integrated into a systemic innovation.	4
simply integrated into a systemic innovation.	3
part of a synergistic innovation.	2
autonomous.	1

Firm industry structure risk is sum of questions 17–20   =   7

Table 10-1 (continued)

Firm Analysis
Firm technological risk is weighted average of large and small project samples from product and process innovation areas.

	Score	Times	Weight	
Large project product innovation	9	×	4	= 36
Large project process innovation	10	×	3	= 30
Small project product innovation	—	×	2	= ___
Small project process innovation	—	×	1	= ___
Subtotal				= 66
Firm technological risk score is subtotal divided by 7				= 9.4

Firm market risk is weighted average of large and small project samples from product and process innovation areas.

	Score	Times	Weight	
Large project product innovation	11	×	4	= 44
Large project process innovation	14	×	3	= 42
Small project product innovation	—	×	2	= ___
Small project process innovation	—	×	1	= ___
Subtotal				= 86
Firm market risk score is subtotal divided by 7				= 12.3

Firm organization risk is weighted average of large and small project samples from product and process innovation areas.

	Score	Times	Weight	
Large project product innovation	10	×	4	= 44
Large project process innovation	6	×	3	= 18
Small project product innovation		×	2	= ___
Small project process innovation		×	1	= ___
Subtotal				= 62
Firm organization risk score is subtotal divided by 7				= 8.8

Risk Profile
The firm's risk profile can be plotted below:

	1	2	3	4	5	6	7	8	9	10	11	12	13	14	15	16
Technology									X							
Market									X							
Organization												X				
Environment											X					
Industry structure						X										
TOTAL =																48.5

Audit Instrument Comments

Along with the numerical analysis it is important to consider that VSI is a member of a much larger firm with a strong financial backing potential and, of particular value in this instance, a strong product distribution system.

The technology factors in the TIPA indicate a tendency to enter into somewhat risky new arenas. Neither of the two newest activities is soundly based in organizational technological experience. Additionally, the market factors are also oriented more toward producer interest than firsthand knowledge of the market. This represents

Table 10-2. Vascular Systems Inc. Innovative Comparison Audit

Compared to your leading competitors (or to all your competitors), how does your firm rate on each of these questions?

	Much Below Average	Below Average	Average	Above Average	Much Above Average
Track Record					
New-product introductions				X	
Costs of production			X		
Success of new products				X	
First mover record			X		
Contribution of new products to sales and profits				X	
Capability of Staff					
Size of R&D staff			X		
Discipline diversity				X	
Experience level of staff				X	
Reputation of staff			X		
Strength of R&D Organization					
Flexibility				X	
Anticipation skills				X	
Ability to execute long-term projects			X		
Reliability of communication			X		
Idea Generation					
Robustness of ideas			X		
Breadth of base in firm from which ideas arise			X		
Mechanisms for evaluating new ideas			X		
Time to Commercialize					
Time from start to market introduction		X			
Time from introduction to full-scale marketing			X		
Time to derive learning curve benefits on costs		X			
Costs/Benefits of R&D					
R&D costs relative to life cycle revenues			X		
Relations among Functional Areas					
Smoothness of transfer from R&D to marketing and manufacturing			X		

Table 10-3. Vascular Systems Inc. Technological Position Audit

List of Product Technologies Base	Investment Level
Blood oxygenators	L
Transducers	L
Key	Investment Level
Vascular access system	SB
List of Process Technologies Base	Investment Level
Basic manufacturing skills	L
Key	Investment Level
Disposable blood-compatible material	SB
Pacing	Investment Level
Gamma ray sterilization	SI

Note: Investment levels include little (L), systematically built (SB), selective investment (SI), and monitoring (M).

a second level of risk. The organizational factors do not exacerbate the market and technological risk as the projects represent firm objectives; and communication, partially due to the small size of the firm, is good. The process innovation seemingly has stronger value for the firm and is reported as more in line with the firm's objectives. The riskiest portion of the project is the combination of a complex regulatory environment (normal in the medical products arena) and heavy reliance on suppliers for unique materials and subcontracting of the gamma ray sterilization process. On the

Table 10-4. Vascular Systems Inc. Industry Placement

Blood oxygenators	
VSI	40%
Six others each with 10%	60%
Transducers	
SH	40%
VSI	20%
Four others each with 10%	40%
Vascular access systems	
VSI	1%
RS	1%
Older technology	98%

other hand, the industry structure is relatively benign. The market can respond to new products without dramatic competitive responses as the market consists of several firms with relatively similar market shares.

The ICA analysis shows a firm that is above average within the industry in pursuit of the key innovation processes. The one major exception to this is in the area of commercialization of new products, where VSI is judged to be slow. Thus, from a competitive perspective the risk factors of the TIPA can be judged to be less serious as the ICA shows some above-average competitive position. The slowness in time to commercialize, though, is a serious caution that must be factored into the managerial judgment about how to proceed. The technological position audit (TPA) reinforces this last concern as it shows only a limited outreach to pacing technology and no connection to emerging technology. Thus, serious changes in the basis of competition seem unlikely for this firm.

The industry placement report indicates three sectors, two of which are relatively evenly held by a limited number of competitors. None of the firms seems to be seriously exhibiting market power in the transducer or the oxygenator sectors. The vascular access system is in its very early stages and needs to gain medical acceptance over the earlier technology. (The contrast here is a vein implant versus repeated venipuncture.)

Linkages to Technology Strategies

For the reader's convenience the strategy selection matrix is reproduced as Table 10-5. Formal linkage to the selection of technology strategies involves concern about the nature of the product, the market, and the customer. For Vascular Systems Inc. the assessment of purchaser sophistication is an important starting point. Then, working up the left-hand side of the matrix, market questions come to the fore. What is the relative size and/or potential of the market? How well does or can the firm comprehend the nature and dynamics of the market? And finally, the last step in this linkage process considers the position of the product within the product life cycle.

Table 10-5. Strategy Selection Matrix

	Product Life Cycle		
	Early D, G	Growth B, E, E′	Mature A, C, E, E′, F, G′, G″, H, I
Is the market well understood?			
Yes		B	A, C, F, G″, H, I
No	D, G	E, E′	E, G′
Is the market large?			
Yes		B	A, C, G′, G″, H, I
No	D, G	E, E′	E, E′, F
Is the purchaser sophisticated?			
Yes	D, G	E′	E′, I
No		B, E	A, C, E, F, G′, G″, H

Is the purchaser sophisticated? Unless asked very carefully, the answer to this question would undoubtedly be yes. While the purchaser is sophisticated about whether a vascular access system versus repeated venipuncture is appropriate, the system itself represents a relatively small part of the patient treatment system and its costs are therefore only a tiny portion of the patient or physician costs. There may be some real saving in nursing costs and some potential simplification in patient management. By and large, however, the purchaser of this system does not employ detailed specifications, detailed acceptance testing, fierce competitive bidding, and the like, in making purchasing decisions and is therefore not a sophisticated purchaser.

Is the market large? There are many illnesses which require constant medication. Although time release capsules and transdermal patches serve many purposes for outpatients, they are not yet considered serious replacement technologies for inpatient medications. On the other hand, the system's relatively low price and the relatively small demonstrable savings that the customer would realize counters such a market size judgment. On balance, however, it is reasonable to assume the market will be large; the most reasonable judgment then is that the potential for high unit volume will provide scale economies.

Is the market well understood? Simply answered, yes. What is the product life cycle stage? Early. When narrowly interpreting these factors, the early stage of the product life cycle would dominate and either a D (producer preference) or a G (product pioneer) strategy is indicated. The basic differences between the two strategies involve technological complexity and thus long-term benefits from experience curve effects and from uncertain imitability. Both these factors provide a relatively defensible first mover advantage for the product pioneer. In this situation technological complexity is not great and successful copying would normally be expected. The firm's basic strengths in other products suggests that in the longer run competition will not be very strong. As the product reaches maturity the continuing investment in manufacturing processes, as indicated by strategy B during the growth stage and strategy A in the mature stage, will allow VSI to maintain a good market share but at conservative margins.

Internal (Managerial) and External (Investor) Perspectives

From the outside investor's perspective the apparent paucity of opportunity keeps this firm from being attractive in the three- to five-year time frame. The relative lack of attention being paid to the technological potential as evidenced by little knowledge of pacing and emerging technology coupled with the market share of the existing product lines suggests that dramatic growth should not be expected. While solid performance should continue, significant upside movement in the VSI valuation is unlikely.

Management, on the other hand, can safely look to a variety of technology strategies. The nature of the medical products market is one that would accept a proven improvement or new product given a strong distribution system. Thus, the reliance of VSI on its parent firm and on the parent firm's distributive power permits VSI to continue a producer preference strategy. VSI would first need to exploit its detailed knowledge of blood transportation systems and particularly biostatic materials as implants and/or as disposables. The monitoring of biostatic material development would be a valuable long-run investment. In the shorter term, market analysis of potential products might direct the firm's current investments into areas where 10–20 percent market share was likely and away from areas where the expected share was less. Thus, technology scanning coupled with medical practice–oriented market research would provide VSI with a substantial intellectual base on which to pursue a producer preference strategy. (This analysis has been drawn from the work of Quirk, 1983.)

Note that the foregoing analysis still requires a significant amount of managerial judgment. The slow development of new products is probably the most dramatic finding and this factor is, of course, suggestive of less than dramatic growth. Thus, as an investment opportunity VSI is not especially attractive. On the other hand, a larger medical products firm with good distribution channels could (and in this case did) provide synergies which an outside investor could not. Obviously, the managerial perspective would be quite different from that of the outside investor.

AN INNOVATION AUDIT OF INTEGRATED PRODUCTS INC.

Integrated Products Inc. (IPI) is an integrated circuit manufacturer that produces products for the digital signal processing industry. It was founded in 1976 and is a rather small player in the overall integrated circuit industry. Its products are 16-bit multipliers, analog-to-digital (A/D) and digital-to-analog (D/A) converters, multiplier-accumulators, and shift registers. The products have application in video digital signal processing, computer-assisted tomography (CAT) and ultrasound equipment, telecommunications, and a range of military uses. The three audit results are shown in Tables 10-6, 10-7, and 10-8. The analysis of these audits follows directly.

Audit Instruments Comments

The technology innovation process audit identifies a great many extant individual risk factors. The rate of technology change is high. There is an orientation toward achieving order of magnitude product improvements. The industry is rapidly changing in regard to both competitors and customers. The technology is both widening and deepening at a rapid rate. And there is reliance on one project champion for each new product innovation.

The innovative comparison audit indicates that IPI has difficulty achieving early production cost reductions necessary to take advantage of the early phase of product introduction when higher prices can be charged and early recoupment of R&D expenses can be accomplished. Overall the ICA shows IPI to be average in comparison with the competitors in the industry. Thus, management concern about the riskiness of the IPI innovation process cannot be mitigated by a strong competitive position. This concern is reinforced by the results of the TPA. The technological position audit indicates a limited effort on the part of IPI to keep in touch systematically with rapidly moving technology. A "custom design" strategy is required to keep up systematically with changes in data signal processing needs, for example, but satisfying customer needs will often require new integrated circuit technology, which in turn requires constant updates of the wafer fabrication capability.

Table 10-6. Integrated Products Inc. Technological Innovation Process Audit

Technology

1. The length of experience that the firm has with the basic technological approach it has selected is:

	<1 year	1–2 years	2–3 years	>3 years
Subsystem technologies	4	3	2	1

2. The depth of technical experience that the firm has with the basic technological approach it has selected is:

	Analysis	Prototype	Use Test	Production
Subsystem technologies	4	3	2	1

3. The source of innovative stimulation for the project is:
   technical literature. 4
   the organization itself. 3
   competitors. 2
   customers. 1
4. The promised performance character of the project is:
   an order of magnitude increase. 4
   a shift of primary performance focus. 3
   a substantial increase. 2
   a modest increase. 1

Project technological risk is sum of questions 1–4   = 9

Market

5. The project faces:
   an undifferentiable replacement market. 4
   a modestly differentiable replacement market. 3
   a significantly differentiable replacement market. 2
   a latent market. 1
6. The market perception is derived from the:
   producer. 4
   producer with limited user input. 3
   user with limited producer input. 2
   user. 1
7. The level of market uncertainty is due to the project:
   being never sold in the market before. 4
   being sold by others in the market before. 3
   being sold through others in the market before. 2
   being sold and serviced by the firm before. 1
8. The project is intended:
   to leapfrog the competition. 4
   to improve performance. 3
   to keep up with competitive performance. 2
   to catch up with competition. 1

Project market risk is sum of questions 5–8   = 9

Organization

9. The project's match to the organization's objectives is:
   not at all. 4
   good, but represents a major new area. 3
   good, but represents a minor new area. 2
   good and in direct support of current mainline work. 1

Table 10-6 Integrated Products Inc. Technological Innovation Process Audit *(Continued)*

10. The project is an important idea of:
a single project champion.	**4**
a small team of technical personnel.	3
a small team of technical and marketing personnel.	2
a systematically defined objective development.	1

11. Cross-functional communication is achieved by:
formal memo.	4
informal liaison.	3
regular face-to-face meetings (or physical colocation).	2
all of the above.	1

12. The project requires:
dramatic changes in normal business practices.	4
significant changes in normal business practices	3
little change in normal business practices	2
no change in normal business practices.	**1**

Project organization risk is sum of questions 9–12   = <u>9</u>

Environment

13. The environment is:
subject to major changes in competitors and outputs.	4
subject to uneven but rapid evolution of outputs.	**3**
subject to smooth but rapid evolution of outputs.	2
subject to well-understood evolution.	1

14. The regulatory climate is:
extremely complex and strict.	4
complex but well understood.	3
well understood and reasonable.	2
loosely constraining and indirect.	**1**

15. The underlying technological bases are:
changing rapidly and unevenly.	**4**
changing rapidly and smoothly.	3
changing smoothly.	2
changing gradually.	1

16. The firm depends on a supplier:
for complexly compatible input.	4
for unique parts or services.	3
for high-value parts or services with second sourcing.	2
for commonly available parts and services.	**1**

Firm environment risk is sum of questions 13–16   = <u>9</u>

Industry Structure

17. Substitution for the firm's products and services by other technologies or from other industrial sectors:
is making rapid inroads in the industry.	4
occurs frequently.	**3**
occurs only occasionally.	2
is not expected to occur in the medium term.	1

18. The industry is reshaping to require:
new competence outside its mainline technology core.	4
widening its mainline technological core.	**3**
deepening its mainline technological core.	2
no change in its mainline technological core.	1

19. The basic industry structure has:

many participants and diverse integration strategies.	**4**
many participants and common integration strategies.	3
a moderate number of participants.	2
few participants.	1

20. The firm's products and services are:

complexly integrated into a systemic innovation.	4
simply integrated into a systemic innovation.	3
part of a synergistic innovation.	**2**
autonomous.	1
Firm industry structure risk is sum of questions 17–20	= <u>12</u>

Risk Profile

The firm's risk profile can be plotted below:

	1	2	3	4	5	6	7	8	9	10	11	12	13	14	15	16
Technology									X							
Market									X							
Organization									X							
Environment									X							
Industry structure												X				
TOTAL																= <u>48</u>

Table 10-7. Integrated Products Inc. Innovative Comparison Audit

Compared to your leading competitors (or to all your competitors), how does your firm rate on each of these questions?

	Much Below Average	Below Average	Average	Above Average	Much Above Average
Track Record					
New-product introductions	_____	_____	_X_	_____	_____
Costs of production	_____	_X_	_____	_____	_____
Success of new products	_____	_____	_____	_X_	_____
First mover record	_____	_____	_____	_____	_X_
Contribution of new products to sales and profits	_____	_X_	_____	_____	_____
Capability of Staff					
Size of R&D staff	_____	_____	_X_	_____	_____
Discipline diversity	_____	_____	_X_	_____	_____
Experience level of staff	_____	_X_	_____	_____	_____
Reputation of staff	_____	_____	_____	_X_	_____
Strength of R&D Organization					
Flexibility	_____	_____	_____	_X_	_____
Anticipation skills	_____	_X_	_____	_____	_____
Ability to execute long-term projects	_____	_____	_X_	_____	_____
Reliability of communication	_____	_X_	_____	_____	_____

Table 10-7 Integrated Products Inc. Innovative Comparison Audit *(Continued)*

Idea Generation					
Robustness of ideas	_____	_____	X	_____	_____
Breadth of base in firm from which ideas arise	_____	_____	X	_____	_____
Mechanisms for evaluating new ideas	_____	_____	X	_____	_____
Time to Commercialize					
Time from start to market introduction	_____	_____	X	_____	_____
Time from introduction to full-scale marketing	_____	_____	X	_____	_____
Time to derive learning curve benefits on costs	_____	_____	X	_____	_____
Costs/Benefits of R&D					
R&D costs relative to life cycle revenues	_____	X	_____	_____	_____
Relations among Functional Areas					
Smoothness of transfer from R&D to marketing and manufacturing	_____	_____	X	_____	_____

Table 10-8. Integrated Products Inc. Technological Position Audit

List of Product Technologies Base	Investment Level
Metal oxide semiconductors	SI
Bipolar semiconductors	L
Key	Investment Level
Digital signal processing	SI
List of Process Technologies Base	Investment Level
Wafer fabrication	SB

Note: Investment levels include little (L), systematically built (SB), selective investment (SI), and monitoring (M).

The firm is a division of a much larger corporation which subscribes to investment for the longer term and basically understands the role of heavy R&D investment for a firm such as this. Senior management in this firm has been drawn from the ranks of applications engineering, which is an indicator of the relationship of the firm to its market. There are several much larger firms doing very well in the integrated circuits business. Thus, IPI faces a need to differentiate itself from firms that have progressed to the commodity portion of the integrated circuit cycle. Normally the commodity portion might be seen as a period of industry maturity, but in this case the rapidly moving technological front requires the major firms to follow a technology leadership strategy to avoid quickly falling behind.

Once again for ease of reference, the strategy selection matrix has been reproduced as Table 10-9. The formal linkage to the selection of technology strategies involves concern about the nature of the product, the market, and the customer. For Integrated Products Inc. the assessment of the purchaser sophistication is an important starting point. Then, working up the left-hand side of the matrix, market questions quickly emerge. What is the relative size and/or potential of the market? How well does or can the firm comprehend the nature and dynamics of the market? And finally, the last step in this linkage process is consideration of the product's position within the product life cycle.

Is the purchaser sophisticated? No. This is evidenced by the firm's decision to work closely with individual customers and to create a synergistic chip design for specific applications. Customers are unable either to provide design specifications or to use competitive bidding in the purchasing process. Is the market large? On a niche-by-niche basis the market is not large. Is the market well understood? On a customer-by-customer basis the market is well understood. What is the stage in the product life cycle? From an application-by-application perspective, it is probably early, but the basic ability to design custom chips is a good example of a mature stage in the life cycle.

Taken together the answers suggest an E (customer preference) strategy, which echoes precisely the general description of the firm. Here the manufacturing process

Table 10-9. Strategy Selection Matrix

	Product Life Cycle		
	Early D, G	Growth B, E, E'	Mature A, C, E, E', F, G', G'', H, I
Is the market well understood?			
Yes		B	A, C, F, G'', H, I
No	D, G	E, E'	E, E', G'
Is the market large?			
Yes		B	A, C, G', G'', H, I
No	D, G	E, E'	E, E', F
Is the purchaser sophisticated?			
Yes	D, G	E'	E', I
No		B, E	A, C, E, F, G', G'', H

must permit some range of flexibility while at the same time providing some scale economies. Sales to individual firms command premium prices since the chips are specialized, but by themselves they are not a major cost component in the customers' competitive position. Rather, the function of the specialized chip will probably be the basis of competition for Integrated Product's customers.

Internal (Managerial) and External (Investor) Perspectives

In the short run this is not a firm that is likely to grow dramatically and earn growth premiums as part of its valuation. In the short to medium term, the firm will make only expensive and hard-earned progress. The basic technology strategy recommended here is a customer preference strategy. The firm has demonstrated an ability to work with customers to create synergistic chip design for specific applications—a niche strategy. Again the importance of exercising managerial judgment is highlighted in the commentary. But it is clear that this firm assumes risk positions by investing in technology without employing a strategy aimed at earning exceptional returns from these risks. (This analysis has been drawn from the work of Giansante and Parris, 1983.)

SUMMARY

This chapter and the last two have focused on the role of technological programs as a framework for analyzing the firms' systematic applications of technology to improving strategic positioning and operational effectiveness. The technological program concept forces management to consider explicitly the technological risk associated with new product and process development and offers some guidance for reducing this risk. An investment in new technology and in the application of that new technology should be made in response to its leverage regarding the firm's position and the industry's maturity. Leverage is possible if the investment promises to change the basis of competition within the industry. The technique of the innovation audit was offered to make more explicit the relationship between the firm's abilities and the appropriate technology strategies that the firm might follow as well as to provide a methodology for creating a priority matrix for assigning resources to the development or monitoring of new technologies based upon leverage now and in the future.

REFERENCES

Giansante, J., and S. Parris. 1983. "An Innovation Audit: Integrated Products, Inc." Los Angeles: Graduate School of Management, University of California, Los Angeles.

Quirk, P. 1983. "Innovation Audit: Vascular Systems Inc." Los Angeles: Graduate School of Management, University of California, Los Angeles.

III

TECHNOLOGICAL CONNECTIONS TO OTHER STRATEGIC ISSUES

The earlier portions of this book have been focused upon the questions of technology and strategy and technology-strategy tools. This focus began in a broad context and continued to narrow as the work progressed. This narrowing has been consciously pursued in order to clearly focus upon the central issue of the book—technology and strategy.

There are several aspects of strategy that rightly demand special consideration by the manager. In these issue areas technology per se plays a role but is not the main focus. Here in Part III we consider some of the other important strategy issues within which technology has a role.

The first chapter of this part, "Thinking about Technology," focuses on the broad sweep of economic development and the role of environmental variables in the encouragement or discouragement of evolutionary or revolutionary development processes. The role of management and the role of entrepreneurship are explored within various environmental contexts.

The second chapter of this part, "Technology, Core Competence, and the Resource-Based View," offers a very different perspective. Within this chapter the core competence idea is carefully articulated. Most firms have a portfolio of abilities that describe their defensible advantage. One competence may be specifically technological while another may be a combination of abilities. Both direct and supporting roles of technology in the building of a competence portfolio are described.

Chapter 13, "Technology and Strategy Issues in Improved Quality," presents another important strategic thrust which relies upon technology in a number of ways but does so within a larger vision. The similarities among the three apparently disparate strategic issues are used as a frame for the presentation of both the visions and the support functions of technology to these visions.

11

Thinking About Technology

Technology can have a strong, direct effect on both competitive strategy and its resultant performance. As technology has the potential to alter the balance of market power, it is an important element in formulating strategy. While the same technology is not available to all, its potential effects can be altered or captured by competitive action. Not surprisingly, performance is determined by the interaction of technologically based strategic moves among competitors. The potential impacts of technology suggest that it plays a principal role as a source of change in both organizational environments and competitive markets. In fact, analysts following Schumpeter's theories (to be discussed shortly) argue that technology is the driving factor behind radical shifts in the market. These theorists suggest strongly that technology will continue to play this role in the future.

Because of the strong role that technology plays, and because its interactions with other forces are complex, it is a problem to manage. Like other forces in the environment, it is possible to affect, but impossible to actually control technology. Although difficult, it is necessary to be both reactive and proactive in formulating strategy. The strategy-making process must take into account the nature of technological change and the ensuing implications to competitive position as well as the possibility of unanticipated technological developments that may arise from competitive circumstances. In either reacting to or forecasting technological change, the nature of technological development must be well understood. Organizations that have achieved a sophisticated understanding of the dynamics of technology are in a better position to develop competencies with which they can react appropriately to environmental and market changes.

TECHNOLOGY AS REVOLUTIONARY OR EVOLUTIONARY

The first half of this chapter contains broad conceptual frames for viewing technology. The ideas presented here are gathered from practitioners of the "dismal science" of economics and from some very practical philosophers of science. These authors have seen the value and importance of technology proven over substantial time periods; to some extent it is these extensive time periods that give the theories their basic plausibility. Their debate is centered on the question of revolution or evolution: Does technology develop smoothly over time or are there significant discontinuities in the process?

This chapter presents four issues as frames for understanding the revolutionary versus evolutionary question posed above. We begin with the idea of technological change as a proactive process—one which is potentially destabilizing. Then technological change is examined as a reactive and incremental process. The analysis of the impacts of social systems and of basic environmental conditions concludes the discussion.

Driving Forces for Technological Change

This conceptual frame focuses initially on the broad societal impacts brought about by technological forces. It then deals with the underlying factors that create such forces. This is a unique economic frame of reference as it contains two very different underlying paradigms. It employs basic economic theory to analyze the impact of technological change on market conditions—a traditional and not unexpected set of concepts. But the very nature of the technological changes and their resultant impact is posited as a natural outcome of certain underlying behavioral characteristics. In this case entrepreneurs pursuing vision (not rationality) create technology, which can and does radically restructure the nature of the marketplace.

Traditional economists looking at technological change would simply predict another equilibrium condition with some shift in the market share among the current competitors. They would be loath to predict a radical market restructuring. The traditional analysis of technological impact would suggest that all too soon the innovator's competitors would be able to readjust and recapture some of the market share lost by virtue of their own improvements. These arguments, while admitting to an innovation-based reason for a certain fluidity in market share, are essentially homeostatic concepts suggesting dynamic readjustment in response to stable conditions. Joseph Schumpeter disagrees.

Considered by many the most influential writer on technological change, Schumpeter (1976) created a framework that is among the most useful and visible models for studying the effects of technology on markets. He described innovation as the driving force of long-term economic progress, as the cause of economic cycles, and as the determinant of the level of competition in industries. Innovation creates new products and new processes, requires new key market competencies, results in new competitors, and hastens the exit of some traditional rivals. Innovation is, in his view, essentially a force for disequilibrium and the cause of revolutionary restructuring of markets. The entire economic system moves toward a new and different state and the return from discontinuous change to preexisting market conditions is virtually impossible.

In some instances, new technology creates whole new markets where none existed previously. The transistor created a massive change in the electronics industry. The popularity of digital computers based on transistor technology spread rapidly. Use of personal computers spread into the home from the office as semiconductor technology became more sophisticated. The "information society" has spread to the office and home. Many substantially new retail and industrial markets have evolved from these technologically driven events, and the major participants in these new markets are equally new. Even in existing markets technology has the power to change the nature of the market. It can effect the intrinsic demand for products, the cost and price structures, and the barriers to entry—it can have a powerful generalized impact on competitive conditions (Marx, 1973; Butler, 1988).

Practically speaking, strategists need to understand the potential that technology has—the potential to disrupt the conditions under which they have been competing. It can significantly change the rules of the game, requiring new decisions about the strategic deployment of resources. The strategic implications that one might take would be very different if one were predicting only a shifting of market share versus a radical change in the basis of competition. Within Schumpeter's framework, the technology effect is cyclical, but discontinuity is, most emphatically, the primary force behind most economic change (Tushman and Anderson, 1986).

Within Schumpeter's model the entrepreneur is the most important figure—the source of innovative activity, of market disequilibrium, and ultimately of economic growth. Through implementing new combinations of the "means of production," in Schumpeter's terms, the entrepreneur's innovative activity pushes the market out of its equilibrium state. His entrepreneur serves as a guidepost for advanced analysis of innovation and diffusion.

Elster (1983) paraphrases Schumpeter on the motivation of entrepreneurs: "[one,] the dream and the will to found a private kingdom, two, the will to conquer, three, the joy of creating." This behavioral drive to take an irrational position coupled with the willingness to take risks is what creates the likelihood of a disjoint or radical innovation rather than the incremental change that a more analytic or rational manager might prefer.

In contrast, the decision maker of neoclassical economics makes rational choices that serve the goal of maximizing profit. He or she innovates to the extent that there is a rational motive for it, in other words, that it results in greater profits than not innovating. This description sounds arid and somewhat mechanical next to Schumpeter's entrepreneur.

In the context of earlier economic analysis, Schumpeter's attention to the personal characteristics of the entrepreneur is revolutionary. His work points out, at an early stage in the development of thought on innovation, these important issues for management. The entrepreneur is a source of change and growth to be reckoned with both inside the firm and out. Inside the firm, entrepreneurial activity is a source of competitive advantage through innovation. The attendant management problems are the cost of fitting such activity into an organization that has some stability. Outside the firm, entrepreneurs tend to disrupt industry norms, increase the intensity of competition, and pressure other firms toward making their own investment in innovation.

Competition and Imitation

The economists Nelson and Winter (1982) emphasize the long-term tendency for firms to compete on the basis of their own "repertoires" and on imitation of their successful rivals. Their model serves as a counterpart to Schumpeter's, since it treats the stable part of the economy/technology life cycle. It is based on the idea, originated by the Carnegie Institute of Technology economists Cyert and March (1963), that much of the decision making among competing firms is based on precedent. Strategists tend to make decisions by matching current problems with ones successfully resolved in the past. They simply apply the previous solution. Moreover, repertoires and competitive strategy formulation generally involve a degree of imitation. In particular, successful firms' approaches to the market are copied by competitors.

Nelson and Winter frame the problem of strategy development as one of differentiation. Successful firms are those that find ways to exploit their unique qualities. In other words, they isolate themselves from the competition and create a monopoly situation through differentiation. Technology provides an avenue through which the firms can evolve continuously and maintain a lead on their competitors by relying upon their unique advantages. Technology is therefore clearly a force in their model—a model based upon a particular evolutionary perspective of industry. Technological change can be influenced by the firm, through R&D investments, for example, and has the potential to provide the firm with a continuous source of differentiation from imitating rivals and a source of competitive advantage. (See also similar work of Chamberlin, 1933; Rumelt, 1974; Lippman and Rumelt, 1982; Barney, 1986; and Teece, 1987.)

Technology is therefore one force in an evolutionary process in which firms assume market positions based on their endowments, their investments, and external market forces. Their potential to maintain differentiated practices in the face of imitation affects their long-term profits.

Innovation and Social Systems

The economic analysis of innovation, as a revolutionary force or an evolutionary force, is limited by its adoption of a simplifying assumption relating to human and organizational behavior. The essence of the assumption downplays the effects of friction within the smooth flowing of societal change. On the contrary, a full analysis of the innovation adoption process must take into account that social systems or milieus are resistant to innovation in rather complicated ways. Thus, the simplification employed in a straightforward (or linear) model of the innovation diffusion process is likely to be misleading. Specifying the user cost–benefit relationship (the traditional economic approach) is a necessary but not sufficient explanation of the process. Similarly, the traditional marketing models of information dissemination and communication are often insufficient. Conversely, a "general systems" analysis of the social system impact provides a richer assumption base for understanding the process. And this richer understanding will enhance strategy formulation and implementation processes.

In simplified terms, the concept of social system refers to an established pattern of relationships which is reasonably well known and stable. Broadly speaking the organization is symbolized by a patterned set of relationships among its members and its functional entities. Generalizing from this, a social system concept also includes the patterned relationship among organizational units—firms and suppliers, government and governed, customers and providers, competitors and competitors. Stability among such relationships is ephemeral, but we can easily accept a notion of relative stability versus rapid change. Due to the inherent complexity of most social systems in the first place, change generally requires the system's members to engage in a fairly compli- cated calculus in order to reach a preferred new equilibrium. This calculus is even more difficult when the change rate is high. Thus, in many ways these general charac- teristics of social systems provide some theoretical limits to the rate at which innova- tion can be adopted.

As asserted earlier, technology and markets have a reciprocal impact. The broad social system within which the changes are embedded affects both the speed and mag- nitude with which a new technology changes markets and organizational environ- ments. General responsiveness to innovation as a matter of culture or industry norms, perceived need of users for a new product or process, communication of the innova- tion, and the nature of information about the innovation—all have significant influence on the rate and direction of adoption. This tendency to adopt or resist, a dimension of the social system, is exacerbated by the more narrowly drawn resistance to change that is a common behavioral feature of most individuals when faced with uncertainty (Tan- nenbaum, 1976).

A firm's ability to sell a new product and the speed with which the product pene- trates the market are generally enhanced when the product has only a limited impact on the social system. On the other hand, significant disruptions, causing a social system to go into disequilibrium, are a potential threat to existing members of the system. Such innovations are likely to be strongly resisted. In operational terms, individuals and groups of people in organizational units are likely to feel threatened by change and are therefore likely to avoid or resist it. In conceptual terms, resistance (either strong or weak) comes from inertia, or the natural tendency of a system to adapt minimally. While diffusion of any innovation faces various resistances, diffusion of an innovation which is moderately or strongly disruptive becomes a very complicated matter. Donald Schon (1963) describes this resistance as "dynamic conservatism"—a force in the sys- tem to restore the system to the old equilibrium.

General systems theory provides Schon with the starting point for his model of the innovation process. His ideas are especially useful for looking at differences in the ways innovations affect the social systems in which they are placed. Schon makes a special point of isolating innovations that destabilize significant portions of their sur- roundings from those that cause a small amount of localized change. For example, the personal computer has fundamentally changed the nature of computing with the possi- ble exception of work requiring very large data bases. Almost all computer usage, office automation systems, word processors, spread sheet, file management capabili- ties, and more, are now available to individuals who once depended on mainframes or on nonautomated methods. On the other hand, the hard disk drive has enhanced per- sonal computing capabilities with only localized effects. It has increased the power of the personal computer without having the same effect on the overall state of comput- ing. The former was "disruptive" and became widely diffused only because of the enormous power it provided for its users. The latter is not disruptive and diffused mainly as an upgrade to an existing system. (See also Henderson and Clark, 1990, and Abernathy and Utterback, 1978, for similar discussions.)

Schon's social system and behavioral orientation are helpful complements to those working on the economics of innovation when more disruptive innovations are consid- ered. Von Hippel (1978), for one, stresses the importance of benefits as an issue in the degree to which any firm is innovative. His empirical findings emphasize that firms have an incentive to innovate if they have the ability to prevent rivals from copying their new products or processes and can keep them from expropriating the returns. In contrast with Schon, those using an economic foundation to study innovation will recommend change that either cannot be easily imitated or can be protected with patents or other entry barriers. But these same innovations are the ones that will inevitably face the most social system resistance.

The innovation adoption process is complex. It is not closed and determined—moving from a given starting point to an outcome that can be forecast. Neither is it linear, or even predictable in a way that permits significantly improved strategic decision making. Learning about innovation by observing or surveying early adopters can significantly reduce costs for later adopters. Such time-dependent economies are an important issue to firms that seek competitive advantage through innovation. (This latter comment refers to the values of "second mover advantage" or "product followers" in certain circumstances.) Management decisions in such cases will interact with events and processes that they will not be able to control, or perhaps even predict.

Diffusion of the system-type innovation is likely to be more complex than the traditional model indicates. An innovation, for example, may not have been completed before diffusion begins, but instead may evolve during the process. Second, and more important, there may be many sources from which the innovation spreads, leading to variations based on local needs and environmental conditions.

Technology and Competitive Environments

When strategists consider questions of innovation and technological change, technology is generally considered as an independent variable in a broad array of environmental factors. As a result, the link between technology and individual firms—with minimal attention to intervening forces—is emphasized in treatments of strategy and technology. Firms are said to react to technology: their R&D investments are tied to the current stage of the life cycle, production processes are based on greatest efficiency given the current technology state, and competitive strategy is geared to technology parameters.

It is possible, however, to draw a more comprehensive picture of the relationship between technology and competitive strategy and to treat technology as an independent variable affecting conditions in the environment. Tushman and Anderson (1986) did this in order to trace the effects of technological discontinuities on competitive conditions. They argue that environmental dimensions of uncertainty, complexity, and munificence depend in part on the state of technology for the industry. By adding this intervening level, the means by which technology influences organizational outcomes can be understood more completely.

When Dess and Beard (1984) conducted a broadly based review of the literature on organizational environments they concluded that environments can be reasonably represented using only three dimensions: munificence, dynamism, and complexity.

Munificence. Firms are most likely to be situated in environments that allow them both to grow and to maintain stability. In such environments firms can gain access to resources sufficient to set up and support coalitions such as R&D consortia, to maintain essential activities during periods of scarcity, and to invest in further innovation. In some analyses, like the learning curve and Boston Consulting Group approaches, munificence is measured by sales growth. In others, such as industrial organization–based strategy studies, munificence is measured by industry profitability.

Dynamism. Environments can also be described by levels of change. Dynamism is measured by constructs such as turnover, the presence or absence of a pattern in change occurring over time, and the predictability of changes. In dynamic industries, firms will try to reduce the level of uncertainty to the maximum extent possible by developing specialists, signing long-term contracts, stockpiling, and integrating vertically.

Complexity. Highly complex industries require that competitors procure and manage many varied inputs and produce a wide range of outputs that permits firms to interact with many other organizations: suppliers, customers, and competitors. Higher complexity means that more factors must be considered when formulating strategy and that there are more variables to contend with when strategy is implemented.

These three dimensions suggest that technology can be applied in a variety of ways. In a munificent environment there is more "space" or "slack" for entrepreneurship both within and outside existing firms. In dynamic environments uncertainty in technological investment provokes the firm into taking action to avoid uncertainty, which tends to put a damper on nascent entrepreneurial behavior. The more complexity that a firm must deal with, the more room there is for isolating mechanisms based upon technology to take hold. Again, such an environment is an opportunity for entrepreneurial activity.

Meta-Level Technological Frames Integrated

For effective management and strategic analysis, the diverse frames must be brought together in a simplified fashion. The apparently divergent issues of entrepreneurship versus management; of revolution versus evolution; of munificence, dynamism, and complexity; and of social system characteristics can be logically arrayed in three broad theoretical arguments. Such logical assemblages provide theory-based grounds for organizational planning and implementation while simultaneously providing fertile ground for empirical verification.

First, the work of Schumpeter, Nelson and Winter, and Schon can be logically intertwined as shown in Table 11-1. The potential effects of the entrepreneur, the manager, and the social system with respect to technologically based shifts in the market are shown. During periods of revolutionary change entrepreneurs seem to play major

Table 11-1. Revolution, Evolution, and Social Systems

	Revolutionary Change	Evolutionary Change
Role of entrepreneur	Major	Minor
Role of manager	Minor	Major
Role of social system	Resistive	Benign

roles; during evolutionary periods they play a more subdued role. Conversely, during periods of evolutionary change effective management assumes a major role, occupying a more subtle role during revolutionary periods. The social system is a resistive force to revolutionary change and benign to evolutionary change.

In practice such a descriptive argument is only academic unless the underlying causal factors are explicitly articulated. Managers need to understand what they can control and to anticipate what they cannot control. There are two factors which empirical analysis would probably show to be causal here: the unevenness of invention and the incalculable complexity of the social system. To bring about revolutions, technological or otherwise, requires ideas or inventions. Serious technological revolutions cause the reconfiguration of a large number of elements—many themselves recently invented or discovered. This is essentially a creative act and not subject to effective analysis; therefore, it is unlikely to be successfully planned and managed. Thus, many creative acts (from many different entrepreneurs or inventors) need to be attempted in order to arrive at a set that is revolutionary.

In a similar fashion, the basic complexity of the social system inhibits revolution as the calculation or determination of the correct bundle of goods, services, and necessary performance parameters cannot not be easily determined. For revolution to occur many entrepreneurs must be active to generate many variations for many different elements so that a successful combination might be formulated. In such a situation it can be argued that the environment selects, in the Darwinian sense, the most successful formula. The evidence used to support such an environmental selection process is the frequent occurrence of industry shakeouts, usually after a dynamic shift in an industry—when the many variations that spring up to take advantage of the changes (i.e., different firms and different products) are inexorably reduced to but a few viable solutions.

Given an appropriate stock of inventions and ideas, entrepreneurial activity is required to generate the many solutions needed within a complex social system to create the possibility of revolutionary technological change. A more modest stock of invention and idea permits only evolutionary change and hence requires only good analytic skills on the part of management to understand (rather than change) the extant social system. Thus, evolutionary development reflects issues that are more or less within the control of the management.

A second summary argument (Table 11-2) connects the Schumpeterian analysis with the environmental conditions concepts of Dess and Beard. This table summarizes how high or low levels of munificence, dynamism, or complexity affect the likelihood of revolutionary or evolutionary change. This argument is presented *ceteris paribus,* that is, all other things being equal. The requisite stock of ideas and inventions, the effects of the social system, and so on, are also required in order to usefully take actions based on this descriptive summary.

The two can then be brought together into a generalized argument involving revolution, evolution, and environmental interaction. Table 11-3 depicts the basic structure of this argument. It suggests that management should be aware of opportunities for revolutionary change in periods of high munificence, low dynamism, and high complexity. Entrepreneurs will see such periods as a time of market opportunity evidenced by munificence, limited uncertainty as evidenced by low dynamism, and good poten-

Table 11-2. Revolution, Evolution, and Environmental Conditions

	Revolutionary Change	Evolutionary Change
Munificence		
High	Likely	Unlikely
Low	Unlikely	Likely
Dynamism		
High	Unlikely	Likely
Low	Likely	Unlikely
Complexity		
High	Likely	Unlikely
Low	Unlikely	Likely

tial for defensible niches or full-fledged technologically driven shifts in the basis of competition due to the degree of complexity the firms are facing. It also suggests that if two of the three conditions are present, the opportunities for revolutionary shifts are still likely. Of course, the table also demonstrates the converse, that evolutionary change is likely to occur when conditions are reversed.

This interpretive analysis assists the organization in assessing the likelihood of revolutionary change in its market. When such an exercise in intellectual assessment is reinforced by considered managerial judgment and vision then the firm can exercise its options to continue its current strategic approach or to begin preparing for a significantly different approach based upon forecasted radical changes in the firm's market. As suggested by the presentation, radical change usually requires many different strategic attempts until an acceptable or better strategy becomes clear. A forecasted radical change thus cannot lead to a prescriptive strategic solution but should stimulate a reexamination of current practice and a search for alternatives.

Table 11-3. Revolution, Evolution, and Environmental Interactions

Munificence							
High				Low			
Dynamism				Dynamism			
High		Low		High		Low	
Complexity		Complexity		Complexity		Complexity	
High	Low	High	Low	High	Low	High	Low
LUL	LUU	LLL	LLU	UUL	UUU	ULL	ULU
REV	EVO	REV	REV	EVO	EVO	REV	EVO

Key: L = likely to support revolutionary change; U = unlikely to support revolutionary change (L and U are drawn directly from Figure 11-2 regarding each category); REV = likely dominates unlikely; EVO = unlikely dominates likely.

CONCEPTUAL ASSESSMENT OF TECHNOLOGICAL POTENTIAL

The second half of the chapter will focus on conceptual frames useful for viewing the technological potential of a situation. While models of markets or environmental levels of technological change are diverse and are drawn from a variety of disciplines— including economics, systems theory, and sociology—they are consistent when it comes to some important themes. In one way or another, they all describe the relationship of technological change to the evolution of organizational environments, and ultimately to the survival of the firms affected by these relationships.

Technological change is described most basically by two variables: (1) the rate at which it affects market structure and firms and (2) its magnitude, or the degree of divergence between the new and the old technology. These ideas are found consistently throughout the literature, and we suggest they are the basic dimensions on which strategists can concentrate when they include technology in their environmental scanning. Technological change can be rapid, discontinuous, and radical at one extreme, leading to complete replacement of products and/or processes—and altering markets and competitors entirely. At the other extreme, it can be slow, adaptive, and normal, enhancing established products and processes and reinforcing the competitive position occupied by incumbents (Abernathy and Utterback, 1978).

Both speed and degree of change are measured relative to the existing technology and to the ability of the general population of firms to respond to such changes. Dimensions of technology are meaningful to strategists only in relation to the adaptability of organizations, markets, industries, and other affected institutions. Change perceived as radical in a stable industry characterized by a typically low rate of change could well be routine—and seen as normal—in a growing or otherwise volatile industry. Similarly, the face of one particular market may change, based on the differential response of various member firms or their ability to control the rate and impact of change.

In the next few sections, some frameworks for analyzing the nature of technological change which use concepts of technological evolution, technological performance curves, and technological states are reviewed. They have been selected for inclusion because they have proved themselves to be useful and important.

Technological Evolution

Since the 1950s there has been a resurgence of interest in the sources, influences, and nature of technological advance. While interest in the relationship between technological advance and economic growth waned during the first half of the twentieth century, contemporary scholars such as Sahal (1981), Basalla (1988), Dosi (1982), and Abernathy and Utterback (1978) have rekindled interest in this line of inquiry.

Sahal's particular interest lies in the patterns of technological innovation and change. The focus of his studies reflects the fact that advances in technology represent a slowly evolving understanding of the potential of the defined technology across many fields, and technological advance results from the progressive exploitation of that potential. In this sense, cumulative learning processes lead to a progressive flow of innovation. Economic variables such as product supply, demand, and factor cost may stimulate or impede innovation efforts, but they always stay within the boundaries defined by the basic constraints on the technology as well as the internal logic of the learning process.

Sahal advances the proposition that technology and technological advances unfold over time. When advances are seen as cumulative processes which cannot be taken out of a temporal sequence of events, then the advances witnessed today can be seen as the result of past accomplishments while advancements of tomorrow will be the result of the technological foundations established today.

Conceptions of Technology. The term technology has numerous connotations. For example, it may connote an object of our material culture, or it may refer to a pool of applied scientific knowledge. The problem of how to operationalize such a broad-based notion is real, however, and, regardless of whether one views technology from a neoclassical economics stance (in terms of a production function) or from what Sahal terms a Pythagorean account (in terms of counting the number of patents, for example), one finds both views are somewhat limited. In fact, our efforts to come to grips with the notion of technology have always been limited by the particular analytic approach adopted. To date, the concept remains ambiguous and ill-defined.

One popular concept is the systems viewpoint, wherein a particular technology is analyzed in terms of its functional properties (Atkinson and Stiglitz, 1969). Sahal argues that this particular view is advantageous in that it takes into account the evolutionary nature of technological change, whereas the production function and the Pythagorean approaches are founded upon an antithesis of evolution. At the same time, Sahal suggests that the three viewpoints are potentially complementary and that each may lend insight to the other two approaches.

The Production Function Concept. The relationship between various technically feasible combinations of factors (inputs) and outputs is generally known as the production function. Within the context of existing technological knowledge, the production function can be represented as a graph using input and output as the dimensions of the axes. A line drawn thorough the points that represent equal production quantities (the so-called isoproduct curve, or isoprod) will be a smooth, convex curve. This represents different combinations of factors that can be employed in the production of a given level of output. Changes that are the result of the development of new techniques will shift the isoprod toward the origin and will imply increased efficiency.

Problems arise in integrating the concept of technological change into the framework of a production function. One may assume a logically pure production function which exhibits all conceivable techniques that could be defined by means of existing theoretical knowledge, but it is first necessary to presume that technology originates in the pure sciences. That this reflects a real-world situation is questionable. It is also seldom feasible to specify the fundamental production function in terms of known physical laws of a theoretical nature. In effect, it is impossible to specify a production process except in the most rudimentary cases. If we adopt a realistic production function, which represents techniques in use, we have a problem distinguishing economic from purely technical factors in production. This objective is unlikely to be met except in extraordinary circumstances. Summarizing, the production function provides a number of broad general options for *macroeconomic* policy. Its ability to *directly measure* a technological innovation process, however, is limited.

The Pythagorean Concept. Two essential elements comprise the Pythagorean concept. First, the concept refers to a count of technological events such as the number of inventions patented. Second, the uniqueness and chronology of an event are crucial. But these two indices have some serious limitations. Merely counting excludes the notion of development of technology from blueprint to mass production. In recent decades, for instance, only half of patented commercial inventions have actually been placed into production (Schmookler, 1966). Chronologies are somewhat unsatisfactory because the making of an innovation is a continuous process, not well described by discrete events. In summary, while the Pythagorean viewpoint does provide a means to measure technology, it lacks a formulation of the production activity.

The Systems View Concept. According to this concept, technology is best conceived and evaluated in terms of its performance or functional characteristics. For example, fuel consumption efficiency may be viewed as one appropriate measure of the state of a jet engine's technology. This concept of technology has many merits. The first is that functional measurements of technology can be objectively measured. Second, these measures have practical utility to engineers and managers compared with the more abstract notions of the neoclassical production function. Third, functional measures of technology make it possible to take into account major and minor innovations. Fourth, changes in the product characteristics can be taken into consideration in the systems view concept; this cannot be done in the neoclassical production function since product characteristics are assumed not to change. Fifth, this view can be applied to a wide range of problem areas while incorporating the idea of the multidimensional nature of innovation diffusion.

There are some limitations, however, and they include a lack of data on the changes in the functional characteristics of technologies over time. In addition, combining the multidimensional attributes of a given technology into a single index poses significant problems relating to data collection. Finally, the systems concept is applicable primarily to the micro level of analysis.

Ideally, an eclectic approach that incorporates the three major conceptions of technology would be most useful. Further inquiry into the possibility of combination, as well as an assessment of the potential benefits, is needed at present. Sahal summarizes by stating that the process of technological development predictably leads to a certain pattern of design and indicates that the pattern will have a significant bearing on subsequent developments. Innovations in any given area will depend on incrementally exploiting the patterns of design. The basic design may be viewed as a guidepost which represents the general direction of technical progress. The implication for the strategist and policymaker is that it is possible to determine the relative success of a technique in terms of the scope of its development.

Technological Performance Curves

Technology life cycles generally take on identifiable patterns. A graphic plot of the relationship between input (resources, effort, investment) and performance of a technology looks like an *S*, as shown in Figure 11-1. In the earliest phase even high investment levels show little change in performance. In the middle phase, where the curve is

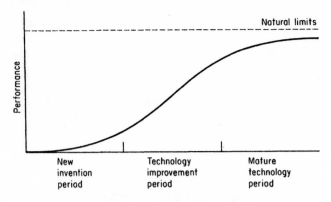

Figure 11-1. Technology S curve.

seen to be steeply rising, rapid performance improvement relative to invested resources is the norm. Finally, in the later, mature phase marginal performance differences are all that can be wrung from a technology even if significant resources are applied.

According to Foster (1986) and others, the efficiency of a technology can generally be expected to change in a predictable sequence. A life cycle effect can therefore be implied. While timing of transitions from one phase in the S curve to another is not revealed, implications for strategic management of the technology are quite clear. One is the clear implication that any technology will reach a stage after which continued investments will produce marginal improvements in performance at best. Afterward, competitive advantage gained from further development is likely to be relatively insignificant. Thus, researchers in strategy and technological change warn of the natural limits to the performance of any technology.

Further, patterns of S curves emerge when technological development is tracked over longer time periods (see Figure 11-2). Typically, a mature technology is replaced, through "radical" change, with a new one best represented by another S curve. Series of S curves are found in many analyses, reflecting the introduction, development, maturity, and replacement of a sequence of technologies with similar applications. Technologies, and the markets that develop around them, are subject to forces moving them toward maturation and replacement. Competitive markets where the rules of the

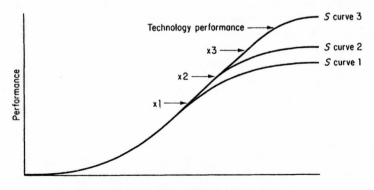

Figure 11-2. Sequence of technology S curves.

game—entry and exit, competitive advantage, market share—are based on a technology are subject to pressure when the technology reaches its natural limits. And then these same competitive markets can be thrown into disequilibrium when the predominant technology is replaced.

The pattern that links these curves together is one of change within, then across, *S* curves. While a single life cycle applies, "normal" science and equilibrium competition, punctuated with process improvements, are realized. For instance, Foster (1986) argues that there are marginal changes in the product, which remains consistent in its technological core. This cycle is played out until the technology reaches a mature stage. Then, a shift to another *S* curve is expected, characterized by radical science and discontinuity in markets. At the point where a mature technology is replaced by a new one, firms assume market positions based on their ability to exploit the new technology (Tushman and Anderson, 1986). As the technology and the market develop, a new technology life cycle takes shape.

Technology States

Abernathy and Utterback (1978) focused on the complex strategic issues of technology, particularly on a concept they called the "technology state." It is actually a description of several states linked by an evolutionary process. It might also be considered a process of technological opportunity, since changes among disparate states may also alter competitive conditions. Abernathy and Utterback offered a three-step process through which high-technology industries evolve over time. Their system closely resembles that proposed by Kuhn (1963) in his overall analysis of the social psychology of scientific development.

According to Abernathy and Utterback's concept, technological innovation evolves through three states, each with distinctive features. These states are the fluid state, the dominant design and transition state, and the specific or mature state. They can be described as follows.

Fluid State. The fluid state refers to the initial stages of product development. Invariably, this beginning phase is marked by trial and error, where product design and manufacturing operations are not organized concretely. Frequent changes in both product and process are common; adaptability and loosely defined methods employed in product development are notable. During this initial phase of product innovation, potential markets have not yet been well defined. This may be a reflection of a lack of consensus on potential applications or utility of an emergent product. The technical nature of the innovation and role of the entrepreneur always have a bearing on the technology-push versus market-pull developments. Since the progress of technological innovation depends on the ability of the firm to establish and develop market niches, companies that capitalize on the fit between technology and the market are most likely to be successful.

Dominant Design and Transition State. A congealing of ideas, concepts, and objectives leads into a dominant design stage. During this stage, a single firm has developed a design for the technological innovation that sets a standard for the industry. At this point, the primary concern is with performance maximization of the particular innovation. Efforts to increase efficiency of both the product and process technology are emphasized. Other companies within the existing technology may generate substantial revenues by introducing incremental variations. These companies may differentiate by emphasizing reliability, service, or unique performance of their product.

Specific or Mature State. The final stage, that of maturity, is associated with the standardization of manufacturing methods and product design. Firms will capitalize on standardization, and economies of scale will result. Innovations will revolve around the dominant design; improvements will be incremental. Abernathy and Utterback believe that the industry reaches a "specific state" where, as a consequence of standardization and stability, resistance to product and process change will emerge. Sources of managerial resistance are derived from the stability of related economic forces—low unit costs, for example—and the fear that managerial careers may be jeopardized by changing what appears to be a "good thing." Significant investments in technological, fiscal, and human capital may present further barriers to change.

Organizations that are currently in the mature state (where incremental innovation is guided by cost reduction) were once smaller, fluid units whose purpose was to generate new-product innovations. For example, the evolution of the electric light bulb readily reveals the three stages of evolution. The light bulb was initially developed in line with a small number of profound technological innovations. During the process of refinement (1905–1955), the product and processes associated with its manufacture became increasingly standardized. Unit costs, direct labor content, and price all dropped, while illumination capacity of the light bulb nearly doubled. Evolutionary improvements were reflected in increased product efficiency, and resulting lower prices were passed on to the consumer. Here one notes the shift from a radical to an evolutionary product innovation. Small-scale units, which were initially flexible and able to make use of general equipment in the production process, are transformed over time to units that utilize automated, high-volume production techniques. We expect that rivalry will evolve away from significant product innovation but not necessarily converge on production efficiency. There are many different means to compete, even when product technology no longer differentiates rivals.

ACHIEVING THE BENEFITS WHILE AVOIDING THE PITFALLS

We can summarize the effects of the level of innovation by comparing information on technology from the frameworks reviewed above with each of the environmental dimensions. Munificence, or the general level of profitability and resources, is increased as a particular technology is accepted by its potential users. Profitability is greatest if there are sources of effective barriers to market entry and the technology cannot be readily duplicated by potential new entrants.

Dynamism, or change resulting in uncertainty for competitors, falls into two types according to Abernathy and Utterback and to the S curve analysis. Change is incremental, process-oriented, and rather predictable during the period of movement along a single S curve. The level of uncertainty is low, and competitors with established positions are expected to maintain them and to increase efficiency. On the other hand, transitions from one S curve to another result in conditions of high uncertainty during which well-developed and trusted methods of competing may no longer apply.

Both niche strategies based upon technological exploitation and revolutionary strategies based upon technological barriers are characterized by complexity. Technological exploitation requires that a technology be tailored to better fit a special class of customer. This tailoring may very well be preemptive if the added costs of operation attributable to such customizing keeps the niche revenues from seeming sufficiently attractive. Major changes in the bases of competition made possible by technological changes can themselves become technological barriers because of the many elements of the firm which now have to change to deal effectively in a new but still complex environment.

Firms must position themselves for change. They may attempt to gain competitive advantage by emphasizing the existing technology, for example, through process innovation and vertical integration. Alternatively, they may develop a prospecting approach, in which they try to position themselves on the leading edge of the next technology. In fact, Tushman and Anderson classify technological and environmental change according to its effect on firms. Changes that require new skills, abilities, and knowledge are disruptive to firms that have established themselves in relation to a particular technology. For them, radical change, from one S curve to another, is competence-destroying. These firms must learn how to participate effectively in markets under a new regime of technology and competitive practices. Competence-enhancing change is more likely to be found in arenas where change is incremental and the technological core of a market is consistent. Competence-enhancing change involves improvement of current ways of managing technology and methods of competing through that improvement.

Technology is described here as a fundamental force for change affecting firms and their environments. There is no science yet of technological change, but there are some helpful conceptual frameworks and guidelines. At the level of broad environmental factors, the impact of technology is gauged by the rate and magnitude of change associated with that technology. They can be fit into frameworks that specify phases of growth, maturity, and replacement for technologies. In each, technology has some impact on the munificence, complexity, and dynamism of competitive environments, and through them on participating firms. Since none of the models presented here is complete by itself, they may be used to complement each other, and to develop a specialized approach that suits the needs of the individual analyst or strategy maker.

REFERENCES

Abernathy, W. J., and J. M. Utterback. 1978. "Patterns of Industrial Innovation," *Technological Review,* 80:40–47.

Atkinson, A., and J. Stiglitz. 1969. "A New View of Technological Change," *Economic Journal* 79:573–78.

Barney, J. 1986. "Types of Competition and the Theory of Strategy: Toward an Integrative Framework," *Academy of Management Review* 11(4):791–800.

Basalla, G. 1988. *The Evolution of Technology.* Cambridge: Cambridge University Press.

Butler, J. 1988. "Theories of Technological Innovation as Useful Tools for Corporate Strategy," *Strategic Management Journal* 9(1):15–29.

Chamberlin, E. 1933. *The Theory of Monopolistic Competition.* Cambridge, MA: Harvard University Press.

Cyert, R., and J. March. 1963. *A Behavioral Theory of the Firm.* Englewood Cliffs, NJ: Prentice-Hall.

Dess, G., and D. Beard. 1984. "Dimensions of Organizational Task Environments," *Administrative Science Quarterly* 29(1):52–73.

Dosi, G. 1982. "Technological Paradigms and Technological Trajectories," *Research Policy* 11:147–62.

Elster, J. 1983. *Explaining Technological Change: A Case Study in the Philosophy of Science.* New York: Cambridge University Press.

Foster, R. 1986. *Innovation—The Attacker's Advantage.* New York: Summit Books.

Henderson, R., and Clark, K. 1990. "Architectural Innovation: The Reconfiguration of Existing Product Technologies and the Failure of Established Firms," *Administrative Science Quarterly* 35:9–30.

Kuhn, T. S. 1963. *The Structure of Scientific Revolutions.* Chicago:University of Chicago Press.

Lippman, S., and R. Rumelt. 1982. "Uncertain Imitability: An Analysis of Interfirm Differences in Efficiency under Competition," *Bell Journal of Economics* 13:418–38.

Marx, K. 1973. *On Society and Social Change,* edited by N. Smelser. Chicago: University of Chicago Press.

Nelson, R., and S. Winter. 1982. *An Evolutionary Theory of Economic Change.* Cambridge, MA: Belknap Press.

Rumelt, R. 1974. *Strategy, Structure and Economic Performance.* Cambridge, MA: Harvard Business School Press.

Sahal, D. 1981. *Patterns of Technological Innovation.* Reading, MA: Addison-Wesley.

Schmookler, J. 1966. *Invention and Economic Growth.* Cambridge, MA: Harvard University Press.

Schon, D. 1963. *The Displacement of Concepts.* London: Tavistock.

Schumpeter, J. 1976. *Capitalism, Socialism and Democracy,* 5th ed. London: Allen and Unwin.

Tannenbaum, R. 1976. "Some Matters of Life and Death," *OD Practitioner* 8(1):1–7.

Teece, D. 1987. "Profiting from Technological Innovation: Implication for Integration, Collaboration, Licensing and Public Policy." In D. Teece, ed., *The Competitive Challenge.* Cambridge, MA: Ballinger.

Tushman, M., and P. Anderson. 1986. "Technological Discontinuities and Organizational Environment," *Administrative Science Quarterly* 31:439–65.

von Hippel, E. 1978. "Users and Innovators," *Technology Review* 80(3):30–39.

12

Technology, Core Competence, and the Resource-Based View

Within the last few years, familiar concepts about competitive strategy have been combined with new ones to reshape the way firms think about strategy. This evolution has gone through two recent stages. The first focused management attention on the concept of core competence. Further evolution has led to a more current view, which has been labeled the "resource-based view" of strategic management.

THE EVOLUTION OF CORE COMPETENCE AND RESOURCE-BASED VIEW

The origin of this development can be traced as far back as 1938 when Barnard first emphasized the existence of strategic factors and their effect on the firm's ability to compete. This emphasis helped focus academic thought and led to evolutionary developments in understanding strategic factors. Increased understanding allowed authors such as Steiner (1969) to move from the idea of existence to the idea of specifying or identifying firms' strategic factors. Further transformations occurred when Porter (1980) and Ohmae (1982) applied the framework outside the firm to the "industrial environment" and began studying requirements for success demanded by industry conditions. More recently, Rumelt (1984) and Wernerfelt (1984) brought the focus back from the industrial level to the firm, a development that led to a more formal statement of the resource-based view. Their work has been enriched by concepts of commitment on the one hand (Ghemawat, 1991) and dynamic capabilities on the other (Teece, Pisano, and Shuen, 1990). Developments of the concept and refinement of the model by each of these scholars has added substantially to our understanding.

Unfortunately, the evolution of these concepts is outpacing the academic profession's ability to generate sound advice on how to implement them. Still, the promise of these newer concepts as a comprehensive approach to strategy formulation is apparent, and there is value in laying out the main issues as they relate to the strategic management of the technology resource.

To accomplish this goal, the chapter is divided into three parts. In the first section, the underlying constructs are identified and described. This section is followed by a brief review of the various streams of thought that contribute to the evolving constructs. Together, these two sections highlight the fundamental shift in perspective that the resource-based view brings to the strategy formulation task. The third section is devoted to a discussion of how the basic ideas can be applied by strategists with special interests in technology.

A Basic Intellectual Framework

An intellectual frame for this chapter is contained in the following statement. "Firms generate profit to the extent that they accumulate rent-producing resources that, in addition to producing economic value, meet tests of scarcity, imperfect imitability, and imperfect tradeability in factor markets." This statement, a succinct summary of the resource-based view, while elegant, requires careful explication. It is important to recognize that some components of the statement refer directly to the operational characteristics of the firm while others refer to strategic opportunities facing the firm.

Organizational resources include formal ownership rights of items such as patents or plant and equipment, lines of credit, a trained work force, locations, contractual supplier connections, operating systems and procedures, and a myriad of other items. They also include more subtle resources, or rather "capabilities," such as reputation, tacit design and/or production know-how, responsive customer relationships, and organizational culture.

Resources and capabilities usually represent significant time investments as they are the result of incremental developments. (Although acquisitions may seem to be instantaneous benefits, they are actually the result of much preparation and negotiation and take much time in integration.) In the course of doing business a firm accumulates resources that represent unique bundles of organizational resources capable of generating revenues from sales in the market. Because of its unique history, each firm follows a different pattern of resource accumulation and thus represents a distinctive capability or a unique variation with regard to rival firms. Revenues (rent production) represent the economic value of the firm's resources from the perspective of the market.

Strategic Values in These Concepts

The strategic element is derived from the concepts of scarcity, uncertain imitability, and uncertain tradeability. If the firm owns a scarce resource, then competitors cannot own that same resource; hence the firm has a defensible advantage. If the firm's method of doing business requires a unique blending of process and know-how, then competitors cannot copy it exactly—and the firm has a defensible advantage. If the firm's unique resources cannot be easily traded because of their inherent nature or because they don't fit into a competitor's operations, then the firm has a defensible position. If all these situations occur simultaneously and the resulting business generates a profit, then this defensible advantage generates a defensible profit stream. Thus, operations can be said to develop resources which provide defensible advantage and these resources can be considered strategic. These positions and advantages, of course, must lead to values for the customer. If the customer doesn't value the differences (real or perceived), then the firm's resources or capabilities will not produce rents.

Capabilities (resources) and core competencies (Prahalad and Hamel, 1990) are closely related, although not identical, concepts. Capabilities at the core of a company's business are the fundamentals developed by taking several generations of products to market. Because they are based on skills, know-how, and other basic qualities, rather than on a company's individual products, they can potentially lead to a strategy that is more flexible and viable over the long term than a firm that does not have a significant investment in capabilities. Often capabilities developed in one market can be effectively deployed in another market. Products eventually become obsolete, but the ability to effectively integrate market research into the development of new products does not become obsolete. This ability is a base for flexibility and growth, whereas the product-based strategy is a base for eventual decay. Thus the long-term viability of the firm may depend more on its capabilities than on its product positioning.

More specifically, the firm's competencies or capabilities in the technological area are often referred to as the firm's *core technology*. Core technology represents a body of knowledge and science, know-how, techniques, tools and artifacts, procedures, and methods that

1. Allows the key value-added activities in the firm to flourish (e.g., an information system that allows custom manufacturing to buyers' specifications with short turnaround)
2. Are embodied in a large portion—or key value-added portion—of a firm's products

Rappaport and Halevi (1991) suggest a new set of strategic rules for choosing areas for developing competencies:

1. Compete on utility, not power. Identify high-value areas that are not yet standardized, and create proprietary technologies that are candidates to become standards.
2. Monopolize "true" sources of added value and encourage competition for complementary assets. If there is competition for the provision of these complementary assets, their costs to the buyer will be driven down and this will make the "monopolized" asset even more attractive.

These new approaches shift attention from the *strategies* of competing firms to the *capabilities* they employ in support of those strategies. The sources of competitive advantage are unique capabilities, and returns are reinterpreted as rents on those capabilities. This juxtaposition of ideas has potential for developing new ways of explaining relationships among technology, organization structure, competitive strategy, and advantage and for describing ways in which firms implement technology strategies more effectively, and thus are more profitable than their competitors. The next section explores these ideas in more detail.

RESOURCE-BASED VIEW

Many scholars have converged on resource-based thinking as a useful way of explaining firms' conduct and profitability. Some now wonder whether this may be the foundation upon which the organizing framework—the paradigm—for strategic management might be built (Teece, Pisano, and Shuen, 1990; Connor, 1991).

One of the basic ideas in resource-based thinking is the important link between profits and unique firm characteristics. Performance is based on the firm's unique capabilities and its competitor's difficulty in imitating them. The logic of strategic differentiation is familiar (Chamberlin, 1962; Rumelt, 1984; Teece, 1985) and has been argued by Porter (1980) as one of the three basic strategies available to the firm. Even where there are other companies in the market, a strategy that is difficult to imitate gives a firm a unique position where it has no direct competition. In this situation the firm actually obtains advantages akin to a monopoly. If it also creates value for customers, then it can expect returns that exceed industry norms. Imitation is the major threat to strategic differentiation; as quickly as competitors start to replicate the special position of the firm in the marketplace, advantages of differentiation, including extraordinary profits, decline.

The positive value of imitation barriers, Rumelt's "isolating mechanisms" (1984), is evidenced by Northern Telecom. This firm pursues advanced research and development on fiber optic transmission equipment employing custom-made instruments and machine tools of its own design. Since Northern Telecom appears to be in a position to control access to such equipment, other competitors will be disadvantaged. In future communications equipment markets other competitors will not be able to develop new equipment as efficiently as Northern Telecom and thus will not have the same strategy options. Because of increased R&D expenses (a direct efficiency impact) Northern Telecom's competitors will either have a price disadvantage or will experience a time lag in introducing new technology (an indirect efficiency impact).

Focusing on capabilities also puts a different spin on ways that firms are structured, raising new issues that could change the outcomes of many strategic decisions. "Outsourcing," participation in alliances, and administration of internal markets as well as external contractual relationships are being reexamined using a criterion often called "best in class."

This approach begins by evaluating the full range of the firms' activities and the capabilities that support them (e.g., procurement, distribution, facility maintenance, information systems, R&D). These activities are then compared with outside sources of supply, and compared with (benchmarked against) competitors. As a general rule, the firm would keep in house only those activities they can perform better than a rival or alternative source—along with the capabilities that support the activities they keep. Thus, the firm's resource base would consist of only those capabilities in which they dominate rivals and dominate outside sources of supply and the related infrastructure to support those capabilities. If the firm's capabilities are best, as suggested by this logic, then, by definition, it has a competitive advantage.

CAPABILITIES AND COMPETENCIES

When one shifts to focusing upon the competitive value of capabilities and competencies instead of on the competitive value of products, far-reaching potential for developing strategic advantage is easily foreseen (Stalk, Evans, and Shulman, 1992). Precursors to strategic management based on models of capabilities began appearing in the academic and business press in the early 1980s (Lippman and Rumelt, 1982; Werner-felt, 1984; Prahalad and Hamel, 1990). While the roots of resource-based thought go back to Chamberlin, and to classical economists like Ricardo, the focus on capabilities is recent enough that not all components of a genuinely coherent approach are yet in place.

Critics argue that this apparently new paradigm is nothing more than the recycling of old ideas. Nevertheless, many researchers, consultants, and managers are writing on capabilities or closely related topics. Thus far, discussions about the domain of capability-based strategy are marked by divergence and disagreement as key concepts, propositions, and terminology are only slowly being refined.

Working descriptions, rather than conclusive definitions, are offered here. To set the framework for this chapter, consider that "capabilities" is an umbrella term for both competencies and resources. It is used to describe those characteristics of firms that make some strategies feasible and allow them to be pursued more effectively or at lower cost than would otherwise be possible. Both competencies and resources are capabilities in the sense that they help to enable strategies, but they can be differentiated from each other. Competencies equate to potential derived from abilities, capabilities, expertise and know-how, technology, knowledge, talent and skill, aptitudes, organizational culture, and values. Resources, on the other hand, can be broadly defined as assets. They include contracts, licenses, intellectual property, trade secrets, and physical resources (Hall, 1992).

Capabilities may be thought of as a platform from which to pursue alternative strategies and market positions. They allow firms to pursue certain strategies more effectively, and they prevent firms from pursuing others by making them too costly or impractical.

Look at the way the regional Bell operating companies (RBOCs) perform basic R&D for communications products of the future. Under AT&T's aegis, these RBOCs historically operated local telephone networks in their respective regions but were not expected to demonstrate abilities in the performance of basic research. Thus, they never developed the competencies needed to effectively pursue basic and applied research.

As independent entities, the RBOCs are faced with a serious problem regarding the evolution of their markets. To accommodate their current needs for a constantly evolving range of telecommunications products and services, the RBOCs have chosen to share their research resources by jointly participating in a research consortium with Bellcore (the current name for the famous AT&T central research facility in Murray Hill, New Jersey, commonly known as Bell Labs). Each RBOC supports basic research in communications technologies at Bellcore, and in return has access to the results of those research efforts.

In addition to the financial commitment, the RBOCs also develop skills at transferring the results of basic research into products and at evaluating the costs and benefits of their participation in the Bellcore consortium. Thus, they have used their historical resource strength (centralized Bell Labs research) to provide an unusual competitive resource of continued shared outsourcing of basic R&D.

Some of these activities and skills can be defined as a capability for acquiring and integrating R&D. As a rule, the RBOCs do not have in-house basic R&D staffs and facilities, having decided that in this case outsourcing R&D is more effective than developing the competence in house. Thus they have little use for the know-how needed to manage such activities or the physical plants required to house them. These companies have, however, established a stable platform for contracting basic R&D. All other things being equal, continuing to rely on this capability is a more efficient option than moving basic R&D in house.

EVOLVING ACADEMIC THOUGHTS ABOUT CAPABILITIES

A capabilities (competence and resource-based) perspective represents an innovative approach that promises to integrate investments with strategies. It leads to two broad classes of comparison. One is a comparison with competitors, which can be used to determine whether one or another specific capability actually differentiates a firm from rivals and is therefore a potential source of competitive advantage. The other is a determination of how best to acquire the capability—whether it is more effective to pursue an arrangement with an outside provider of the capability, as the RBOCs have, or to bring it in house.

Capabilities, according to Wernerfelt's definition (1984), are resources that enable rivals to pursue strategies. Each competitor has a different bundle of resources. Thus certain strategies may prove more compatible with the firm's unique capabilities and therefore prove more efficient than others. There are markets in which multiple strategies have value and the different strategic efficiencies, while affecting market share, do not preempt profitable performance.

For this chapter a few general examples of technological resources serve to explicate the issues as well as to ground the issues in technologically relevant bases. Capabilities are relevant to both process and product technologies. The discussion of process technologies can be clustered in terms of efficiency or flexibility and in terms of integration stage. Product technologies can be grouped in terms of output values or process values. The nature of the product market and the product life cycle connects these resources to appropriate strategies as suggested in Chapter 5. Some examples follow.

1. Flexible manufacturing capabilities are often batch process–oriented and increasingly are supported by serious investment in computer-aided design and manufacturing (CAD/CAM) resources. These processes allow shifts in products within a broad range, allowing the firm to effectively respond to shifting market demand. Flexibility is purchased at a cost, as such manufacturing processes are necessarily less efficient than dedicated long-run oriented manufacturing process approaches.

2. An efficiency focus in the manufacturing arena reduces unit cost by balancing product lines and tailoring productive units to the specific process. It also demonstrates a commitment to competing on a low unit cost basis, since a tailored manufacturing process is a firm-specific asset, and thus has little value in other applications. The demonstrated commitment serves as a market signal and affects competitors' decisions regarding strategy selection.

3. Integration activities refer to control over forward or backward stages of production. Encouraging suppliers to specialize to meet specific requirements and/or purchasing critical suppliers to ensure successful sourcing arrangements are examples of weak and strong forms of backward integration. Walmart's unique electronic data inter-

change (EDI) supply system reduces paperwork significantly while also reducing inventory costs, costs of stock-outs, and the like. Walmart requires all suppliers to be compatible with this EDI system and thus reaps cost-saving strategic advantages from a weak form of backward vertical integration.

When faced with distribution problems in regions where it had limited market penetration, Trebor-Sharp integrated forward. By purchasing wholesaling operations (a strong form of integration) Trebor-Sharp could achieve distribution benefits since costs at each wholesale site were shared by competitors. The increased volume made investment in computerized logistics and distribution systems worthwhile. Aside from an increase in revenues and a reduction of costs in the acquired wholesale business, an increase in revenues from market penetration for the firm's own products was also achieved. As this example indicates, owning or controlling distribution channels may permit unique technological investments to have significant payoffs for the firm.

4. Product technology as a resource refers to the firm's ability to produce niche or general-purpose products. This ability has elements of research and development, of customer or market research, and of manufacturing skills which underlie its effectiveness. The value of this ability is reflected in customer satisfaction and eventually in reputational capital.

5. The development process itself creates organizational and individual intellectual capital as described in Chapter 8. This resource directly affects the firm's ability to maintain a pipeline of new products and its ability to direct its future intellectual capital investment projects toward strategic ends.

An important dimension for technology strategists is the degree to which assets are specialized or generalized. Some observers argue that competitive advantage is the result of specialized assets that are at the same time difficult to imitate or buy (Ghemawat, 1991). Managers must invest in assets with little alternative use value to outperform others in their markets. A specialized asset base can constrain a company from pursuing all but a specific set of strategies permitted by its asset base. On the other hand, companies seeking flexibility might theoretically maintain generic asset bases, which would permit them to adjust quickly to changing market conditions without the costs sustained by specialist firms that try to move with the market.

The application of the generalist approach to technology-intensive industries is apparent. In these industries, exogenous changes, especially as driven by technology, are a continuous force on companies to adapt, sometimes in fundamental ways. The generalist approach is well developed in the strategic management literature, particularly when contingency models are included.

Of concern when employing a technological generalist approach is the advent of higher performing alternative technologies. Thus, the ability to easily climb the performance curve in the firm's core technology through the use of a generalist approach does not mean that the firm will be able to successfully shift core technologies. This was seen clearly in the vacuum tube industry, where manufacturers that failed to convert to the production of integrated circuits became rapidly obsolete.

Criteria to evaluate technological assets are identical to those for capabilities in general. Recent developments in resource-based theory can be of assistance in evaluation. Amit and Schoemaker (1993) employ a nine-factor list for assessing the value of a firm's resources. They look at resource scarcity, low tradeability, inimitability, limited substitutability, appropriability, durability, complementarity, and overlap with industry strategic factors. Peteraf (1993) has a somewhat shorter list. She argues that competitive advantage is derived from resources that exhibit heterogeneity, ex-post limits to competition, imperfect mobility, and ex-ante limits to competition.

For strategists, the degree of anticipated durability (i.e., whether the assets are sources of short- or long-term advantage) is a key issue. Several of the dimensions from each of these two lists can be used to estimate the duration effect of the firm's resources, technological or other.

Resource Scarcity

If assets are hard to obtain—that is, if they do not have the character of a commodity— then a longer horizon is expected. Some firms are distinguished by their ability to obtain these assets. For example, Sony's product development skills in physics and engineering for blue light lasers represent a serious investment in the development of intellectual capital. This type of an experience curve advantage is difficult for others to approach, and thus Sony is expected to dominate the field for an extended period.

Imperfect Imitability

Imperfect imitability also leads to durable advantage. Assets characterized this way are usually proprietary and their exact nature is poorly understood and hard to explain. The more difficult it is to imitate assets, the longer the firms controlling them have advantages.

For almost a decade, the Laboratory for Electronics had a unique approach to detecting radar signals using an interrupted continuous wave (ICW) to permit an accuracy which few competitors could match. The circuitry that provided this competitive edge was hard to emulate and created a durable advantage. (The advantage was eventually lost to a substitute technology, inertial guidance.) Assets that are proprietary, tacit, or otherwise nonobvious in ways that they might be imitated are sources of durable advantage.

Value Production

When technological assets are valued by the marketplace, more durable advantage can be expected. The asset must make the final product or service more effective in its end use, lower in cost to the next purchaser, or advantageous in some other way. For example, Walmart's coordinated inventory control system avoids stockouts at its retail stores and allows cost and price reductions by just-in-time (JIT) inventory management. The company takes further steps to reduce the cost of its logistics systems by planning backhauls for delivery trucks using the same information system.

Imperfect Tradeability

Imperfect tradeability means that the asset can have firm-specific value and durable advantages. An early study comparing aircraft design capabilities in the United States and the United Kingdom showed that the U.K.'s design resources were more efficient. The cause of this difference was attributed to a nontradeable resource.

In the United Kingdom, members of the various aircraft design firms each spent their entire career in the same firm. Thus, they exhibited great familiarity with the intricacies of aircraft design and particularly with the very complex technological interrelationships. When a designer had to initiate a change the full technological implication of the change could be quickly assessed as the designers knew all the potential impacts of their responsibilities on other design efforts. When an opportunity to surpass specification or a problem in achieving specification arose the ramifications were easily ascertained and the appropriate members of the team were notified. This led to rapid problem identification and problem solving and eventually resulted in less expensive design efforts.

By contrast in the United States, the aircraft design force migrates from firm to firm; it is the rare individual who remains with a single firm over the span of a career. Thus, each firm must create its own system of design coordination and orient new members of the technical staff to its specificities. The resulting system as compared to the U.K. system is more formal and bureaucratic. This endemic lack of informal familiarity and the resulting formality in signoff procedures and required paper trails is inherently less efficient and therefore more expensive than the United Kingdom's.

Since the U.K. "familiarity and informal coordination system" is not tradeable on the market and thus cannot be easily acquired by a U.S. firm, it provides the U.K. firm with a durable advantage, particularly with respect to the impact of change (external and internally generated) on the design process and its outcomes.

CAPABILITIES AND TECHNOLOGY MANAGEMENT

Finally, after outlining these academic concerns, it is important to present some direct technological implications for the possible implementation of a resource-based strategic program. The following steps and activities provide a framework for translating these ideas into practice in the arena of technology management:

1. Identify capabilities that are available or that may be needed in the future. These capabilities may reside in the product development technology portfolio or in the manufacturing technology portfolio.
2. Benchmark capabilities versus those of rivals and potential entrants. Entrants are often initially niche players for some very narrow application area. On occasion these entrants offer substitute processes, for instance, inertial guidance for ICW.
3. Benchmark capabilities versus those of alternative suppliers. These determinations are critical for acquisition or outsourcing decisions.
4. Develop and reinforce capabilities that suit strategies and lead to advantage. Particular attention should be paid to technological approaches which promise future "best-in-class" performance.
5. Phase out capabilities that don't lead to advantage. Strategy formulation, then, is conceiving what the platform should look like as well as developing and reinforcing competencies. Therefore, a key element of strategy formulation is investing in competencies that fit the strategies managers intend to pursue.

The technology mapping technique presented in earlier chapters provides one mechanism for determining the strategic platform. The technology programming concept, which depicts different levels of investment in different technological approaches, helps fill out the technological basis of the strategic platform.

Under competitive pressures, this resource-based view of competencies is necessary but not sufficient. It still begs the question of competitive advantage. A competitive firm must differentiate itself from rivals if it is to be profitable. Forging an intellectual link between competencies and strategy provides an opportunity to rethink the basis on which differentiation might be achieved. In particular, best-in-class competencies within a given niche may be a source of advantage.

Capabilities and strategies should be reciprocally related. A firm should follow strategies for which it has supporting capabilities. Strategies should be built on the firm's defensible capabilities. A corollary statement is that the firm should invest in capabilities which support current, effective strategies. The clear interdependence between capabilities and strategies is normally the mark of a successful firm.

A simple example of this phenomenon is found in the writing instrument industry. BIC and Mont Blanc are both successful competitors in the industry. BIC manufacturing capabilities are based on a minimalist design which contains only seventeen parts, and the product is manufactured in a highly automated, capital-intense, high-volume operation. BIC's distribution strategy matches its design and manufacturing capabilities and its ubiquitous stick pen can be purchased almost everywhere: discount stores, convenience stores, pharmacies.

Mont Blanc's manufacturing competence also emanates from its product design approach. The multiple parts, the fineness of the nibs, the expensive materials—all lead to a process with higher labor intensity and lower volume. The competence is matched with a distribution strategy that relies on image and thus has far fewer outlets. In both cases, the strategies adopted by these firms match their competencies and are appropriate and successful.

SUMMARY

Competencies, resources, and capabilities are new ways to think about strategy and competition. Capabilities limit the range of feasible strategies and may help to differentiate a firm for competitive advantage. Although implementation problems have not yet been solved, thinking in these terms has potential for giving companies a competitive edge and represents a potentially important tool for strategic planners.

REFERENCES

Amit, R., and P. J. Schoemaker. 1993. "Strategic Assets and Organizational Rent," *Strategic Management Journal* 14:33–46.

Barnard, C. I. 1938. *The Functions of the Executive.* Cambridge, MA:Harvard University Press.

Chamberlin, E. 1962. *The Theory of Monopolistic Competition: A Reorientation of the Theory of Value,* 8th ed. Cambridge, MA: Harvard University Press.

Connor, K. 1991. "A Historical Comparison of Resource-Based Theory and Five Schools of Thought within Industrial Organization Economics: Do We Have a New Theory of the Firm?" *Journal of Management* 17:121–54.

Ghemawat, P. 1986. "Sustainable Advantage," *Harvard Business Review,* September–October, pp. 53–58.

Ghemawat, P. 1991. *Commitment: The Dynamic of Strategy*. New York: Free Press.

Hall, R. 1992. "The Strategic Analysis of Intangible Assets," *Strategic Management Journal* 13(2):135–44.

Hamel, G. and C. K. Prahalad. 1989. "Strategic Intent," *Harvard Business Review*, May–June, pp. 63–76.

Lippman, S., and R. Rumelt. 1982. "Uncertain Imitability: An Analysis of Interfirm Differences in Efficiency under Competition," *Bell Journal of Economics* 13:418–53.

Ohmae, K. 1989. "Managing in a Borderless World," *Harvard Business Review*, May–June, pp. 152–61.

Peteraf, M. A. 1993. "The Cornerstones of Competitive Advantage: A Resource-Based View," *Strategic Management Journal* 14:179–91.

Porter, M. 1980. *Competitive Strategy*. New York: Free Press.

Prahalad, C., and G. Hamel. 1990. "The Core Competence of the Corporation," *Harvard Business Review*, May–June, pp. 7–91.

Rappaport, A., and R. Halevi. 1991. "The Computerless Computer Company," *Harvard Business Review*, July–August, pp. 69–80.

Rumelt, R. 1984. "Toward a Strategic Theory of the Firm." In R. Lamb, ed., *Competitive Strategic Management*. Englewood Cliffs, NJ: Prentice-Hall.

Stalk, G., P. Evans, and L. Shulman. 1992. "Competing in Capabilities: The New Rules of Corporate Strategy," *Harvard Business Review*, March–April, pp. 57–69.

Steiner, G. A. 1969. *Top Management Planning*. New York: Macmillan.

Teece, D. 1985. "Multinational Enterprises, Internal Governance, and Economic Organization," *American Economic Review* 75:233–38.

Teece, D., G. Pisano, and A. Schuen. 1990. "Firm Capabilities, Resources, and the Concept of Strategy." Consortium on Competitiveness and Cooperation CCC Working Paper 90-8, Center for Research in Management, University of California at Berkeley.

Wernerfelt, B. 1984. "A Resource-Based View of the Firm," *Strategic Management Journal* 5:171–80.

13

Technology and Strategy Issues in Improved Quality

In the 1970s and early 1980s, the basic focus of large firms was to develop adequate products and services. Management often warned employees not to overdesign, or "gold plate," their work. This idea was reflected in orientation programs for new technical employees: "Your A grades are admirable *but* striving for A's is now past. You must learn to aim for C quality designs." Under this management philosophy an appropriate design *met*, but did not *exceed*, the needs of the customer. Similarly, proof of effectiveness for an investment or a procurement became "this is an adequate product," and any mention of excellence was considered poor practice.

Such a philosophy is clearly inappropriate in today's competitive marketplace. The basis for competition has shifted significantly in the last decade. Now, competition for markets in several technological areas, from memory chips to automobiles, is being driven by a combination of price containment and high quality—both affected by technological advance and a focus on excellence.

At a broader level, indirect concerns arose due to the apparently parallel national issues of trade and competitiveness. At the base of these concerns was the diminution of the United States's technological dominance. This dominance, a temporary artifact of World War II, was replaced by a return to balanced international technological competence as early as the mid-1960s (Vernon and Kapstein, 1991). With the restoration of technological balance the trade position began eroding until it became an international crisis.

Hayes and Abernathy forcefully articulated the national question in their 1980 article, "Managing Our Way into Economic Decline." Their argument focused U.S. national concern on the negative competitive consequences of a short-term, financially oriented perspective. They pointed to a need to invest in productivity-enhancing equipment and to improve the quality of our technology in general. Their analysis stimulated further conceptual development and more substantive concern with global competition. After further work, Wheelwright and Hayes (1985) concluded that a "world-class" corporation must be excellent in all operational aspects—technology and manufacturing, marketing and finance, design and quality, and the like. Thus, the issue of excellence was joined with the question of competitiveness.

Quality and quality improvement now represent very important dimensions of competitive behavior as market forces require an increased emphasis on excellence. Whereas excellence is easy to articulate as a goal, it is elusive as a practical guide for corporate behavior. To achieve excellence more and more firms are focusing their attention on a complex and multifaceted approach to quality called *total quality management* (TQM).

The creation of the Malcolm Baldrige National Quality Award in 1987 has stimulated many firms to engage in substantial review of their way of doing business. Practical investment in TQM, the philosophy underlying the Baldrige Award, has increased rapidly. The interest level generated by this award has been very high and over 200,000 requests for Baldrige applications have been received by the U.S. Department of Commerce since the enabling legislation. While comparatively few applications have actually been filed, many firms use the application's award structure as a template for their quality efforts. The National Center for Manufacturing Sciences has found the most succinct way of expressing these quality concerns with their slogan "Exceeding Partner Expectations."

Exploration of the Baldrige Award structure, the Wheelwright and Hayes world-class concept, and other writings on TQM demonstrates effects on the entire operation of the firm—and its suppliers. TQM is an extraordinarily complex idea containing a multitude of issues, which makes simple explanations difficult. This is a systemic idea that does not fit neatly into the nine technology strategies of Chapter 4 and thus is treated here as a separate chapter.

The explanation of the relationship among TQM, technology, and strategy begins with the explication of the fundamental assumptions of the TQM philosophy. Then, using the Baldrige application as a frame, the central issues and the techniques that are part of the TQM process are discussed. In the second half of the chapter, various technology roles which are supported by TQM are presented and then blended with strategic issues to complete the explanation.

TOTAL QUALITY MANAGEMENT

Total quality management represents a firm-wide effort that involves all operational areas. The systemic TQM character requires a very different approach to management than many other systems aimed at improving only a few parts of the firm. In this sense, TQM represents a "management philosophy" with some underlying techniques. One method of explaining the TQM philosophy is by tracing several fundamental assumptions.

The Fundamental Basis of TQM

In practice TQM fundamentals are variously employed—some firms adopting all, others a selected few. The inherent complexity of the system prevents firms from fully adopting TQM overnight and is one of the reasons for the unevenness found in practice. Additionally, TQM itself is not meant as a formula; rather, it is a template or an envelope of underlying assumptions for guiding corporate decision making and action. Table 13-1 systematically describes this template.

Table 13-1. The Total Quality Management Template

1. *Quality must really count.* The first step in the process of TQM is the full commitment of top management to a program that is lifelong in character. It is possible for individual managers to effectively adopt TQM within their local domain, but their efforts will have far more leverage with wide community support. Since firms' convey, by their behavior, which goals are most important, if quality—total quality—is not one of these goals, then an extensive TQM program will be sabotaged by underinvestment of resources and energies. Thus, total commitment by top management is a prerequisite.

2. *Quality goals must be determined.* TQM is about the achievement of quality goals. The program requires a thoughtful determination of just what these goals should be. Quality is not easy to define and many issues must be considered within the goal-setting process. An understanding of the relationship among in-process steps and their effect on final outcomes is required. Then, clear, challenging, but reasonable goals must be selected and articulated.

3. *The main goal should be customer satisfaction.* The basic reason for TQM is to create products and services of value to the customer. Thus, customers should be involved in the determination of quality goals and customer satisfaction should be heavily weighed in any TQM system. While customer satisfaction is the ultimate TQM target, many activities in the firm seem only distantly connected to this goal. The various in-process steps that eventually lead to customer satisfaction need a clear focus rather than an amorphous goal. Intermediate goals must be established. Thus, a successful TQM system requires numerous in-process goals which link upward toward the achievement of the top-level goal. To operationalize and simplify this idea employees can be shown that their "customer" is the next step in the work flow. Goals can then be set by interactions between individual employees who receive and those who produce—in a process step–by–process step fashion.

4. *Measurements must be created.* Once the goals have been set it is important to establish measurements and measurement processes which show how well the goals have been met. Measurement is necessary at all steps within the firm's process. That is, measurement should focus on the steps to achieving the goals as well as the goals themselves.

5. *Employee involvement is necessary.* While customers are important in helping create end-product quality goals, employees are equally important in creating in-process quality goals. Involvement increases detailed understanding of organizational processes and employee commitment to the goals.

6. *Actual performance should be public.* Actual performance must be swiftly and clearly made known to the employees. The posting of results in a public place should enable employees to understand how well they are doing and whether they are improving. For improvement, "experiments," or new ways of proceeding, must be attempted. To understand whether a new procedure is working well, timely feedback is required. This is a basic requirement for establishing a correct understanding of the linkage between action and result.

7. *Continuous improvement must be an important issue.* Over time, the organization usually applies increasing sophistication to TQM. The quality goal set should be constantly reviewed as to *salience, relevance,* and *achievement.* Goals should be continuously improved with regard to each of these three elements. Targets for the firm as a whole and the various in-process steps should be constantly revised to be more salient and relevant. With experience, goals should be set higher as improved methods permit better results.

8. *Competitive benchmarking should be used.* A solely internal determination of quality potential will usually understate possible attainment. Performance of other units within the corporation and of competitors is minimally necessary in order to obtain a good sense of feasible targets. The goals set based upon such a performance benchmark study should be compared with similar measures and achievements of direct competitors. It is not unusual to use a firm in a different industry as a benchmark for one or another element in the matrix of goals. For instance, a manufacturing firm might look at the performance of a distribution company to understand feasible distribution targets.

9. *Supplier partnership should be employed.* To achieve TQM goals suppliers should be included in the organization's plans and joint goals should be considered. Suppliers are very important contributors to quality service and innovation and should be encouraged to join the firm's quality efforts.

The Macolm Baldrige National Quality Award

These nine fundamentals circumscribe the general issues of TQM. Specific issues can be seen in the Malcolm Baldrige National Quality Award application form. Table 13-2 shows 1990 and 1991 award categories and their weights. The adjustment in the

Table 13-2. The Baldrige Award Template

	1990	1991
1.0 Leadership	**100**	**100**
1.1 Senior executive leadership	30	40
1.2 Quality values	20	15
1.3 Management for quality	30	25
1.4 Public responsibility	20	20
2.0 Information and analysis	**60**	**70**
2.1 Scope and management of quality data and information	35	20
2.2 Competitive analysis and benchmarks	—	30
2.3 Analysis of quality data and information	25	20
3.0 Strategic quality planning	**90**	**60**
3.1 Strategic quality planning process	40	35
3.2 Quality leadership indicators in planning	25	—
3.3 Quality goals and plans (priorities)	25	25
4.0 Human resource utilization	**150**	**150**
4.1 Human resource management	30	20
4.2 Employee involvement	40	40
4.3 Quality education and training	40	40
4.4 Employee recognition and performance measurement	20	25
4.5 Employee well-being and morale	20	25
5.0 Quality assurance of products and services	**150**	**140**
5.1 Design and introduction of quality products and services	30	35
5.2 Process quality control	25	20
5.3 Continuous improvement of processes	25	20
5.4 Quality assessment	15	15
5.5 Documentation	10	10
5.6 Quality assurance, assessment, and improvement of support services and business processes	25	20
5.7 Quality assurance, assessment, and improvement of suppliers	20	20
6.0 Quality results	**150**	**180**
6.1 Quality of products and services	50	90
6.2 Comparison of quality results	35	—
6.3 Business process, operational and support service improvement	35	50
6.4 Supplier quality improvement	30	40
7.0 Customer satisfaction	**300**	**300**
7.1 Knowledge of customer requirements and expectations	50	30
7.2 Customer relationship management	30	50
7.3 Customer service standards	20	20
7.4 Commitment to customers	20	15
7.5 Complaint resolution for quality improvement	30	25
7.6 Customer satisfaction determination	50	20
7.7 Customer satisfaction results	50	70
7.8 Customer satisfaction comparison	50	70

weighting system is a reflection of the TQM fundamental of continuous improvement. Salience and relevance have been reevaluated based upon Department of Commerce experience, external analysis, and critique.

Some TQM Techniques

Two basic techniques—statistical process control (SPC) and competitive benchmarking—are associated with TQM. The application of SPC recognizes that TQM is actually a process. Many of the measures implied in the Baldrige schema are measures of ongoing processes such as complaint resolution, employee involvement, and quality results. Competitive benchmarking, on the other hand, targets achievable results by studying others and then focusing the firm on a path toward matching the quality potential revealed by the competitive studies.

Statistical Process Control. While the essence of statistical process control is the establishment of a target and an acceptable range centered in this target, the real story is the basic idea represented by this technique. First and foremost, this technique is based on the three concepts of measurement, presentation, and control.

There are several foci and specific techniques which SPC can employ. It can focus on "loss functions," which help quantify the losses resulting from process variability (Ferguson, 1989; Taguchi, Elsayed, and Hsiang, 1989; Taguchi and Konishi, 1989; Naguib, 1992). Or SPC can include orthogonal array techniques to experimentally explore the interactions among key parameters (causal factors) and parsimoniously determine how to reduce process variance (Ferguson, 1989; Taguchi, Elsayed, and Hsiang, 1989; Taguchi and Konishi, 1989; Naguib, 1992). In its most basic use, statistical process control focuses on the graphical presentation of process-performance results with statistically determined upper and lower control limits (Juran, 1945, 1989; Deming, 1950, 1982; Ferguson, 1989; Naguib, 1992). Control limits establish the widest variation from standard that is acceptable and provide a method of determining the drift in a process early enough to take corrective action before the control limits are violated.

The SPC measurement issues involve target selection and measured process-variance statistics. The control chart target selected can be a product specification such as a diameter, an organizational phenomenon such as absenteeism, or a customer satisfaction measure such as rejects or complaints. The second measurement concept involves understanding the normal process variance around the targeted mean. Knowledge of this variance allows management to judge how important improvement in the process should be and consequently provides information for priority setting.

The second most important factor to the SPC approach is the question of continuous improvement. The "loss function" of Taguchi (Ferguson, 1989) measures the losses due to deviation from target. By studying the losses and evaluating their consequences management can find a more robust evaluation of the variance and a more sophisticated method of setting priorities. The Taguchi approach is supplemented by "activity-based costing" in some settings (Naguib, 1992).

With a knowledge of the value of variance reduction, then, the other key feature of the Taguchi method can be employed. He recommends assorting the possible causal factors into orthogonal dimensions so that an experiment which varies along one dimension would yield clear information about the causal relationship. In this manner a parsimonious experiment can be carried out to determine the various effects of each causal factor (Ferguson, 1989; Naguib, 1992). Improvement targets can be assigned cost priorities and simple experimentation can determine effective improvement actions.

The causal elements need some connection to customer values; without this the cost frame may be misleading. For instance, one delivery firm has assessed its variance in terms of the obvious performance issues of timely and reliable service. This firm's improvement focus was clear, and the targeted mean and variance in these dimension improved dramatically. Unfortunately, it did not look to its billing department, and difficulties in accurate billing led to significant customer dissatisfaction. A much wider concept of customer value was needed so that impacts from support areas could be included in the management TQM model. The firm's early focus on direct production was an effective starting point and improved the ability to deliver. Unfortunately, the firm's narrowly defined dimensions of customer value prevented it from avoiding customer loss.

In the main the SPC approach supports measurement, presentation, and employee involvement, control, and improvement. All these are fundamentals of total quality management. Generally, SPC looks at the internal working of the firm. This tendency to be internally focused can be balanced by another central TQM technique—competitive benchmarking.

Competitive Benchmarking. A second major technique associated with TQM is competitive benchmarking. This technique can be used directly for competitive assessment, as a potentiator for a technology-push perspective, or as a tool for a market-pull perspective. The benchmarking process per se is described first and then the three possible perspectives are explored.

The benchmarking system described here is called quality functional development (QFD) and was popularized by Yoji Akao's 1990 book (*Business Week,* 1991). The system begins with the customer. Table 13-3 describes the system in a step-by-step fashion.

Through various forms of customer research, customer demands are determined. These demands are weighted by importance. Customers are then asked to rate the firm and the firm's competitors on how well they meet these demands. This provides a customer-driven, externally based, competitive benchmark. The next step is to consider the functional characteristics of the firm's offerings and assess how they relate to customer demands. Then the firm and the firm's competitors' offerings are reverse-engineered to assess their actual performance in each functional category. From this product/process design targets are set.

Obviously, this cycle should be repeated as customer demands change and competitors improve. In addition to these externally driven benchmarking issues it is possible to compare many in-process measures and other absolute measures which are not driven by the market analysis. Thus, many executives also see benchmarking as a search for best practice (Camp, 1989). In this use benchmarking contributes directly to target setting for efficiency.

Basically, firms use benchmarking to measure how well they are doing and how well others are doing. If the measures are purely in-process or technical end-result measures, then the underlying management issue is that of efficiency and representa-

Table 13-3. The Quality Functional Development Process

1. Assess customer demands. Various forms of market research are employed to determine which product or service attributes are important parts of the purchase decision.

2. Assess customer priorities. The market research is especially focused on importance ratings of the various demands to help drive improvement priorities.

3. Assess customer satisfaction. The central competitive benchmark question is how well the firm's offerings measure against the offerings of competitors.

4. Determine functional characteristics. This information is turned into design specification by first identifying the functional characteristics of the firm's product or service.

5. Assess relationship between functional characteristics and customer satisfaction. With the product/service functional structure in mind, it is necessary to assess how important each design parameter is to the satisfaction of one or the other demand.

6. Determine competitors' functional performance. Reverse engineering of competitor's products or services permits the firm to identify comparative functional measures, a second form of benchmarking.

7. Assign functional performance and customer satisfaction targets. Then functional performance targets can be set and resulting customer satisfaction rating assessed.

tive of a technology-push strategy. If the measures are purely customer demands and satisfactions, then the underlying management issue is market share and represents a market-pull strategy. When the benchmarking process includes a mixture of customer demands/satisfactions with internal in-process and technical result comparisons, then the management issue is balancing share and efficiency goals and represents an economically sound "buyer value" strategy.

The Nature of TQM Benefits

Does TQM work? This can be answered at several levels. At the lowest level of evaluation Naguib (1992) reports results from a five-year effort at a microelectronics wafer fabrication facility: a 74 percent increase in yield, a sevenfold decrease in customer returns, 114 percent increase in shipments with a 24 percent decrease in work force, 142 percent increase in revenues, and a 25 percent annual reduction in unit manufacturing costs, on-time delivery increases to 100 percent level, benchmark studies showed increased customer satisfaction, and improved employee satisfaction. He also reported several barriers: (1) employees feared downsizing; (2) improvement had to be implemented on a project-by-project basis and allowed to stabilize before moving to the next improvement; (3) balancing the TQM process-oriented management with the simultaneous need for result-oriented management; (4) changing managerial roles to emphasize coaching and training; and (5) new coordination issues between the wafer fabrication facility and the rest of the corporation. He concludes with "we consider ourselves to be at the early steps of a long never ending journey of continuous quality improvement" (Naguib, 1992, p. 13).

At a broader level of analysis is the 1991 U.S. General Accounting Office (GAO) report which studied Baldrige Award participants. The findings were reported in three broad categories: employee measures, operating indicators, and financial performance. In the employee category the GAO found an average annual percentage improvement in satisfaction, attendance, and safety of 1–2 percent, a decreased turnover of 6 percent, and increased suggestions submitted of 17 percent. The operating indicators show a somewhat higher percentage rate improvement than the employee measures. Reliability, order processing time, errors, and costs of quality showed an annual improvement rate of 9–12 percent, on-time delivery, product lead time, and inventory turnover 5–7 percent. The average annual percentage improvement in financial performance indicators was 1–2 percent in return on asset and on sales, 9 percent in sales per employee, and 14 percent in market share. In each of the comparison areas some negative results were also found.

The GAO study looked at the benefits from a sample of the very best TQM practitioners. *Business Week* (1991) chose to look at a much broader sample. Here the variance in the application of TQM elements can be observed. In a sample of 250 firms, some 85 percent use customer satisfaction and employee involvement as part of their quality strategy but only 60 percent use competitive benchmarking and supplier partnerships. Thus, American industry exhibits a wide variation in approaching the quality opportunity.

David Garvin (1991) in his interview study of firms submitting Baldrige applications presents some comparisons between low, medium, and high scorers. In low-scoring applicants the leadership category is strongest but does little to pull the rest of the organization along. In general these low-rated firms articulated the philosophy but didn't engage in the difficult task of definition and measurement. In the medium-scoring applicants, the leadership function is stronger. These firms also exhibit strong direct quality activities, human resource utilization, and customer satisfaction. The medium-scoring firms present an incomplete innovation; that is, they pursue the task in several areas but do not approach the task systemically. In high-scoring companies all categories are very strong and the systemic nature of the TQM activities is clearly noticeable.

What do these studies imply about technology and strategy? How is TQM related to improved defensible advantage? Since TQM is a totally systemic management approach, it should not be surprising if the benefits of TQM arise from many areas. The explication of the TQM, strategy, and technology issues employs several perspectives in order to capture the systemic nature of TQM and relate directly to the concerns of this book.

TQM AND TECHNOLOGY

The strategy question is best approached in two stages. Operational-level groundwork is necessary before proceeding to the exploration of strategic options. Thus, the general exploration of the operational impact of TQM and technology precedes the analysis of TQM, technology, and strategy. This exploration is used to set the underlying parameters for the next stage.

The TQM process provides an abundance of information which guides operational-level analysis and decision making by providing management with a method of assigning priorities. For instance, the TQM-derived information about buyer value or customer satisfaction is a major aid in defining priorities. This information can be integrated with TQM benchmarking information to add some competitive perspective into priority setting by blending what has high customer leverage with what would most differentiate the firm from its competitors. Such priorities would then be supplemented by various traditional financial analyses.

The technology role in TQM occurs at many different levels and is widespread throughout the organization. The major impact can be seen in manufacturing, product design, information systems, and improved quality analysis. These, of course, interact with each other due to the systemic nature of the TQM approach. The technological development of the manufacturing process is the most obvious arena of impact. But this is overly simplistic as product design specifications require both a "buyer value" dimension and a "producibility" dimension. Product and process improvements are only part of the story. There is significant investment in information technology and in the direct statistical and analytic elements of the TQM process itself.

TQM, Technology, and Manufacturing Processes

The manufacturing process has two distinct and interactive elements: technological effectiveness and work group effectiveness. Manufacturing technologies which exhibit more stability, which adapt more readily, and which can be operated with greater precision will be one source of increasing ability to deliver quality products. But much of the benefit from TQM arises from work group effectiveness. Abernathy, in his 1980s study of competitiveness in the automobile industry (personal communication, 1982), concluded the $1500 per car advantage of Japanese manufacturers was more attributable to the work group management system than the technological effectiveness. More recently Lieberman (1991) concurred when he indicated that the increased effectiveness of new methods such as just-in-time inventory management arises more from altered work group behavior than from direct cost reductions.

A focus on TQM will definitely require an increased emphasis on the technologies employed in the manufacturing process. It will require a search for variances in the current system and methods for limiting those variances. Normally, reducing the limitations of the current manufacturing process will be the first avenue of attack and will probably provide significant opportunities for improvement.

The second avenue of attack will involve the redesign of the manufacturing process to incorporate new technologies of promise. This will require direct investment in design, equipment, and installation. It will also require careful planning because changing technologies and processes are always disruptive. The value of various new manufacturing technologies can be assessed in part by reference to TQM customer satisfaction data and competitive benchmarking data. Thus, the TQM studies will help determine priorities for the various improvement choices.

Along the way, the TQM system provides work groups with data which allows them to monitor their own progress toward improved quality. The ability to understand work group outcomes permits the work group to experiment with alternative approaches. This is the beginning step in the development of increased work group effectiveness.

These two avenues represent starting points and, of course, they reflect medium-term opportunities. In the longer term, serious attention must be focused upon a third avenue of improvement which blends product and manufacturing design. Major improvement opportunities are created when product and process designers effectively work in concert.

TQM, Technology, and Product Design

The benchmark studies reveal customer satisfaction issues (buyer values) and performance capabilities of outside firms. These studies are the information base for
improved product specifications. To achieve a better overall performance envelope
new technologies will have to be examined and continued innovation will be required.
Thus, the basic TQM documentation will provide stimulation and information for better reaching the goals of high quality and customer value.

It is insufficient to simply use TQM information to drive product design. The perspective of management must be the joint design of the product/manufacturing process.
These question of joint design must be viewed in the medium term and the long term.
The product design approach must consider product improvement and the corollary
issue of producibility. It must also see how product technologies will play themselves
out over the longer term and how manufacturing technologies will do the same.

TQM, Technology, and Information Systems

TQM cannot be successfully achieved unless serious thought is given to the information requirements of the system. Under a TQM approach the information system will
have to seriously attend to new information demands and to new methods or techniques for bringing that information to bear on operations.

If the outcomes of operations are not known, then the improvement process can
move ahead only by employing intuition. The information system must accommodate
many more measures of performance so that employees at all levels of the organization
can become aware of the quality of their work and the trends in that quality. This will
require, in many cases, establishing new measurements and new measures.

In addition to the increased need for information there is an increased demand for
providing information in a useful format to the employees at their work site. This
implies providing key information to the employees in an understandable manner—
often not a trivial challenge as this involves innovation in presentation as well as
employee training to enhance comprehension. While appropriate presentation of information at the work site is often challenging, it is a necessary but not sufficient condition for TQM. Additionally, the information must be timely so employees can clearly
understand how their actions are affecting their goals. Without a timely information
connection between action and result, diagnosis of opportunities for improvement
becomes considerably more difficult.

TQM, Technology, and Quality Analysis

TQM has spawned heightened interest in many techniques which assist in analysis of
quality and in the determination or diagnosis of opportunities to improve quality.
These techniques bridge from simple audit techniques, to somewhat more complex statistical process control analysis, to the more complex analytics such as the Taguchi
method (Taguchi and Konishi, 1989). The main impact of TQM is to increase the

sophisticated employment of available techniques in an effort to determine causal connections between choices and/or actions and outcomes.

TQM and Technology in the Corporation

The operational impact of TQM on the organization is seen and felt at all levels. This is because TQM is a total organizational system. The obvious impact in the manufacturing process is misleading unless corporate leadership also understands the systemic connections between supply and design, between manufacturing and distribution, between service and logistics, and so on. The interrelationship of these elements requires serious attention to information systems on the one hand and serious increases in the sophistication of analytic capabilities on the other hand.

TQM AND STRATEGY

How does TQM, a systemic intervention, affect the firm's strategic positioning? The discussion that has preceded this section does not clearly suggest the role that TQM can play in corporate strategy. In the GAO study (1991) increases were found in various in-process costs and satisfaction measures. Financial performance showed limited improvement although market share showed significant improvement. The resulting mixed message suggests a need to look a bit more closely at TQM and strategy.

Seven basic strategic action steps were proposed in Chapter 5 and summarized in Chapter 6. These steps, which include three broad areas for corporate investments, are used as a basis for a more fine-grained analysis of TQM and strategy. In Table 13-4 (repeated from Chapter 6) investments in manufacturing processes, in product R&D, and in governance are the actions generally available to the corporation. These actions lead to defensible competitive advantage through creation of cost, informational, or regulatory barriers.

The discussion of TQM, technology, and strategy will follow the three basic action foci: product, process, governance. Each of the three foci, of course, has subsidiary issues, some of which turn out to be interrelated. The subcategories in this structure

Table 13-4. Technology Actions and Competitive Barriers

Action	Type of Barrier Created
Invest in productivity	Cost/price or cost/reputation
Invest in capacity	Cost/market size
Invest in flexibility	Cost/market size
R&D for new general products	Information barriers
R&D for new niche products	Information barriers
R&D for hierarchical design	Information barriers
Negotiate hierarchical governance	Contractual/regulatory barriers

serve as reminders that in any given market there will normally be more than one viable strategy; thus, managerial judgment is still a major tool in the development and/or the selection of specific strategic choices.

TQM and Product R&D Strategies

The three general categories of product R&D aim at very different markets. The R&D effort for general products seeks a product that broadly serves its market. In most instances resulting general products have a performance envelope which customers judge to range from acceptable to exceptional. These qualities of the envelope are determined by individual customers in their own specific application of the product. Here TQM is one approach to the marketing question of customers' desires and thus can make a significant contribution in the assignment of priorities to the R&D technology portfolio.

Niche products can be created on a number of dimensions, but for simplicity two general niche categories will be used in this discussion. One general niche category—performance specialization—reflects the firm's choice to offer products that have dominant characteristics in a specific application. This differentiates the niche product from the products aimed at a general market. Here the technology-based strategic question reflects which technologies yield the necessary performance and perhaps how wide a range of niches could be attacked with such technology. In contrast to the broad marketing issues of a general-purpose product, a specialization niche product requires a sharper knowledge of buyers' actual needs.

This sharper knowledge requirement normally leads to a close and detailed relationship with the customers and with their specific applications of the firm's product. Such a detailed relationship has all the characteristics of a weak form of hierarchical governance. That is, there is some interaction between the customer and firm (sometimes called "direction") and this interaction affects the firm's decision making. Customer satisfaction is, of course, very important as niches are comparatively small. The TQM focus on customer satisfaction identifies buyer needs and drives the technology decision.

The other niche approach is to focus on the low-cost portion of the market. In the design of a low-cost niche product the firm must be more aware of the producibility aspects of the selected technology. The market awareness does not have to be appreciably better than for the design of a general-purpose product. The technological impact here comes from the TQM uses of quality analysis and internal information system improvements.

The third product design target is hierarchical design. The term hierarchical design refers to products which are designed specifically to work with another manufacturer's products—with or without assistance from the other firm. Third-party software, communications protocols that connect one technology with another, and clone computers represent hierarchical design products. R&D for hierarchical design requires good liaison and/or information flow between levels in a product chain.

Here anticipating changes in the products at the next hierarchical level is necessary. Developing good information sources and/or agreements is critical to success. The technological strategy focuses on prediction of both subsystem and component-level developments as well as higher level embodiments of these technologies. This prediction is aided when collaboration is possible.

Here we have a slightly stronger form of a governance system as the firm's decision is defined by decisions at the next level in the hierarchy. When they are shared, as in the Toyota procurement system, the innovative flow goes both ways. A firm whose products greatly assist the next-level firm's sales is more likely to achieve good cooperation, thus reinforcing the hierarchical product strategy. The customer satisfaction, producibility, reliability, and value analysis elements of TQM go a long way toward the effective design of a complementary hierarchical product.

TQM and Process Investment Strategies

There are three generic actions which a firm can take when the focus of its strategy is on manufacturing processes. These actions include investment in productivity, capacity, and flexibility. TQM studies will assist the firm in distinguishing which of these three approaches will have the most leverage with the customer. So from a strategic viewpoint, the TQM system helps to set priorities.

Internal to the investment opportunities are the more detailed performance features generated by the TQM systems, which lead to increases in the effective management of the productive process. They do not directly indicate a technology strategy but do clearly direct the tactical questions about how best to carry out such a strategy.

TQM and Governance Negotiation Strategies

The last of the three broad categories of strategic actions involves governance issues. Here the question of formal vertical or horizontal integration opportunities can be addressed. The TQM process in this setting is one instrument which allows two firms to assess their business practice compatibilities. Since TQM normally requires very good relationships with suppliers, a backward vertical integration opportunity would more easily be assessed. Forward vertical integration may not start from as rich a mutual understanding as backward vertical integration, depending on the nature of the preestablished links. In this strategic setting TQM provides a rich information base as one of several issues that need to be attended to when the strategic question suggests a governance-oriented strategy.

TQM and Strategy in the Corporation

The basic contribution of TQM to corporate strategy is in the assignment of priorities for investment in product and/or process technologies. Since product development cannot effectively be accomplished without a concern for the required productive processes, all investment decisions have a stake in the information developed from a TQM system. Detailed productive improvement information coupled with detailed customer satisfaction measures provides the firm with an unusually rich understanding of the extant situation and perhaps a forecast of improvement, which then, in turn, is a substantial base for assessing the potential benefits to be derived from a proposed technological investment.

TQM, TECHNOLOGY, AND STRATEGY

The systemic nature of TQM permeates the entire corporation and extends beyond the bounds of the firm to supplier, customer, and competitor. This information base and the implied forecasted improvements lay a solid basis for the competitive assessment of alternative technological investment. Thus, TQM contributes substantively as well as substantially to the firm's ability to analyze its opportunities and to apply the sort of analysis recommended in the earlier chapters of this book.

REFERENCES

Akao, Yoji, ed. 1990. *Quality Function Deployment: Integrating Customer Requirements Into Product Design,* trans. G. Mazur. Cambridge, MA: Productivity Press.

Business Week. 1991. "No.1—And Trying Harder," in *Business Week* bonus issue, *The Quality Imperative.*

Camp, R. C., 1989. *Benchmarking: The Search for Industry Best Practices That Lead to Superior Performance.* Milwaukee, WI: Quality Press.

Deming, W. E. 1950. *Some Theory of Sampling.* New York: Wiley.

Deming, W. E. 1982. *Quality, Productivity, and Competitive Position.* Cambridge, MA: MIT Press.

Ferguson, I. 1989. "Taguchi Methods and Parameter Design." In *Proceedings, First Conference on Tools and Techniques for TQM.* London: IFS Ltd.

Garvin, D. A. 1991. "How the Baldrige Award Really Works," *Harvard Business Review,* November–December, pp. 80–95.

Hamilton, M. R., A. I. Mendelowitz, and R. I. Fogel. 1991/92. "TQM at GAO," *GAO Journal* 14:39–47.

Hayes, R. H. and W. J. Abernathy. 1980. "Managing Our Way to Economic Decline," *Harvard Business Review,* July–August, pp. 67–77.

Juran, J. M. 1945. *Management of Inspection and Quality Control.* New York: Harper and Brothers.

Juran, J. M. 1989. *Juran and Leadership for Quality: An Executive Handbook.* New York: Free Press.

Lieberman, M. 1991. "Just-in-Time Management." Lecture presented at Anderson Graduate School of Management, University of California, Los Angeles.

Malcolm Baldrige National Quality Award. 1990. Application Guidelines. Washington, DC: National Institute of Standards and Technology, United States Department of Commerce.

Malcolm Baldrige National Quality Award. 1991. Application Guidelines. Washington, DC: National Institute of Standards and Technology, United States Department of Commerce.

Naguib, H. 1992. "The Implementation of Total Quality Management (TQM) in a Semiconductor Manufacturing Operation." San Francisco: International Semiconductor Manufacturing Science Symposium, June. (mimeo)

Taguchi, G., E. Elsayed, and T. Hsiang. 1989. *Quality Engineering in Production Systems.* New York: McGraw-Hill.

Taguchi, G., and S. Konishi 1989. *Orthogonal Arrays and Linear Graphs: Tools for Quality Engineers.* Dearborn, MI: American Supplier Institute.

United States General Accounting Office. 1991. "Management Practices: U.S. Companies Improve Performance Through Quality Efforts." Washington, DC: U.S. GAO, May.

Vernon, R., and E. B. Kapstein. 1991. "National Needs, Global Resources," *Daedalus,* pp. 1–22.

Watson, J. E. and T. W. Hopp. 1991/92. "The Private Sector's Experience with Total Quality Management," *GAO Journal* 14:34–38.

Wheelwright, S., and R. H. Hayes. 1985. "Competing through Manufacturing," *Harvard Business Review,* January–February, pp. 99–109.

IV

TECHNIQUES FOR MANAGING TECHNOLOGY STRATEGIES

Increased effectiveness of the technology-based firm begins with the mastery of the *conceptual frame* that was presented in Part I of this book. It is then important to develop skills in the *techniques for diagnosing* situations and selecting appropriate technology strategies. Good diagnostic skills then lead to the selection of plans and action steps which meld the technological with the strategic.

The result of the diagnostic process is the selection of actions which are strategically positioned to create value for the firm. Execution of these actions must be effectively handled or the hoped-for benefits are unlikely to occur. To aid the execution or implementation process *techniques for managing* and implementing technology-driven actions are explored now.

In the first four chapters in this section of the book, managerial issues raised in the course of executing a technologically based strategy are examined. Presented in the first, "Technology Management Techniques," is a survey and a synthesis of various quantitative and qualitative management methods. The first part of the chapter covers the main technology management techniques. The final part of the chapter offers a synthesis of the seemingly discordant quantitative and qualitative approaches into a framework—an "adaptive rationality model"—which permits analysis and judgment.

Chapter 15, "Selecting Appropriate Technological Substrategies," begins with the premise that each industry situation presents a firm with alternative strategy opportunities. These may be opportunities in the form of choices between existing mainline strategies or varieties of differentiation approaches aimed at a particular niche. The chapter then looks at some of these situations more carefully, demonstrating, even within the same overall firm strategy, technological substrategies can be different.

Chapter 16, "Structuring the Organization for Advantage: The Technological Innovation Dimension," begins with the presentation of a two-by-two-by-two typology of innovation. Then the chapter identifies the structural issues that are associated with the various innovation dimensions. By linking these two analyses, the executive is able to select an effective organizational structure by determining the sort of innovation the firm is pursuing.

Chapter 17, "External Acquisition of Technology," explores the increasingly important need and benefits of the external sourcing of technology. One of the major trends in the current world situation is the deepening and the widening of the technological needs of the corporation and the spreading of technological competences. Thus, many more options for the strategic acquisition of technology are available for consideration. Here the life cycle timing and the strategic role of various partnering approaches are explored.

14

Technology Management Techniques

Relying mainly on their own instincts and experience, managers develop formulas for successfully managing their firms' competitive strategy. Their formulas provide the nuts and bolts of management—those activities that are performed within the envelope of overall strategy. They include methods of planning, forecasting, running new ventures, or introducing new products. Within technology-based firms, each of these management activities is much more complex and subject to surprises than similar activities in markets where technology is less a factor.

This chapter contains a review of several common and tested approaches employed by skilled technology managers. These methods allow managers to be proactive (where proactivity is possible) and/or to avoid being ambushed either by competitors' moves or by technological change. After presenting important techniques for forecasting planning and managing technology, a higher level synthesis of these techniques will be offered. This synthesis will balance the strengths and weaknesses of the various techniques. Hard-nosed analytical method will be blended with more judgmental techniques to form an "adaptive rationality model" which will strengthen the manager's hand in pursuing the firm's technologically assisted strategy.

A SURVEY OF TECHNOLOGY MANAGEMENT TECHNIQUES

In earlier chapters, two technology management approaches were developed in some depth. Technology mapping and innovation auditing were introduced as approaches for blending external and internal analyses for the selection of appropriate technologically assisted strategies. Underlying these two approaches are many specific technology management techniques. In the broadest sense, all the techniques focus upon planning and monitoring. Sometime the monitoring is for planning purposes, as in forecasting; sometimes it is for purposes of implementation, as in evaluation and feedback. The most common technology management techniques can be easily divided into six general categories.

The demands of high-technology firms require that much greater emphasis be placed on anticipating and positioning the firm for technological change than is necessary in other industries. Technology directly affects the firm's ability to perform effectively within its markets as competitors seek varying forms of advantage. Technological change itself is an external force so difficult to predict that managers are often puzzled about how to plan for it effectively. Even so, a requisite for successful competitive positioning is the planning of new-technology development processes, which in turn require that externally based technological change be forecast as early and accurately as possible.

Through investment in R&D, firms have opportunities to exert more control on the state of technology and the changes occurring in their market segments. If, for instance, a firm focuses upon a technology that is both basic and key to its current competitive advantage, an appropriate investment pattern quickly becomes evident. Additionally, if the firm asks which technology is most likely to soon change the nature or bases of competition and which technology in the longer run will change these bases again, then R&D proactivity can be effectively directed. This phenomenon, originally shown in Chapter 8, is repeated in Table 14-1.

Conversely, if the firm does not strategically invest in R&D, then it is either limited to reacting to new products and processes introduced by others, or it must engage in other nontechnologically based strategies in order to develop its own form of competitive advantage.

Successful response to both internal and external change is predicated upon a thoughtful search for information about technology and technological potential. Broadly speaking, the information sought can be used to provide basic awareness and can serve as input to the firm's formal planning process. There are, of course, a number of channels through which potentially important information may be sought. The most direct are the various technology-based or scientific journals in related fields. Some of these journals focus so frequently on key issues that they should be canvassed on a regular basis. Others with apparent peripheral interest can be monitored through search services and computerized data bases. Journal sources are likely to be limited in two important ways, however. First, because of the time lag between completing research and getting it into print, information can be months or years old—perhaps too old to be of use. Second, in order to be of interest to a wide audience, journal-based information is often very general and therefore of less use in specific planning problems. Still, these sources are valuable in sharpening the firm's search for more detailed and specific acquisition of information.

The search for information also has a behavioral aspect. In Chapter 8 the concept of technological programming was presented. The output of the programming process was the increase in individual and organizational intellectual capital. Peters and Waterman

Table 14-1. Technology Category and Technology Program Investment Level

Technology Category	Investment Level
Base technology	Needs little
Key technology	Systematically built
Pacing technology	Selective investment
Emerging technology	Monitored

(1982) present a method of increasing both types of intellectual capital by scanning and creating new concepts of technology and environment. Their method can be summarized in four steps. The first is the development of a cohort of management and technology specialists who know their fields thoroughly and can evaluate new information in an informed way. Second, the firm must be represented at trade, technical, and professional meetings so information can be gathered both formally at presentations and symposia and informally through conversations with various representatives. Third, it is very important to foster informality and good communication within the firm so that awareness of different technologically driven potentials is widespread and syntheses for new development efforts can occur more easily. Fourth, decision-making authority should be brought closer to the best available information to decrease response time through decentralization in the organizational structure. (This latter recommendation is the central theme of Lorsch and Lawrence's [1965] work on organizing for product innovation.)

To be of optimal value to the organization, information gathering through internal R&D or external sources must be integrated into a foresight and/or planning framework. The techniques employed by firms in high-technology industries to accomplish this task can be grouped into six categories (Goodman, 1984).

Trend Extrapolation

Assuming that it is not interrupted by radical change, historical data may be used to depict technological development. Performance characteristics such as materials and costs can be plotted over time to trace the history, and then extrapolated to predict the future development of new products. This assumption has been central to the RAND Corporation's cost analysis work and to the work of Herman Kahn, who characterized his forecasts as a "surprise-free future." Uncertainty and interaction effects can be accommodated in these extrapolations and models can be constructed to incorporate stochastic processes to simultaneously evaluate several independent variables. Range estimates and sensitivity analysis also can be employed to develop contingency plans from this analysis. The information added by including uncertainty is often not worth the complication unless the final performance parameters have a wide range of possible results (Abernathy, 1969).

Curve Matching

More sophisticated than trend extrapolation is the inclusion of a life cycle effect, which can be depicted with an S curve. The S curve analysis recognizes that the pattern of technological development is often predictable. Slow rates of change are experienced in the revolutionary or product introduction phase. Then, as a critical mass of information develops about the cluster of relevant technologies, the rate of change increases until the innovation begins to reach its natural limitation. As further increases become incremental, the rate of change slows.

Many technologies have been tracked accurately through S curves, and it is generally accepted that technological change can be forecast with a fair degree of rigor. In contrast to trend extrapolation, the S curve analog gives planners ranges within which to expect specific changes in the development patterns of any technology. The startup phase, with performance increasing at a low rate, is replaced by very rapid performance growth as knowledge increases cumulatively. Finally, during the mature phase further progress comes very slowly—the principal benefits of the technology having been achieved.

Application of S curve matching requires first that the key performance variables be identified and historical observations be obtained. Comparison of these points with the superimposed S curve helps planners to assess the current stage of technology development and the likely timing of inflection points between stages.

Delphi

Where there is less of a data base for a technology or where expected discontinuous change makes curve fitting or matching tenuous, planners may call on expert opinions for their forecasts. Delphi is a technique for obtaining the opinions of an expert panel on an important technological development and for creating a convergent forecast of future changes.

The procedure first requires selection of a panel of expert respondents. A questionnaire is created to solicit forecasts of the arrival of a technology, its performance characteristics, the necessary precursor conditions, and other parameters. Next statistics are calculated that describe the judgment of the panel as a whole. Upper and lower quartile respondents are then asked to comment on the underlying reasons for their optimism or pessimism. These comments and the statistical analysis of the overall set of answers are returned to the experts, who are asked to reflect on this information package so they can adjust their estimates. This process continues through several iterations until the estimates converge on a commonly agreed upon set of results. This final product, the consensus estimate, is the forecast upon which technological and strategic plans are made.

Relevance Trees

This is a graphic/analytic method for matching strategic and technological problems with an array of possible solutions. The final output is a series of intermediate-level objectives which can serve as an input device for a Delphi study. One example of a relevance tree is shown in Table 14-2. At the first level of the tree, a product or process objective of rather broad scope is identified. As the second, a first-cut array of solutions is matched with the problem. At the third level, each solution is evaluated using a similar set of functional criteria. At the fourth level, functional solutions are suggested for each of the problems along with the research projects that will prove or disprove the feasibility of each solution. This final level of the tree presents planners with an array of research projects required in the immediate future. These projects will identify just which combination of technologies will actually meet the overall or fundamental objective of the exercise. The likelihood of successfully following through the various levels of the relevance tree and the timing associated with trying all needed solutions are often then estimated with the Delphi panel.

Table 14-2. Sample Relevance Tree

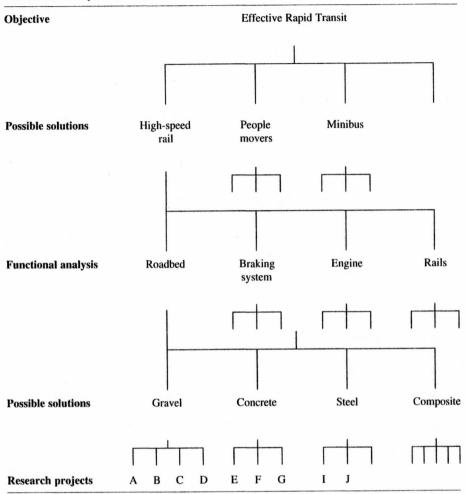

Objective	Effective Rapid Transit
Possible solutions	High-speed rail People movers Minibus
Functional analysis	Roadbed Braking system Engine Rails
Possible solutions	Gravel Concrete Steel Composite
Research projects	A B C D E F G I J

Scenarios

For a planner who sees the future as a set of closely related events, the extrapolation or estimation of a single stream of events may seem inadequate. Instead, a group of forecasts covering several simultaneous streams of events over a wide range of categories may be preferable. In looking at technological developments, for example, competitive market changes and the evolution of government regulation may all be predicted and combined into an integrated forecast. Managers may want to use a single planning exercise to evaluate several scenarios distinguished by differing underlying assumptions.

The first step is the identification of a baseline scenario or one that is surprise-free—a straightforward extrapolation of current trends. Extreme scenarios are then posited, still based on plausible assumptions but intended to represent boundary conditions for the future, rather than most likely states. Finally, variations of the surprise-free scenario which incorporate some elements of the extremes may be generated in order to capture some permutations of technological and competitive changes.

The following steps have been laid out:

1. Develop a data base to establish a requisite baseline of historical data.
2. Identify the firm's objectives as innovations must be measured against the firm's capabilities and profit requirements.
3. Identify relevant organizational and environment variables to model the factors that will determine performance outcomes when technological change occurs.
4. Select an array of surprise-free and extreme scenarios and variations as needed for planning purposes.
5. Develop detailed versions of the selected scenarios (well-defined procedures for creating detailed scenarios using planning teams are available from published sources).
6. Analyze implications of the scenario set and integrate them with the strategic plan to be used as a basis for a critique of the firm's mission and for developing contingency plans.

Cross Impact Analysis

This is a matrix technique that allows planners to examine the extent to which a technological change affects a number of other products, processes, and technologies. Like

Table 14-3. Sample Cross-Impact Matrices

Product–Product Matrix (based upon the impact on sales of complementary products)

		MC	S1	PR	MO	SP
Microcomputer	(MC)	1.0	0.0	0.3	1.0	1.0
S-100 Buss	(S1)	0.1	1.0	0.0	0.0	0.0
Printer	(PR)	0.3	0.0	1.0	0.0	0.0
Modem	(MO)	0.3	0.0	0.1	1.0	0.0
Surge protector	(SP)	0.1	0.0	0.0	0.0	1.0

Technology–Technology Matrix (based upon the impact of developments in one technology on the other technologies)

		NA	CD	LO	HI	MW
Network analysis	(NA)	1.0	0.3	0.0	0.0	0.0
Circuit design	(CD)	0.0	1.0	0.5	0.5	0.3
Lo-freq design	(LO)	0.0	0.1	1.0	0.1	0.1
Hi-freq design	(HI)	0.0	0.1	0.1	1.0	0.2
Microwave design	(MW)	0.0	0.0	0.1	0.1	1.0

Product–Technology Matrix (based upon the impact of developments in one technology on the sales of specific products)

		MC	S1	PR	MD	SP
Network analysis	(NA)	0.2	0.0	0.0	0.1	0.1
Circuit design	(CD)	0.4	0.1	0.3	0.3	0.2
Lo-freq design	(LO)	0.3	0.1	0.3	0.3	0.2
Hi-freq design	(HI)	0.2	0.0	0.0	0.0	0.0
Microwave design	(MW)	0.0	0.0	0.0	0.0	0.0

scenarios (and unlike most other forecasting and planning methods) cross-impact analysis does not assume that technologies and products are independent of one another. By accounting for interaction effects in a simple way, cross-impact analysis increases the sophistication of forecasts at low cost. Table 14-3 is one example of a cross-impact matrix taken from Goodman and Lawless (1984), where it is suggested that three matrices should be created. The first is a product–product matrix that illustrates the impact of one product on the sales of complementary products. The second matrix shows the impact of technological development in one technology upon the technological development in another. The final matrix demonstrates the impact of the improvement of specific technologies upon the sales of various products of interest. Combined, they allow planners to evaluate virtually all key interactions. The matrices can be cross-multiplied and weighted with potential returns, producing a figure of merit for the technology which can be used in resource allocation decisions.

EVALUATION OF TECHNOLOGY PLANNING METHODS

Each of the techniques just described has direct relevance to the technology mapping technique introduced in earlier chapters. Several of the techniques explicitly help to establish the rate of change of various underlying technologies. Thus, they provide important input to the analysis of subsystem functional needs and the relevant technologies which could alter the bases of satisfying these needs.

These techniques represent common industrial practice. Each takes a particular differentiated approach useful for solving some issue of high-technology management. Taken as whole they raise the question of fit between standard technology management techniques and the requirements of strategic decision making in high-technology environments. Considering its importance, this idea of fit between technology and strategy does not usually get enough scrutiny.

When it comes to methods offered by academics, scientists and researchers, and managers from technology companies, highly rational procedures and decision-making rules are recommended over loosely defined "organic" measures. In general, the methods provide the strategists with tools with which to structure a complex decision situation and to make the optimal feasible decision. These techniques best fit problems with well-defined parameters and a high degree of certainty.

The rest of this chapter is devoted to an evaluation of technology management methods with particular emphasis on the question of fit between available strategic analysis techniques and the realities of the high-technology environment. High-rationality methods, for example, may be completely inappropriate under the high-uncertainty and rapid change found in high-technology environments. A number of researchers (Mintzberg, 1973; Lindblom, 1979) argue against the use of rational methods in turbulent environments. In essence, they say that some highly rational methods should be avoided despite their intuitive appeal because they rely on certainty and structure—indeed, in addition to *not* improving strategy, they may even lead a company away from a successful course. On the other hand, low-rationality methods, because of their lack of direction and confusion, also may endanger the firm. Additionally, though one finds a wide range of strategy–technology integration techniques, there is no organizing concept within which to understand their use, costs, and capabilities. Neither is there any indication of the ways that complementary methods might fit together into a coherent technology strategy.

Presented here is an integrative model of the technology-strategy formulation process based on a comprehensive evaluation of the integration methods currently available. In explaining the model it is most useful to first describe and summarize the major types of existing technology management techniques, categorizing them according to their degree of rationality. This new analytic framework accommodates uncertainty and change in technology management and allows the use of techniques of various degrees of rationality, as appropriate. The adaptive rationality model calls on the strategy maker to cycle between a global, loosely defined viewpoint and focused, rational, analytic techniques. It allows for use of a wide array of analytic tools in their proper context and for incremental learning as the analysis converges on an acceptable solution. First the methods and their degrees of rationality are discussed, and then the adaptive rationality model is presented.

Methods for Technology-Strategy Analysis

These methods are generally designed to increase either the consideration given to technology issues or the involvement of technology function managers in strategy making. Within the following framework, a wide assortment of methods are screened from a survey of over seventy recent articles that have been drawn systematically from both the academic and practitioner-oriented literature. The analysis involves several steps. First, each integration method is isolated. Next, like methods are placed into homogeneous groups to simplify evaluation. The grouping procedure uses similarity among the methods in three characteristics: purpose (e.g., to evaluate R&D project proposals or to do comprehensive planning), concept (e.g., a portfolio method or a set of generic strategies), and procedure (e.g., an expected value method or a set of lessons from excellent companies). This part of the evaluation results yields several groups of methods.

Second, the groups are classified according to their level of rationality. A three-point rating of high, moderate, or low is employed. Trade-offs among cost, need, and feasibility make the question of level of rationality important to this assessment. Strategy–technology integration methods described here as highly rational follow the comprehensive or synoptic model in the general business strategy literature (Andrews, 1971; Schendel and Hofer, 1979). Generally, they rigorously define their input data requirements, the output consisting of strategy indications, and the processes of strategy identification and evaluation. At the other extreme, low-rationality methods are relatively unfocused, giving the strategist only the broadest guidance on the management of technology functions.

While they offer optimal feasible strategies for issues that fit into their frameworks, high-rationality methods are expensive, respond slowly to problems, and do not often fit real-world decision situations. Additionally, the issues of the appropriateness of a strategy formulation technique to a particular setting has also been raised (Mintzberg, 1973).

In turbulent environments where high uncertainty and complexity intervene, the drawbacks of the comprehensive techniques are increased. On the other hand, low-rationality methods may not give sufficient direction to be used effectively by strategists. In short, it is clear that serious attention should be given to the level of rationality of strategy–technology integration methods so that they may be carefully evaluated.

Strategy–technology integration methods in the three groups that follow are classified by their level of rationality—high, moderate, or low. Each rationality level is described in terms of its differentiating characteristics. Integration method groups belonging to each of the levels are listed. Then in-depth discussions and evaluations of each level are presented along with examples of individual methods belonging to each.

High Rationality Methods. In conceptual terms, high-rationality decision making is selecting "optimal choices in a highly-specified and clearly-defined environment" (March and Simon, 1958). In practical terms, it consists of techniques designed to make explicit and systematic decisions about new products, R&D investment, process innovations, and the like. Methods typed as "high rationality" exhibit the following specific characteristics:

1. Strategies are keyed to a few well-defined environmental conditions.
2. Procedures, decision rules, and threshold values are used, and precisely specified.
3. There is high cause–effect expectation; outcomes from strategies are well defined.

There are two broad groups of methods which meet these criteria of specificity, procedural clarity, and well-defined cause and effect models. They are:

1. Matrix methods for integrating technology and competitive strategy.
2. Project selection and planning processes for innovations.

Strategists planning for technology–strategy integration must cope with both high levels of complexity and high levels of uncertainty (Balthasar, Boschi, and Menke, 1979). To fit technology-strategy issues into the high-rationality approach requires rigorous definition and measurement. In general, this is accomplished by the simplification and categorization of the otherwise complex and uncertain elements inherent in the situation. Relationships are quantified and formulas developed, where possible; otherwise well-defined heuristics are employed (Ward 1981).

Levine and Yalowitz (1983), Boschi and Barjon (1983), and Pappas (1984) use matrix analysis for fitting R&D strategies with the firm's plans. These matrices, in one form or another, categorize the competitive situation and the potential technological responses, thus directing the firm to the correct response. Others increase the thoroughness of technological planning in order to reduce surprises and to systematically encompass more situational elements. Buijs (1979) and Linn (1983) both recommend corporate plans that include comprehensive planning for technology. Dean (1984) goes even further by applying network analysis to the planning and management of innovative ventures. The contribution of high-rationality methods in explicit, structured analyses should be more comprehensive than unanalyzed, incremental approaches which rely on serendipity for success.

The drawbacks of the deployment of high-rationality techniques arise from their poor fit to many problems inherent in technology integration. Specification of actions and outcomes is difficult under uncertainty; prescribed procedures are unresponsive to change; and important information may be lost in fitting the issues into a defined framework (Mintzberg, 1973; Lindblom, 1979). Where improperly used, the results can be wasted time and resources and poor timing of decisions. Additionally, managers are likely to ignore rational plans and analysis if they are untimely and if there is a feeling that they do not add to the understanding of the problem (Lawless, 1982).

Moderate Rationality Methods. While less specific in terms of processes than the high-rationality methods, moderate-rationality methods are nonetheless specific in their content. They are designed to provide broad, yet operational, guidance to decision makers. A method fits this category if:

1. It keys on broadly described environmental conditions (e.g., scenarios),
2. It describes classes of problems or issues,
3. It suggests broad guidelines or generic strategies,
4. Within the guidelines, managers can pick or create strategies to fit their individual problems, or
5. Outcomes are described in broad terms.

There are two major groups of moderate-rationality methods:

1. Broad prescriptions for integrating technology and strategic management, and
2. Generic strategies, internal and external, for managing technology.

For the most part these methods are mainly guidelines for decision making that depend on certain factors common to a wide range of strategy-making situations. They should apply equally well to a variety of organizations, technologies, industries, and markets. Generic strategies (Porter, 1980) are typical of this level of rationality. Traditionally, it is the authors' experience that moderate-rationality guidelines for strategy–technology integration are the synthesis of decision-making patterns.

Some of these methods help position the firm's innovations against its rivals in the high-technology market (Ansoff and Stewart, 1967; Cooper and Schendel, 1976; Linn, 1983). The group also includes broad guidelines for investing in R&D (Goodman, 1984; Johnson, 1984), in product innovation (Crawford, 1980), or in continuing product development projects (Balachandra, 1981). Williams (1983) suggests that broad strategies could be based on technological evolution and competitive pressure. Heany (1983) categorizes product innovations on the amount of variance from current products while White and Graham (1978) use a set of innovation merit factors.

Depending on indicators of market, technology, and firm conditions, managers are led to one or another of these methods as a foundation on which to build their individual approaches to integrating technology with strategy. These methods avoid most of the drawbacks of the high-rationality group. They are more adaptable to individual applications simply because they are less specific. On the other hand, they can be criticized as too simple and broad for operational strategy making in particular applications. Such suggestive guidelines puts the burden of interpretation on the decision maker.

The two techniques of innovation auditing and technology mapping fit clearly into this category of moderate-rationality methods. In both, systematic questions are asked and the results are blended into guidelines for selecting strategic approaches. In both techniques, the systematic framework is emphasized to create a more comprehensive set of dimensions for analysis while simultaneously providing range for the judgment of the executive in the final selection of strategic action.

Low Rationality Methods. The principal feature of this group is that the prescriptions tend to be very general. Issues are partially defined, either by choice or by constraint. Methods may be rather specific regarding preferred results, but they lay out only minimal means or procedures. Instead they suggest conditions and guidance under which managers can work toward their objectives. Specifically a method fits in this category if:

1. It suggest ways to conceptualize issues and problems,
2. It describes issues rather than prescribes solutions, and generally leaves managers to define specific responses, or
3. It offers guidance rather than actionable strategies.

Three major groups of methods are found in this category:

1. Models of technology management process,
2. Themes for technology management emerging from successful companies, and
3. Factors affecting technology management results.

In terms of specification and rigorous definition, low-rationality methods have something in common with Quinn's (1980) "logical incrementalism." His model for strategy making proposes that only goals and broad guidelines should be laid out in a plan, leaving managers to their own devices in accomplishing the firm's objectives. In applying these approaches to strategy–technology integration, Hettinger (1982) says top management must know where it wants to go but not articulate its objective in detail. Without specifying procedures, both Ward (1981) and Petroni (1983) suggest organizational structure reforms to increase the effectiveness of the technology functions in competition.

Lessons for effective technology management gleaned from consulting practice and from observation are also common. Rosenbloom and Kantrow (1982) suggest broad, experience-based guidelines for managing corporate research. Frohman (1982), Maidique and Hayes (1984), and McGinnis and Ackelsburg (1983) list practices that will help companies manage corporate research well. Finally, there are descriptions of conditions for successful technology management. Fernelius and Waldo (1980) list factors affecting innovation in companies. Horwitch and Prahalad (1976) describe technological innovation management in differing contexts. Ford and Ryan (1981) use the technology life cycle to help decide the disposition of the firm's technology.

These methods are best attuned to the high uncertainty and complexity of the technological environment. They allow for adaptability and flexibility in managing unique situations. They all have serious flaws, however, that come from their level of abstraction. Because it is very difficult to know how to implement them in practical situations, they must be supplemented with other guidance to help managers know how to put them into effect.

THE ADAPTIVE RATIONALITY MODEL

Firms that count technology as a significant influence on their competitive success must operate in ambiguous environments (Cohen and March, 1974). These situations present threats to strategy makers who are overly rational. They are vulnerable to exigencies that do not fit their framework: inaccurate forecasts, unpredicted conditions, incorrect assumptions, and unexpected decision outcomes. The rational manager can spend time and money on strategic plans and decision aids that are not used, or that lead the company astray. On the other hand, those who are undirected and overly reactive may not see the cumulative effects on their incremental decisions until they have stepped out of the envelope within which their firms can survive. While both high- and low-rationality approaches have their place in strategically managing technology, they must be used in balance with each other. The issue of the appropriate use of strategy formulation methods—particularly in the context of strategy–technology integration—is not generally recognized in the literature, so little help is available. Instead, various methods are presented with virtually no guidance on their limitations, costs, or benefits. However, a framework similar to ones previously applied to the analysis of general strategy-making problems may help to improve technology-strategy decision making. Called the *adaptive rationality model* (ARM), the method is in the tradition of Goodman, Huff, Abonyi, and Lawless (1977), Goodman and Huff (1978), and Quinn (1980). The model is presented in Figure 14-1.

Under the adaptive rationality model, technology-strategy formulation is laid out as an iterative process, moving from macro to micro methods and back, until a satisfactory action program is ready for execution. Information from control systems is used to evaluate the performance of strategies after they are implemented and to adapt them as required. Following is a description of the ARM as a process, formally illustrating all of its essential parts. This process description does not attempt to portray the use of the model in an actual application. In use the model must adapt to the real-world complexity and is less linear than presented here.

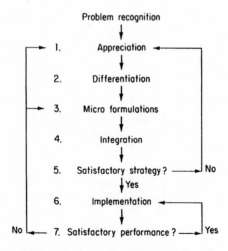

Figure 14-1. Adaptive rationality model flow diagram.

Appreciation

In the initial phase, the appreciation phase, low-rationality methods are used to create a "macro view"—a rich, holistic understanding of the issue at hand (Vickers, 1965). In Richard Rumelt's view (1979), the proper role of strategy is to frame a complex, uncertain situation so that analyzable problems can be identified. Data are collected based on their potential importance, rather than on their fit to a particular algorithm. The strategy maker must maintain an open mind and avoid being locked into a single perspective early on, particularly where there is high uncertainty, as any strategy once chosen limits the manager's options. It then puts the organization on a course of collecting certain kinds of information and pursuing some actions while excluding others (Huff, 1982).

The *purpose* of the appreciation is (1) to develop a reference framework on the issue to support further analysis and decision making; (2) to visualize the relationships among all parts of the issue and between the issue and the environment; and (3) to accommodate "squishy" (Strauch, 1974) aspects of the issue—those that do not lend themselves to rigorous analysis.

The *task* of the appreciation phase is: (1) to accumulate and structure information while avoiding evaluation; (2) to develop multiple viewpoints on the issues (from different models, sources, perspectives of involved parties); and (3) to put the issue in the broad context, avoid detail, look for connections among the issue and other activities, the mission, and the environment.

The *devices* employed in the appreciation phase are: situation analysis, critical issues lists, descriptive scenarios, nominal group techniques, and brainstorming.

Differentiation

In the differentiation phase the strategic issue is divided into smaller problems that fall within the realm of the organization that has decided to apply a high-rationality method. Conceptually, this phase is similar to the organizational structure problems of the "differentiation–integration" process described by Lawrence and Lorsch (1967) or in the decomposition problems in management science (Wagner, 1969). In an attempt to minimize the interactions among variables and to attack issues with only a limited need to refer to larger issues, issues are isolated by the analyst based upon a judgment of the intensity with which they are related to each other. Micro issues that result are small in scope compared with the macro view and are more likely be suitable for and benefit from high-rationality analytical techniques.

The *purpose* of differentiation is to segment the appreciation analytically into analyzable micro issues, those that are "small" and well defined.

The *task* of differentiation is to isolate parts of the appreciation based upon (1) minimizing the intensity of connections among the elements; (2) finding an analytical fit with available solution methods; (3) finding a fit with the size and complexity limits of available solution methods; and (4) employing other judgmental logics which are situationally appropriate.

The *devices* employed in differentiation rely on heuristics that isolate and cluster problem characteristics and then exploit "near decomposability" (Simon and Ando, 1961; Simon, 1981).

Micro Formulations

Next, in the micro formulation phase, the strategy maker attempts to identify the best strategy for each of the micro issues. This is an opportunity to apply expected-value analysis, discounted cash flow analysis, and other rigorous methodologies as appropriate. High-rationality methods permit managers to study the well-defined aspects of problems in technology strategy. Additionally, managers may be able to better analyze issues that do not fit available methods simply because these are relatively simpler and smaller than the issues from which they are derived.

The *purpose* of the micro formulation phase is the identification of the best strategy for each of the micro issues.

The *task* of this phase is to select formulation and solution methods and apply them to the micro issues as appropriate.

The *devices* employed in this phase include net present-value methods, expected value methods, portfolio methods, and lessons drawn from excellent companies.

Macro Integration

In the macro integration phase, these results are combined into an overall strategy so that consistency among the solutions, proper budgeting of resources, and fit with the environment are assured. The strategy maker selects a comprehensive framework like a scenario or a decision tree to fit the micro issue formulations and to create a complete overview of the issue.

The *purpose* of the macro integration phase is to formulate a unified strategy set.

The *task* is to evaluate and combine micro strategies in the context of the appreciation, to look for conflicts, unintended results, gaps, and the like.

The *devices* that can be employed here include decision trees, fault trees, scenario building, and value analysis.

Formulation Check

In the macro integration phase, discrepancies between the appreciation and the results of the micro formulations are further explored. Often the problem or issue needs to be addressed differently within the appreciation and possibly differentiated using alternative decision priorities. Thus, the analytic process continues to iterate—alternating between low- and high-rationality analysis—until, as indicated in this formulation check phase, continuing produces no net benefit. When the strategy maker is satisfied that this is the best available strategy set—it should be implemented. In this way, the high- and low-rationality approaches, while philosophically different, operate as complements in the strategy formulation process.

The *purpose* of the formulation check phase is to decide whether to continue the strategy formulation phase by moving on to the implementation phase or by returning to the appreciation phase.

The *task* of this phase is to evaluate the current strategy set in terms of expectations (likelihood of success, and other results) and constraints and to decide if the current solution is adequate.

The *devices* employed here are estimates of expected results, pro forma budgets, and the development of an implementation issues list.

ARM strategy making is still not complete, however, since performance data must be employed to adjust the strategies after they are implemented. The model formalizes the monitoring of strategies once in place as a means for management to learn about their suitability under uncertainty. The model includes the implementation and performance check phases in strategy formulation consistent with Quinn's idea (1980) that implementation and formulation should be considered part of the same process rather than as discrete elements. He cites the importance of incremental learning by decision makers as a means of achieving the best possible fit of strategies within the extant environmental conditions. This critical interaction between formulation and implementation is also supported by Goodman and Huff (1977) in their discussion of strategy making in ambiguous situations.

Implementation

The *purpose* of the implementation phase is to execute the actions developed in the several earlier formulation phases.

The *task* of the implementation phase is to allocate resources and to transfer information, instructions, and incentives to line managers.

The *devices* of this phase are differentiation, delegation, information systems operations, and goal-setting methods such as management by objectives.

Performance Check

The *purpose* of the performance check is to evaluate the impact of the selected strategy set on strategy–technology integration issues and upon overall firm performance.

The *task* of the performance check is to create a set of performance standards, to collect data, and to evaluate performance.

The *devices* employed here are performance measures, goals, information from control systems, decision support systems and their precursor management information systems.

In summary, the ARM is a procedural model for strategy formulation in high-uncertainty, complex environments like those of high-technology industries. It gives the strategist a framework within which to evaluate and fit together the various analytic methods of high, moderate, or low rationality. It also provides a framework within which knowledge gained from evaluation of strategies before implementation and from actual performance can be used as a basis for adapting the selected strategy. It is clear that the major techniques posed in this book, technology mapping and innovation auditing, fit rather well into the micro formulation, the macro integration, and the formulation check stages of this adaptive rationality model.

SUMMARY

Despite the sizable array of techniques for strategic management of the technology functions, decision makers should not be blamed for relying on their own devices instead of the published results of practice or of management research. The potentially applicable techniques are numerous and diverse, with little guidance offered on their utility and net benefits. The question of the appropriateness of high-rationality strategy methods in turbulent high-technology environments is often not adequately addressed. The solution to the problem of selecting a strategy–technology integration method may very well be found in a framework such as the one suggested here. The adaptive rationality model helps to narrow the range of methods employed and to match the rationality level of the methods to the issues of concern. The iterative nature of the model further strengthens the strategist's assurances that analysis has appropriately blended the high- and low-rationality perspectives.

REFERENCES

Abernathy, W. J. 1969. "Parallel Strategies in Development Projects," *Management Science* 15(10):B486–B505.

Andrews, K. 1971. *The Concept of Corporate Strategy.* Homewood, IL: Irwin.

Ansoff, I., and J. Stewart. 1967. "Strategies for a Technology-Based Business," *Harvard Business Review,* November–December, pp. 71–82.

Balachandra, R. 1981. "Critical Signals for Making Go–No Go Decisions in New Product Development," *Journal of Product Innovation Management* 1(2):92–100.

Balthasar, H., R. Boschi, and M. Menke. 1979. "Calling the Shots in R&D," *Harvard Business Review,* May–June, pp. 151–160.

Boschi, R., and M. Barjon. 1983. "Strategy in R&D." Paper presented at the annual meeting of the Strategic Management Society, Paris.

Buijs, J. 1979. "Strategic Planning Product Innovation—Some Systematic Approaches," *Long Range Planning* 12(3):23–34.

Cohen, M., and J. March. 1974. *Leadership and Ambiguity.* New York: McGraw-Hill.

Cooper, A., and D. Schendel. 1976. "Strategic Response to Technological Threats," *Business Horizons,* February, pp. 61–69.

Crawford, C. 1980. "Defining the Product Innovation Charter," *Sloan Management Review,* Fall, pp. 3–12.

Dean, B. 1984. "The Management of Innovative Start-up Firms," *Technical Memorandum No 548.* Cleveland: Case Western Reserve University.

Fernelius, W., and W. Waldo. 1980. "The Role of Basic Research in Industrial Innovation," *Research Management* 23:36–40.

Ford, D., and C. Ryan. 1981. "Taking Technol-

ogy to Market," *Harvard Business Review,* March–April, pp. 117–126.

Frohman, A. 1982. "Technology as a Competitive Weapon," *Harvard Business Review,* May–June, pp. 97–104.

Goodman, R. A. 1984. "Strategic Planning and Decision-Making Techniques." in Balderson, J. P. Birnbaum, R. A. Goodman, and M. Stahl, eds., *Modern Management Techniques in Engineering and R & D.* New York: Van Nostrand Reinhold.

Goodman, R., and A. Huff. 1978. "Enriching Policy Premises for an Ambiguous World." In J. Sutherland, ed., *Management Handbook for Public Administrators.* New York: Van Nostrand Reinhold.

Goodman, R., A. Huff, G. Abonyi, and M. Lawless. 1977. "An Alternative World-View for Policy Analysis and Policy Making (or Beyond Systems Theory)," *Proceedings of the Third Annual Southeastern Meeting of the Society for General Systems Research,* New Orleans: Society for General Systems Research.

Goodman, R., and M. Lawless. 1984. "A Cascading Matrix Method for the Development of a Technological Figure-of-Merit." In R. Goodman and J. Pavon, eds. *Planning for National Technology Policy.* New York: Praeger.

Heany, D. 1983. "Degree of Product Innovation," *Journal of Business Strategy* 3:3–14.

Hettinger, W. 1982. "The Top Technologist Should Join the Team," *Research Management* 25:7–10.

Horwitch, M., and C.K. Prahalad. 1976. "Managing Technological Innovation—Three Ideal Modes," *Sloan Management Review,* Winter, pp. 77–89.

Huff, A. 1982. "Industry Influence on Strategy

Reformulation," *Strategic Management Journal* 32:119–32.

Johnson, S. 1984. "Comparing R & D Strategies of Japanese and U.S. Firms," *Sloan Management Review*, Spring, pp. 25–34.

Lawless, M. 1982. "A Policy and Process Model of the Implementation of Computer Models in Criminal Justice Agencies," *Applications in Management Science*, 2:212–31.

Lawrence, P., and J. Lorsch. 1967. "Differentiation and Integration in Complex Organizations," *Administrative Science Quarterly* 12(1):1–47.

Levine, S., and M. Yalowitz. 1983. "Managing Technology: Key to Business Growth," *Management Review*, September, pp. 44–48.

Lindblom, C. 1979. "Still Muddling, Not Yet Through," *Public Administration Review* 39:517–26.

Linn, R. 1983. "A Sectoral Approach to Strategic Planning for R&D," *Research Management* 26:33–40.

Lorsch, J., and P. Lawrence. 1965. "Organizing for Product Innovation," *Harvard Business Review*, January–February, pp. 109–27.

Maidique, M., and R. Hayes. 1984. "The Art of High Technology Management," *Sloan Management Review*, Winter, pp. 17–31.

March, J., and H. Simon. 1958. *Organizations*. New York: Wiley.

McGinnis, H., and J. Ackelsburg. 1983. "Effective Information Management: Missing Link in Strategic Planning?" *Journal of Business Strategy*, 4(1):59–66.

Mintzberg, H. 1973. "Strategy Making in Three Modes," *California Management Review*, Winter, pp. 44–54.

Pappas, C. 1984. "Strategic Management of Technology," *Journal of Product Innovation* 1(1):30–35.

Peters, T., and R. Waterman. 1982. *In Search of Excellence: Lessons from America's Best-Run Companies*. New York: Warner Books.

Petroni, G. 1983. "The Strategic Management of R&D, Part 2—Organizing for Integration," *Long Range Planning* 16(2):51–65.

Porter, M. 1980. *Competitive Strategy*. New York: Free Press.

Quinn, J. 1980. *Strategies for Change: Logical Incrementalism*. Englewood Cliffs, NJ: Prentice-Hall.

Rosenbloom, R., and A. Kantrow. 1982. "The Nurturing of Corporate Research," *Harvard Business Review*, January–February, pp. 115–23.

Rumelt, R. 1979. "Evaluation of Strategy: Theory and Models." In D. Schendel and C. Hofer, eds., *Strategic Management*. Boston: Little, Brown.

Schendel, D., and C. Hofer, eds. 1979. *Strategic Management*. Boston: Little, Brown.

Simon, H. 1981. *The Science of the Artificial*. Cambridge, MA: MIT Press.

Simon, H., and A. Ando. 1961. "Aggregation of Variables in Dynamic Systems," *Econometrica* 29:111–38.

Strauch, R. 1974. *A Critical Assessment of Quantitative Analysis as a Policy Analysis Tool*. Santa Monica, CA: Rand Corporation, P-5282.

Vickers, G. 1965. *The Art of Judgement*. New York: Basic Books.

Wagner, H. 1969. *Operations Research*. Englewood Cliffs, NJ: Prentice-Hall.

Ward, P. 1985. "Planning for Technological Innovation—Developing the Necessary Nerve," *Long Range Planning* 14(2):59–71.

White, G., and M. Graham. 1978. "How to Spot a Technological Winner," *Harvard Business Review*, March–April, pp. 146–152.

Williams, J. 1983. "Technological Evolution and Competitive Response," *Strategic Management Journal* 4(1):55–65.

15

Selecting Appropriate Technology Substrategies

In Chapter 14 the roles of various methodological approaches in the study of technology–strategy integration were outlined. In this chapter, the technology question is pursued in more detail—relying upon research results—to expose the technological alternatives in strategy implementation. Both the technological mapping and the innovation auditing techniques help direct the analyst toward a short list of technology strategies. The manager exercising executive judgment can select a final choice from this list. In this chapter are research results which reflect the real-life choices made when technological substrategies are deployed in the pursuit of corporate-level strategies.

Because of rapid change and high complexity, a manager operating in a high-technology environment may well look for help in determining a sound competitive strategy. A strategist consulting the literature—either academic- or practitioner-oriented—will find a high level of consensus on two premises. First, the "technology functions" (corporate and divisional R&D, production engineering, and product and process innovation management) can be potent competitive weapons (Lawless and Rossy, 1984), but they are rarely exploited by corporate management (Maidique and Patch, 1980; Jelinek and Burstein, 1982). Second, when it comes to methods available for accomplishing the integration of technology with strategy, there's a lot of conventional wisdom, but little actual research.

It is commonly said that firms that successfully tie the technology functions into strategy will perform better than those that do not (Bright, 1964; Schoonhoven, 1983; Wheelwright, 1984). In determining the best method of effectively managing technology functions in relation to the firm's competitive position, several questions should be asked: What sorts of technology management patterns exist? What is the nature of the interaction between technology and strategy? Is there a "correct" combination of technology and competitive strategy (one that makes for better performance)? And in responding to these queries it is important to concentrate on the question of fit between competitive strategy and technology substrategy.

SUPPORT FOR STRATEGY–TECHNOLOGY INTEGRATION

The literature on the management of research, development, and innovation almost uniformly recommends that the technology areas be integrated with strategy making and planning for reasons that should eventually translate to better performance for the firm. The rationale for integration is broad, and it includes the promise of more successful product introduction, greater production economies, protection of products from appropriation by competitors, avoidance of conflict, and more. Justification for integration often includes one or more of the following general statements.

1. Many decisions for managing technology functions span long time frames, deploy large portions of a firm's available resources, and are difficult to change once commitments are made. They are, therefore, the concern of top management and are strategic in nature (Wheelwright, 1984).

2. Production decisions, including currency in product innovation, manufacturing, and transportation costs (Skinner, 1978), have direct impact on the firm's competitive position. Defining the firm's technology as it affects the ability to maintain distinctive competitive advantage is, therefore, central to market success (Frohman and Bitondo, 1981; Williams, 1983; Goodman, 1984).

3. Technology projects compete for resources with other activities and investments within the firm. There should be an allocation method that reflects a wide-ranging view of the company's ability to support the mix of proposed activities available to it (Ramsey, 1981; Buggie, 1982; Hertz and Thomas, 1983).

4. Organization structures and processes intended specifically to promote innovation are generally associated with high administrative costs (Quinn, 1979; Cooper, 1981; Lawless, Feinberg, Glassman, and Bengston, 1981) as well as opportunity costs and external effects. They may either limit or enhance the firm's ability to execute its other critical tasks.

5. In the technology functions, there is often high task uncertainty and a corresponding intense need for information to be gathered, processed, and transferred during task performance (Galbraith, 1973, 1977). Managing uncertainty and developing adequate information systems to support the technology functions are strategic issues.

6. A tendency for organizational units, including those involved with the technology functions, to suboptimize has been noted. They pursue parochial goals regardless of their impact on other units, and perhaps on the organization as a whole (Cyert and March, 1963). Meanwhile, coordination among several departments appears related to successful commercialization of new products (Mansfield, 1981). Product innovation requires interaction among R&D, marketing, product engineering, and production (Ford and Ryan, 1981; Buggie, 1982). Differentiation among these units drives the need for integration (Lawrence and Lorsch, 1967).

7. The values, worldview, and orientation toward corporate goals of scientists are likely to differ from those of managers, and from what is needed for the competitive success of the firm (Parker, 1977; Petroni, 1983a). While the importance of this issue varies with the technology function (Ritti, 1982), it poses problems of communication and goal congruity to some degree in all.

This list is not intended to be exhaustive, only to convey some of the concerns that cause many of the authors in technology management to promote strategy–technology integration. As Weil and Cangemi (1983) point out in their review of the evolution of thought on technology and strategy, integration is the dominant theme emerging from the received literature. This proposition finds support in the work of respected scholars writing on R&D, production, and innovation. Given the need for strategy–technology integration, a wide array of responses is available to managers. In the following section, current methods for enhancing integration are reviewed.

DEFINITIONS OF STRATEGY AND SUBSTRATEGY

This chapter uses basic economic concepts to lay out the relationship between strategy and technology in business unit strategy making. It presents a set of accepted, well-articulated ideas that tie technology to competition in a fairly direct way. Industrial organization is a branch of economics specifically designed to describe the structure and profitability of markets. It has traditionally been used by regulators to assess the level of competition in industries, especially for purposes of deciding on the need for antitrust intervention. Federal decisions on mergers, acquisitions, and divestitures are based in part on industrial organization (IO) analysis. Michael Porter (1980, 1985) was a pioneer in adapting IO models to firm-level use. Instead of industry profitability, the key issue is individual firm profitability. Strategists, now conversant with industrial organization concepts, uniformly accept the premise that the performance of firms results from their individual behaviors, market structure, and underlying environmental conditions (Scherer, 1980). The outcome of competitive strategy, the firm's position among market forces, affects its performance.

Market Competence

Further, a firm can be conceptualized as a "nexus," or meeting ground, for a set of contracting relationships among the factors of production (Jensen and Meckling, 1976), each factor contributing some expertise or capability that allows the firm to compete effectively. This abstraction on the abilities of firms to compete has a particular advantage for thinking about the strategy–technology connection.

Additionally, we can use the construct that each firm is a unique array of competencies. These are factors of production, or tools for getting things done, that are organized around a particular set of objectives. They can be interpreted more broadly as *market competencies*—abilities to respond to, and to influence, all market forces that can affect profitability (Lawless, 1986). Competitive strategies, or the market behavior of individual firms, result from investments that management makes to develop market competencies. A firm's competitive strategy then is recognized in the pattern of market competencies used to obtain profits through its market position. The technology functions are a subset of these competencies through which firms try to develop competitive advantage over their rivals. It may be through the technology directly (e.g., by taking a leading-edge position in new products, by being a product pioneer or product leader) or through the many ways in which technology supports or promotes other competencies (e.g., through flexible manufacturing where firms in commodity markets provide customized products in response to customer need).

The market competence concept is based on the notion that strategies are decomposable (Simon, 1981), that they consist of components that are interesting for their individual contribution to performance as well as for their part in overall strategy. It is preceded in management thinking by the concept of "distinctive competence," a term coined by Selznick (1957) in his classic studies of the Tennessee Valley Authority where he observed that special capabilities tend to emerge as a normal process of organizational evolution. The aspect of distinctiveness in relation to competitors has been added and developed since (Andrews, 1971; Snow and Hrebiniak, 1980; Grant and King, 1982). Now distinctive competence generally is defined as a set of skills that a firm can muster that are unique among its rivals. More important, however, the competence is strategically important and makes a real difference in the firm's competitive performance. It gives the firm an edge over others when competing in the same markets. In relation to this part of the strategy literature, the market competencies concept focuses on factors contributing to competitive success. First the complete array of relevant abilities, activities, and "things organizations do" (Snow and Hrebiniak, 1980) must be identified so they can be aggregated into strategy and substrategy types. Only at this stage are propositions made about the uniqueness of firms' approaches to market position and their effectiveness.

The potential for an elegant, generalizable approach is the motivation for the market competence model. Its basic goal is to provide a means to describe competitive strategy using the characteristics of firms that directly relate to their market positions. Such a framework supports the selection of variables for a numerical taxonomy of competitive strategies through a focus on market forces and market competencies.

An array of relevant *market forces* is identified using market structure analysis from industrial organization theory (Porter, 1980, 1985; Scherer, 1980). These are the parts of the firms' environments that affect performance. Corresponding *market competencies* are abilities developed by firms to respond to, and to influence, the various market forces that they face. Borrowing from Lawrence and Lorsch's (1967) concept of organizational differentiation we can develop a model in which organizations develop departments to deal individually with discrete parts of their diverse environments. In the market competence model, firms' competencies have specific roles vis-á-vis particular market forces. When an array of market competencies appropriate to an environment is identified, patterns can be searched out. Competitive strategy types emerge as groups of firms place their emphasis differently among market competencies. Competitive strategies are interpreted as *patterns of market competencies* used by firms to maintain an acceptable configuration of relations with market forces.

Table 15-1 summarizes the main parts of the model, which are explained further in following sections. It shows market forces, their relation to the firm, and three market competencies relevant to each force. The market forces are taken from Porter's model (1980). These market competencies are not exhaustive. They were chosen for purposes of illustration and are intended only to show some of the possibilities. Having been summarized, the market competence model is described more completely as a technique to support competitive strategy taxonomy.

Theoretical Foundations of the Market Competence Model

Fundamentally, this approach views competitive strategy as ex-post results of decision behavior, that is, as deliberate, emergent strategy (Mintzberg, 1978). This is an appro-

Table 15-1. Market Forces, Relations, and Sample Market Competencies

Market Forces	Firm's Relation	Sample Market Competencies
Buyers	Value creation/need satisfaction	Collect intelligence on buyer needs
		Bundle goods and services
		Customize product features
Competitors	Competition/cooperation	Joint R&D venturing
		Maintain standard industry practice
		Offer lowest priced product
New entrants	Deny entry to served market	Maintain high product innovation rate
		Patent products and processes
		Product differentiation advertising
Substitutes	Reduce attractiveness of substitutes to buyers	Price on par with substitutes
		Advertise brand name
		Tie special service into installed base
Suppliers	Bargaining, integration	Maintain multiple sources
		License, acquire, develop the input
		Maintain ability to use substitutes

priate interpretation of competitive strategy for research where performance evaluation is the ultimate goal. In previous studies using the same tack, strategy is inferred through configurations of resource allocation (Hambrick, 1983) or through the stated intentions of management (Dess and Davis, 1984). The market competence model posits that competitive strategy can be observed through the characteristics of firms that reflect management's activity in seeking preferred market position. In contrast to previous approaches, competitive strategy is identified through its artifacts—firms' infrastructure and capabilities. Several basic ideas are brought together in the model.

First, the key outcome of competitive strategy is each firm's position among the *market forces* that affect its performance. The idea is consistent with industrial organization theory, where relevant market forces are those affecting overall market attractiveness and the relative position of individual firms. In a framework developed by Scherer (1980), various market forces affecting performance—under broad categories of basic conditions, market structure, and firm conduct—are identified and related to each other. The focus, however, is on industries as the unit of analysis, not individual firms. Some nuances of market strategy for firms (e.g., coordination among functional areas) are lost unless reinterpreted. Therefore, Porter's model (1980) is chosen for this discussion because of its wide adoption in strategy making at the firm level. It identifies relevant market forces as customers, competitors, suppliers, new entrants, and substitutes. In the market competence model, each has potential impact on performance and thus requires a response from the firm.

Second, firms develop *market competencies* in order to maintain and improve position among market forces. They are capabilities necessary if they are going to carry on essential relationships with various environmental actors at satisfactory levels. Market competencies consist of combinations of capital goods, personnel skills, methods of management, production, marketing, and other elements that contribute to each capability. Examples are provided in Table 15.1.

The definition of market competencies in this model parallels the concept of differentiation basic to organization theory (Lawrence and Lorsch, 1967). There, firms develop individual departments which respond to different demands from their environments. The more diverse the environments in which firms operate, the more varied are their departments. Environment affects the design of all units with which it interacts, and therefore organizational structure as a whole. In the present model, market competencies are articulated by firms in order to deal with heterogeneous market forces.

The model posits that market forces are reciprocally related to firms' market competencies. The former strongly influence management to develop particular abilities and to deemphasize others. On the other hand, market competencies affect the market forces relevant to the firm. A feasible set of market competencies is that which firms already have in place, can develop inhouse, can contract, or can acquire. It directs each firm toward some market relationships and away from others, and it attempts to influence its environment where possible. Given a set of market forces, for instance, limited production scale and detailed knowledge of the needs of particular buyers might cause the firm to seek a small but hospitable market niche.

Third, strategies emerge from *patterns of relative importance* placed on market competencies. For all firms affected by similar market forces there is a particular set of relevant strategies. Firms facing the same market forces place their emphasis differently among relevant market competencies. Each firm's competitive strategy therefore consists of its market competencies taken together and weighted by their importance for achieving its preferred market position. Competitive strategy types are determined by patterns of emphasis among firms' market competencies. Table 15-2 illustrates the way that market competencies, emphasized differently by management of two groups of firms, result in different strategy types. In this hypothetical example, firms place low, medium, or high importance on market competencies listed in Table 15.1. Based on these ratings, strategy 1 might be called "buyer-oriented bundling." A descriptive name for strategy 2 is "low-price commodity production." Other strategy types could be defined where still other patterns of importance are differentiated.

Table 15-2. Two Illustrative Strategy Types Derived from Market Competencies

Sample Market Competencies	Importance	
	Strategy 1	Strategy 2
Collect intelligence on buyer needs	High	Low
Bundle goods and services	High	Low
Customize product features	High	Low
Joint R&D venturing	Medium	Low
Maintain standard industry practice	Low	High
Offer lowest priced product	Low	High
Maintain high product innovation rate	Medium	Low
Patent products and processes	Medium	Low
Product differentiation advertising	High	Low
Price on par with substitutes	Low	High
Advertise brand name	High	Medium
Tie special service into installed base	High	Low
Maintain multiple sources	Medium	High
License, acquire, develop the input	Medium	High
Maintain ability to use substitutes	Medium	High

In summary, the basic elements in the market competencies model are *market forces* with which firms interact, *market competencies* with which they respond to their competitive environment, and various *patterns of importance* placed on particular market competences by firms as they seek their preferred market position.

Competitive strategy classification holds an important current position in the development of a competitive strategy paradigm and has potential for a larger future role. In particular, numerical taxonomy creates a path that allows researchers to answer more sophisticated questions about strategy definition and performance.

The market competence model has potential for a broader role in studying strategic behavior than can be developed in this presentation. The range of substrategies (e.g., in functional areas like production or marketing) consistent with a particular competitive strategy can be tested. The model can reduce current limitations on analyzing major components of competitive strategies and their effects on performance. Moreover, distinctive competence can be studied as part of an array of market competencies. The model can explain more precisely than was previously possible, why firms develop different specializations differently when participating in similar markets.

Substrategies from Market Competence

Substrategies have been extensively studied, particularly by researchers interested in distinctive competence. The definition and use of the substrategy concept here is consistent with the literature. Substrategies are simply patterns of market competencies held together by a particular task or problem subsidiary to overall competitive strategy. They are evaluated for their individual contribution to the firm's ability to generate profits, and for their role in the effectiveness of competitive strategy as a whole. They could, for example, be defined by a market force, a traditional functional area such as marketing, production, or a special project.

Of course, the set of market competencies of most interest is technology substrategy, that is, the activities and decisions involved in managing R&D, engineering, product and process innovation, and production. Technology is firmly established in the innovation literature as a coherent set of issues that affect competitive success (Quinn, 1979; Bitondo and Frohman, 1981; Frohman, 1982; Maidique and Hayes, 1984; Pappas, 1984; and others). As a factor in innovative ability and efficiency, technology can help promote competitive advantage—and even monopoly conditions—in product markets. Additionally, since it may involve specialized assets, large investments, and organizational integration issues, technology also has a strong influence on market entry, vertical integration, and organization structure (Klein, Crawford, and Alchian, 1978; Lawless, 1986 Goodman, 1986). Among those writing in the field there is general agreement that technology can be a potent competitive weapon, but it is rarely exploited to full potential by corporate management (Maidique and Patch, 1980; Jelinek and Burstein, 1982), and that integration of technology management with strategy making is necessary for market success. Clearly the performance of all firms would improve if technology were well managed by strategists (Bright, 1964; Schoonhoven, 1983; Wheelwright, 1984). Despite the appeal of these arguments, little empirical evidence exists of their validity or importance (Lawless, 1986).

COMPETITIVE STRATEGY AND TECHNOLOGY SUBSTRATEGY

The subject of substrategies in general, and technology and competitive strategy in particular, is treated widely throughout the literature. In Quinn's (1980) work, substrategies are described as groupings of activities and decisions interacting principally around the accomplishment of a major strategic goal. Substrategies have been studied in the context of organizational structure (Chandler, 1962; Lawrence and Lorsch, 1967; Rumelt, 1986), strategy hierarchy (Parsons and Shils, 1951; Miles and Snow, 1978; Schendel and Hofer, 1979), and formulation and implementation (Quinn, 1980; Hrebiniak and Joyce, 1984; Hammermesh, 1986). Although not a necessary condition, substrategies may be pursued in functional areas such as marketing and finance.

Technology substrategy is defined as the activities and decisions involved in managing R&D, engineering, product and process innovation, and production. These functions are widely noted in the innovation literature for producing a coherent set of issues that affect competitive success (Quinn, 1979; Bitondo and Frohman, 1981; Frohman, 1982; Maidique and Hayes, 1984; Pappas, 1984; and others). As a factor in both innovative ability and efficiency, technology directly affects performance in product markets. Since it can involve specialized assets, large investments, and organization-wide information systems, strategic decisions on market entry, vertical integration, and organization structure are also affected (Klein, Crawford, and Alchian, 1978; Goodman, 1986; Lawless, 1987). There is general agreement that technology can be a potent competitive weapon but seldom is fully exploited by corporate management (Maidique and Patch, 1980; Jelinek and Burstein, 1982), and that integration of technology management with strategy making is necessary for market success (Bright, 1964; Schoonhoven, 1983; Wheelwright, 1984). Despite the appeal of these arguments, empirical evidence is sparse. Some technology typologies classify firms according to their innovative abilities (Ansoff and Stewart, 1967; Freeman, 1974); however, they are supported only by anecdotal data. Miller's research is virtually the only extant survey analysis of technology and strategy, and he finds no significant correlation of technology with financial performance (1984).

In a survey of 125 manufacturing firms (Lawless, 1987) variables were derived by reference to the market competence model and firms, sampled randomly from specified Standard Industrial Codes industries, were clustered into competitive strategy types based on 46 different strategy dimensions. The firms were clustered a second time based on 26 technology substrategy dimensions, then both classifications were matched to see the relation between competitive strategy and technology substrategy types. Four competitive strategy types, three technology substrategy types, and seven combined competitive strategy–technology substrategy types are described next.

Competitive Strategies

A preliminary factor analysis identified four underlying factors among the variables used to classify competitive strategies: product innovation, responsiveness and service, sales and distribution, and efficiency and control. These are latent dimensions behind the competitive strategy types. Next, the cluster analysis yielded four competitive strategies: product innovation, promotion and distribution, customer service, and weak responsiveness. Numerous market competencies were weighted heavily across all four strategy types. They include responsiveness to customer needs, product quality and features, and quality control training for employees. Some qualitative differences among strategies tend to be obvious, others rather subtle. Briefly the differentiating characteristics of each competitive strategy type can be described as follows.

Product Innovation. The goal of the product innovation strategy is to provide state-of-the-art products with high value added, and to make frequent improvements. The innovation process, including evaluation of new products, is important. Sales representatives are technically skilled, and they work to support the product. They also scan competitors' moves. Tie-ins are made with other firms' products, and the firm contracts for components for their own products. Response to changes in customer needs, quality control training for employees, and product quality had highest mean importance of all strategy types. The firm tends to deemphasize efficiency and control as well as sales and marketing.

Promotion and Distribution. The promotion and distribution strategy could also be called a generalist strategy. More competencies and factors are assigned high mean importance than in any other strategy category. The sales and distribution factor, though, has most emphasis. Promotion and advertising—both corporate and for individual products—in specialized media are priorities. Distribution is also part of the strategy, through both a large number of outlets and wide geographical coverage. Personal selling by representatives and presence at trade shows and conventions are important.

Customer Service. Market competencies for firms employing a customer service strategy correspond most closely with the responsiveness and service factor. They include delivery dependability and product service. The strategy also emphasizes long-range planning and coordination between marketing and production.

Customer Support. This strategy requires an orientation toward customer service that is only weakly differentiated from other competitive strategies. Standing alone, this type emphasizes competencies that load heavily on responsiveness and service, including delivery dependability and delivery speed. On the other hand, each heavily weighted competence has the same or higher mean value in at least two other strategy types. Thus, while service is the focus of this type, it is relatively undistinguished in qualitative terms.

Initially in terms of highlighted characteristics, this taxonomy appears different from previous classifications, such as those based on Porter's (1980) or Miles and Snow's (1978) conceptual models. Using this classification system, new aspects of competitive strategies can be seen. It does not reinvent the wheel; there are substantive similarities to existing strategy typing studies (Dess and Davis, 1984; Smith, Guthrie, and Chen, 1986). Product innovation, for example, in both the factor and cluster analysis, tends to align with Miles and Snow's "Prospector" (1978) and is confirmed in Hambrick's study (1983). The efficiency and control factors correspond closely with

Porter's "cost leader" generic strategy (1980) and with the findings of Dess and Davis (1984) and Snow and Hrebiniak (1980). Sales and distribution and customer service are less easy to match to precedents in the literature. This may be due to the larger representation of customer orientation—the buyer-seller role—among variables in this model. In summary, however, similarities with previous work tend to validate some parts of this analysis through precedent and to complement earlier empirical classification results.

Technology Substrategies

Five underlying factors were found in the technology competence data. Two of the factors relate to importance placed on integrating technology with competitive strategy formulation. One is strategy–technology integration, the role of technology in strategy making. The other is functional area–technology integration, the relation between R&D and production, finance, and marketing. The remaining factors—product innovation, product and process development, and production—involve degree of innovative abilities.

The technology clusters turn out to be a subset of the nine technology strategies defined earlier. They are "product pioneer," "product leader," and "product follower." Following is a brief description of each.

Product Pioneer. All firms in the product pioneer classification place high importance on all variables related to leading-edge technology competencies: forecasting, basic and applied R&D, highly skilled R&D personnel, and product development. Additionally, production competencies, particularly quality control, are important. The approach extends to management practices as well. Product development teams, innovation champions, and innovation incentives are part of the substrategy. Of the three clusters, heaviest emphasis is placed on measures that integrate technology with competitive strategy formulation, especially soliciting technology input to strategic planning and involving top management with technology plans.

Product Leader. Many of the same competencies as product pioneer are emphasized in the product leader strategy, but with lower mean importance ratings. Other competencies, most of them reflecting leading-edge technology, are deemphasized, including basic R&D, innovation incentives, and technology forecasting. In production, process R&D and coordinated manufacturing operations have low mean values. Other mean values indicate less emphasis on ties between R&D and other functional areas (finance in particular) than the product pioneer type.

Product Follower. Firms in the product follower cluster differ significantly from the other two. Heaviest emphasis is placed on production competencies: simple, adaptive manufacturing, quality control monitoring, and technically skilled production personnel. These firms are also characterized by the low level of importance they place on most R&D and innovation competencies and the small role given to strategy–technology integration. Technology's relations with other functional areas and with overall competitive strategy formulation are also deemphasized. Production competencies, whether driving other strategy-making concerns or neglecting them, are the focus of this type.

Aspects of technology competencies factors and clusters coincide closely with previous classifications at the *competitive strategy* level. Miles and Snow's types (1978) can be distinguished on grounds of responsiveness to change (Smith, Guthrie, and Chen, 1986). There are clear parallels between their prospector and product pioneer, and between their defender and the product follower types.

Innovative ability and integration are both broadly developed characteristics of strategy in conceptual as well as empirical analysis (e.g., Miller and Friesen, 1980; Maidique and Hayes, 1984). There is, however, no precedent for isolating them in substrategies rather than as part of a competitive strategy. Innovative ability, integration— and other strategic dimensions-might well take on significantly different values within a single competitive strategy.

COMPETITIVE STRATEGY–TECHNOLOGY SUBSTRATEGY COMBINATIONS

Comparison of firms by joint membership in strategy and technology substrategy clusters reveals seven combinations with relatively high incidence. Table 15-3 shows the cross-tabulation of competitive strategy–technology substrategies (CSTSs).

The analysis indicates that there is substrategy variation within strategy types. Except for promotion and distribution, each competitive strategy is matched with two technology substrategies. There is not simply a single, typical technology substrategy. Additionally, variation assumes a recognizable pattern. Besides the seven populated CSTS types, five contain fewer than three firms, or none at all. (These five, considered outliers, are not treated further.) On the other hand, the smallest among the populated cells has a membership of twelve firms. There is not a pattern of strong tendency to

Table 15-3. Competitive Strategy/Technology Substrategy Cross-Tabulation Frequency and Percentage

Competitive Strategy	Technology Substrategy			
	Product Pioneer	Product Leader	Product Follower	Total
Product innovation	17	16	1	34
	13.6%	12.8%	0.8%	27.2%
Promotion and distribution	14	3	1	18
	11.2%	2.4%	0.8%	14.4%
Customer service	12	29	0	41
	9.6%	23.2%	0.0%	32.8%
Customer support	0	18	14	32
	0.0%	14.4%	11.2%	25.6%
Total	43	66	16	125
	34.4%	52.8%	12.8%	100.0%

follow typical substrategies. Instead, comparable numbers of firms within a competitive strategy type follow different substrategies. Given a competitive strategy type, multiple technology substrategies are pursued, yet some CSTSs are avoided. In short, there is structure as well as variation in the technology substrategies.

Product innovation firms follow product pioneer or product leader substrategies with almost identical frequencies. The pattern has obvious face validity, reinforced by the virtual absence of product innovation–product follower firms. Reasons for the relatively high frequency of promotion and distribution matched with product pioneer, and almost no other substrategies, are less clear initially. However, further analysis shows they emphasize first mover product innovation, combined with their marketing competencies, in order to achieve high sales volume and growth. Among strategic goals, creating demand for new products, getting to market first with new products, product differentiation, and brand loyalty are considered high priority. Some of their technology effort is devoted to process innovation too, since efficiency in inventory and manufacturing are stressed. Of the four competitive strategies, this promotion and distribution type is the most homogeneous.

It is not a coincidence that the customer service competitive strategy does not fit well with the substrategy product follower. Instead, firms split two to one between product leader and product follower. They appear to combine relative innovative ability with service, perhaps following the IBM model.

Finally, one strategy alone shows high frequency in combination with the product follower substrategy. It is competition based on service that is only weakly distinguished relative to the other strategy types. Customer support also occurs significantly more frequently when combined with the product leader substrategy, and none with product pioneer. The result may be interpreted as an undifferentiated competitive strategy driven in some firms by manufacturing competencies like efficiency, and in others by a moderate level of innovative ability.

SUMMARY

Within this chapter two advanced conceptual models have been presented that relate competitive strategy to technology substrategy. In the market competence model, firms' competitive position can be decomposed, or broken down, into individual competence to cope with market forces. This provides detailed means to assess position and lays a foundation for analyzing substrategies.

The relation of competitive strategy to technology substrategies is the subject of much speculation. In Lawless's study of competitive strategy–technology substrategy integration several combinations were found to be similarly profitable. These provide grounds on which to speculate on equifinality of substrategies—the potential for more than one technology management approach to be consistent with a given competitive strategy. This means that technology integration with competitive strategy is a more complex, less determined process than the literature generally indicates. This conclusion, of course, is entirely consistent with the techniques of technology mapping and innovation auditing as well as the message contained in the adaptive rationality model, all of which emphasize the requirement for executive judgment in the final analysis.

REFERENCES

Andrews, K. 1971. *The Concept of Corporate Strategy.* Homewood, IL: Irwin.

Ansoff, I., and J. Stewart. 1967. "Strategies for a Technology-Based Business," *Harvard Business Review,* November–December, pp. 71–82.

Bitondo, D., and A. Frohman. 1981. "Linking Technological and Business Planning," *Research Management* 24:19–23.

Bright, J. 1964. *Research Development and Technological Innovation.* Homewood, IL: Irwin.

Buggie, F. 1982. "Strategies for New Product Development," *Long Range Planning* 15(2):22–31.

Chandler, A. 1962. *Strategy and Structure: Chapters in the History of the Industrial Enterprise.* Cambridge, MA: MIT Press.

Cooper, A. 1981. "Strategic Management: New Ventures and Small Business," *Long Range Planning* 14(3):39–45.

Cyert, R., and J. March. 1963. *A Behavioral Theory of the Firm.* Englewood Cliffs, NJ: Prentice-Hall.

Dess, G., and P. Davis. 1984. "Porter's (1980) Generic Strategies as Determinants of Strategic Group Membership and Organizational Performance," *Academy of Management Journal* 27:467–88.

Ford D., and C. Ryan. 1981. "Taking Technology to Market," *Harvard Business Review,* March–April, pp. 117–26.

Freeman, C. 1974. *The Economics of Industrial Innovation.* Baltimore, MD: Penguin.

Frohman, A. 1982. "Technology as a Competitive Weapon," *Harvard Business Review,* May–June, pp. 97–104.

Frohman, A., and D. Bitondo. 1981. "Coordinating Business Strategy and Technical Planning," *Long Range Planning* 14(6):58–67.

Galbraith, J. 1973. *Designing Complex Organizations.* Reading, MA: Addison-Wesley.

Galbraith, J. 1977. *Organizational Design.* Reading, MA: Addison-Wesley.

Goodman, R. A. 1984. "Strategic Planning and Decision-Making Techniques." In J. Balderston, P. Birnbaum, R. A. Goodman, and M. Stahl, eds., *Modern Management Techniques in Engineering and R & D.* New York: Van Nostrand Reinhold.

Goodman, R. A. 1986. "Some Thoughts on the Technological Dimension of Vertical Integration." Working paper, Graduate School of Management, University of California, Los Angeles.

Grant, J., and W. King. 1982. *The Logic of Strategic Planning.* Boston: Little, Brown.

Hambrick, D. 1983. "Some Tests of the Effectiveness and Functional Attributes of Miles and Snow's Strategic Types," *Academy of Management Journal,* 26:3–26.

Hammermesh, R. 1986. *Making Strategy Work.* New York: Wiley.

Hertz, D., and H. Thomas. 1983. "Decision and Risk Analysis in a New Product and Facilities Planning Problem," *Sloan Management Review,* Winter, pp. 17–31.

Hrebiniak, L., and W. Joyce. 1984. *Implementing Strategy.* New York: MacMillan.

Jelinek, M., and M. Burstein. 1982. "The Productive Administrative Structure: A Paradigm for Strategic Fit," *Academy of Management Review* 7(2):242–52.

Jensen, M., and W. Meckling. 1976. "The Theory of the Firm: Managerial Behavior, Agency Costs, and Ownership Structure," *Journal of Financial Economics* 11:5–50.

Klein, B., R. Crawford, and A. Alchian. 1978. "Vertical Integration, Appropriate Rents, and the Competitive Contracting Process," *Journal of Law and Economics* 21:297–326.

Lawless, M. W. 1986. "Competitive Strategy, Technology Strategy, and Performance." University of Colorado working paper.

Lawless, M. W. 1987. "The Structure of Strategy: A Taxonomic Study of Competitive Strategy and Technology Substrategy." University of Colorado working paper.

Lawless, M. W., A. Feinberg, A. Glassman, and R. Bengston. 1981. "The Role of the Change Agent in Management Science Implementation," *Omega* 10(2):107–14.

Lawless, M. W., and G. Rossy. 1984. "The Impact on Financial Performance of Integrating Corporate Strategy with Technological Functions," Paper presented at the annual meeting of the Strategic Management Association, Barcelona.

Lawrence, P., and J. Lorsch. 1967. "Differentiation and Integration in Complex Organizations," *Administrative Science Quarterly* 12(1):1–47.

Maidique, M., and R. Hayes. 1984. "The Art of High Technology Management," *Sloan Management Review,* Winter, pp. 17–31.

Maidique, M., and P. Patch. 1980. "Corporate Strategy and Technological Policy." Harvard Business School Note 9-679-033, Rev.3.

Mansfield, E. 1981. "How Economists See R & D," *Harvard Business Review,* November–December, pp. 98–106.

Miles, R., and C. Snow. 1978. *Organizational Strategy, Structure and Process.* New York: McGraw-Hill.

Miller, A. 1984. "Technology, Strategy, and Performance—What Are the Links?" In B. Bozeman, M. Crow, and A. Link, eds., *Strategic Management of Industrial R & D.* Lexington, MA: Lexington Books.

Miller, D., and P. Friesen, 1980. "Archetypes of

Organizational Transition," *Administrative Science Quarterly* 25:268–99.

Mintzberg, H. 1978. "Patterns in Strategy Formulation," *Management Science*, 24(9):934–48.

Pappas, C. 1984. "Strategic Management of Technology," *Journal of Product Innovation Management* 1(1):30–35.

Parker, R. 1977. "Human Aspects of the R & D Organization," *Research Management* 20:34–38.

Parsons, T. and E. A. Shils 1951. *Toward a General Theory of Action*. Cambridge, MA: Harvard University Press.

Petroni, G. 1983a. "The Strategic Management of R & D, Part 2—Organizing for Integration Long Range Planning," *Long Range Planning* 16(2):51–64.

Petroni, G. 1983b. "Strategic Planning and Research and Development—Can We Integrate Them?" *Long Range Planning* 16(1):15–25.

Porter, M. 1980. *Competitive Strategy*. New York: Free Press.

Porter, M. 1985. *Competitive Advantage: Creating and Sustaining Superior Advantage*. New York: Free Press.

Quinn, J. 1979. "Technological Innovation, Entrepreneurship, and Strategy," *Sloan Management Review*, Spring, pp. 19–30.

Quinn, J. 1980. *Strategies for Change: Logical Incrementalism*. Homewood, IL: Irwin.

Ramsey, J. 1981. "Selecting R&D Projects for Development," *Long Range Planning* 14(1):83–92.

Ritti, R. 1982. "Work Goals of Scientists and Engineers." In M. Tushman and W. Moore, eds., *Readings in the Management of Innovation*. Boston: Pitman.

Rumelt, R. 1986. *Strategy, Structure and Eco-*

nomic Performance. Cambridge, MA: Harvard Business School Press.

Schendel, D., and C. Hofer, eds. 1979. *Strategic Management: A New View of Business Policy and Planning*. Boston: Little, Brown.

Scherer, F. 1980. *Industrial Market Structure and Economic Performance*. Cambridge, MA: Harvard Business School Press.

Schoonhoven, C. 1983. "Strategy and Performance in High Technology Corporations." Paper presented at the annual meeting of the Western Academy of Management, Santa Barbara, CA.

Selznick, P. 1957. *Leadership in Administration: A Sociological Interpretation*. Evanston, IL: Row Peterson.

Simon, H. 1981. *The Sciences of the Artificial*. Cambridge, MA: MIT Press.

Skinner, W. 1978. *Manufacturing in the Corporate Strategy*. New York: Wiley.

Smith, K., J. Guthrie, and M. Chen. 1986. "Miles and Snow's Typology of Strategy, Organizational Size, and Performance." Paper presented at the national meeting of the Academy of Management, Chicago.

Snow, C., and L. Hrebiniak. 1980. "Strategy, Distinctive Competence, and Organizational Performance," *Administrative Science Quarterly* 25:317–36.

Weil, E., and R. Cangemi. 1983. "Linking Long Range Research to Corporate Planning," *Research Management* 26:32–39.

Wheelwright, S.C. 1984. "Manufacturing Strategy: Defining the Missing Link," *Strategic Management Journal* 5(1):77–91.

Williams, J. 1983. "Technological Evolution and Competitive Response," *Strategic Management Journal* 4(1):55–65.

16

Structuring the Organization For Advantage: The Technological Innovation Dimension

In Chapter 4, a basic theoretical position about the elements of a defensible competitive advantage was laid out. The theory explored preemptive and regulatory barriers as well as both subtle and explicit barriers to information flow. Those theoretical concepts were then applied to nine technology strategies. Earlier chapters focused on some broad conditions necessary to permit the organization to effectively employ the theory. These conditions involved the communication and coordination aspect of the technology–strategy interface and were further developed in later chapters as the potential for merging quantitative and qualitative strategy-making techniques through an adaptive rationality model was presented.

In this chapter the focus is the organizational issues that assist or complicate the firm's choices and actions in its attempt to create and defend a competitive position. An *innovation typology* that provides an analytic structure for making appropriate choices regarding organizational issues is developed. The selection of *organizational design* features compatible with the critical elements of the innovation typology improve the firm's ability to achieve in practice the defensible advantage predicted by the earlier theoretical analyses.

REORIENTATION VERSUS VARIATION: DEGREE OF CHANGE

Before developing the innovation typology, it is first necessary to define *innovation*. Widely used as a key concept in the marketplace, innovation is often synonymous with "new and improved," and advertisements are found widely for such products throughout the print and broadcast media. In a similar vein, concern for innovative techniques or business practices fill the pages of the business journals. Business firms are, in fact, inundated with a morass of undifferentiated exhortations, all promising to deliver the benefits of innovation. By contrast, relatively few advertisers emphasize "tried and true."

Commentary and conventional wisdom both suggest that increased innovation is the cure for many contemporary problems. Many believe that the "energy crisis" can be abated by the development of cost-effective alternative sources of energy, that new approaches are the key to substantially improving mass transportation approaches, and that increased productivity will increase export potential, which in turn will increase the level of domestic employment.

Much of the recent literature on management focuses on the value of entrepreneurship or intrapreneurship as the key to world-class competitive capabilities (Wheelwright and Hayes, 1985); numerous recent publications conclude that those firms which master the innovation process are quite likely to be the same firms that the general public identifies as exemplars of excellence (Deal and Kennedy, 1982, Peters and Waterman, 1982; Kanter, 1983; Peters and Austin, 1985). Innovation and entrepreneurship are seen as primary criteria for improving the firm's productivity and competitiveness.

The Misuse of the Concept Innovation

Underlying this rather simple view of innovation is a basic societal interest in the concept of the "new" (Hofstede, 1980). Given the interest in innovation and the ready acceptance that innovative techniques receive, businesses respond by assigning resources to advertising, marketing, and product development for the express purpose of capitalizing upon the consumer's apparent need for the new. Many consumer products are planned with specified renewal cycles in mind. Automobiles are new every year, textbooks are revised every four years, and new improved soap powders are scheduled for every three years.

Capturing the marketplace value of "new" through planned renewal cycles serves to divert resources from innovation of a more significant character. Under such pressures, the *innovation image* has been employed in circumstances which serve only to confuse our understanding of true innovation. The introduction of two candy bars wrapped into a single package (rather than being wrapped and sold separately) is very likely to be heralded as an innovation. As a result, the common connotation of the word innovation has been severely diffused—so much so that it now borders on the trivial (Schon, 1963). The endemic misuse of the term is a serious problem, particularly to executives who want to engage in innovation as a business strategy or needing to understand its effects within the competitive marketplace.

A Clarifying Definition of the Concept of Innovation

When Richard Normann (1969) writes about innovation he distinguishes between variation and reorientation. His concept of "product variation" would include the wrapped candy bars and many other changes that alter, in some form, the dimensionality of a product. But his product variations are limited to rather straightforward changes in product dimensions—longer shelf life, speed, smoothness, improved reliability, and the like. By contrast, "reorientation" refers to changes that dramatically and simultaneously alter several dimensions. The introduction of the transistor into radio products altered size, performance, power demand, repair costs, overall costs, portability, and so on. A change which impacts on multiple dimensions is the characteristic sign of a reorientation.

Normann's distinctions are doubly important because there are corollary organizational impacts. Fundamentally, product variations are normally used to extend the life cycle during a product's mature or declining stage. Although these comparatively minor variations frequently offer very attractive returns on investment and maximize the value of the current process technology, they are organizationally "conservative"—they have relatively minor impact upon the distribution of power within the firm.

By contrast, a major reorientation can significantly alter the organizational power distribution. While organizational executives focus their time on the new idea and divert resources to the new area, the remainder of the firm, if it is running smoothly, will require and therefore receive less attention. This rather subtle "power shift" effect may have a much greater impact upon the firm's resistance to innovation than the more obvious financial risk issues.

SOME ORGANIZATIONALLY RELEVANT DIMENSIONS OF INNOVATION

Innovation, whether reorientation or variation, is a reflection of the internal organizational positioning of the firm's innovative units, the character of technological interdependencies in a particular innovation, and the character of external technological interdependencies. The intersections of these three dimensions can be represented simply in a two-by-two-by-two diagram yielding an eight-cell innovation typology. Each cell is unique, and the implied organizational design relating to each is similarly unique. The dimensions of the typology are represented by dichotomous variables. The first is the familiar dichotomy of *product or process,* the second pair is *individual or synergistic,* and the final dichotomy is *autonomous or systemic.*

The Product–Process Dimension

Many authors make a distinction between product and process. This distinction, well grounded in normal industrial practice, will be used here even though it oversimplifies the balance of organizational activities involved in either type of innovation (Besserye, 1985). It is clear from even a cursory look at corporate organizational charts that the industrial norm is separation of product and process research and development into two departments. The same cursory study will often show product R&D reporting at a higher organizational level than process R&D. While this is a reflection of distinct differences in the relative status of the two R&D units, it does not necessarily reflect the firm's strategic emphasis. In general, the strategic emphasis placed upon product or process innovation varies in accordance with the stages of the product life cycle (Abernathy and Utterback, 1978).

In an ongoing organization, the struggle to create a new product is normally quite demanding. During the early phases of the life cycle the organization must focus on product innovation, and the organizational stresses experienced at this stage are those associated with the concept of reorientation. Once widespread distribution has been accomplished, the strategic focus shifts to process innovation and the investment focus is on cost savings and margin widening in anticipation of the ensuing life cycle phases. During this mature phase the organizational stresses are usually characterized by the concept of variation. As the market begins to decline, the strategic emphasis shifts back to product innovation, but at this time, in order to extend the product life, the focus is not on reorientation but rather on variations (new features, colors, etc.). The resultant organizational stresses in this phase can easily be characterized as relatively minor perturbations.

The Individual–Synergistic Dimension

The second dimension of this typology is the individual versus synergistic dichotomy. Many innovations in both the product and process areas occur through creative effort aimed at an individual functional area. In the fashion industry, for example, mechanical pattern cutting will be replaced by laser cutting. In dishwashers, mechanical controls are being replaced by programmable controls. In each of these examples, progress has occurred and the customer will realize benefits, but only a single function has been affected. Sewing, pressing, pattern layout, and so on, are still the same even if the cloth is cut by a laser. The basic washing mechanism is unaffected by the change in the control system. Adjustments in interconnections or packaging may be necessary, but in the main these individual functional improvements will not require creative and interdependent efforts from multiple functional areas.

The concept of synergistic innovation is defined as a result obtained from the creative, concomitant development of several functional areas. This can occur in two distinct manners. The simultaneous but essentially independent development of several functional areas is one form of synergistic innovation. Conversely, synergistic innovation can occur when there is significant interdependence among several functional areas in the development of a new product or process. Most products which are described as "next generation" fit this latter definition quite well. In order to meet performance specifications for the "next generation" appellation, all functional areas have to be "tuned" to fit together and yield the required system performance improvements.

The first of these forms of synergy can be illustrated by the development of the pocket transistor radio. American manufacturers initially employed the transistor as a power-saving device. The "new" design of portable radios was marked by an increase in reliability and a decrease in power requirements. The then current typewriter-sized portable radio was only modestly decreased in size. This initial phase was an individual product variation. A second wave of development, originating in Japan, resulted in a major decrease in the size of the antenna, the tuning condenser, and the speaker. Breakthroughs in other functional areas had to be achieved before a true innovation was accomplished and the pocket-sized transistor radio became a reality (White and Graham, 1978). Note in this example each of the functional areas developed essentially independently but the resultant new product would have been unsuccessful in tapping what turned out to be a latent new market unless all of the functional improvements had been successfully accomplished.

Another type of synergistic innovation occurs when there is a need for the close interaction among several functional areas in the development of a new product or process. The early development of the slotted array radar antenna required concurrent development in three separate functional areas. It was necessary not only to create an antenna for airborne radar navigation without moving parts (i.e., one which could alter the search pattern of the radar beam electronically rather than by rotating the antenna itself) but also to create an antenna that had a minimum physical profile so as to not alter the aerodynamics of the airplane. To succeed, a new approach in microwave amplification was needed to solve the profile problem, and then a new approach to radar transmission and reception was needed to create the electronic search patterns. Central to this development was the need to create a precision method of cutting slots in the array such that the final accuracy of the system was not compromised by a manufacturing process with too wide a dimensional tolerance. The final accuracy of the antenna was dependent upon both the accuracy inherent in the electronic and microwave design and the precision with which the slots were cut in the microwave array during the manufacturing process.

The Autonomous–Systemic Dimension

The third and final dimension in this typology is the autonomous versus systemic dichotomy. Fundamentally, innovations are often substitutes for existing products and represent a new method for accomplishing current user functions. These are termed autonomous innovations. Car radios, for example, were first designed using vacuum tubes. Later when these tubes were replaced by transistors, the public experienced little or no change in the radio function. Thus, the transistorized car radio was a simple (and simplifying) replacement for the earlier design. The pocket-sized transistor radio discussed earlier is also an autonomous innovation as all the changes occurred within the radio. The product was able to become economically viable without other firms, functions, or situations adjusting their functions.

A systemic innovation, by contrast, is one that requires major adaptations by many organizations. When, for example, the coin-operated or home dry cleaning machine was developed it could not be successfully marketed. The difficulty was not in the machine itself but in the pressing of the dry-cleaned clothing. The pressing equipment required was very expensive and potentially dangerous steam and hydraulic "mangles," which could not be designed to be accommodated within the home environment. When new materials were developed for clothing, the required pressing technology became simpler. Thus, the chemical industry had to develop new fibers for clothing and the textile industry had to develop new weaving techniques before an innovation in the consumer hard goods industry had any value (Schon, 1963).

Similar problems and opportunities can be seen in the current development status of electronic funds transfer. This systemic innovation has been delayed considerably because of the many organizations and sectors of society which must adapt their business practices in order to benefit from the innovation.

Innovation Typology

To create an innovation typology each of these three dimensions must be interrelated. Table 16-1 illustrates the eight-cell typology with an example of different innovations shown parenthetically within each cell.

Cell I represents an autonomous, individual, product innovation that stands alone as a more effective replacement for another product through the enhancement of a single functional dimension. The example is the repackaging of an otherwise unchanged product—juice. The advent of "boxed juice" is a variation that seems to please parents and teachers while giving children new options for their lunches. Simultaneously, children can now more safely and conveniently carry liquids from home. Concerns about bringing empty containers home, about disposing of cans or carrying glass, have all but vanished. The change (on an individual dimension) is solely in the package, not in the juice. The resulting new product is autonomous in the marketplace with no need for other products or outside organizations to make adaptations.

By way of contrast, cell II represents an autonomous, individual, process innovation and an example of this is the manufacture of carbon film resistors. Beginning with the deposit of an even coating of carbon upon a ceramic core, the excess carbon must then be ground off in a spiral pattern to provide a path for the electricity to follow from one end of the core to the other. The accuracy of the resistive value depends upon the evenness of the carbon deposit and the accuracy of the spiral path. In the traditional manufacturing process the spiral path has been accomplished with a grinding wheel technology. Recently the grinding wheel has been replaced by a laser grinder, which is considerably more accurate. In addition to its accuracy, the laser grinder does not require the frequent readjustment or replacement that the older grinding wheel did. This process change has improved the individual dimension of productivity. Because there was no need to alter any other portion of the manufacturing process, the improvement can be classified as autonomous.

The pocket transistor radio in cell III was previously described as a synergistic product innovation that could stand alone in the marketplace. Its success depended upon the simultaneous improvement of several functions. The complexity of this development was not further complicated by the need to negotiate with organizations external to the firm. Thus, it serves as a good example of an autonomous, synergistic, product innovation.

Table 16-1. Innovation Typology

Innovation		Product	Process
Autonomous	Individual	I (boxed juice)	II (laser grinding)
	Synergistic	III (pocket transistor radio)	IV (CAD/CAM)
Systemic	Individual	V (home dry cleaner)	VI (weaving new fabrics)
	Synergistic	VII (videodisc)	VIII (just-in-time manufacturing)

Computer-aided design and computer-aided manufacturing (CAD/CAM) in cell IV is the process innovation equivalent of the previous example. To use shoe manufacturing as an example, the whole process begins with the designer. As a first step a three-dimensional representation of a new shoe design is drawn on a computer screen. When the designer is satisfied with this picture, a software program is run to automatically "explode" the shoe design into the several pattern pieces it requires. A second program "grades" the design, that is, it creates a family of pattern pieces for each size that the company intends to manufacture. A third program "nests" the design. This program accepts an "order" depicting how many pairs of each size are desired. It then lays out the pattern pieces on the raw leather in such a manner as to maximize leather usage and to minimize leather waste. The final program drives a cutting device, which cuts the leather according to the nested and graded pattern layout.

CAD/CAM, as this example suggests, is the result of complex and interdependent developments which require changes in the structure of both design and manufacturing processes. It is sufficiently complex that firms tend to select modular steps as they move slowly toward the fuller exploitation of the CAD/CAM potential. Its potential in the longer run will be realized when CAD/CAM becomes a fully integrated design and manufacturing process. This example fits well into the autonomous, synergistic, process innovation category.

The "home" dry-cleaning machine of cell V is an example of a product whose basic design required only the change of an individual dimension (the cleaning fluid) but whose success was complexly related to major innovations in two other industrial sectors. This systemic, individual, product innovation was relatively inexpensive to develop but became economically viable only after many years when the chemical industry developed new fibers and then the textile industry developed new weaving techniques. Organizations external to the firm do not always appreciate the possible benefits of "joint" or "coordinated" actions in the development of new technologies. Thus, the chemical industry did not anticipate the benefits for the dry-cleaning industry. Major time lags are a likely result of pursuing systemic innovations unless some coordination can be achieved. Reduction of such time lags occurred when the chemical industry successfully was able to demonstrate to the textile industry the benefit of a "coordinated" development program utilizing the newly developed fibers.

To more rationally plan its R&D efforts, TRW developed a systematic technology map of a large number of potential future systems within which it expected to play a role (North and Pike, 1969). The timing of the critical events necessary for the development of each system was initially estimated. The firm then decided to defer research commitments until the precursor critical events by other firms had been realized. Though this long-range R&D planning made sense, what was missing was any appreciation of the strategic value of accelerating system development through joint efforts with relevant outside firms.

The process innovation analog to the home dry-cleaning machine can be found in the weaving technology portion of this example. To become economically viable, developments of new fibers by the chemical industry necessitated new developments in the textile industry as well. Now the process for weaving fabrics from the new fibers (an individual dimension of the manufacturing process) required joint organizational efforts of the chemical industry and the textile industry. This classifies as a systemic, individual, process innovation and is a good example of cell VI.

The development of the videodisc shown in cell VII is an example of systemic, synergistic, product development. This requires not only the complex tuning of numerous design elements but the establishment of common standards and the cooperation of the many firms that produced video software. Without such industry cooperation, the lack of products available on videodisc would inhibit market development. With broad standardization, new media, service facilities, and product enhancements (of a "plug-compatible" nature) would develop through entrepreneurial activity and the basic value of the videodisc in the marketplace would be improved significantly.

The epitome of cell VIII is the process innovation referred to as "just-in-time" manufacturing. The essence of just-in-time manufacturing is the dramatic reduction of both basic and work-in-process inventory through the careful attuning of manufacturing processes and planning efforts. Extensive coordination within the firm and among all of the firm's suppliers is required so that components and subassemblies arrive in a timely fashion. This is an example of systemic, synergistic, process innovation—a technology-assisted cost reduction strategy.

ORGANIZATIONAL COUNTERPOINTS TO THE INNOVATION PROCESS

The typology developed can be associated with a matching organizational structure. There are unique combinations of structural dimensions which seem most effective for each of the different cells in the typology. There are three dimensions of structure which seem most affected by the three dimensions of the innovation typology: *uncertainty about the market and its performance needs, complexity of the interdependencies among the various technical specialties,* and *complexity of interdependencies with organizations in the firm's external environment.* Each issue was selected to match with the dimensional issues of the innovation typology.

Much of the recent literature on strategy focuses upon the basic question of how most effectively to structure the firm once the firm's strategy has been determined (Chandler, 1962, 1977; Rumelt, 1976). Most of this work pointed to the development of the multidivisional firm as a necessary response to the management of ever-widening product lines and narrowing market niches. As products became increasingly specialized to meet the demand of a niche (usually due to competitive pressures) the traditional functional form of organization became overburdened. Coordination costs increased considerably and margins were narrowed by these cost increases. The conclusion was clear: organizational structure must be adjusted to match with organizational strategy.

These studies tended to look at the broader aspects of organizational structure and not at the finer details. The innovation typology developed above allows a considerably more detailed analysis of the structural question. However, the innovation typology is a necessary but not a sufficient consideration as an organization's structural design exists within an overall context or culture of the firm. The importance of such contexts has been emphasized in recent studies of organizational culture, which in turn suggest that the answers to some critical questions regarding organizational processes must be ascertained as a precursor to the detailed design of an organization's structure.

The Organizational Process Context of Structural Design

The way that the firm's activities (or organizational processes) are conducted can be consistent with organizational strategy or at variance with it. Sonja Sackmann's (1985) studies of three distinctly different divisions within a large firm demonstrates the connection between strategy and organizational processes. In her study of a multidivisional manufacturing firm it became clear that the strategy of customized manufacture and a high level of customer service could be effectively delivered only if the organizational process culture emphasized, selected for, and rewarded localized problem solving. That is, the firm's managers expected its people to be receptive to problem solving rather than blame finding and to take initiative when problems surfaced. New employees from general manager to clerk were selected with these criteria in mind and were not retained past their probationary period if they were unable to adapt responsibly. At all levels within the organization, problems were addressed as soon as they were recognized and resolved at as low a level as possible. In this fashion, design variation requests from customers could often be handled directly on the shop floor with only limited intervening engineering processes. Changes in a customer's order could be worked into the production schedule and the supporting distribution and accounting functions quickly adjusted to the changes.

Sackmann's study suggests that organizational process culture must be matched to organizational strategy as a precursor to the question of matching organizational structure to organizational strategy. If innovative activity is to be a cornerstone of corporate strategy, then an appropriate organizational process culture must be selected.

In earlier studies (Vickers, 1965; Schon, 1972) about the management of complexity under conditions of turbulent environments (Emery and Trist, 1965), the efficacy of detailed planning to achieve organizational control was shown to be insufficient. Rather, what appeared to provide the necessary compensating, homeostatic pressures were agreements about the underlying assumptions and organizational processes that supported these values. The value of selecting the correct organizational structure is strongly enhanced if the question of organizational process culture has been previously resolved.

The organizational process culture that favors innovation can be described as one that has explicit plans for innovation but also has a responsible tolerance for failure. Many firms have the former but few have the latter. Yet tolerance for failure is critical to success.

What does responsible tolerance for failure mean and why is it important? During an interview, one very senior project manager illustrated this idea by pointing out of his office window to a fenced area filled with many unusual large pieces and structures. He identified this area as the "turkey farm." All of the items piled in the yard had been failures. If the turkey farm did not exist, he commented—that is, if there had been no failures—then it would be a sign that the company was not trying hard enough to stretch the state of the art. In fact, many later successes were directly related to the knowledge gained from these earlier failures.

A project failure often leads directly to a later organizational success. If project management were severely chastised for failure, then only conservative projects would be proposed and variations rather than reorientations would result. The benefits of downstream payoffs from project failures have been found by others in several diverse technologies (Clarke, 1968; Goodman and Abernathy, 1971; Abernathy, 1978).

To be responsible, however, the process culture should not tolerate failure because of poorly conceived work or mismanagement. But failures that result from stretching and attempting new technological approaches with good contingency planning must be acceptable if innovation is to be a key element in an organization's strategy.

In the context of this discussion on the precursor question of organizational process culture it has been assumed that some organizations explicitly choose to use the reorientation form of innovation as an organizational strategy. For many organizations or individual units within organizations there are technology strategies which require variations or slow but constant improvement in order to achieve the creation or maintenance of a defensible competitive advantage. This latter situation requires a more traditional organizational process culture.

Organizational Structure

For the purposes of this discussion organizational structure is defined as a pattern of stable relationships. This includes hierarchy and several other structural concepts. This definition allows for the inclusion of both the traditional ideas about structure as role definitions and role relationships and the newer ideas about the organizational process culture.

A successful innovation is one that resolves all the necessary areas of uncertainty. This includes technological uncertainty (the actual performance characteristics of a technology and how the technology interacts with other technologies), use uncertainty (the actual rather then the envisioned use to which the product will be put), and process uncertainty (the management control of the uncertainties in the information flow and interaction among organizational units) (Goodman and Abernathy, 1978). Broadly speaking, a good understanding of the market, the possible product and process technologies, and organizational relationships is necessary to transform technologies into products and then products into use.

In this light an organizational structure typology can be built in a fashion that is parallel to the innovation typology. The structural question can be described by employing three dichotomous dimensions in a two-by-two-by-two typology. The three dichotomies are *simple versus complex access to market information, project versus matrix organizational form,* and *simple versus complex boundary-spanning units.* The resulting eight-cell structural model overlays the earlier eight-cell innovation model.

Simple versus Complex Access to Market Information

The market information dimension describes an organization's ready access to knowledge of the market. In organizations where the product line is rather stable, the organization develops a good understanding of the market and can easily adapt to normal demand variations. This situation often stimulates innovative variations rather than the more complex reorientations. In a well-understood market, however, competitive pressure can stimulate a technological strategy which attempts to alter the basis of competition and results in an innovation characterized as a complex reorientation. Product innovation is a reflection of the organization's desire to be creative and is successful only when the organization has relatively complete market information.

When the technology strategy is focused upon manufacturing there is a simple access to market information since user needs are identifiable and are fully contained within the firm itself. Needs are similar in the product development situation but the potential market informants are all on the payroll. Manufacturing management is not shy in expressing its needs to the manufacturing research units of the organization.

Project versus Matrix Organizational Form

The project form of organization was designed for situations when coordination of complexity is more important than functional excellence. Within the project form of organization, personnel from all of the functional specialties are assigned directly to the project. The project manager must exercise direct technical supervision over all personnel, regardless of specialty, and must exercise responsibility for reviewing their performance. With direct authority the project manager can closely control the coordination between and among the various technical specialties as the design evolves. Thus, the project manager has control over the detailed trade-offs that are often required to complete a project.

In contrast, the matrix form of organization is designed for situations when functional excellence is more important than the coordination of complexity. Such situations occur when the core technology of the innovation dominates the expected result and the supporting technologies can adapt relatively easily once the core idea has been proven and detailed. When installing a microprocessor-based control system for a consumer hardgood such as a dishwasher, the dominant technology is the software design since standard microprocessors are normally selected. Aside from the control panel design, the dishwasher design remains unchanged. In situations such as these the functional specialties report to their functional managers and not to the project manager. Complex trade-off decisions are not required and the project manager's role becomes one of coordination rather than direction. The functional managers strive to have their personnel deliver innovative changes that conform to company standards and technological area standards. Thus, the firm has few new issues to solve and seeks minimum perturbations in its organizational processes.

Simple versus Complex Boundary-Spanning Units

The requirement for simple or complex boundary-spanning units can be determined by ascertaining the firm's location on a continuum which describes the entities in the firm's "relevant environment" (Dill, 1958), those organizations and processes in the environment which effect the firm's abilities to achieve its objectives. At one end of this continuum the firm can effectively represent its relevant environment as if it contains clusters of homogeneous units behaving in predictable fashion. At the other extreme, the firm can effectively represent its relevant environment as a matrix of unique and complexly interrelated entities whose behavior is dependent upon the specific situation. In the former case simple boundary-spanning units are all that is necessary, and market-oriented sales, advertising, and research structures are sufficient. In the latter case, the internal boundary-spanning unit is very complex and often contains an in-house specialist for each entity and process in the relevant environment. Thus, the unit might contain forecasters and negotiators, liaison and information system designers, and the like.

Dimensional Relationship between Structure and Innovation

The eight cells of the innovation typology shown in Table 16-2 describe significant organizational differences. Key to the differences between product and process innovation is the fact that in process innovation use uncertainty is very low as the organization itself is the customer. By contrast, within a product innovation effort the need for good information from the outside market or user community is high and this information can be ascertained only after a variety of user research probes have been attempted.

Turning this discussion around, inherent uncertainties about users and the use of innovation are conceptually similar in product and process technology, but the easy managerial access to information about the requirements and specifications needed for process design allows use uncertainty to be reduced through simple structural devices such as formal design signoff processes, cross-functional coordinating committees, and periodic design review processes. In the product example, customer needs are not easily clarified and the manager's ability to quickly reduce use uncertainty requires complex structural patterns that include market research, early test programs, iterative trials, and complex coordination among the various internal entities.

The requirement for significant intergroup coordination efforts is the major difference between individual and systemic innovations. Individual innovations usually require only a rudimentary coordination effort and can be handled within the functional area of the firm sponsoring the innovation. These coordination activities do require a clear planning and progress monitoring system and often require adjustments in other functional activities. A manager to exercise project control and coordination is needed. Personnel related to this innovation are assigned within each of the functional areas as coordination linchpins to the project manager, who exercises project control and provides necessary coordination and who has responsibility in addition to his or

Table 16-2. Summary Innovation Typology

Innovation Type	Dimensional Combination		
Type I	Product	Individual	Autonomous
Type II	Process	Individual	Autonomous
Type III	Product	Synergistic	Autonomous
Type IV	Process	Synergistic	Autonomous
Type V	Product	Individual	Systemic
Type VI	Process	Individual	Systemic
Type VII	Product	Synergistic	Systemic
Type VIII	Process	Synergistic	Systemic

her responsibilities in the standard functional organization—a so-called matrix form of organization (Davis and Lawrence, 1977).

A synergistic innovation is best handled by either a pure project organizational form or an intensified matrix form. The coordination and detailed trade-off requirements of the synergistic innovation mean that a much more intensive communication flow must exist. This is particularly important as the technical developments require compromises and trade-offs among the many elements involved in the project. Progress is accomplished and control exercised by reciprocal adjustments (Thompson, 1967). Most appropriate is the pure project form with all technical specialties being removed from their functional units and reassigned to report solely to the project manager.

If the synergistic innovation is not all-encompassing in its effects, then an intensified matrix organization would be the logical choice. In this form the transfer of personnel to the project would include only the functional areas participating directly in the area of synergy. Supporting functional areas would then remain in a matrix relationship with only linchpin relationships for reasons of monitoring and reporting progress.

The distinction between autonomous and systemic innovation is seen mainly in the nature of the boundary-spanning organizational units. In an autonomous innovation, the boundary-spanning units are marketing and product service. Information about the details of market need and use can be determined through these channels and eventually reflected in product design. A systemic innovation requires informal and perhaps formal relationships with many organizations in the environment. It is interesting to note that these organizations may not all be in the same field. Government agencies, universities, and other organizations may participate.

The systemic innovation process can be the result of a grasped opportunity such as the home dry-cleaning machine or a purposeful effort by a systems integrator such as the Northrop F-20 Tigershark development or a firm choosing a just-in-time manufacturing process. In all cases, the members of the innovating organization set must, at a minimum, receive or acquire information about plans and progress toward implementation of those plans from the many organizations that make up the domain of the innovation. Because the difficulties in the management and coordination of such directed interorganizational systems (DIOS) are relatively distinct they are also quite challenging (Lawless, 1980).

Systemic innovations frequently require activities within each of the relevant organizations that do not contribute significantly to the accomplishment of each unit's organizational mission. To be a successfully directed or managed inter-organizational system, the first requirement is the creation of a shared understanding of the innovation opportunity (the so-called problematique) among the interrelated autonomous organizations. Beyond the problematique, it is then necessary to obtain a clear view of the organizational system's structure and the expected relationships among each of the components. Then a managing system would need to be created to divide and determine the appropriate priority for the various tasks that must be accomplished.

On the other hand, an opportunistic systemic innovation requires several boundary-spanning units that specialize in the acquisition of information from each type of organization in the domain of the innovation. One example of such a boundary-spanning unit is a legislative monitoring unit which is needed to scan for local, state, and federal regulatory changes that are frequently sources of either enabling conditions or constraints. At a different level, in the procurement department a special unit might be created to evaluate capability and product plans of potential suppliers of key material.

In the case of firms interested in becoming major suppliers of solar energy systems, reliance upon the technological progress of suppliers of photovoltaic cells is a necessary evil. Unless or until they are able to bring down the price per peak kilowatt hour by a factor of twenty there is not likely to be a major market for solar energy systems. Thus, it is important to keep up with the research and development programs and progress of the many firms and institutes pursuing photovoltaic research and development. Organizations such as systems developers, distributors, and power utilities in the larger environment may be approached frequently so that the groundwork for merging forces has been established prior to the time when such action is deemed appropriate. These mergers may be formal collaborations such as joint ventures or informal collaborations through the constant sharing of information among the relevant set of firms. Systemic innovation requires complex, diverse boundary-spanning units.

A COMBINED INNOVATION AND STRUCTURE TYPOLOGY

This discussion used each of the three dimensions of the innovation typology as a building block for a comprehensive structural argument. The structural highlights for each dimension have been articulated. What remains is to bring the separate discussions together into a single summary presentation. The three structural dimensions of need for market information, project–matrix coordination needs, and nature of boundary-spanning units are thus summarized in Table 16-3.

Since Table 16-3 is an overlay of Table 16-1, it is helpful to recall the examples from the earlier discussion to further explicate the meaning of the organizational recommendations. Assume that a firm believes that a packaging improvement such as boxed juice (a product variation that is individual and autonomous) can provide a defensible advantage. Then (as shown in Table 16-3, cell I) the firm should pursue three specific organizational actions. First, since the firm has a high need for market information, it should initiate market research to create the package specifications and to design a package that is consistent with consumer preference. Designing a package that is inconsistent with consumer preference may destroy the potential advantage. In this case, the project or product manager can coordinate the package development without having direct responsibility for functional specialists (a matrix organization) since creation of a project organization would be very costly and might reduce the benefit/cost ratio to an unhealthy level.

The resulting product can be moved through normal distribution channels that require only a simple boundary-spanning unit since the creation of a new and complex distribution system for a product variation would be prohibitively expensive. Thus, while the product innovation "boxed juice" might very well have a significant potential competitive value, it could have been severely weakened if inappropriate organizational structures and processes had been employed.

One more example will show how Table 16-3 can be used to obtain the greatest benefit from a potentially valuable technology strategy. The earlier example for cell IV, an autonomous, synergistic, process innovation, was CAD/CAM. Detailed

Table 16-3. Innovation Typology and Organizational Conditions

Innovation		Product	Process
Autonomous	Individual	**I** High need for market information Matrix organization Simple boundary-spanning unit	**II** Low need for market information Matrix organization Simple boundary-spanning unit
	Synergistic	**III** High need for market information Project organization Simple boundary-spanning unit	**IV** Low need for market information Project organization Simple boundary-spanning unit
Systemic	Individual	**V** High need for market information Matrix organization Complex boundary-spanning unit	**VI** Low need for market information Matrix organization Complex boundary-spanning unit
	Synergistic	**VII** High need for market information Project organization Complex boundary-spanning unit	**VIII** Low need for market information Project organization Complex boundary-spanning unit

specification for such a system can and must be generated internally to conform to the nature of the firm's products and product markets. To actually make this project functional an enormous amount of detailed design process and manufacturing process information is necessary. It is virtually impossible, however, to satisfy every organizational unit within the firm. Thus, as the project develops, detailed technical trade-offs will be necessary. This would normally call for a full project organization as the delays associated with a matrix organization facing detailed interdependency would stretch the scheduled completion far beyond acceptable limits. The firm needs only a simple boundary-spanning unit as the need for outside information is basically limited to the extant CAD/CAM hardware and software. This would easily fall under the purview of any effective purchasing organization. Here again the stress has been to show that the selection of any other type of organizational structure would quite probably lead to higher costs and schedule delays, which would severely weaken the value of an otherwise appropriate technology strategy.

A Digression into the Organizational Issue of Coordination

For most parts of an organization, coordination can be accomplished through planning (Thompson, 1967) and by using specified kinds of information in regularly scheduled reports, whereas for most innovations the use of known categories in regularly scheduled reports provides insufficient control. The complex interdependencies inherent in innovation require coordination through a process called reciprocal adjustment (Thompson, 1967). This means that each of the involved functional areas must be prepared to continually adjust and readjust its plans and designs to accommodate changes required by development in other functional areas. Since this necessitates detailed coordination efforts, the normal hierarchical flow of information and decision making is too clumsy and unwieldy for this process.

Typically, as information flows upward through the organization, it is summarized and loses detail as it rises from one level to the next. Thus, information generated at level three which flows up to level one and then down to another group at level three will not have the detail necessary for the complex readjustment process. Conversely, when personnel at the lower level come to an understanding of the process and needs, they usually do not have sufficient information about the management and the coordination of the work to move easily from understanding to action.

Lorsch and Lawrence (1965) suggest an effective conceptual compromise. They argue that cross-functional coordinating committees are valuable in the innovation process and that the membership of these committees should be comprised of midrange managers (i.e., personnel low enough in the hierarchy to understand and seek, when necessary, the detailed technological issues while at the same time being high enough in management to make informed, action-oriented decisions). This approach seems to give the management–technical detail trade-off good balance while simultaneously providing a mechanism for timely decision making.

Finally, it is important to look at the firm's resource allocation/budgeting process. Seldom are funds budgeted for innovative development adequate to actual project costs. In most organizations, rather than holding a pool of contingency funds for overruns within a fiscal year, readjustments are made in second-year or third-year budgets. The critical point is the significance in innovative areas of the underestimation of required resources, whether they are funds, facilities, space, or personnel. Explicit planning and control changes must be incorporated into the organization's general planning and control system to deal with the real uncertainties of innovative behavior. It is somewhat beyond the scope of this discussion to suggest such planning and control procedures. It is important, however, to understand that the uncertainties of the process are unavoidable but must be anticipated and accepted, and coping mechanisms must be designed to handle the results of such uncertainty.

INNOVATIONS, LIFE CYCLES, AND STRUCTURE

This chapter emphasized the importance of selecting appropriate organizational structure and showed how an inappropriate selection can severely reduce the potential of an otherwise valuable technology strategy. The matching of cells from the innovation typology with cells in the organizational structure typology has been presented along with an implicit assumption that the firm was facing only one innovation and that the normal processes of the firm were simply waiting for the innovation to be complete before swinging into action. In reality, the contemplated innovation is typically an addition to the firm's ongoing business. Quite logically then, the innovation typology and the organizational recommendations that ensue from the earlier analysis must be considered within the context of an ongoing firm.

In addition to the innovation typology–organizational structure analysis there are two phenomena that should be explored. One is related to the concept of product and process life cycle. The second phenomenon is the concurrent undertaking of many developments in both product and process. At the very least, these phenomena taken together suggest that structural patterns within firms must be continually adjusted to the ever-changing patterns of stability and innovation.

An innovation passes through a life cycle that begins with the seed of an idea and ends with standardized production of what is perceived as a normal portion of the main core of the business. Within this cycle, product or process variations are quickly absorbed into the "everyday" management of the firm while product or process reorientations are only slowly moved into the core of the firm.

In a general sense, the earlier phases of an innovation require extensive coordination in the form of reciprocal adjustments. That is, complex trade-offs must be made among the many technical discipline bases and the many functional organizational units in order to fit the new ideas into current production schedules, to order new machines or design and build new tooling, to launch into new markets, to purchase critical components, and so on. The skill at making these trade-offs requires a project manager with skills enough to select the appropriate organizational form—either a matrix or full project. In fact, depending upon the innovation, the firm might very well have several organizations of each type operating concurrently. Only after the launch and growth phases have passed and the product maturity phase has been reached can the normal planning methods and functional management skills effectively manage the product. Thus, within a single firm one may concurrently find new project organizations, mature project organizations, and some project organizations that are winding down. And, in fact, project organizations will be seen as overlays upon the current functional organization that is effectively managing the majority of the firm's product line.

Implied rather clearly is the idea that the organizational demands presented by a particular innovation are not only ever changing as partial solutions are developed and progress is accomplished, but in addition many innovations are simultaneously occurring. The resultant organizational complexity often creates a large measure of difficulty for senior management. Thus, there is a natural tendency to simplify the organization and to ignore the otherwise subtle debilitating effect of selecting the wrong structure for a particular development.

SUMMARY

In this chapter, a typology of innovation was employed as the background for an organizational design argument. In general the design question was focused upon the reduction of uncertainty and the coordination of complexity. In this way, a structural concept was created and matched with the innovation typology. The appropriate selection of organizational features to match with specific technology strategies is necessary if the strategies are to be useful in fulfilling potential promises.

REFERENCES

Abernathy, W. J. 1978. *The Productivity Dilemma: Roadblocks to Innovation in the Automobile Industry*. Baltimore, MD: Johns Hopkins University Press.

Abernathy, W. J., and J. M. Utterback. 1978. "Patterns of Industrial Innovation," *Technological Review* 80:40–47.

Besserye, C. 1985. "Middle Managers as Innovators: The Initiation of Organizational Innovations," Ph.D. diss. proposal, Graduate School of Management, University of California, Los Angeles.

Chandler, A. 1962. *Strategy and Structure: Chapters in the History of the Industrial Enterprise*. Cambridge, MA: MIT Press.

Chandler, A. 1977. *The Visible Hand: The Managerial Revolution in American Business*. Cambridge, MA: Belknap Press.

Clarke, R.W. 1968. "Innovation in Liquid Propellant Rocket Technology," *Final Report Task 7910-05*. Holloman Air Force Base, New Mexico, Office of Aerospace Research, March.

Davis, S. M., and P. R. Lawrence. 1977. *Matrix*. Reading, MA: Addison-Wesley.

Deal, T. E,. and A. A. Kennedy. 1982. *Corporate Cultures: The Rites and Rituals of Corporate Life*. Reading, MA: Addison-Wesley.

Dill, W. 1958. "Environment as an Influence on Managerial Autonomy," *Administrative Science Quarterly* 2:409–43.

Emery, F. E., and E. L. Trist. 1965. "The Causal Texture of the Environment," *Human Relations* 18(1):21–32.

Goodman, R. A., and W. J. Abernathy. 1971. "Summary of a Workshop on Dimensional Analysis for Design, Development and Research Executives." Working paper, Graduate School of Management, University of California, Los Angeles.

Goodman, R. A., and W. J. Abernathy. 1978. "The Contribution of 'NEW BOY' Phenomena to Increasing Innovation and Development in New Technology," *R & D Management*, 9(1):31–41.

Kanter, R. M. 1983. *The Change Masters*. New York: Simon and Schuster.

Hofstede, G. 1980. *Culture's Consequences: International Differences in Work-Related Values*. Beverly Hills, CA: Sage.

Lawless, M. 1980. "Toward a Theory of Policy Making for Directed Interorganizational Systems." Ph.D. diss. Graduate School of Management, University of California, Los Angeles.

Lorsch, J., and P. Lawrence. 1965. "Organizing for Product Innovation," *Harvard Business Review*, January–February, pp. 109–122.

Normann, R. 1969. "Some Conclusions from Thirteen Case Studies of New Product Development." Stockholm: Swedish Institute of Administrative Research, UPM-RN-100.

North, H. Q., and D. Pike. 1969. "Technological Probes of the Future," *Harvard Business Review*, May–June, pp. 68–83.

Peters, T. J., and N. Austin. 1985. *A Passion for Excellence: The Leadership Difference*. New York: Random House.

Peters, T. J., and R. H. Waterman. 1982. *In Search of Excellence: Lessons from America's Best-Run Companies*. New York: Warner Books.

Rumelt, R. 1976. *Strategy, Structure and Economic Performance*. Cambridge, MA: Harvard Business School Press.

Sackmann, S. 1985. "Cultural Knowledge in Organizations: The Link between Strategy and Organizational Processes." Ph.D. diss. Graduate School of Management, University of California, Los Angeles.

Schon, D. 1963. *The Displacement of Concepts*. London: Tavistock.

Schon, D. 1972. *Beyond the Stable State*. London: Maurice Temple Smith.

Thompson, J. D. 1967. *Organizations in Action: Social Science Bases of Administrative Theory*. New York: McGraw-Hill.

Vickers, G. 1965. *The Art of Judgement*. New York: Basic Books.

Wheelwright, S. C., and R. H. Hayes. 1985. "Competing through Manufacturing," *Harvard Business Review*, January–February, pp. 99–109.

White, G., and M. B. W. Graham. 1978. "How to Spot a Technological Winner," *Harvard Business Review*, March–April, pp. 146–52.

17

External Acquisition of Technology

By definition a firm's technology strategy must include the acquisition of technology, either through internal investment in R&D and process development or by employment of external sources. The external acquisition of technology is a straightforward issue when the technology acquired is in the form of raw materials, components, or equipment. It becomes more complicated when the mode of acquisition includes licensing, joint venturing, or outright acquisition of subsidiaries.

The need to acquire technology creates basic tensions between the desire to use the best technology (often found outside the firm) and the desire for control (weakened by reliance on outside sources). These tensions become central debating points among senior management as opportunities and/or problems arise. Although strategic tensions are endemic, the rate of external acquisition is rapidly increasing. To frame these tensions and the underlying opportunities, a strategic analytic approach should be pursued. A framework for this analysis is developed from ideas presented in earlier chapters. Potential pitfalls are explored and some cautionary tales illuminate key issues.

THE BASIC TENSION

If we consider the origins of technological advances over the last century we can detect often unrecognized sources of distortions. In the early part of the century, basic scientific capability was distributed relatively evenly throughout the industrial world. Scientific breakthroughs critical to a wide range of industrial and consumer products occurred in Asia and Europe as well as in North America (IITRI, 1968). On the whole, however, these three regions were rather evenly matched during this early period.

World War II and the resulting disruption of the Asian and European economies and physical infrastructures allowed North America to assume technological dominance. The immense technological and scientific advances stimulated by the war effort led to a rapid increase in the technological content of postwar civilian products and services. The ensuing technological dividends from the enriched portfolio of technology made the North American dominance even more striking.

Within the United States, it was assumed that the newly emerging pattern of technological dominance was permanent and that it derived from an educational, scientific, and industrial lead that would remain unsurpassed. Not surprisingly, this dominance eroded as other industrialized regions retooled and rebuilt their industrial and educational bases. Great surges in technology from the cornucopia of war efforts began to reach maturity, and the resulting benefits slowed considerably over the next few decades, setting the stage for a redress of the "unusual" North American dominance and restoration of equity among the various players of the industrialized world. The broad-scale technological domination of North America was in truth an *artifact* of World War II.

In writing about national needs and global resources, Vernon and Kapstein (1991) explored this question, focusing their concern on the appropriate bases for national technology policy making. By analogy their focus has direct implications for a technology-based firm facing international competition. As a basis for strategy making (or in their case, national policy making), it is more reasonable to assume that North American dominance in technology has been replaced by relative equity among the three regions that make up the bulk of the industrialized world. North America's earlier technological dominance was replaced with technological *balance* within the industrial world as early as 1966.

There are several ways in which this balance leads to strategic tension. In many corporations the competitive strategy requires the very best in underlying technology. For some it is manufacturing technologies; for others it is product technologies. A review of the list of technologies related to electronic components presented in Chapter 5 illustrates the wide range of necessary competencies (Goodman and Pavon, 1984). Because of developments such as fiber optic applications and opto-electronics on the product side and wafer fabrication techniques on the manufacturing side, the approximately ninety technologies reported as necessary for maintaining a competitive position in this field has since escalated even further. Few firms can have the very best underlying technology in all competitively relevant areas.

A detailed examination of the sources of technological developments and the nature of the expertise relevant to these developments indicates that important developments are occurring in firms of all sizes both domestic and foreign. These developments must be identified and evaluated, and their impact must be blended into the firm's strategic thinking.

In most firms, important technology must be acquired externally. Increasing needs for technological acquisition strains the normal strategic process. The firm must be aware of technological progress that may (or may not) be made by suppliers of critical technologies. Finding a good strategy-making process which factors in the firm's external reliance upon critical technological input is a very difficult issue.

The basic tension of competing in technology-dependent situations is clear. The external acquisition of technology provides the *benefit* of improved competitive position while simultaneously *loosening* corporate control over strategic results. Because of this the form and nature of external acquisitions remains very fluid and firms are continually reevaluating their portfolios of external technologies. The explosion and dispersion of technological competence is proceeding so fast that the benefit–control tension is currently being overwhelmed by the absolute need to acquire access to new technologies for important competitive reasons.

CHANGING TIMES

Basic trends indicate three factors that affect the firm's need to acquire external technology. The first factor, asserted previously, relates to the regional (Asia, North America, Europe) balance of technological competence. The second factor is the explosion of scientific knowledge that requires more specialized and thus narrower and deeper training of technologists. The third is the blending of technologies from several industries.

The first factor suggests that the best technologies may not be located within the firm. The second factor suggests that the cost of being a broad-range specialist is likely to be very high. The third factor suggests that the future may not resemble the past and may require very different expertise.

One instance of this can be seen in the extent to which external acquisition practices have evolved among American multinational firms. In a study of the top four American multinational firms in five industries the rate of external acquisition increased approximately 600 percent over the last decade (Komaran, 1993). Table 17-1 contrasts the 1976–1980 period with the 1986–1990 period on several dimensions. The five industries studied are chemicals, medical instruments, pharmaceuticals, electronic components, and computers/peripherals. Two basic classes of acquisitions, event-oriented and institutional, are reported. Event-oriented acquisitions include licensing and joint efforts such as the development of complementary products. These efforts do not take on a formal organizational relationship. Institutional events include the creation or

Table 17-1. External Acquisition of Technology by American Multinational Firms

Industry	Acquisition Event		Acquisition Institution	
	Licensing	Joint Efforts	Subsidiary	Collaboration
1976–1980				
Chemical	17	45	18	35
Medical Instruments	4	7	20	3
Pharmaceutical	7	7	16	5
Electronics	2	4	13	13
Computers	5	4	13	15
Total	35	67	80	71
1986–1990				
Chemical	42	100	105	205
Medical	23	20	42	44
Pharmaceutical	22	12	32	50
Electronics	45	71	28	166
Computers	96	97	78	295
Total	228	300	285	760

Adapted from Komaran, 1993, by permission.

acquisition of a subsidiary firm or the creation of a joint venture. These activities result in the creation of formal "establishments" and have well-bounded corporate forms.

The chemical industry once dominated the external acquisition landscape. More recently, chemicals, although still strong, were supplanted by computers and peripherals. The most powerful indicator of the significance of external technology is the almost tenfold increase in licensing and in institutional forms of collaboration.

It seems clear that prior to 1980, formal acquisitions of subsidiary companies fit better into the firms' comfort zone than other forms of technology acquisition. The chemical industry, the most mature of the five industries studied, is the sole exception. It is also technologically true that there are few chemicals which by themselves account for a significant market share of the industry as a whole. That is, the chemical industry encompasses an incredibly wide range of products when compared to the other four industries.

The data suggest that during the later period, all forms of external acquisition fell within the firms' comfort zone. This demonstrates corporate learning capabilities which provide the firm with a more robust portfolio of potential actions.

Not shown in the data, but powerful in its absence, is the very small number of institutional relationships that link these top twenty American multinational firms with university and government entities. The absence of this link suggests that the transfer of the technology generated in these two major institutions is a personal or personnel process.

From the university perspective these transfers occur primarily through employment of university students (upon graduation) or research faculty. The former is fine but probably inefficient because new hires have limited power to bring technology to bear until seasoned by the firm in the sense of "best practice." The latter provides the firm with some short-run benefits but threatens to erode the basic research base, which is the main generator of the science necessary for technologically driven industries.

The government laboratory transfer is most likely through publications and recruitment. Again, the publication route is fine but inefficient, and recruitment threatens to erode the government's technological capabilities. In either circumstance, the university-based and government-based store of technological knowledge seems underexploited.

To summarize the changing times, a few comparative statements are useful. Table 17-2 demonstrates how quickly and massively the firms' action in the study has shifted. Total external acquisitions rose from 254 to 1573, a 615 percent increase.

Table 17-2. Period-to-Period Analysis of Technological Acquisitions by American Multinationals Firms

	1976–1980		1986–1990	
Total acquisitions	254		1,573	
Mechanisms and strategic intent				
Events	102	40%	527	34%
Institutions	152	60%	1,048	66%
Domestic	164	65%	1,104	70%
Foreign	90	35%	469	30%

While the increase between the two periods was massive, there was a significant shift toward institutional methods of acquisition. Thus, the corporate form of acquisition shifted from 60 percent of the total to 66 percent of the total. Most noticeable was the shift in domestic sourcing of acquisitions. While foreign acquisition of technology increased from 90 to 469, a 521 percent increase, the domestic increase was even greater. Domestic sourcing moved from 65 percent of the total to 70 percent of the total.

The tremendous increase shown in technological acquisition by large American multinational firms has demonstrated that the modern firm would be unwise to rely solely upon a strategy of in-house research and development. This conclusion, then, leads to a new question: How can a firm strategically determine which technologies to acquire and which technologies to ignore? The answer requires omniscience, an attribute no firm possesses, but a strategic framework for analysis is helpful.

FRAMEWORK FOR ANALYSIS

The framework for analysis presented here represents a synthesis of the frameworks presented earlier. The framework contains two broad conceptual elements: technology mapping and technology programming. These two elements taken together highlight the buyer value perspective of product development and provide a more efficient base for subsequent product development. This framework balances the market-pull and technology-push paradigms. The technology-push aspect of strategy is contained in the technological programming perspective while the market-pull aspect is intrinsic to the technology mapping perspective.

Technology Mapping

The technology mapping process is depicted in Figure 17-1, which is repeated from Chapter 6. This seven-step process begins with the general mapping of the technologies represented in the firm's current product line. This general mapping provides the contextual dynamics of the technological developments in the industry over time and helps to reflect the real-time dynamics of competitive shifts in underlying technology. It shows the simultaneous occurrence of rapid transformations and slow step-by-step evolutions.

The next three steps go together and highlight the role of the market-pull or buyer value perspective. A systems block diagram of the product is created using current classes of products. Within each subsystem block key parameters are identified. These key parameters represent the buyers' wishes, demands, or concerns. Then technologies which have potential for making progress along these dimensions are identified. These three steps provide the firm with a portfolio of technological competencies with which it must be concerned.

These needs can be assessed with respect to various strategic investment decisions, including levels of investments, nature of investments, and external versus internal processes of development. These decisions, of course, change over time. Questions

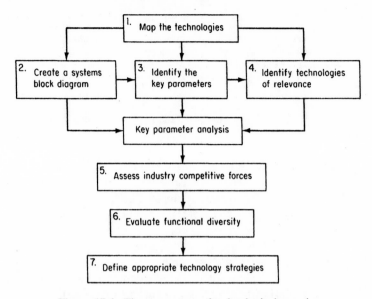

Figure 17-1. The seven steps of technological mapping.

about the proprietary value of the development as well as its inherent nature and whether it requires a critical mass or minimum outlay affect the level of investment a firm may make. The nature of the development ranges from simple monitoring (for a technology that is seen as far into the future, e.g., high-temperature superconductivity) to more systematic development (for the next product generation). The external versus internal questions refer to the potentially lower cost of acquisition versus the potentially lower proprietary position of acquisition.

The remaining three steps of the technology mapping process include the assessment of competitive forces, an evaluation of how the products and thus the technology will need to be moderated as product use becomes functionally diverse. Finally, these concepts are merged and an appropriate technology strategy is selected.

A cursory example of technology mapping begins with the creation of a systems block diagram. Electronic funds transfer (EFT) is used as an example and the EFT generic block diagram is shown in Figure 17-2. The diagram depicts retail elements

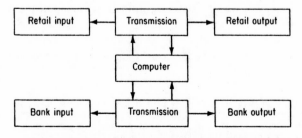

Figure 17-2. Electronic funds transfer block diagram.

Table 17-3. Electronic Funds Transfer Retail Input Key Parameter List

---

Style: print data, keystrokes, voice, magnetic strips, microprocessors, visuals (visage or fingerprint)
Use characteristics: simplicity, speed, reliability, ruggedness
Costs: investment, training, operating

---

connected by transmission and computational elements to a financial institution. These elements of the product arena serve as the focus of the next step, which involves the identification of key parameters.

Key parameter identification involves two kinds of assessment. First, the functional elements of the block must be identified. Table 17-3 lists the functional parameters identified in the retail input block of the example. The list contains three categories: style, use characteristics, and costs. Style of input, the first category, encompasses print data, keystrokes, voice, magnetic strips, microprocessors, and visuals. Use characteristics include simplicity, speed, reliability, and ruggedness. The third category consists of investment costs, training costs, and operating costs. These must be assessed in light of customer priorities and user populations. In this example a priority rating for each of these parameters is established by studying two customer constituencies: retail operators and retail customers.

This step is followed by identification of technologies which affect or promise to affect the parameters of interest. The technologies with the most leverage become target technologies for development or acquisition. The technologies with the most promise become targets for the future capture.

The technologies of relevance for the retail input block of the EFT example are listed in Table 17-4. The three categories employed are sensors, converters, and user technology. Sensors include keyboards, scanners of many types such as print, voice, fingerprint, pen pads, and magnetic readers. Converters, devices which digitize information, are summarized as analog-to-digital conversion in this example. User technologies include psychology of cognition, consumer behavior, and human factors.

These technologies need to be assessed from both present perspectives and potential contributions to improving the product key parameter performance. This assessment, in conjunction with the earlier priority determination of the buyer value or market-pull nature of the parameters, should lead to a portfolio of technological competencies. Competencies which the firm does not have need to be developed or acquired.

Thus, the technology mapping process aims at helping the firm identify its technological needs from a strategic perspective. A fuller description of the process in earlier chapters includes three other steps which further solidify the strategic view. First, the identification of competitive forces brings an evaluation of the current and future bases of competition into the picture. Second, an evaluation of functional diversity adds a

Table 17-4. Electronic Funds Transfer Retail Input Technologies of Relevance

---

Sensors: keyboards, scanners (print, voice, fingerprint, pen pads, magnetic readers)
Converters: analog to digital, etc.
User technology: psychology of cognition, consumer behavior, human factors

---

wider definition of customer and allows the firm to weigh the key parameters and relevant technologies with regard to their performances in niches. And finally the selection of appropriate strategies reminds the analyst of two issues: that each industry can simultaneously sustain several strategic approaches and that the approach selected has specific implications for the definition of the required technology portfolio.

Technological Programming

The issues derived from the technology mapping approach must be blended into technology programs which extend over time and beyond any specific product development. Figure 17-3 depicts technology programming in a unique fashion. The goal of the organization is portrayed as the development of individual and organizational intellectual capital. This goal is achieved by importing knowledge about technology, market data, and external environment. These sources of knowledge are transformed by various technology programs into intellectual capital, or core competence. In this figure, product development is shown as a by-product of the technology programs.

There are two important underlying technological phenomena that make this very important. When an organization decides to develop a new product, it selects technological approaches to use in each of the new product's subsystems. Technological approaches should be chosen for their potential contribution to delivering or improving the performance of the key parameters *and* because they can be reduced to practice in the time required by the product's window of opportunity.

Reduction to practice is seldom successful unless the firm has significant experience with the technological approach in the use environment. It often takes a year or so of active experimentation with a new technological approach before an organization builds sufficient intellectual capital to successfully deploy it within the constricted time frame of a product development (Abernathy and Goodman, 1972).

The examination of the technologies with potential for improving key parameters as derived from the technology mapping process helps define the nature of the technology program that should be undertaken by the firm. Thus, technology programs must proceed apace without a specific product in mind until such time as the technology under question is sufficiently mastered. Such mastery reduces the risk of deploying a specific technology in product development.

Technology programs include several levels of investment, some through acquisi-

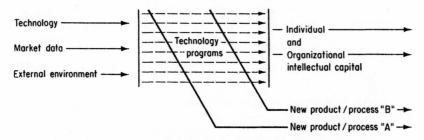

Figure 17-3. The generic flow of technology programs

Table 17-5. Strategic Importance of Technology and Development Strategy

Technology Category	Development Strategy
Base technology	Needs little
Key technology	Systematically built
Pacing technology	Selective investment
Emerging technology	Monitoring

tion, some through internal development, and others hybrids of the two. The technological portfolio represented by the technology programs is related to investment costs versus strategic benefit. A simple explanation of the latter is contained in Table 17-5. Four categories of technology— base, key, pacing, and emerging—are arrayed in this table (Arthur D. Little, 1971). From a strategic perspective, base technologies are those required to manufacture the products and are widely held by all participants in the industry. These base technologies require little development and thus little investment. Key technologies are those which distinguish the organization from the competition and which need to be systematically developed. They require substantial investment.

Pacing technologies are those which hold promise for competitive improvement in the future and which either operate directly on the key parameters or have potential to significantly alter the bases of competition, thus requiring the organization to reevaluate its strategy. Pacing technologies need to be selectively developed and require significant investments. They fit into the technology program by building core competencies and permit effective integration into new products because they lead to the establishment of substantial bases of intellectual capital. Emerging technologies hold broad promise for the longer term. These technologies need to be monitored so that their development does not come as a surprise. The monitoring effort requires little investment.

The strategic framework for analysis offered here employs technology mapping to help determine the technology portfolio by assessing the market priorities. Technology programming is added to help the firm focus on building its technology portfolio in anticipation of new product development. Thus, technology mapping and technology programming, taken together with extant core competencies and estimated investment cost, aid firms in determining which technology to develop internally and which to acquire on the outside.

The basic tension of using the very best technology at the risk of relaxing corporate control requires careful navigation. The acquisition route creates significant strategic benefits while requiring cautionary behavior to avoid paying too dearly for such benefits.

SOME CAUTIONARY TALES

To appropriately appreciate the benefits of external acquisition of technology, some "cautionary tales" need to be explored. Many an acquisition attempt has foundered on one or another of the potential pitfalls. In structure, a technology acquisition exhibits asymmetric knowledge and thus uncertainty on both sides of the exchange. The inherent issue is that the acquiring firm does not know the technology very well and the providing firm does not know the value in use of its technology. This generic uncertainty is also compounded by the firms' inability to know exactly how future products and product lines will evolve.

Cautionary tales can be clustered into four categories defined by issues of ownership, evolution, repeat contracting, and governance and control. This four-issue set is explored using the two examples of licensing and joint venturing, chosen because they represent two extreme situations.

In a licensing situation no research and development expenses are incurred and aside from a fixed initial payment further costs are incurred only when sales are made. Royalty payments reduce the firm's per-unit advantage and make the per-unit costs higher for licensees than for competitors who have developed their own technology. If the technology does not represent a significant portion of the total costs, then this issue is unimportant. In a joint venture, however, significant resources are committed to the venture and a corporate form is created. This permits a wider deployment of the technology after it is developed and perhaps reaps more financial returns as technological modifications for diverse applications require few contractual modifications or renegotiations.

Issues Related to Ownership

The tension between the licensee and the licensor occurs in two non–cost-related elements. The first elements are the limitations placed on the license. The terms of the license often limit the application of the technology and/or the geographical market. The second elements are the further development of the technology by the licensee in order to make the technology more effective in the specific market. Ownership of these further developments, if permitted, is frequently a source of conflict. On the other hand, a license which does not permit development or requires the development problem to be passed back for solution by the licensor is likely to result in other forms of conflict about value and/or priority.

In the joint venture situation, more resources are committed but the value of ownership clearly resides with the "corporate entity"—the joint venture itself. Any further development of the technology is owned by the venture. Recent research indicates that joint ventures' payoffs often occur outside the venture, in the parent firms. These benefits help build core competencies in new marketing approaches and in the use of joint ventures to acquire technology, and there are other so-called soft benefits (Kreiner, 1993).

The ownership issue also creates exit barriers. As partner firms' markets or structures change with time, the value to one or the other shifts but the commitment still exists. It is not unusual for firms to honor their commitments to a joint venture partner even though their own restructuring has made the venture less interesting (Kreiner, 1993).

Issues Related to Evolution

Further development of a technology is complicated by the differing priorities of the two firms with regard to the question of which partner benefits most. A corollary problem is the structuring of incentives for the evolution of the technology. The licensee has more relevant information about its particular market niche and benefits that will accrue. The licensor can pass evolutionary technology along to other licensees and perhaps reap benefits from the broader market. Thus, the licensee has no incentive to consider evolution with broad impacts. In the joint venture, the corporate form ameliorates these issues but the differences in the ultimate market for the partners still distorts incentives to innovate.

Issues of Repeat Contracting

In some circumstances, arrangements are time-limited and/or apply to a limited phase of development (e.g., the precompetitive phase). When the value of the technology has been established and firms have designed their products around a specific technology, conditions are created that make the next round (renewal of license, further joint work) one of shifting bargaining power. The more product-specific the technological development, the more value it has for an individual firm and the more it strengthens the other firm's bargaining position. This so-called holdup phenomenon is another source of potential conflict.

Issues of Governance and Control

The final concern involves governance and control, but it is specifically founded in concerns about direction and growth. Often partners will have differing views about directions technological development should take and how fast it should move. This derives from the characteristics of different markets, differences in overall strategies, and varying abilities to apply resources. Loss of control and direction is another potential source of conflict.

ACQUISITION ISSUES

The firm also faces the basic tension inherent in the choice of having the best underlying technology versus having absolute control over its development. With the increasing complexity of technology and the geographical widening of competence it is less and less likely that any firm can be the sole technological master of its fate. The recent 600 percent increase in the external acquisition of technology among the twenty top high-technology American multinationals is evidence of this limitation. The firm must seek technology, but it should do so in light of market-driven priorities and strategic, targeted technological programs. This method of identifying the required technological portfolio permits the firm to choose internal development or external acquisition subject to the cautions that are implied in the basic tension statement. The benefits of technology must be contrasted with the risks of loosening control.

REFERENCES

Abernathy, W. J., and R. A. Goodman. 1972. "Strategies for Development Projects: An Empirical Study," *R & D Management* 2(3), 125–29.

Arthur D. Little, Inc. 1981. "The Strategic Management of Technology." New York: Arthur D. Little, Inc.

Goodman, R. A., and J. Pavon. 1984. *Planning for National Technology Policy.* New York: Praeger.

IIT Research Institute. 1968. *TRACES (Technology in Retrospective and Critical Events in Science).* Chicago: IITRI, December 15.

Komaran, R. 1993. "The Evolution of the External Acquisition of Technology by American Multi-National Firms." Ph.D. diss., Anderson Graduate School of Management, University of California, Los Angeles.

Kreiner, K. 1993. "The Art of Managing EUREKA-Projects: Lessons from a Longitudinal Study." Copenhagen: Copenhagen Business School, EUREKA Management Research Institute. (draft)

Vernon, R., and E. B. Kapstein. 1991. "National Needs, Global Resources," *Daedalus*, pp. 1–22.

18

The Elements of Strategic Action: Analysis, Formulation, and Implementation

The general theme of this book is the creation of defensible competitive advantage—advantage that is obtained through strategic analysis, formulation, and implementation. The specific focus of this book is technology's unique contribution in each of the three activities. This contribution is maximized when the firm's strategic program is purposively interwoven with its technological program. Strategic effectiveness relies upon the firm's ability to creatively manage the interactions between the technologists and the strategists.

On the technology side, the firm employs the past to explain the present since current technological solutions always represent the firm's embodiment of past scientific advances. Current solutions are based upon existing science and conditioned by the firm's ability to transform the science base into products and processes. This transformation process always adds a time delay between the creation of scientific knowledge and the development of viable products. But this also means that the basis for products of the future is in today's science. Thus, an analysis of the development time delay and the current state of scientific knowledge can be employed to foresee the rate and direction of future development. Such foresight is necessary in order to anticipate new competitive opportunities as well as new competitive challenges.

To integrate technological understanding into the strategic process, the firm must understand the mechanisms by which a firm can create a defensible position and the role that technology can play in assisting the firm in the execution of such a strategy. It must see the role of technology as a dynamic one. The firm must develop a sophisticated understanding of the uncertainties that are basic to the development process and that are the result of competitive reaction to technological issues.

To be able to establish market positions the firm must analyze its capabilities and its opportunities and then engage in specific actions or develop appropriate technology. Whether the firm wishes to be reactive or proactive, its analysis and planning systems, its action steps, and its strategic control systems must reflect this intent. Most markets support several participants—some who play the role of dominant supplier, some who do quite well as lower technology low-price competitors, and/or some who are higher technology niche competitors. Some even do well through adopting a mixed position. Regardless of which strategy the firm selects, its technologically oriented actions must be consistent with this choice. Thus, strategic analysis of technology is a prerequisite for selecting strategic action.

THE TECHNOLOGY-STRATEGY MODEL

Strategy making does not begin de novo with a clean slate and unlimited options. It is instead a real-life process afflicted by the firm's past history, which is relied upon as a basis for action and as a basis for understanding. A firm's options are limited by the management's worldview, by the firm's actual situation, and by its abilities to envision the future. While the strategy formulation process is under way, real-time decisions are being made and implemented by current management, by competitors, and by a host of environmental players. Thus, the nature of the firm's underlying position is constantly in flux even while the management is carefully considering new and better strategic possibilities. These dynamics force the firm to characterize strategy making as an unending process which requires continual monitoring of the underlying assumptions upon which it is based.

Strategy can be considered the creation of a defensible competitive advantage. The advantage arises from the failure of the so-called perfect market. In the real world this failure can result from information delays and blockages, high costs of information, imperfect imitability, artificial differentiation, preemptive moves, or regulatory barriers.

Looking at the nature of technology provides a window on a series of technology strategies which will generate greater than average returns for investors. The selection of the appropriate technology strategy requires an analysis of the nature of the potential market failure, an understanding of the market itself, and the competitive position of the product or process technology. This analysis suggests which of the nine strategies described in Chapter 4 should be selected: technological commodity search, preemption, productive efficiency, producer preference, production flexibility, customer preference, product pioneer/product leader/product follower, vertical integration (forward/backward), or complementary technology.

THE STRATEGY FORMULATION MODEL

When an action-taking perspective is considered the role of metaphor becomes preeminent. Most action plans are extremely detailed and the complexities of real organizations often mean that personnel within the firm are asked to complete specific tasks without a comprehensive understanding of the task's role in the overall strategic plan. Metaphor is a linguistic device for establishing the basic context of a set of ideas—in this case a strategic plan. The metaphor of defensible competitive advantage provides a very powerful image about the benefits of investing in opportunities provided by the failure of the market.

The ability to integrate the firm's technological processes and strategic processes is subject to a great deal of misunderstanding and tension. In the strategist's view, technology creates many problems because of associated underlying uncertainties. These uncertainties guarantee that today's strategic plan will veer off target in one way or another before the full benefits of the plan can be reaped. The embedded base of technology and current customers for that technology are a constraint on revolutionary changes in favor of evolutionary change. Strategists are similarly distressed by technologists' frequently unreliable estimates. The strategists' responses when estimates seem unreliable demonstrate a basic misunderstanding of the technological process. The standard request for more detailed planning is not consistent with a process whose core is "discovery" and whose success is based in an iterative process coupled with a high degree of complex intuition.

This standard request for more detail in the planning process makes technologists inherently suspicious of strategists. The technologists want to get on with the discovery process and not delay their work to develop detailed plans when this detailed approach is at variance with the process of discovery. Because the technologists are rarely included in the firm's strategy-making councils they frequently suspect that the strategies that are handed down to them are out of touch with the actual capabilities of the technological staff. Thus, the two groups have a poor history of effective communication and only a limited base of shared understanding.

One way of dealing with these tensions is the employment of an adaptive rationality model. A strategy maker under conditions of endemic ambiguity needs both rigor and creativity. The seven steps of an adaptive rationality planning system employ techniques that vary from loosely structured to highly structured. Thus traveling from problem identification to appreciation requires multiple perspectives and input from multiple constituencies. The analytic process alternates between low- and high-rationality analysis as it moves in an iterative fashion through differentiation, micro formulation, integration, strategic assessment, implementation, and performance evaluation.

This movement back and forth between techniques provides opportunities for key participants to draw upon their own strengths. Technologists and strategists play important roles and through these tools they are able to develop communication channels that are consistent with the underlying issues that derive from within their own task environment.

THINKING ABOUT TECHNOLOGY

After surveying the broad literature on technology it is possible to cluster most of it into two broad categories. Within the first category the ideas of technology are considered as an externality. Technology is seen as a force that is constantly changing the playing field and a force which must be understood and accurately forecast if the strategy-making process is to be effective in locating a defensible position. The other category posits technological processes as an internal force. The mastery or not of certain technologies affects the firm's ability to execute a particular technology strategy and is of direct concern in the strategy formulation process once the opportunities in the environment have been identified.

Technological change is generally described by its rate, its diffusion, and its degree of radicalness. Some technologies expand for a time at a dramatic rate, others evolve slowly. Some technologies have an extremely diffuse functional application; others have only narrow but clearly defined applications. Some technologies represent a radical departure from the past, others are adaptive.

Some of the externally oriented literature on technology provides a window on the sources of technological change—science, economic conditions, government policy—and offers a method for understanding the general rate and direction of change over a broad horizon. Other literatures help in forecasting the shaping of technology from a competitive perspective by addressing issues such as emerging technologies, patterns of diffusion, appropriateness of technology, and market positioning.

The internally oriented literature on technology relates the technology function to a wider range of firm infrastructure systems. The substrategies in marketing, finance, human resources, manufacturing, and/or distribution may or may not fit well with a particular technology strategy. Within the literature it is not uncommon to find an analysis of industry by comparative or contrasting common features of a group of competitors—so-called strategic groups. This leads to suggestions that the difficulty that firms face in being able to successfully move from one group to another is directly related to the complexity of the functional substrategies that are employed. The more complex the substrategy, the more difficult the adjustment for the different market segment.

Within this text the external focus is mirrored in the technology mapping technique and the internal focus is integrated into the innovation auditing technique.

TECHNOLOGY MAPPING

Over many centuries, the history of technology has been a fascinating subject. Ideas about the role of technology in society have been considered by anthropologists, historians, and economists. Technology has become a significant variable in the explanation of the development of the world as we know it.

In recent decades, the history of technology has taken on a different role. Rather than being solely used for explanation, the history of technology has been cast in a predictive role. This new role can be seen in the movement toward the creation of technology policy occurring at national levels in major industrial states and in the development of the discipline of technological assessment for both competitive analysis and in measuring potential ill effects. The field of technological forecasting has developed as an important part of strategy formulation at the firm level.

The technique of technology mapping is aimed at assisting the corporation to make better decisions about the selection of the appropriate technology strategy. To that end it focuses on several perspectives: perspectives about the rate of changes in the technology; perspectives about the nature of the changes and their contribution to firm's success or failure; and perspectives about the role of outsiders in the fortunes of the firm. In this sense the technology mapping process provides an external view. When used as a basis for firm-level decision making it is a process that requires thoughtful and detailed analysis in order to be successful.

As a starting point, the technique of technology mapping requires the creation of several building blocks. One is a detailed history of the underlying scientific and developmental breakthroughs that were the forerunners of the first viable product. Others include information about the history of performance parameter improvements, the history of functional (use) diffusion, the sources of innovative stimulation, and the nature of the various industry participants.

While the synthesis of a set of building blocks into a perspective is a creative act, such an act can be guided by broad principles. The basic synthesis needs to reflect two foci. One focus should try to summarize the map in terms of the ever-changing bases for competitive advantage. The second focus should adopt the dual perspective of investor and manager. The investor perspective is to identify those areas within the industry where rapid appreciation of firm valuation is likely to occur. The managerial perspective is to identify the technology strategies that are must likely to be effective over the longer run.

INNOVATION AUDIT

The innovation audit is another useful analytic tool. The development of a firm's abilities to employ technology strategies relies upon a clear understanding of the nature of the technology function. For this purpose the concept of managing technology within programs can greatly help the firm balance the long run against the short run and thus manage the intersection of the strategic interest with operational effectiveness.

Basically, implementation of technology programs represents the conscious desire to further develop subsystem technology as well as to study new approaches to the solution of the functional benefits offered by one or another technology. The technological program includes analysis and selective investment in new approaches—so-called pacing technologies—which offer dramatic changes in the bases of competition. This conscious analysis also requires that emerging technologies be constantly monitored, since these technologies threaten to change the basic competitive relationships within the industry. Maintenance of these investment and programmatic foci is critical to anticipating competition, functional substitution, and the reduction of risk in new product and process development. This latter benefit arises from the reduction of the uncertainties related to the application of such technologies.

By learning to appreciate the nature of uncertainties—technological, use, and managerial—appropriate investment priorities can be established. By adding to this an analysis of market maturity and firm positioning these priorities can be further refined. The basic output of a technological program concept is the development of intellectual capital for the firm and for the individuals in the firm. This in turn allows for far more effective reduction to practice of the various underlying technologies in a new-product or new-process development.

The basic audit technique follows from this analytic perspective and adds a three-instrument research tool, which relates to the firm's innovation process, its comparative position, and its preparative position. The technological innovation process audit identifies the firm's normal processes for large and small innovations in either product and process. Related to the wide range of literature on effective project management, this audit instrument is framed as a risk analysis. The innovation comparison audit is a report of the firm's effectiveness in introducing new technology as compared to the rest of the industry. The technological positioning audit is an analysis of the firm's preparatory position vis-à-vis base, key, pacing, and emerging technologies. These audits taken together provide the foundation for recommended management action.

The implications that can be drawn from these perspectives are to be examined from the perspectives of short- and long-run action. Basically, the framework of the audit can be integrated with the idea of corporate value creation. Often a firm's investors have a short-term perspective about value creation, whereas the senior management has a somewhat longer perspective. Within these two frames a conceptual analysis of the three audit instruments should be conducted by applying the product and market situation questions outlined in Chapter 5. Recommendations can then be derived from the nine technology strategies of that chapter.

TECHNOLOGY-STRATEGY TECHNIQUES

Implementation of a strategic approach can be assisted by the appropriate use of several technology-strategy techniques. The useful techniques fall into a number of categories. The overall operational techniques involve assessment and environmental scanning as context for strategy formulation and strategy control. An array of technological forecasting approaches ranging from rudimentary to sophisticated coupled with a variety of market analysis tools and competitor analysis provide the firm with a data base for strategy formulation. Central to the firm is the formal ability to maintain and to replicate this contextual assessment.

With the contextual data base in place, further organizational effectiveness is ensured through the application of project selection, project planning, and project control methods. (These approaches require some adjustment when applied to new venture start-up.) Additionally, the question of implementation is far more difficult than planning since it is confounded by communication problems, by motivational problems, and by commitment problems.

There are also techniques that can be used to successfully blend technological developments occurring concurrently within the firm. Thus, the successful connection of strategy analysis and strategy formulation, the selection and execution of a project, can be accomplished only with coordinated marketing, manufacturing, and finance activities. These must be part and parcel of the firm's positioning analysis, and effective liaison, perspective sharing, issue identification, and the like, must occur for operational effectiveness to follow effective strategic processes.

STRATEGY AND SUBSTRATEGY

As was indicated earlier, most markets support several participants, with some playing the role of dominant supplier and some doing quite well as lower technology price competitors or higher technology niche competitors. For many firms, similar overall strategies can be supported by quite different substrategies. Thus high-performing firms employing similar strategies are frequently found to have different technological substrategies and may very well employ different substrategies within other functions as well.

Through a clustering analysis of a large sample of firms four strategy types were identified. While the underlying detail of each firm and its classification into categories is unique, the analysis suggested four competitive strategy types. These types are similar in character to many of the common strategic types reported in the literature.

The broad-scale competitive strategies empirically identified are similar to some of the characterization identified and analyzed in the earlier section on strategic models. Initially these models were identified as product innovator, promotion and distribution focus, customer service, and customer support. Within the product innovator strategy an early mover advantage was expected. The promotion and distribution strategy relied heavily on smoothly functioning production processes with reasonably stable technology. The customer service and customer support strategies were more closely allied with a market-driven need, perhaps a customer preference model.

With one exception, successful firms in each of the competitive strategy categories were able to choose from two technology substrategies. For instance, product innovators were either product pioneers or product leaders. Customer service strategies employed the same two substrategies, although the product leader type predominated. Customer support allowed either product leader or product follower. Only promotion and distribution evidenced but a single substrategy, that of product pioneer. This test of the concept of technology strategy begins to demonstrate the ability of several strategies to simultaneously compete effectively within the same marketplace.

ORGANIZATIONAL STRUCTURING

An essential understanding of innovation is a prerequisite for beginning a study of the firm's internal abilities to deal with innovation and execute successfully one or another technology strategy. A clear distinction must be drawn between variations and reorientations (changes that dramatically and simultaneously affect several product dimensions). Variations are organizationally conservative, whereas reorientations often cause organizational disturbances and a certain degree of "power shift."

This concept can then be effectively expanded to create a typology of innovation. Beginning with the standard *product–process* dichotomy, a first-level elaboration would be used to determine whether the innovation was *individual* or *synergistic*. Individual refers to a one-dimensional innovation that does not rely on any significant adjustments in other dimensions of the product or process for its success. A synergistic innovation refers to a need for interactive adjustment between or among several dimensions in order to achieve the intended breakthrough. This two-by-two schema can then be converted into a more powerful analytical tool by adding to it the concepts of *autonomous* and *systemic*. An autonomous innovation is a direct substitute for another product or process. A systemic innovation requires adaptation on the part of many organizations in order for it to be a success. These concepts then lead to an eight-cell, two-by-two-by- two typology of innovation.

A similar analysis then can be made of the organizational implications of the typology. From the perspective of organizational structuring there are three dimensions of special interest. One dimension refers to simple versus complex access to market information. A second dimension refers to selection of a project or a matrix organizational form. The third dimension refers to the need for simple versus complex boundary-spanning units.

The innovation typology has a direct relationship to these issues. For instance, product innovation requires complex access to market information while process innovation requires simple access to market information. Individual innovation can be effectively handled through the use of a matrix organization, whereas synergistic innovation requires a project organization. Autonomous innovation can be pursued with a simple boundary- spanning unit, but systemic innovation requires complex boundary-spanning units. Thus the innovation typology can be blended with organizational structuring issues to yield an eight-cell matrix of typology structure matches.

ACTION IMPLICATIONS

The basic action implications of the foregoing material focuses upon the perspective of the technology strategy, the need for an adaptive rationality model in strategy formulation and assessment, the application of technological mapping concepts for external appreciation, and the application of innovation audit techniques to frame ensuing corporate decision making.

The overall approach described here has been used extensively over the last several years, often with powerful results. Its application has helped many firms to audit and confirm their current plans and strategies. Other firms have been able to strengthen their technological programs by identifying weaknesses or oversights. On occasion, the approach has been employed to provide a basis of outside evaluation when seeking venture funds. The approach has also helped some firms by providing the analytic basis for their search for and acquisition of a merger partner whose technology portfolio and innovative skills will blend and create a sustainable advantage in a dynamic industry segment. Thus, the promise of these techniques can be seen in such outcomes that offer the firm opportunities for creating defensible competitive advantage in an ever-changing and challenging world.

Bibliography

Abernathy, W. J. *Decision Strategies in R & D Projects.* Los Angeles: Graduate School of Business, University of California, Los Angeles, August 1969.

——. *The Productivity Dilemma: Roadblocks to Innovation in the Automobile Industry.* Baltimore, MD: Johns Hopkins University Press, 1978.

Abernathy, W. J., K. Clark, and A. Kantrow. *Industrial Renaissance.* New York: Basic Books, 1983.

Abernathy, W. J., and R. A. Goodman. "Strategies for Development Projects: An Empirical Study," *R & D Management* 2(3): 125–29 (1972).

Abernathy, W. J., and J. M. Utterback. "Patterns of Industrial Innovation," *Technological Review* 80: 40–47 (1978).

Ackoff, R. *A Concept of Corporate Planning.* New York: Wiley, 1970.

Andrews, K. *The Concept of Corporate Strategy.* Homewood, IL: Irwin, 1971.

Ansoff, I., and J. M. Stewart. "Strategies for a Technology-Based Business," *Harvard Business Review*, November–December 1967, pp. 71–82.

Argyris, C., and D. Schon. *Organizational Learning: A Theory of Action Perspective.* Reading, MA: Addison-Wesley, 1978.

Arthur D. Little, Inc. *The Strategic Management of Technology.* New York: Arthur D. Little, Inc., 1981.

Ashby, R. *An Introduction to Cybernetics.* London: Methuen, 1964.

Atkinson, A., and J. Stiglitz. "A New View of Technological Change," *Economic Journal* 79: 573–78 (1969).

Balachandra, R. "Critical Signals for Making Go–No Go Decisions in New Product Development," *Journal of Product Innovation Management* 1(2): 92–100 (1981).

Balderson, J., P. Birnbaum, R. A. Goodman, and M. Stahl. *Modern Management Techniques in Engineering and R&D.* New York: Van Nostrand Reinhold, 1984.

Balthasar, H., R. Boschi, and M. Menke. "Calling the Shots in R & D." Paper presented at the annual meeting of the Strategic Management Society, Paris, 1983.

Barber, B., and R. Fox. "The Case of the Floppy-Eared Rabbits: A Case of Serendipity Gained and Serendipity Lost." In B. Barber and W. Hirsch, eds., *The Sociology of Science.* New York: Free Press of Glencoe, 1962.

Barnett, W. "The Organizational Ecology of a Technological System," *Administrative Science Quarterly* 25: 31–60 (1990).

Basalla, G. *The Evolution of Technology.* Cambridge: Cambridge University Press, 1988.

Battelle. "Interactions of Science and Technology in Innovative Processes: Some Case Studies." Columbus: Battelle, March 19, 1973.

Bennis, W. *The Unconscious Conspiracy: Why Leaders Can't Lead.* New York: AMACOM, 1976.

Besserye, C. "Middle Managers as Innovators: The Initiation of Organizational Innovations." Ph.D. diss. proposal, Graduate School of Management, University of California, Los Angeles, 1985.

Bitondo, D., and A. Frohman. "Linking Technological and Business Planning," *Research Management* 24: 19–23 (1981).

Boschi, R., and M. Barjon. "Strategy in R & D." Paper presented at the annual meeting of the Strategic Management Society, Paris, 1983.

Brandt, S. C. *Strategic Planning in Emerging Companies.* Reading, MA: Addison-Wesley, 1981.

Bright, J. *Research Development and Technological Innovation.* Homewood, IL: Irwin, 1964.

Brown, A. E. "New Definitions for Industrial R&D," *Research Management* 15: 55–57 (1972).

Buggie, F. "Strategies for New Product Development," *Long Range Planning* 15(2):22–31 (1982).

Buijs, J. "Strategic Planning Product Innovation—Some Systematic Approaches," *Long Range Planning* 12(3): 22–31 (1979).

Business Week. January 16, 1984, pp. 78–82.

Business Week. January 30, 1984, pp. 50–58.

Business Week. "No.1—And Trying Harder," in *Business Week* bonus issue, *The Quality Imperative,* 1991.

Camp, R. C. *Benchmarking: The Search for Industry Best Practices That Lead to Superior Performance.* Milwaukee, WI: Quality Press, 1989.

Chamberlin, E. *The Theory of Monopolistic Competition: A Reorientation of the Theory of Value,* 8th ed. Cambridge, MA: Harvard University Press, 1962.

Chandler, A. *Strategy and Structure: Chapters in the History of the Industrial Enterprise.* Cambridge, MA: MIT Press, 1962.

———. *The Visible Hand: The Managerial Revolution in American Business.* Cambridge, MA: Belknap Press, 1977.

Christensen, C. R., K. R. Andrews, J. L. Bowers, R. G. Hammermesh, and M. L. Porter. *Business Policy,* 5th ed. Homewood, IL: Irwin, 1982.

Clarke, R. W. "Innovation in Liquid Propellant Rocket Technology," *Final Report Task 7910-05.* Holloman Air Force Base, New Mexico, Office of Aerospace Research, March 1968.

Clemens, D., M. K. Ganobcik, E. Gerhardt, and L. McCracken. "Monoclonal Antibodies for Cancer," Los Angeles: Graduate School of Management, University of California, Los Angeles, 1984.

Cohen, M., and J. March. *Leadership and Ambiguity.* New York: McGraw-Hill, 1974.

Connors, K. "A Historical Comparison of Resource-Based Theory and Five Schools of Thought within Industrial Organization Economics: Do We Have a New Theory of the Firm?" *Journal of Management* 17: 121–54 (1991).

Cooper, A. "Strategic Management: New Ventures and Small Business," *Long Range Planning* 14(3): 39–45 (1981).

Cooper, A., and D. Schendel. "Strategic Responses to Technological Threats," *Business Horizons,* February 1976, pp. 61–69.

Cordero, J. "Desarollo de las Matrices Productos/Tecnologias del Sector de Componentes Electronicos." In J. Pavon and R. A. Goodman, *La Planaficacion del Desarollo Tecnologico.* Madrid: Centro para el Desarollo Tecnologico Industrial, 1981.

Crawford, C. "Defining the Product Innovation Charter," *Sloan Management Review,* Fall 1980, pp. 3–12.

Cyert, R., and J. March. *A Behavioral Theory of the Firm.* Englewood Cliffs, NJ: Prentice-Hall, 1963.

Dalkey, N. C., and O. Helmer. "An Experimen-

tal Application of the Delphi Methods to the Use of Experts," *Management Science* 9: 458–67 (1963).

Dasgupta, P., and J. Stiglitz. "Industrial Structure and the Nature of Innovative Activity," *Economic Journal,* 90:266–93 (1980).

Davis, S. M. and P. R. Lawrence, *Matrix* Reading, MA: Addison-Wesley, 1977.

Deal, T.E., and A.A. Kennedy. *Corporate Cultures: The Rites and Rituals of Corporate Life.* Reading, MA: Addison-Wesley, 1982.

Dean, B. "The Management of Innovative Start-up Firms," *Technical Memorandum No. 548.* Cleveland: Case Western Reserve University, 1984.

Deming, W. E. *Quality, Productivity, and Competitive Position.* Cambridge, MA: MIT Press, 1982.

———*Some Theory of Sampling.* New York: Wiley, 1950.

Dess, G., and D. Beard. "Dimensions of Organizational Task Environments," *Administrative Science Quarterly* 29: 52–73 (1984).

Dess, G., and P. Davis. "Porter's (1980) Generic Strategies as Determinants of Strategic Group Membership and Organizational Performance," *Academy of Management Journal* 27: 467–88 (1984).

Dill, W. "Environment as an Influence on Managerial Autonomy," *Administrative Science Quarterly* 2: 409–43 (1958).

Dosi, G. "Technological Paradigms and Technological Trajectories," *Research Policy* 11 147–62 (1982).

Eisenhardt, K. "Agency Theory: An Assessment and Review," *Academy of Management Review* 14 (1): 57–74 (1989).

Elster, J. *Explaining Technological Change: A Case Study in the Philosophy of Science.* New York: Cambridge University Press, 1983.

Emery, F. E. "The Next Thirty Years: Concepts, Methods and Anticipations," *Human Relations* 20(3) 71–92 (1967).

Emery, F. E., and E. Trist. "The Causal Texture of the Environment," *Human Relations* 18(1): 21–32 (1965).

Ferguson, I. "Taguchi Methods and Parameter Design." In *Proceedings, First Conference on Tools and Techniques for TQM.* London: IFS Ltd., 1989.

Fernelius, W., and W. Waldo. "The Role of Basic Research in Industrial Innovation," *Research Management* 23: 36–40 (1980).

Ford D., and C. Ryan. "Taking Technology to Market," *Harvard Business Review,* March–April 1981, pp. 117–26.

Forrester, J. *Industrial Dynamics.* Cambridge, MA: MIT Press, 1961.

Foster, R. *Innovation—The Attacker's Advantage.* New York: Summit Books, 1986.

Freeman, C. *The Economics of Industrial Innovation.* (Baltimore, MD: Penguin, 1974.

Freeman, C., et al. *Success and Failure in Indus-trial Innovation.* Centre for the Study of Industrial Innovation, University of Sussex, 1972.

Frohman, A., "Managing the Company's Tech-nological Assets," *Research Management* 23: 20–24 (1980).

———. "Technology as a Competitive Weapon," *Harvard Business Review,* May–June, 1982, pp. 97–104.

Frohman, A., and D. Bitondo. "Coordinating Business Strategy and Technical Planning," *Long Range Planning* 14(6): 58–67 (1981).

Galbraith, J. *Designing Complex Organizations.* Reading, MA: Addison-Wesley, 1973.

———. *Organizational Design.* Reading, MA: Addison-Wesley, 1977.

Galbraith, J., and D. Nathanson. *Strategy Imple-mentation: The Role of Structure and Process.* St. Paul, MN: West, 1978.

Garvin, D. A. "How the Baldrige Award Really Works," *Harvard Business Review,* Novem-ber–December 1991, pp. 80–95.

Giansante, J., and S. Parris. "An Innovation Audit: Integrated Products, Inc.," Los Ange-les: Graduate School of Management, Univer-sity of California, Los Angeles, June 12, 1983.

Goodman, R. A. "Dual Perspectives on the Strategic Employment of Technological Verti-cal Integration: As National Policy and as Corporate Policy," Los Angeles: Graduate School of Management, University of Califor-nia, Los Angeles, 1989.

———."Some Thoughts on the Technological Dimension of Vertical Integration," working paper, Graduate School of Management, Uni-versity of California, Los Angeles, 1986.

———."Strategic Planning and Decision-Mak-ing Techniques." In Balderson, J. P. Birn-baum, R. A. Goodman, M. Stahl, *Modern Management Techniques in Engineering and R&D.* New York: Van Nostrand Reinhold, 1984.

———. *Temporary Systems: Professional Development, Manpower Utilization, Task Effectiveness and Innovation.* New York: Praeger, 1981.

Goodman, R. A., and W. J. Abernathy. "The Contribution of 'NEW BOY' Phenomena to Increasing Innovation and Development in New Technology," *R & D Management* 9(1): 31–41 (1978).

———."Summary of a Workshop on Dimen-sional Analysis for Design, Development and Research Executives," working paper, Graduate School of Management, University of Califor-nia, Los Angeles, 1971.

Goodman, R. A., and A. S. Huff. "Enriching Pol-icy Premises for an Ambiguous World." In John Sutherland, ed., *Management Handbook for Public Administrators.* New York: Van Nostrand Reinhold, 1978.

Goodman, R. A., A. S. Huff, G. Abonyi, and M. Lawless. "Policy Making and Policy Analysis in an Ambiguous World," *Proceedings of the Third Annual Southeastern Meeting of the Society for General Systems Research,* New Orleans: Society for General Systems Research, 1977.

Goodman, R. A., and J. Pavon. *Planning for National Technology Policy.* New York: Praeger, 1984.

Grant, J., and W. King. *The Logic of Strategic Planning.* Boston: Little, Brown, 1982.

Hambrick, D. "Some Tests of the Effective-ness and Functional Attributes of Miles and Snow's Strategic Types," *Academy of Man-agement Journal* 26: 3–26 (1983).

Hamilton, M. R., A. I. Mendelowitz, and R. I. Fogel. "TQM at GAO," *GAO Journal* 14: 39–47 (Winter 1991/92).

Hammermesh, R. *Making Strategy Work.* New York: Wiley, 1986.

Hayes, R., and W. J. Abernathy. "Managing Our Way to Economic Decline," *Harvard Busi-ness Review,* July–August 1980, pp. 67–77.

Heany, D. "Degrees of Product Innovation," *Journal of Business Strategy* 2: 3–14 (1983).

Hempel, R. "Building a Total R & D Effort at Alcoa," *Research Management* 22: 27–30 (1979).

Henderson, R., and K. Clark. "Architectural Innovation: The Reconfiguration of Existing Product Technologies and the Failure of Established Firms," *Administrative Science Quarterly* 35: 9–30 (1990).

Hertz, D., and H. Thomas. "Decision and Risk Analysis in a New Product and Facilities Plan-ning Problem," *Sloan Management Review,* Winter 1983, pp. 17–31.

Hettinger, W. "The Top Technologist Should Join the Team," *Research Management* 25: 7–10 (1982).

Hofstede, G. *Culture's Consequences: Interna-tional Differences in Work-Related Values.* Beverly Hills, CA: Sage, 1980.

Horwitch, M., and C. Prahalad. "Managing Technological Innovation—Three Ideal Modes," *Sloan Management Review,* Winter 1976, pp. 77–89.

Hrebiniak, L., and W. Joyce. *Implementing Strategy.* New York: Macmillan, 1984.

Huff, A. "Industry Influence on Strategy Refor-mulation," *Strategic Management Journal* 3(2): 119–32 (1982).

Hughes, T. *Networks of Power.* Baltimore, MD: Johns Hopkins University Press, 1988.

IIT Research Institute. *TRACES (Technology in Retrospective and Critical Events in Sci-ence).* Chicago: IITRI, December 15, 1968.

Jelinek, M., and M. Burstein. "The Productive Administrative Structure: A Paradigm for Strategic Fit," *Academy of Management Review* 7(2): 242–52 (1982).

Jensen, M., and W. Meckling. "The Theory of the Firm: Managerial Behavior, Agency Costs, and Ownership Structure," *Journal of Financial Economics* 11: 5–50 (1976).

Johnson, S. "Comparing R & D Strategies of Japanese and U.S. Firms," *Sloan Management Review*, Spring 1984, pp. 25–34.

Juran, J. M. *Juran and Leadership for Quality: An Executive Handbook*. New York: Free Press, 1989.

————*Management of Inspection and Quality Control*. New York: Harper and Brothers, 1945.

Kanter, R. M. *The Change Masters*. New York: Simon and Schuster, 1983.

Klein, B., R. Crawford, and A. Alchian. "Vertical Integration, Appropriate Rents, and the Competitive Contracting Process," *Journal of Law and Economics* 21: 297–326 (1978).

Knight, K. "A Study of Technological Innovation—The Evolution of Digital Computers." Ph.D. diss., Graduate School of Industrial Administration, Carnegie Institute of Technology, 1963.

Komaran, R. "The Evolution of the External Acquisition of Technology by American Multi-National Firms. Ph.D. diss., Anderson Graduate School of Management, University of California, Los Angeles, 1993.

Kreiner, K. "The Art of Managing EUREKA-Projects: Lessons from a Longitudinal Study." Copenhagen: Copenhagen Business School, EUREKA Management Research Institute, 1993. (draft)

Kuhn, T. S. *The Structure of Scientific Revolutions*. Chicago: University of Chicago Press, 1963.

Lamarck, J. B. *Zoological Philosophy*, translated by H. Elion. New York: Hafner, 1963.

Lawless, M. W. "The Adaptive Rationality Model: Managing Strategy–Technology Integration" Paper presented at the annual meeting of the Strategic Management Association, Barcelona, 1984.

————."Competitive Strategy, Technology Strategy, and Performance," University of Colorado working paper, 1986.

————."A Policy and Process Model of the Implementation of Computer Models in Criminal Justice Agencies," *Applications of Management Science* 2: 212–31 (1982).

————."The Structure of Strategy: A Taxonomic Study of Competitive Strategy and Technology Substrategy," University of Colorado working paper, 1987.

————."Toward a Theory of Policy Making for DirectedInterorganizational Systems." Ph.D. diss. Graduate School of Management, University of California, Los Angeles, 1980.

Lawless, M. W., A. Feinberg, A. Glassman, and R. Bengston. "The Role of the Change Agent in Management Science Implementation," *Omega* 10(2): 107–14 (1981).

Lawless, M. W., and G. Rossy. "The Impact on Financial Performance of Integrating Corporate Strategy with Technological Functions." Paper presented at the annual meeting of the Strategic Management Association, Barcelona, 1984.

Lawrence, P., and J. Lorsch. "Differentiation and Integration in Complex Organizations," *Administrative Science Quarterly* 12: 1–47 (1967).

Levine, S., and M. Yalowitz. "Managing Technology: Key to Business Growth," *Management Review*, September 1983, pp. 44–48.

Lewin, K. "Frontiers in Group Dynamics: Concept, Method, and Reality in Social Science, Social Equilibria and Social Change," *Human Relations* 1(1): 5–41 (1947).

Lieberman, M. "Just-in-Time Management." Lecture presented at Anderson Graduate School of Management, University of California, Los Angeles, 1991.

Liebler, W. J. "Impact of Public Policy on Drug Innovation and Pricing." In *Public Policy Research in the Drug Industry*. Washington, DC: American Enterprise Institute, 1976.

Lindblom, C. "Still Muddling, Not Yet Through," *Public Administration Review* 39: 517–26 (1979).

Linn, R. "A Sectoral Approach to Strategic Planning for R&D," *Research Management* 26: 33–40 (1983).

Lippman, S., and R. Rumelt. "Uncertain Imitability: An Analysis of Interfirm Differences in Efficiency under Competition," *Bell Journal of Economics* 13: 418–38 (1982).

Lorsch, J., and P. Lawrence. "Organizing for Product Innovation," *Harvard Business Review*, January–February 1965, pp. 109–22.

Maidique, M., and R. Hayes. "The Art of High Technology Management," *Sloan Management Review*, Winter 1984, pp. 17–31.

Maidique, M., and P. Patch. "Corporate Strategy and Technological Policy," Harvard Business School Note 9-679-033, Rev. 3/1980.

Malcolm Baldrige National Quality Award 1990 Application Guidelines. Washington, DC: National Institute of Standards and Technology, United States Department of Commerce.

Malcolm Baldrige National Quality Award 1991 Application Guidelines. Washington, DC: National Institute of Standards and Technology, United States Department of Commerce.

Mansfield, E. "How Economists See R & D," *Harvard Business Review*, November–December 1981, pp. 98–106.

March, J., and H. Simon. *Organizations*. New York: Wiley, 1958.

Marquis, D. G., and D. M. Straight, Jr. "OrganizationalFactors in Project Performance." Working paper, School of Management, MIT, Cambridge, MA, August 1965.

McGinnis, M., and J. Ackelsberg. "Effective Innovation Management: Missing Link in Strategic Planning?" *Journal of Business Strategy* 4:59–66 (1983).

McKelvey, B. "Expectational Noncomplimentarity and Style of Interaction between Professional and Organization," *Administrative Science Quarterly* 14:21–32 (1969).

———. *Organizational Systematics: Taxonomy, Evolution, Classification.* Berkeley: University of California Press, 1982.

Merriam-Webster Dictionary. New York: Pocket Books, 1974.

Miles, R., and C. Snow. *Organizational Strategy, Structure and Process.* New York: McGraw-Hill, 1978.

Miller, A. "Technology, Strategy, and Performance—What Are the Links?" In B. Bozeman, M. Crow, and A. Link, eds., *Strategic Management of Industrial R&D.* Lexington, MA: Lexington Books, 1984.

———. "A Taxonomy of Technological Settings, with Related Strategies and Performance Levels," *Strategic Management Journal* 9: 239–54 (1988).

Miller, D., and P. Friesen. "Archetypes of Organizational Transition," *Administrative Science Quarterly* 25: 268–99 (1980).

Mintzberg, H. *The Nature of Managerial Work.* Englewood Cliffs, NJ: Prentice-Hall, 1973.

———. "Patterns in Strategy Formulation," *Management Science* 24(9) 934–48 (1978).

———. "Strategy Making in Three Modes," *California Management Review* 16: 44–54 (Winter 1973).

Mooz, W. E. *The B-X: A Hypothetical Bomber Cost Study.* Santa Monica, CA: Rand Corporation, July 1965, RM-4635-PR.

Naguib, H. "The Implementation of Total Quality Management (TQM) in a Semiconductor Manufacturing Operation." San Francisco: International Semiconductor Manufacturing Science Symposium, June 1992. (mimeo).

Nelson, R., and S. Winter. *An Evolutionary Theory of Economic Change.* Cambridge, MA: Belknap Press, 1982.

Normann, R. "Some Conclusions from Thirteen Case Studies of New Product Development," Stockholm: Swedish Institute of Administrative Research, 1969, UPM-RN-100.

North, H. Q., and D. Pike. "Technological Probes of the Future," *Harvard Business Review,* May–June 1969, pp. 68–83.

Pappas, C. "Strategic Management of Technology," *Journal of Product Innovation Management* 1(1): 30–35 (1984).

Parker, R. "Human Aspects of the R & D Organization," *Research Management* 20: 34–38 (1977).

Parsons, T., and E. A. Shils. *Toward a General Theory of Action.* Cambridge, MA: Harvard University Press, 1951.

Peck, M. J., and F. M. Scherer. "The Weapons Acquisition Process: An Economic Analysis," Division of Research, Harvard University, 1962.

Peters, T. J., and N. Austin. *A Passion for Excellence: The Leadership Difference.* New York: Random House, 1985.

Peters, T. J., and R. H. Waterman. *In Search of Excellence: Lessons from America's Best-Run Companies.* New York: Warner Books, 1982.

Petroni, G., "Strategic Planning and Research and Development—Can We Integrate Them?" *Long Range Planning* 16(1): 15–25 (1983).

———."The Strategic Management of R & D, Part 2—Organizing for Integration Long Range Planning," *Long Range Planning* 16(2): 51–64 (1983).

Phillips, P., and A. M. Pulos, "Machine Vision," Los Angeles: Graduate School of Management, University of California, Los Angeles, 1986.

Porter, M. *Competitive Advantage: Creating and Sustaining Superior Advantage.* New York: Free Press, 1985.

———.*Competitive Strategy.* New York: Free Press, 1980.

Prahalad, C., and G. Hamel. "The Core Competence of the Corporation," *Harvard Business Review,* May–June 1990, pp. 7–91.

Quinn, J. *Strategies for Change: Logical Incrementalism.* Homewood, IL: Irwin, 1980.

———. "Technological Innovation, Entrepreneurship, and Strategy," *Sloan Management Review,* Spring 1979, pp. 19–30.

Quirk, P. "Innovation Audit: Vascular Systems Inc.," Los Angeles: Graduate School of Management, University of California, Los Angeles, June 9, 1983.

Ramsey, J. "Selecting R & D Projects for Development," *Long Range Planning* 14(1): 83–92 (1981).

Ritti, R. "Work Goals of Scientists and Engineers." In M. Tushman and W. Moore, eds., *Readings in the Management of Innovation.* Boston: Pitman, 1982.

Rosenbloom, R. S. "Managing Technology for the Longer Term: Notes from a Managerial Perspective." Boston: Harvard Business School, 1984. (mimeo)

Rosenbloom, R. S., and A. Kantrow. "The Nurturing of Corporate Research," *Harvard Business Review,* January–February 1982, pp. 115–23.

Rowe, A., R. Mason, and K. Dickel. *Strategic Management and Business Policy.* Reading, MA: Addison-Wesley, 1982.

Rumelt, R. "Evaluation of Strategy: Theory and Models." In D. Schendel and C. Hofer, eds., *Strategic Management.* Boston: Little, Brown, 1979.

———.*Strategy, Structure and Economic Performance.* Cambridge, MA: Harvard Business School Press, 1976.

———. "Toward a Strategic Theory of the Firm." In R. Lamb, ed., *Competitive Strategic Management.* Englewood Cliffs, NJ: Prentice-Hall, 1984.

Sackmann, S. "Cultural Knowledge in Organizations: The Link between Strategy and Organizational Processes." Ph.D. diss., Graduate School of Management, University of California, Los Angeles, 1985.

Sahal, D. *Patterns of Technological Innovation.* Reading, MA: Addison-Wesley, 1981.

Schendel, D., and C. Hofer, eds. *Strategic Management: A New View of Business Policy and Planning.* Boston: Little, Brown, 1979.

Scherer, F. *Industrial Market Structure and Economic Performance.* (Cambridge, MA: Harvard Business School Press, 1980.

Schmookler, J. *Invention and Economic Growth.* Cambridge, MA: Harvard University Press, 1966.

Schon, D. *Beyond the Stable State.* London: Maurice Temple Smith, 1972.

———. *The Displacement of Concepts.* London: Tavistock, 1963.

Schoonhoven, C. "Strategy and Performance in High Technology Corporations." Paper presented at the annual meeting of the Western Academy of Management, Santa Barbara, CA, 1983.

Schumpeter, J. *Capitalism, Socialism and Democracy*, 5th ed. London: Allen and Unwin, 1976.

Selznick, P. *Leadership in Administration: A Sociological Interpretation.* Evanston, IL: Row Peterson, 1957.

Simon, H. *Administrative Behavior.* New York: Macmillan, 1957.

———. *The Sciences of the Artificial.* Cambridge, MA: MIT Press, 1981.

Simon, H., and A. Ando. "Aggregation of Variables in Dynamic Systems." *Econometrica* 29: 11–138 (April 1961).

Skinner, W. *Manufacturing in the Corporate Strategy.* New York: Wiley, 1978.

———. "Manufacturing—Missing Link in the Corporate Strategy," *Harvard Business Review*, May–June 1969, pp. 136–45.

Sloan, A. P., Jr. *My Years with General Motors.* New York: Doubleday, 1963.

Smith, A. *An Inquiry into the Nature and Causes of the Wealth of Nations.* London: W. Strahan and T. Cadell, 1776.

Smith, K., J. Guthrie, and M. Chen. "Miles and Snow's Typology of Strategy, Organizational Size, and Performance." Paper presented at the national meeting of the Academy of Management. Chicago, 1986.

Snow, C., and L. Hrebiniak. "Strategy, Distinctive Competence, and Organizational Performance," *Administrative Science Quarterly* 25: 317–36 (1980).

Stalk, G., P. Evans, and L. Shulman. "Competing in Capabilities: The New Rules of Corporate Strategy," *Harvard Business Review*, March–April 1992, pp. 57–69.

Steiner, G. *Top Management Planning.* New York: Macmillan, 1969.

Steiner, G., J. Miner, and E. Gray. *Management, Policy and Strategy.* New York: Macmillan, 1982.

Strauch, R. *A Critical Assessment of Quantitative Analysis as a Policy Analysis Tool.* Santa Monica, CA: Rand Corporation, 1974, P-5282.

Taguchi, G., E. Elsayed, and T. Hsiang. *Quality Engineering in Production Systems.* New York: McGraw-Hill, 1989.

Taguchi, G., and S. Konishi. *Orthogonal Arrays and Linear Graphs: Tools for Quality" Engineers.* Dearborn, MI: American Supplier Institute, 1989.

Teece, D. "Multinational Enterprises, Internal Governance, and Economic Organization, *American Economic Review* 75: 233–38 (1985).

Teece, D., G. Pisano, and A. Schuen. "Firm Capabilities, Resources, and the Concept of Strategy." Consortium on Competitiveness and Cooperation CCC working paper 90-8, Center for Research in Management, University of California at Berkeley, 1990.

Thompson, J. D. *Organizations in Action: Social Science Bases of Administrative Theory.* New York: McGraw-Hill, 1967.

Tolstoy, L. *War and Peace*, translated by Louise and Aylmer Maude. London: Oxford University Press, 1941. Originally published in 1863–69.

Trist, E. "Urban North America." Toronto: Town Planning Institute of Canada, 1968.

Tushman, M., and P. Anderson. "Technological Discontinuities and Organizational Environment," *Administrative Science Quarterly*,, 31: 439–65 (1986).

Twiss, B. *Managing Technological Innovation.* London: Longman, 1980.

United Nations Educational, Scientific and Cultural Organization. "Méthode de Détermination de Priorité dans le Domains de la Science et de la Technologie," Science Policy Document No. 40. Paris: UNESCO, 1969.

United States General Accounting Office. "Management Practices: U.S. Companies Improve Performance Through Quality Efforts." Washington, DC: U.S. GAO, May 1991.

Vancil, R., and P. Lorange. *Strategic Planning Systems.* Englewood Cliffs, NJ: Prentice-Hall, 1977.

Vernon, R., and E. B. Kapstein. "National Needs, Global Resources," *Daedalus*, 1991, pp. 1–22.

Vickers, G. *The Art of Judgement.* New York: Basic Books, 1965.

Von Hippel, E. "Users and Innovators," *Technology Review* 80(3): 30–39 (1978).

Wagner, H. *Operations Research.* Englewood Cliffs, NJ: Prentice-Hall, 1969.

Ward, P. "Planning for Technological Innovation—Developing the Necessary Nerve," *Long Range Planning* 14(2): 59–71 (1981).

Watson, J. E. and T. W. Hopp. "The Private Sector's Experience with Total Quality Management," *GAO Journal* 14: 34–38 (Winter 1991/92).

Weil, E., and R. Cangemi. "Linking Long Range Research to Corporate Planning," *Research Management* 26: 32–39 (1983).

Weiss, A. R., and P. H. Birnbaum. "Technological Infrastructure and the Implementation of Technological Strategies." Graduate School of Business Administration, University of Southern California, 1988. (mimeo)

Wernerfelt, B. "A Resource-Based View of the Firm," *Strategic Management Journal* 5: 171–80 (1984).

Wheelwright, S. C., "Manufacturing Strategy: Defining the Missing Link," *Strategic Management Journal* 5(1): 77–91 (1984).

Wheelwright, S. C., and R. H. Hayes. "Competing through Manufacturing," *Harvard Business Review*, January–February 1985, pp. 99–109.

White, G., and M. B. W. Graham. "How to Spot a Technological Winner," *Harvard Business Review*, March–April 1978, pp. 146–52.

White, W. "The Research Survey—A Way to Bridge the Gap between Market and Laboratory," *Research Management* 21:14–20 (1978).

Williams, J. "Technological Evolution and Competitive Response," *Strategic Management Journal* 4(1): 55–65 (1983).

Williamson, O. *The Economic Institutions of Capitalism.* New York: Free Press, 1985.

———. *Markets and Hierarchies: Analysis and Antitrust Implications.* New York: Free Press, 1975.

Woodward, J. *Industrial Organization: Theory and Practice.* London: Oxford University Press, 1965.

Index